Autographs

A REFERENCE AND PRICE GUIDE FOR SPORTS AND CELEBRITY AUTOGRAPHS

Autographs

A REFERENCE AND PRICE GUIDE FOR SPORTS AND CELEBRITY AUTOGRAPHS

PRESENTED BY BECKETT PUBLICATIONS

Page 1: Kathy Ireland, supermodel; page 2–3: Nomar Garciaparra, baseball; page 5: Tom Cruise and Nicole Kidman, actors; page 6: Michael Jordan, basketball

The prices in this book are based solely on the knowledge and experience of the staff of Beckett Sports Collectibles and Autographs magazine, along with dealers across the country. All figures are in U.S. dollars and are for informational purposes only.

First Edition: April 1999
Beckett Corporate Sales and Information (972) 991-6657

YOUR VALUE GUIDE

When it comes to reporting on values for secondary market collectibles, Beckett Publications is recognized and respected worldwide as the most trusted authority. Founded in 1984 by Dr. James Beckett, the company has sold millions of price guide books and magazines to collectors of sports cards, sports memorabilia, toys and other licensed collectible products.

Presently, Beckett Publications publishes eight popular monthly magazines on collectibles. They are *Beckett Baseball Card Monthly*, *Beckett Basketball Card Monthly*, *Beckett Football Card Monthly*, *Beckett Hockey Collector*, *Beckett Sports Collectibles and Autographs*, *Beckett Racing & Motorsports Marketplace*, *Beckett Hot Toys* and *Beckett Sci-Fi Collector*.

This reference book is intended to provide an objective and unbiased representation of values for the subject collectibles on the secondary market. The independent pricing contained in this guide reflects current retail rates determined just prior to printing. They do not reflect for-sale prices by the author, distributors or any retailers of collectibles or memorabilia who've contributed their skills and knowledge to the production of this guide. All values are in U.S. dollars and are for informational purposes only.

The values published in this guide were compiled in a joint effort by a staff of full-time expert Beckett Publications analysts and independent contributors knowledgeable in this field of collecting. The information was gathered from actual buy/sell transactions at collectibles conventions, hobby shops and on-line sites, and, to a lesser extent, from buy/sell advertisements in hobby publications, for-sale prices from collectibles dealers' catalogs and price lists, as well as discussions with leading hobbyists in the U.S. and Canada.

Great care and diligence were taken in determining the prices reported within this book. Our desire to supply independent pricing that is more accurate and reliable than what may be supplied by any other source is paramount to our efforts. It is also a prime reason why the Beckett name is synonymous with collecting and memorabilia. Collectors have come to know Beckett as "The Hobby's Most Reliable and Relied Upon Source."™

CONTENTS

FOREWORD 9

BASEBALL 11

BASEBALL AUTOGRAPHS PRICE
GUIDE 17

BASKETBALL 55

BASKETBALL AUTOGRAPHS PRICE GUIDE . . .61

FOOTBALL 77

FOOTBALL AUTOGRAPHS PRICE GUIDE 83

HOCKEY 115

HOCKEY AUTOGRAPHS PRICE GUIDE 121

BOXING / OTHER SPORTS 143

BOXING / OTHER SPORTS PRICE GUIDE . .149

UPPER DECK AUTHENTICATED 161

UPPER DECK AUTHENTICATED PRICE
GUIDE 163

CELEBRITY AUTOGRAPHS 169

CELEBRITY AUTOGRAPHS PRICE GUIDE . . .175

AUTOGRAPHED TRADING CARDS PRICE
GUIDE 183

Babe Ruth, baseball

BY SCOTT JOHNSON

"Why do you collect autographs?"

It's a fair question. Why would anyone care about having a collection of famous people's signatures?

For some, the attraction is the potential monetary reward. Autographs rarely decrease in value. Years ago, a signed photo of Teddy Roosevelt could be acquired just by writing a letter to the White House. For the cost of postage, you could own something that today has a value in the $3,000 range. Better than the stock market over the same period.

For others, it is a chance to hang on to an important memory. Imagine if you were in attendance when Mark McGwire hit his record-breaking home run; any item with McGwire's autograph will evoke vivid memories of that great day. And what an item to display when telling the story to your grandchildren.

Historians see autographed items as a way of reconstructing the details of the past that are sometimes neglected in the textbooks. For example, you could read a history book and learn about the Civil War. But you are really there when you hold a handwritten letter from a Confederate soldier to his wife, describing that day's activities and how much he missed being home.

Personally, I began collecting autographs quite by accident. After watching a Jack Lemmon movie, I was so impressed that I felt I should write him a complimentary letter. I did not expect any response at all, but a week later there was an 8x10 photo in my mailbox, signed "To Scott, Best Wishes, Jack Lemmon." I was astounded, and immediately hooked. Was it really this easy to get an authentic signed photo just by writing a letter to a celebrity?

Over the years I have found that it is not always that easy — some celebrities use secretaries to sign for them, some use a machine (called an autopen), and some simply do not respond to mail. However, many famous people do indeed respond to a sincere letter from a fan; I have thousands of authentic signatures to attest to that, many of them the result of a simple request through the mail.

By owning someone's autograph, I have captured a brief moment in time, and attached to that is a great book I've read, or a memorable movie I have watched, or some other reason to take note of the celebrity involved. I have also become a little more knowledgeable about certain areas. I have autographs from Bob Heft (designer of our current 50-star U.S. flag), Clyde Tombaugh (only American to ever discover a planet — Pluto) and other notable people I might not have heard of otherwise.

Whatever your reason for collecting autographs, you will discover that it's just plain fun. The first time you open your mailbox, and you see one of your large stamped envelopes, and your heart does a little jump as you wonder whose autographed photo is in there . . . from that moment, you will know why we do it, and chances are you will be hooked, too. ▪

FOREWORD

Mickey Mantle

COLLECTING BASEBALL AUTOGRAPHS

It was 1967, I was 11, and I was on my way to my first Major League Baseball game. My father was driving us both over to the game in his red 1963 Chevrolet Impala. It was an hour or so drive from our home in New Jersey to Yankee Stadium in the Bronx. Like all of the other kids in the neighborhood, the "normal" ones anyway, I was a Yankees fan, or should I say a Mickey Mantle fan.

The Yankees of the late '60s were far removed from their past glories as a baseball dynasty and Mantle, once the best center fielder in the league, was now playing first base in what would be his next to last year as a major leaguer. Injuries, age and more than 2,000 games had taken their toll, but none of this mattered that August afternoon as I caught my first real-life glimpse of Yankee Stadium.

As we took our seats on the first base side of the stadium, the Yankees were on the field warming up. I'll never forget how green the field looked, the sound of the bat against the ball and the tremendous feeling of history that seemed to emanate from every crevice of the immense stadium. And there he was, his back to us at first base catching infield practice warm-ups, the bold number "7" emblazoned on his back. There was no mistaking Mickey Mantle for anyone else. I had heard it said one time that if you were making a movie and you called central casting to find someone to play the part of a baseball player, they would send you Mickey Mantle. He just looked like a ballplayer. The game wasn't particularly memorable. I had hoped to see The Mick hit one of his prodigious home runs that day but none were forthcoming. I did see him get a hit though, one of the 2,415 he would hit in his career, but it was a slow dribbler that just barely squeezed past the outstretched gloves of the second baseman and the shortstop.

After the game I suggested that we stick around outside the exit door of the stadium and try to meet Mantle and maybe even shake his hand, get an autograph or talk a little baseball (I was very naive then). While we stood outside the stadium with a dozen or so other fans who all seemed to have had the same idea, we were able to get a half dozen or so autographs of some of the other players like Bill Monbouquette and Tom Tresh. Mel Stottlemyre in particular was

BY JIM STINSON

especially pleasant and even chatted with me for a few moments before heading off. Mantle, however, was a no-show. Years later I learned that he had his own secret entrances and exits that he used to avoid the fans when he wanted to be left alone. Nevertheless, on this August evening, the damage had already been done: I had become an autograph collector.

The hobby of collecting baseball autographs has changed considerably since then, with some of the most dramatic changes happening in the last few years. But in reality the hobby of collecting autographs of baseball players has been around for a very long time. The charismatic and immensely popular Babe Ruth during his lifetime probably did as much, if not more, than any other ballplayer to popularize the simple notion of putting pen to paper. It became a way of remembering the moment when we mere mortals were able to, for a few short seconds, have our own lives intersect with those of our heroes.

Ruth was not the first ballplayer to be asked for an autograph, but he certainly was asked often and was by all

Chipper Jones

accounts almost always willing to oblige. Sometimes he even requested a chair as he was leaving the ballpark so he could sit and sign for the many fans wanting his autograph. A long-time collector once told me of the time he actually met the Babe. The Yanks were in town to play his home team of Cleveland. This young collector and his father actually were bold enough to find their way up to Ruth's hotel room and knock on his door. The Babe answered, clad in a bathrobe and slippers, and greeted the young man and his father with the familiar "Hi ya kid" and actually invited them in. He signed the baseball the youngster had brought and even offered him a piece of cake and a glass of milk. That was the Babe.

Ryne Sandberg

Collectors in those days who were unable to meet with their favorite stars in person could write them care of the ball club. Many would enclose in their letter a penny postcard with the collector's address already written on it so that all the player need do is autograph the card and drop it in a mail box. It was an inexpensive and easy way for a collector to obtain an autograph. Called government postcards today, these have become a popular medium for collectors.

The postmark with the date the item was mailed and the place it was mailed from imprinted on the reverse provide a form of built in provenance that insures (but does not guarantee) an autograph's authenticity.

The 1933 book "Who's Who in Major League Baseball" by Speed Johnson proved to be a valuable aid to collectors. Along with the various biographies, photos, facts and statistics on the many active players in the book, it also listed their home addresses. And the home addresses of more than 34 retired immortals such as Honus Wagner, Mordecai Brown, Johnny Evers, Tris Speaker, Grover Alexander and more. The hobby of autograph collecting was off and running.

In the 1960s Jack Smalling introduced his first "Baseball Address List." In those days just a couple of pages long, it would soon grow into a book that Smalling updated every couple of years with a comprehensive listing of the known whereabouts and addresses of every player who had ever donned a major league uniform. Collectors were surprised to find that with a simple SASE and a short note to one of the former players in the book

Mark McGwire

they were almost sure to get a reply.

In the 1970s the card collecting phenomenon literally exploded onto the hobby scene and baseball card shows (then called "conventions") began popping up all over the country. Many of the card show promoters would invite a former player or two to sign autographs to help boost the attendance. As card collecting and the nostalgia that accompanied it grew, so too did autograph collecting. Big name stars such as Mickey Mantle, Willie Mays, Joe DiMaggio, Ted Williams, Stan Musial, Sandy Koufax and many more appeared as signing guests at the card shows with promoters charging a fee for their autograph (at that time an unheard of concept). While the pros and cons of signing for pay are still being argued, few can deny that for many of today's hobbyists, their first introduction to the excitement of

Hank Aaron

autograph collecting came at these shows.

Today collecting baseball autographs has eclipsed coin and stamp collecting as this country's most popular hobby. Why? Because it's fun, it's nostalgic and it's a way for many of us to connect with the simplicity of being a kid again. ▪

Cal Ripken Jr.

ALBERT BELLE

LOU BOUDREAU

GEORGE BRETT

JIM BUNNING

Retired Players

Aaron, Hank-(1982)

3 X 5	.12.00
8 X 10 Photo	.25.00
Canceled Check	.25.00
Gold HOF Signed Postcard	.30.00
Perez-Steele Signed Postcard	.25.00
Signed Bat	.175.00
Single Signed Ball	.50.00

Alexander, Grover Clev. (1938) d. 1950

3 X 5	.350.00
8 X 10 Photo	.700.00
B&W HOF Signed Postcard	.1500.00
Single Signed Ball	.4000.00

Alston, Walter-(1983) d. 1984

3 X 5	.25.00
8 X 10 Photo	.100.00
Canceled Check	.75.00
Gold HOF Signed Postcard	.150.00
Single Signed Ball	.850.00

Anson, Cap-(1939) d. 1922

3 X 5	.1500.00
Signed Document	.3500.00

Aparicio, Luis-(1984)

3 X 5	.8.00
8 X 10 Photo	.20.00
Gold HOF Signed Postcard	.15.00
Perez-Steele Signed Postcard	.15.00
Signed Bat	.75.00

Single Signed Ball 25.00

Appling, Luke-(1964) d. 1991

3 X 5	.5.00
8 X 10 Photo	.20.00
Gold HOF Signed Postcard	.20.00
Perez-Steele Signed Postcard	.50.00
Single Signed Ball	.75.00

Ashburn, Richie-(1995) d. 1997

3 X 5	.8.00
8 X 10 Photo	.20.00
Canceled Check	.30.00
Gold HOF Signed Postcard	.20.00
Perez-Steele Signed Postcard	.25.00
Signed Bat	.125.00
Single Signed Ball	.50.00

Averill, Earl-(1975) d. 1983

3 X 5	.15.00
8 X 10 Photo	.75.00
Gold HOF Signed Postcard	.30.00
Single Signed Ball	.400.00

Baker, Frank-(1955) d. 1963

3 X 5	.200.00
8 X 10 Photo	.600.00
B&W HOF Signed Postcard	.1200.00
Single Signed Ball	.3500.00

Bancroft, Dave-(1971) d. 1972

3 X 5	.150.00
8 X 10 Photo	.300.00
Gold HOF Signed Postcard	.600.00
Single Signed Ball	.3500.00

Banks, Ernie-(1977)

3 X 5 . . . . .8.00

8 X 10 Photo 20.00

Canceled Check 50.00

Gold HOF Signed Postcard 20.00

Perez-Steele Signed Postcard 30.00

Signed Bat 175.00

Single Signed Ball 40.00

Barlick, Al-(1989) d. 1995

3 X 5 . . . . .5.00

8 X 10 Photo 20.00

Canceled Check 30.00

Gold HOF Signed Postcard 15.00

Perez-Steele Signed Postcard 15.00

Single Signed Ball 60.00

Barrow, Ed-(1953) d. 1953

3 X 5 .75.00

8 X 10 Photo 250.00

Canceled Check 150.00

Single Signed Ball 3500.00

Beckley, Jake-(1971) d. 1918

3 X 5 . . . . .1500.00

Signed Document 3500.00

Bell, Cool Papa-(1974) d. 1991

3 X 5 .15.00

8 X 10 Photo 50.00

Gold HOF Signed Postcard 35.00

Perez-Steele Signed Postcard 75.00

Single Signed Ball 300.00

Bench, Johnny-(1989)

3 X 5 .10.00

8 X 10 Photo 25.00

Gold HOF Signed Postcard 25.00

Perez-Steele Signed Postcard 30.00

Signed Bat 175.00

Single Signed Ball 45.00

Bender, Chief-(1953) d. 1954

3 X 5 . . . . .150.00

8 X 10 Photo 350.00

Canceled Check 750.00

Single Signed Ball 3500.00

Berg, Moe d. 1972

3 X 5 . . . . .100.00

8 X 10 Photo 400.00

Single Signed Ball 1250.00

Berra, Yogi-(1972)

3 X 5 . . . . .8.00

8 X 10 Photo 20.00

Gold HOF Signed Postcard 20.00

Perez-Steele Signed Postcard 25.00

Signed Bat 150.00

Single Signed Ball 40.00

Bottomley, Jim-(1974) d. 1959

3 X 5 . . . . .200.00

8 X 10 Photo 400.00

Single Signed Ball 3500.00

Boudreau, Lou-(1970)

3 X 5 . . . . .5.00

8 X 10 Photo 12.00

Canceled Check 40.00

Gold HOF Signed Postcard 10.00

MAX CAREY

TED WILLIAMS

JUAN GONZALEZ

KEN GRIFFEY JR.

STAN COVELESKI

SANDY KOUFAX

Perez-Steele Signed Postcard 25.00

Signed Bat 50.00

Single Signed Ball 30.00

Bresnahan, Roger-(1945) d. 1944

3 X 5 . . . . .400.00

Signed Document 1500.00

Single Signed Ball 6000.00

Brett, George

3 X 5 .15.00

8 X 10 Photo 35.00

Signed Bat 175.00

Single Signed Ball 60.00

Brock, Lou-(1985)

3 X 5 . . . . .5.00

8 X 10 Photo 20.00

Gold HOF Signed Postcard 15.00

Perez-Steele Signed Postcard 15.00

Signed Bat 75.00

Single Signed Ball 35.00

Brouthers, Dan-(1945) d. 1932

3 X 5 . . . . .1500.00

Signed Document 3500.00

Brown, Mordecai-(1949) d. 1948

3 X 5 .300.00

8 X 10 Photo 1000.00

Canceled Check 750.00

Single Signed Ball 4500.00

Bunning, Jim (1996)

3 X 5 . . . . .5.00

8 X 10 Photo 15.00

Gold HOF Signed Postcard 15.00

Signed Bat 50.00

Single Signed Ball 35.00

Burkett, Jesse-(1946) d. 1953

3 X 5 .450.00

8 X 10 Photo 1200.00

B&W HOF Signed Postcard . . .1500.00

Single Signed Ball 4500.00

Campanella, Roy-(1969) d. 1993

3 X 5 .300.00

8 X 10 Photo 800.00

Single Signed Ball 3600.00

Carew, Rod-(1991)

3 X 5 . . . . .5.00

8 X 10 Photo 20.00

Gold HOF Signed Postcard 20.00

Perez-Steele Signed Postcard 25.00

Signed Bat 175.00

Single Signed Ball 40.00

Carey, Max-(1961) d. 1976

3 X 5 .15.00

8 X 10 Photo 125.00

B&W HOF Signed Postcard 75.00

Canceled Check 75.00

Gold HOF Signed Postcard 60.00

Single Signed Ball 500.00

Carlton, Steve-(1994)

3 X 5 . . . . .5.00

8 X 10 Photo 20.00

Gold HOF Signed Postcard 20.00

Perez-Steele Signed Postcard 35.00

Signed Bat 75.00

Single Signed Ball 35.00

Cartwright, Alexander-(1938) d. 1892

3 X 5 . . . . .750.00

Signed Document 2500.00

Cash, Norm d. 1986

3 X 5 .25.00

8 X 10 Photo 50.00

Single Signed Ball 300.00

Chadwick, Henry-(1938) d. 1908

3 X 5 . . . . .1500.00

Signed Document 3500.00

Chance, Frank-(1946) d. 1924

3 X 5 .600.00

Signed Document 2000.00

Single Signed Ball 7500.00

Chandler, Happy-(1982) d. 1991

3 X 5 .10.00

8 X 10 Photo 25.00

Canceled Check 125.00

Gold HOF Signed Postcard 20.00

Perez-Steele Signed Postcard 25.00

Single Signed Ball 100.00

Charleston, Oscar-(1976) d. 1954

3 X 5 . . . . .1000.00

Signed Document 3000.00

Single Signed Ball 6000.00

Chesbro, Jack-(1946) d. 1931

3 X 5 . . . . .1000.00

Signed Document 3000.00

Cicotte, Eddie d. 1969

3 X 5 . . . . .350.00

Clarke, Fred-(1945) d. 1960

3 X 5 . . . . .150.00

8 X 10 Photo 400.00

B&W HOF Signed Postcard 650.00

Single Signed Ball 3000.00

Clarkson, John-(1963) d. 1909

3 X 5 . . . . .1500.00

Signed Document 3500.00

Clemente, Roberto-(1973) d. 1972

3 X 5 . . . . .300.00

8 X 10 Photo 700.00

Canceled Check 1200.00

Single Signed Ball 3600.00

Cobb, Ty-(1936) d. 1961

3 X 5 . . . . .300.00

8 X 10 Photo 1500.00

B&W HOF Signed Postcard . . .1200.00

Canceled Check 400.00

Single Signed Ball 3500.00

Cochrane, Mickey-(1947) d. 1962

3 X 5 . . . . .75.00

8 X 10 Photo 450.00

B&W HOF Signed Postcard 350.00

Canceled Check 200.00

REGGIE JACKSON

ROGER CLEMENS

DIZZY DEAN

DAVID JUSTICE

MARK GRACE

BILL DICKEY

BABE RUTH

Single Signed Ball 2500.00

Colavito, Rocky

3 X 5 . . . . .10.00

8 X 10 Photo 20.00

Canceled Check 25.00

Single Signed Ball 40.00

Collins, Eddie-(1939) d. 1951

3 X 5 .100.00

8 X 10 Photo 500.00

B&W HOF Signed Postcard . . .1200.00

Single Signed Ball 3500.00

Collins, Jimmie-(1945) d. 1943

3 X 5 .800.00

8 X 10 Photo 2000.00

Single Signed Ball 5000.00

Combs, Earle-(1970) d. 1976

3 X 5 . . . . .20.00

8 X 10 Photo 125.00

Canceled Check 100.00

Gold HOF Signed Postcard 40.00

Single Signed Ball 2000.00

Comiskey, Charles-(1939) d. 1931

3 X 5 .450.00

8 X 10 Photo 1500.00

Single Signed Ball 6000.00

Conigliaro, Tony d. 1990

3 X 5 . . . . .75.00

8 X 10 Photo 175.00

Single Signed Ball 600.00

Conlan, Jocko-(1974) d. 1989

3 X 5 .15.00

8 X 10 Photo 35.00

Gold HOF Signed Postcard 15.00

Perez-Steele Signed Postcard 50.00

Single Signed Ball 150.00

Connolly, Tom-(1953) d. 1963

3 X 5 .350.00

8 X 10 Photo 750.00

B&W HOF Signed Postcard . . .1200.00

Single Signed Ball 3500.00

Connor, Roger-(1976) d. 1931

3 X 5 .1000.00

Signed Document 3000.00

Single Signed Ball 8000.00

Coveleski, Stan-(1969) d. 1984

3 X 5 .15.00

8 X 10 Photo 50.00

Gold HOF Signed Postcard 25.00

Single Signed Ball 500.00

Crawford, Sam-(1957) d. 1968

3 X 5 .125.00

8 X 10 Photo 500.00

B&W HOF Signed Postcard 300.00

Gold HOF Signed Postcard 350.00

Single Signed Ball 2000.00

Cronin, Joe-(1956) d. 1984

3 X 5 .20.00

8 X 10 Photo 100.00

B&W HOF Signed Postcard 50.00

Canceled Check 125.00

Gold HOF Signed Postcard 35.00

Single Signed Ball 750.00

B&W HOF Signed Postcard 150.00

Gold HOF Signed Postcard 175.00

Single Signed Ball 750.00

JOE DIMAGGIO

Cummings, Candy-(1939) d. 1924

3 X 5 .1800.00

Signed Document 5000.00

Delahanty, Ed-(1945) d. 1903

3 X 5 .2000.00

Signed Document 7000.00

Cuyler, Kiki-(1968) d. 1950

3 X 5 .250.00

8 X 10 Photo 600.00

Single Signed Ball 3000.00

Dickey, Bill-(1954) d. 1993

3 X 5 .15.00

8 X 10 Photo 50.00

B&W HOF Signed Postcard 50.00

Canceled Check 250.00

Gold HOF Signed Postcard 35.00

Perez-Steele Signed Postcard 75.00

Single Signed Ball 300.00

Dandridge, Ray-(1987) d. 1994

3 X 5 .10.00

8 X 10 Photo 20.00

Canceled Check 35.00

Gold HOF Signed Postcard 20.00

Perez-Steele Signed Postcard 15.00

Single Signed Ball 75.00

JACKIE ROBINSON

Dihigo, Martin-(1977) d. 1971

3 X 5 .600.00

Signed Document 2000.00

Single Signed Ball 4000.00

Dawson, Andre

3 X 5 .5.00

8 X 10 Photo 15.00

Signed Bat 125.00

Single Signed Ball 25.00

DiMaggio, Dom

3 X 5 .10.00

8 X 10 Photo 20.00

Canceled Check 50.00

Single Signed Ball 100.00

Day, Leon-(1995) d. 1995

3 X 5 .10.00

8 X 10 Photo 40.00

Canceled Check 100.00

Single Signed Ball 125.00

DiMaggio, Joe-(1955)

3 X 5 .75.00

8 X 10 Photo 125.00

B&W HOF Signed Postcard 175.00

Gold HOF Signed Postcard 150.00

Perez-Steele Signed Postcard . . .250.00

Signed Bat 1800.00

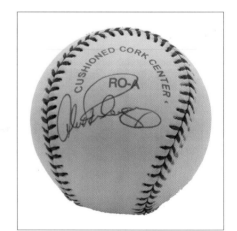

ALEX RODRIGUEZ

Dean, Dizzy-(1953) d. 1974

3 X 5 .75.00

8 X 10 Photo 200.00

BABE RUTH

LEO DUROCHER

CAL RIPKEN JR.

Single Signed Ball 250.00

DiMaggio, Vince d. 1986

3 X 5 . . . . .35.00

8 X 10 Photo 100.00

Single Signed Ball 300.00

Doby, Larry-(1998)

3 X 5 . . . . .5.00

8 X 10 Photo 15.00

Signed Bat 80.00

Single Signed Ball 30.00

Doerr, Bobby-(1986)

3 X 5 . . . . .5.00

8 X 10 Photo 15.00

Canceled Check 25.00

Gold HOF Signed Postcard 7.00

Perez-Steele Signed Postcard 10.00

Signed Bat 75.00

Single Signed Ball 25.00

Drysdale, Don-(1984) d. 1993

3 X 5 . . . . .15.00

8 X 10 Photo 40.00

Gold HOF Signed Postcard 40.00

Perez-Steele Signed Postcard 50.00

Single Signed Ball 150.00

Duffy, Hugh-(1945) d. 1954

3 X 5 . . . . .300.00

8 X 10 Photo 1000.00

B&W HOF Signed Postcard . . .1500.00

Single Signed Ball 3000.00

Durocher, Leo-(1994) d. 1991

3 X 5 . . . . .25.00

8 X 10 Photo 40.00

Single Signed Ball 175.00

Evans, Billy-(1973) d. 1956

3 X 5 . . . . .200.00

8 X 10 Photo 800.00

Single Signed Ball 3500.00

Evers, Johnny-(1946) d. 1947

3 X 5 . . . . .400.00

8 X 10 Photo 1200.00

Single Signed Ball 4500.00

Ewing, Buck-(1939) d. 1906

3 X 5 .1500.00

Signed Document 5000.00

Faber, Red-(1964) d. 1976

3 X 5 . . . . .50.00

8 X 10 Photo 125.00

Gold HOF Signed Postcard 100.00

Single Signed Ball 1500.00

Feller, Bob-(1962)

3 X 5 . . . . .5.00

8 X 10 Photo 12.00

B&W HOF Signed Postcard 25.00

Gold HOF Signed Postcard 10.00

Perez-Steele Signed Postcard 20.00

Single Signed Ball 25.00

Ferrell, Rick-(1984) d. 1995

3 X 5 . . . . .8.00

8 X 10 Photo 20.00

Canceled Check 30.00

Gold HOF Signed Postcard 10.00

Perez-Steele Signed Postcard 15.00

Single Signed Ball 60.00

Fingers, Rollie-(1992)

3 X 5 . . . . .5.00

8 X 10 Photo 15.00

Canceled Check 35.00

Gold HOF Signed Postcard 15.00

Perez-Steele Signed Postcard 20.00

Signed Bat 50.00

Single Signed Ball 25.00

Fisk, Carlton

3 X 5 . . . . .8.00

8 X 10 Photo 20.00

Signed Bat 125.00

Single Signed Ball 50.00

Flick, Elmer-(1963) d. 1971

3 X 5 .50.00

8 X 10 Photo 150.00

B&W HOF Signed Postcard 350.00

Gold HOF Signed Postcard 500.00

Single Signed Ball 1500.00

Ford, Whitey-(1974)

3 X 5 . . . . .8.00

8 X 10 Photo 20.00

Canceled Check 35.00

Gold HOF Signed Postcard 20.00

Perez-Steele Signed Postcard 25.00

Signed Bat 100.00

Single Signed Ball 35.00

Foster, Rube-(1981) d. 1930

3 X 5 . . . . .2500.00

Signed Document 8000.00

Fox, Nellie-(1997) d. 1975

3 X 5 . . . . .150.00

8 X 10 Photo 400.00

Canceled Check 600.00

Single Signed Ball 1800.00

Foxx, Jimmie-(1951) d. 1967

3 X 5 . . . . .250.00

8 X 10 Photo 700.00

B&W HOF Signed Postcard 800.00

Single Signed Ball 3000.00

Frick, Ford-(1970) d. 1978

3 X 5 .50.00

8 X 10 Photo 150.00

Gold HOF Signed Postcard 125.00

Single Signed Ball 1500.00

Frisch, Frankie-(1947) d. 1973

3 X 5 .50.00

8 X 10 Photo 175.00

B&W HOF Signed Postcard 250.00

Canceled Check 250.00

Gold HOF Signed Postcard 250.00

Single Signed Ball 1800.00

Furillo, Carl d. 1989

3 X 5 .25.00

8 X 10 Photo 75.00

BOB FELLER

JIMMIE FOXX

CRAIG BIGGIO

FRANKIE FRISCH

Memorable Moments

Box Score Highlights of Musial's Career

Of the 3,000-plus games in which Stan Musial played, some stand out above the others. There was the day he pumped out five hits in a game for the fourth time in one season, the afternoon when he socked a record five home runs in a double-header and the day in Chicago when he joined the elite 3,000-hit class. The box scores of these and other memorable games in The Man's fabulous baseball career follow:

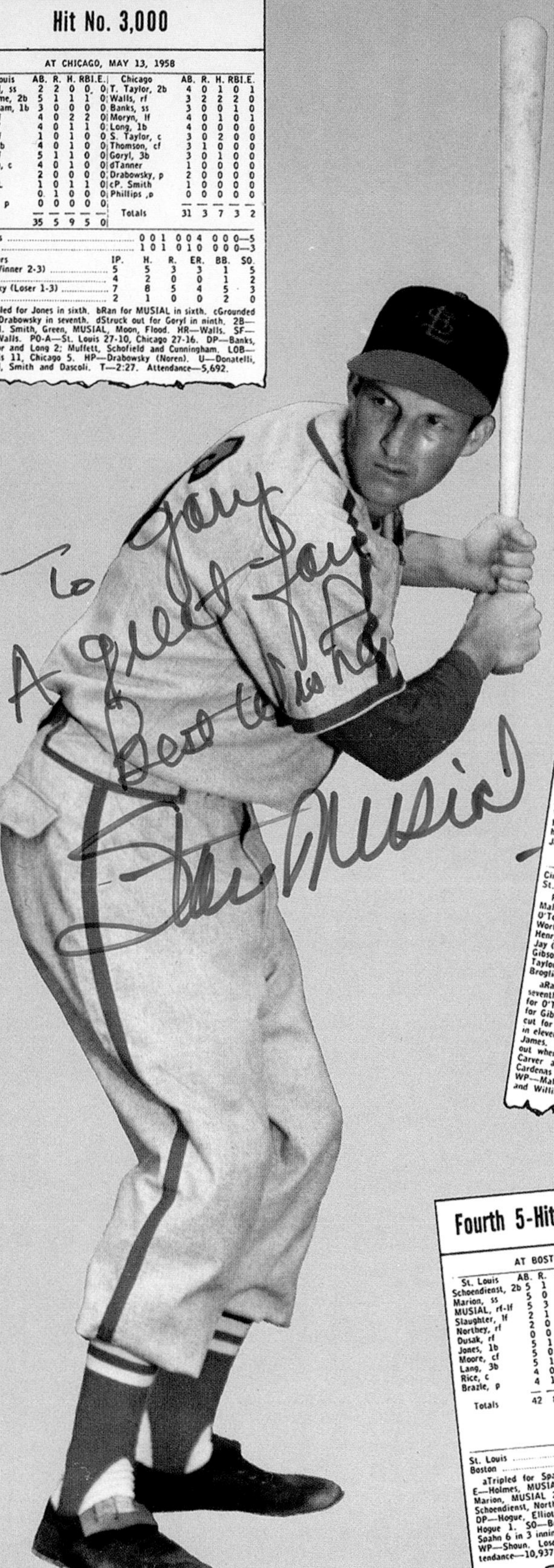

To Gary
A great fan
Stan Musial

Hit No. 3,000

AT CHICAGO, MAY 13, 1958

St. Louis	AB.	R.	H.	RBI.	E.	Chicago	AB.	R.	H.	RBI.	E.
Schofield, ss	2	2	0	0	0	T. Taylor, 2b	4	0	1	0	1
Blasingame, 2b	5	1	1	1	0	Walls, rf	3	2	2	2	0
Cunningham, 1b	3	0	0	0	0	Banks, ss	3	0	0	1	0
Noren, lf	4	0	2	2	0	Moryn, lf	4	0	1	0	1
Moon, cf	4	0	1	1	0	Long, 1b	4	0	0	0	0
Flood, cf	1	0	1	0	0	S. Taylor, c	3	0	2	0	0
Boyer, 3b	4	0	1	0	0	Thomson, cf	3	1	0	0	0
Green, rf	5	1	1	0	0	Goryl, 3b	3	0	1	0	0
H. Smith, c	4	0	1	0	0	dTanner	1	0	0	0	0
Jones, p	2	0	0	0	0	Drabowsky, p	2	0	0	0	0
aMUSIAL	1	0	1	1	0	cP. Smith	1	0	0	0	0
bBarnes	0	1	0	0	0	Phillips, p	0	0	0	0	0
Muffett, p	0	0	0	0	0	Totals	31	3	7	3	2
Totals	35	5	9	5	0						

St. Louis	0 0 1	0 0 4	0 0 0—5
Chicago	1 0 1	0 1 0	0 0 0—3

Pitchers	IP.	H.	R.	ER.	BB.	SO.
Jones (Winner 2-3)	5	5	3	3	1	5
Muffett	4	2	0	0	1	2
Drabowsky (Loser 1-3)	7	8	5	4	5	3
Phillips	2	1	0	0	2	0

aDoubled for Jones in sixth. bRan for MUSIAL in sixth. cGrounded out for Drabowsky in seventh. dStruck out for Goryl in ninth. 2B—Walls, H. Smith, Green, MUSIAL, Moon, Flood. HR—Walls. SF—Banks, Walls. PO-A—St. Louis 27-10, Chicago 27-16. DP—Banks, T. Taylor and Long 2; Muffett, Schofield and Cunningham. LOB—St. Louis 11, Chicago 5. HP—Drabowsky (Noren). U—Donatelli, Crawford, Smith and Dascoli. T—2:27. Attendance—5,692.

Debut in Pro Baseball

AT HUNTINGTON, W. VA., JUNE 18, 1938

Williamson	ab	r	h	rbi	Huntington	ab	r	h	rbi
Johnson, ss	5	1	1	0	Oleks, 2b	3	1	0	0
Carlen, 2b	5	1	2	0	Eastham, 1b	3	0	0	0
Hickey, cf	5	1	1	0	Marshall, cf	3	2	2	0
Hensley, 3b	3	2	0	0	Paul, 3b	3	1	2	1
Sessi, rf	4	2	4	3	Mincy, rf	3	1	0	0
Doyle, 1b	4	0	2	1	Semenko, lf	3	3	1	1
Flannery, lf	4	0	0	1	Sandlock, c	4	1	3	2
Beaman, c	5	1	1	1	Rapol, ss	3	0	1	0
MUSIAL, p	2	0	1	0	Mahan, p	0	0	0	1
DeFame, p	0	0	0	0	Lamanna, p	3	0	2	3
Youngblood, p	2	0	0	0					
Totals	39	8	12	6	Totals	28	9	11	8

Williamson	0 4 0	0 0 0	3 0 1—8
Huntington	1 1 0	2 2 2	0 1 x—9

Two-base hits—Sessi 3, Johnson, Marshall, Semenko, Sandlock. Home run—Carlen. Errors—Williamson 3, Huntington 1. Double play—Sessi and Johnson. Bases on balls—Off MUSIAL 3, off Lamanna 3, off Mahan 2, off DeFame 3, off Youngblood 2. Struck out—By MUSIAL 1, by Lamanna 8, by Mahan 2, by Youngblood 2. Hits—Off MUSIAL 6 in 3⅓ innings, off DeFame 0 in 1⅔ innings, off Youngblood 5 in 3 innings, off Mahan 2 in 5 innings, off Lamanna 10 in 4 innings. Wild pitch—Mahan. Winning pitcher—Mahan. Losing pitcher—DeFame. Left on bases—Williamson 7, Huntington 10. Umpires—Rhein and Yow.

First Game in Majors

AT ST. LOUIS, SEPTEMBER 17, 1941 (SECOND GAME)

Boston	AB.	R.	H.	O.	A.	St. Louis	AB.	R.	H.	O.	A.
Sisti 3b	4	0	0	1	1	Brown, 3b	4	0	1	0	3
Rowell, lf	4	0	1	2	0	Hopp, cf	3	1	0	4	0
Dudra, 1b	4	0	1	8	1	MUSIAL, rf	4	0	2	1	0
Demaree, rf	4	1	0	1	0	Mize, 1b	4	0	0	13	2
Miller, ss	3	1	1	3	2	Crabtree, lf	4	1	1	0	0
E. Moore, cf	3	0	1	4	1	Crespi, 2b	3	0	1	4	4
Cooney, cf	1	0	0	0	0	Marion, ss	2	0	0	1	3
Roberge, 2b	3	0	0	1	6	Mancuso, c	2	0	0	3	0
Berres, c	3	0	0	2	0	Lanier, p	3	1	1	1	1
Tobin, p	3	0	1	2	2	Totals	29	3	6	27	13
Totals	32	2	5	24	13						

Boston	0 0 0	0 0 0	2 0 0—2
St. Louis	0 0 2	0 0 0	0 0 1—3

None out when winning run scored. Runs batted in—MUSIAL 2, Miller, E. Moore, Crabtree. Two-base hits—MUSIAL, Rowell. Three-base hit—Miller. Home run—Crabtree. Double plays—E. Moore, Miller and Dudra; Marion and Mize. Bases on balls—Off Tobin 3, off Lanier 1. Struck out—By Tobin 2, by Lanier 3. Umpires—Goetz, Reardon and Conlan.

Farewell Appearance

AT ST. LOUIS, SEPTEMBER 29, 1963

Cincinnati	ab	r	h	rbi	St. Louis	ab	r	h	rbi
Rose, 2b-lf	6	0	3	0	Flood, cf	7	1	2	0
Harper, rf	6	0	0	0	Groat, ss	4	0	0	0
Pinson, cf	5	0	1	0	Maxvill, ss-2b	3	0	1	1
Neal, 2b	0	0	0	0	MUSIAL, lf	3	0	2	1
Robinson, lf-cf	6	0	0	0	aKolb, rf	1	1	0	0
Coleman, 1b	5	1	2	0	gBeauchamp	1	0	0	0
Edwards, c	2	0	0	0	Shannon, rf	1	0	0	0
bKeough	1	0	0	0	Boyer, 3b	6	0	4	0
Pavletich, c	3	1	1	0	White, 1b	5	0	2	0
Cardenas, ss	6	0	2	0	James, rf-lf	5	0	0	1
Kasko, 3b	5	0	0	2	McCarver, c	5	0	0	0
Maloney, p	2	0	0	0	Javier, 2b	3	0	0	0
cSkinner	1	0	1	0	eAltman	1	0	1	0
O'Toole, p	0	0	0	0	Buchek, ss	2	0	1	0
dGreen	1	0	0	0	Gibson, p	2	0	0	0
Worthington, p	0	0	0	0	fClemens	0	0	0	0
Henry, p	0	0	0	0	Taylor, p	0	0	0	0
hWalters	1	0	0	0	iSawatski	1	0	0	0
Jay, p	1	0	0	0	Broglio, p	1	1	0	0
Totals	51	2	10	2	Totals	51	3	13	3

Cincinnati	0 0 0	0 0 0	0 0 2	0 0 0	0 0—2
St. Louis	0 0 0	0 0 2	0 0 0	0 0 0	0 1—3

Pitchers	IP.	H.	R.	ER.	BB.	SO.
Maloney	7	5	2	2	2	11
O'Toole	1	1	0	0	0	0
Worthington	⅓	1	0	0	2	1
Henry	1⅔	1	0	0	0	1
Jay (L. 7-18)	3⅓	5	1	1	0	3
Gibson	9	7	2	2	1	11
Taylor	2	1	0	0	2	1
Broglio (Winner 18-8)	3	2	0	0	1	2

aRan for MUSIAL in sixth. bStruck out for Edwards in seventh. cSingled for Maloney in eighth. dPopped out for O'Toole in ninth. eSingled for Javier in ninth. fWalked for Gibson in ninth. gStruck out for Kolb in tenth. hPopped out for Henry in eleventh. iCalled out on strikes for Taylor in eleventh. 2B—Flood, Rose, Maxvill. SH—Harper. SF—James. E—Boyer, Groat. PO-A—Cincinnati 40-13 (one out when winning run scored), St. Louis 42-12. DP—McCarver and Groat; McCarver, Buchek and Maxvill; Neal, Cardenas and Coleman. LOB—Cincinnati 12, St. Louis 13. WP—Maloney, Gibson, Broglio 2. U—Barlick, Weyer, Vargo and Williams. T—3:45. Attendance—27,576.

Record 5 Homers in Twin-Bill

AT ST. LOUIS, MAY 2, 1954

FIRST GAME

New York	AB.	R.	H.	O.	A.	St. Louis	AB.	R.	H.	O.	A.
Williams, 2b	4	1	1	2	1	Moon, cf	5	2	2	2	0
Dark, ss	4	0	1	0	2	Schoendienst, 2b	3	3	0	3	3
Thompson, 3b	4	1	1	1	4	MUSIAL, rf	4	3	4	4	0
Irvin, lf	3	2	2	2	0	Jablonski, 3b	5	0	1	0	2
Mueller, rf	4	0	1	0	0	Repulski, lf	5	1	2	2	0
Mays, cf	3	0	0	2	0	Alston, 1b	4	1	4	8	1
Lockman, 1b	4	1	1	9	1	Grammas, ss	2	0	0	1	1
Westrum, c	4	1	2	7	2	aHemus, ss	3	0	1	0	0
Antonelli, p	2	0	0	1	1	Rice, c	3	0	0	6	1
Hearn, p	0	0	0	0	0	Staley, p	1	0	0	1	2
Picone, p	0	0	0	0	0	bLowrey	1	0	0	0	0
cHofman	1	0	0	0	0	Brazle, p	1	0	0	0	0
Totals	33	6	9	24	11	Totals	37	10	14	27	10

New York	0 0 0	3 2 1	0 0 0— 6
St. Louis	2 0 1	1 2 0	0 4 •—10

Pitchers	IP.	H.	R.	ER.	BB.	SO.
Staley	5	7	5	5	0	3
Brazle (Winner 1-0)	4	2	1	1	2	3
Antonelli	4·	6	6	5	3	4
Hearn (Loser 0-2)	3⅓	8	4	4	2	2
Picone	⅔	0	0	0	0	0

·Pitched to three batters in fifth.

aForced Jablonski for Grammas in fifth. bCalled out on strikes for Staley in fifth. cCalled out on strikes for Picone in ninth. E—Dark, Thompson. RBI—Moon, Alston 2, MUSIAL 6, Hemus, Thompson, Irvin 2, Mueller, Lockman, Westrum. 2B—Thompson, Irvin, Repulski. HR—Moon, MUSIAL 3, Alston, Lockman, Westrum, Irvin. SH—Staley, Hearn. DP—Schoendienst, Grammas and Alston; Jablonski, Schoendienst and Alston. LOB—New York 3, St. Louis 9. T—2:48.

SECOND GAME

New York	AB.	R.	H.	O.	A.	St. Louis	AB.	R.	H.	O.	A.
Lockman, 1b	2	1	0	10	1	Moon, cf	4	0	1	2	0
Dark, ss	5	0	0	2	1	Schoendienst, 2b	5	2	2	2	2
Thompson, 3b	4	1	1	0	2	MUSIAL, rf	4	3	2	4	1
Irvin, lf	4	1	1	0	0	Jablonski, 3b	5	1	3	1	0
Mueller, rf	5	3	5	2	0	Repulski, lf	4	1	0	3	0
Mays, cf	4	0	1	6	0	Alston, 1b	2	0	1	7	0
St. Claire, c	4	1	2	3	1	Grammas, ss	3	0	0	2	3
hAmalfitano	0	0	0	0	0	Poholsky, p	0	0	0	0	1
Westrum, c	0	0	0	1	0	gLowrey	0	0	0	0	0
Samford, 2b	1	0	0	0	1	Deal, p	0	0	0	0	0
aRhodes	1	1	1	0	0	Sarni, c	2	0	0	2	0
Wilhelm, p	1	0	0	0	1	dHemus, ss	2	0	0	0	0
Jansen, p	2	0	1	0	2	Presko, p	1	0	0	0	1
Liddle, p	1	0	0	1	0	Lint, p	0	0	0	0	0
bTaylor	0	0	0	0	0	Wright, p	1	0	0	0	0
cHofman, 2b	4	1	1	2	3	eFrazier	1	0	1	0	0
						fMiller	0	0	0	0	0
Totals	38	9	13	27	12	Rice, c	1	0	0	4	0
						Totals	35	7	10	27	8

New York	0 0 0	8 0 0	0 0 1—9
St. Louis	3 0 0	0 3 0	1 0 0—7

Pitchers	IP.	H.	R.	ER.	BB.	SO.
Liddle	3	3	3	3	3	0
Wilhelm	3	6	4	4	0	3
Jansen (Winner 1-0)	3	1	0	0	2	1
Presko	3⅓.	4	3	3	3	0
Lint (Loser 1-1)	⅓	3	5	5	2	0
Wright	2⅓	4	0	0	0	1
Poholsky	1	0	0	0	0	0
Deal	2	2	1	1	0	0

aSingled for Samford in fourth. bAnnounced for Liddle in fourth. cHomered for Taylor in fourth. dFlied out for Sarni in sixth. eDoubled for Wright in sixth. fRan for Frazier in sixth. gWalked for Poholsky in seventh. hRan for St. Claire in ninth. E—None. RBI—Alston 3, MUSIAL 3, Jablonski, Mays 3, Hofman 3, Mueller 2, Jansen. 2B—Schoendienst, Frazier, Alston, Mueller, Thompson. 3B—Mueller, Schoendienst. HR—Hofman, MUSIAL 2, Jablonski. SB—Jablonski. SF—Mays. DP—Thompson, Hofman and Lockman; Jansen, Dark and Lockman. LOB—New York 9, St. Louis 7. HP—Liddle (Moon), Deal (St. Claire). U—Ballanfant, Barlick, Warneke and Donatelli. T—2:58. Attendance—26,662.

Fourth 5-Hit Game of '48 Season

AT BOSTON, SEPTEMBER 22, 1948

St. Louis	AB.	R.	H.	O.	A.	Boston	AB.	R.	H.	O.	A.
Schoendienst, 2b	5	1	1	2	1	Holmes, rf	3	0	1	1	0
Marion, ss	5	0	1	2	6	Dark, ss	4	0	0	2	2
MUSIAL, rf-lf	5	3	5	4	0	M. McCormick, lf	4	0	0	4	0
Slaughter, lf	2	1	1	0	0	Elliott, 3b	4	0	0	1	1
Northey, rf	2	0	1	0	0	F. McCormick, 1b	4	0	0	8	2
Dusak, rf	0	0	0	1	0	Conatser, cf	4	1	2	3	0
Jones, 1b	5	1	2	12	0	Masi, c	4	0	2	4	0
Moore, cf	5	0	1	2	0	Sisti, 2b	4	0	0	2	0
Lang, 3b	5	1	3	0	3	Spahn, p	0	0	0	0	1
Rice, c	4	0	1	4	0	aSturgeon	1	1	1	0	0
Brazle, p	4	1	1	0	4	Barrett, p	0	0	0	0	0
Totals	42	8	17	27	14	Hogue, p	0	0	0	0	1
						bRyan	1	0	0	0	0
						Shoun, p	0	0	0	0	1
						Lyons, p	1	0	0	2	1
						Totals	34	2	6	27	9

St. Louis	0 1 2	4 0 1	0 0 0—8
Boston	0 0 1	0 0 0	1 0 0—2

aTripled for Spahn in third. bPopped out for Hogue in fifth. E—Holmes, MUSIAL, Jones. RBI—Rice, Slaughter, Jones, Brazle, Marion, MUSIAL 2, Northey, Dark, Masi. 2B—MUSIAL, Lang 2, Schoendienst, Northey, Conatser, Masi. 3B—Sturgeon. HR—MUSIAL. DP—Hogue, Elliott and F. McCormick. BB—Brazle 1, Barrett 1, Hogue 1. SO—Brazle 4, Spahn 1, Barrett 1, Shoun 1. Hits—Spahn 6 in 3 innings, Barrett 4 in ⅔, Hogue 2 in 1⅓, Shoun 3 in 2. WP—Shoun. Loser—Spahn. Umpires—Robb, Pinelli and Gore. Attendance—10,937.

STAN THE MAN, INC.

Stan Musial

Single Signed Ball 350.00

Galvin, Pud-(1965) d. 1902

3 X 5 .1500.00

Signed Document 4000.00

Gehrig, Lou-(1939) d. 1941

3 X 5 .1000.00

8 X 10 Photo 4500.00

Single Signed Ball 8000.00

Gehringer, Charley-(1949) d. 1993

3 X 5 . . . . .15.00

8 X 10 Photo 40.00

B&W HOF Signed Postcard 35.00

Gold HOF Signed Postcard 25.00

Perez-Steele Signed Postcard 75.00

Single Signed Ball 175.00

Gibson, Bob-(1981)

3 X 5 . . . . .5.00

8 X 10 Photo 20.00

Gold HOF Signed Postcard 15.00

Perez-Steele Signed Postcard 20.00

Signed Bat 100.00

Single Signed Ball 30.00

Gibson, Josh-(1972) d. 1947

3 X 5 .600.00

Signed Document 1500.00

Single Signed Ball 5000.00

Gilliam, Jim d. 1978

3 X 5 . . . . .20.00

8 X 10 Photo 75.00

Single Signed Ball 600.00

Gomez, Lefty-(1972) d. 1988

3 X 5 . . . . .15.00

8 X 10 Photo 50.00

Canceled Check 125.00

Gold HOF Signed Postcard 20.00

Perez-Steele Signed Postcard 75.00

Single Signed Ball 350.00

Goslin, Goose-(1968) d. 1971

3 X 5 .100.00

8 X 10 Photo 300.00

Gold HOF Signed Postcard 400.00

Single Signed Ball 2000.00

Greenberg, Hank-(1956) d. 1986

3 X 5 . . . . .50.00

8 X 10 Photo 200.00

B&W HOF Signed Postcard 150.00

Gold HOF Signed Postcard 100.00

Perez-Steele Signed Postcard . . .300.00

Single Signed Ball 800.00

Griffith, Clark-(1946) d. 1955

3 X 5 .200.00

8 X 10 Photo 600.00

B&W HOF Signed Postcard 750.00

Single Signed Ball 3500.00

Grimes, Burleigh-(1964) d. 1985

3 X 5 . . . . .15.00

8 X 10 Photo 75.00

Canceled Check 60.00

Gold HOF Signed Postcard 25.00

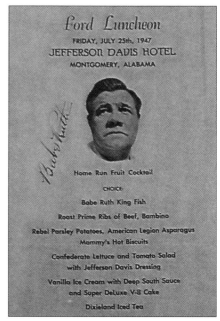

BABE RUTH

NOMAR GARCIAPARRA

TED WILLIAMS

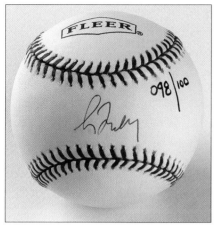

GREG MADDUX

Charles Gehringer (signature)

CHARLEY GEHRINGER

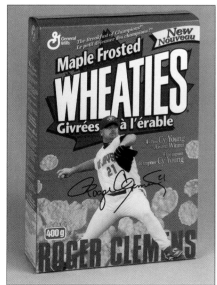

ROGER CLEMENS

Perez-Steele Signed Postcard . . .200.00

Single Signed Ball 300.00

Grove, Lefty-(1947) d. 1975

3 X 5 . . . . .40.00

8 X 10 Photo 200.00

B&W HOF Signed Postcard 150.00

Canceled Check 125.00

Gold HOF Signed Postcard 125.00

Single Signed Ball 2000.00

Hafey, Chick-(1971) d. 1973

3 X 5 . . . . .40.00

8 X 10 Photo 150.00

Gold HOF Signed Postcard 400.00

Single Signed Ball 2000.00

Haines, Jesse-(1970) d. 1978

3 X 5 . . . . .25.00

8 X 10 Photo 125.00

Canceled Check 100.00

Gold HOF Signed Postcard 100.00

Single Signed Ball 1200.00

Hamilton, Billy-(1961) d. 1940

3 X 5 .1000.00

8 X 10 Photo 2000.00

Single Signed Ball 5500.00

Harridge, Will-(1972) d. 1971

3 X 5 . . . . .40.00

8 X 10 Photo 200.00

Single Signed Ball 2500.00

Harris, Bucky-(1975) d. 1977

3 X 5 . . . . .40.00

8 X 10 Photo 200.00

Gold HOF Signed Postcard 150.00

Single Signed Ball 1500.00

Hartnett, Gabby-(1955) d. 1972

3 X 5 . . . . .75.00

8 X 10 Photo 175.00

B&W HOF Signed Postcard 250.00

Canceled Check 250.00

Gold HOF Signed Postcard 400.00

Single Signed Ball 2000.00

Heilmann, Harry-(1952) d. 1951

3 X 5 .350.00

8 X 10 Photo 800.00

Single Signed Ball 3500.00

Herman, Billy-(1975) d. 1992

3 X 5 . . . . .10.00

8 X 10 Photo 35.00

Canceled Check 60.00

Gold HOF Signed Postcard 15.00

Perez-Steele Signed Postcard 25.00

Single Signed Ball 125.00

Hodges, Gil d. 1972

3 X 5 .100.00

8 X 10 Photo 300.00

Single Signed Ball 1200.00

Hooper, Harry-(1971) d. 1974

3 X 5 . . . . .30.00

8 X 10 Photo 125.00

Canceled Check 75.00

Gold HOF Signed Postcard 150.00

Single Signed Ball 750.00

Hornsby, Rogers-(1942) d. 1963

3 X 5 . . . . .200.00

8 X 10 Photo 600.00

B&W HOF Signed Postcard 450.00

Single Signed Ball 3000.00

Howard, Elston d. 1980

3 X 5 . . . . .100.00

8 X 10 Photo 350.00

Single Signed Ball 1000.00

Hoyt, Waite-(1969) d. 1984

3 X 5 . . . . .20.00

8 X 10 Photo 75.00

Canceled Check 125.00

Gold HOF Signed Postcard 50.00

Single Signed Ball 450.00

Hubbard, Cal-(1976) d. 1977

3 X 5 . . . . .50.00

8 X 10 Photo (Baseball) 150.00

Single Signed Ball 1000.00

Hubbell, Carl-(1947) d. 1988

3 X 5 . . . . .15.00

8 X 10 Photo 50.00

B&W HOF Signed Postcard 50.00

Canceled Check 75.00

Gold HOF Signed Postcard 25.00

Perez-Steele Signed Postcard 75.00

Single Signed Ball 250.00

Hubbs, Ken d. 1964

3 X 5 . . . . .30.00

8 X 10 Photo 150.00

Single Signed Ball 700.00

Huggins, Miller-(1964) d. 1929

3 X 5 . . . . .600.00

8 X 10 Photo 1800.00

Single Signed Ball 4500.00

Hunter, Catfish-(1987)

3 X 5 . . . . .5.00

8 X 10 Photo 15.00

Gold HOF Signed Postcard 7.00

Perez-Steele Signed Postcard 10.00

Signed Bat 50.00

Single Signed Ball 30.00

Irvin, Monte-(1973)

3 X 5 . . . . .5.00

8 X 10 Photo 15.00

Canceled Check 25.00

Gold HOF Signed Postcard 10.00

Perez-Steele Signed Postcard 15.00

Signed Bat 75.00

Single Signed Ball 30.00

Jackson, Joe d. 1951

3 X 5 . . . . .5000.00

Jackson, Reggie-(1993)

3 X 5 . . . . .10.00

8 X 10 Photo 25.00

Gold HOF Signed Postcard 50.00

Perez-Steele Signed Postcard 50.00

Signed Bat 250.00

Single Signed Ball 60.00

JUAN GONZALEZ

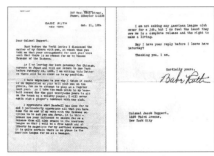

BABE RUTH

KEN GRIFFEY JR.

TONY GWYNN

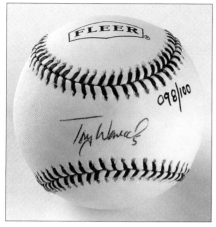

TONY WOMACK

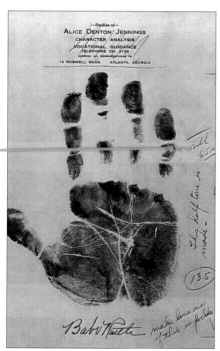

LEFTY GROVE

BABE RUTH

Jackson, Travis-(1982) d. 1987

3 X 5	.25.00
8 X 10 Photo	.75.00
Gold HOF Signed Postcard	.40.00
Perez-Steele Signed Postcard	.75.00
Single Signed Ball	.350.00

Jenkins, Ferguson-(1991)

3 X 5	.5.00
8 X 10 Photo	.12.00
Canceled Check	.25.00
Gold HOF Signed Postcard	.10.00
Perez-Steele Signed Postcard	.15.00
Signed Bat	.75.00
Single Signed Ball	.25.00

Jennings, Hughie-(1945) d. 1928

3 X 5	.700.00
8 X 10 Photo	.2000.00
Single Signed Ball	.7000.00

Jensen, Jackie d. 1982

3 X 5	.25.00
8 X 10 Photo	.50.00
Canceled Check	.100.00
Single Signed Ball	.175.00

Johnson, Ban-(1937) d. 1931

3 X 5	.350.00
8 X 10 Photo	.1000.00
Single Signed Ball	.3500.00

Johnson, Judy-(1975) d. 1989

3 X 5	.15.00
8 X 10 Photo	.50.00

Gold HOF Signed Postcard	.40.00
Perez-Steele Signed Postcard	.60.00
Single Signed Ball	.250.00

Johnson, Walter-(1936) d. 1946

3 X 5	.400.00
8 X 10 Photo	.1500.00
B&W HOF Signed Postcard	.1200.00
Canceled Check	.1000.00
Single Signed Ball	.5000.00

Joss, Addie-(1978) d. 1911

3 X 5	.1500.00
Signed Document	.4500.00

Kaline, Al-(1980)

3 X 5	.8.00
8 X 10 Photo	.20.00
Gold HOF Signed Postcard	.15.00
Perez-Steele Signed Postcard	.20.00
Signed Bat	.125.00
Single Signed Ball	.35.00

Keefe, Tim-(1964) d. 1933

3 X 5	.1000.00
Signed Document	.3000.00
Single Signed Ball	.12000.00

Keeler, Willie-(1939) d. 1923

3 X 5	.1000.00
Signed Document	.2500.00
Single Signed Ball	.10000.00

Kell, George-(1983)

3 X 5	.5.00

8 X 10 Photo 12.00

Canceled Check 25.00

Gold HOF Signed Postcard 7.00

Perez-Steele Signed Postcard 15.00

Signed Bat 75.00

Single Signed Ball 25.00

Kelley, Joe-(1971) d. 1943

3 X 5 .1200.00

8 X 10 Photo 3000.00

Single Signed Ball 7500.00

Kelly, George-(1973) d. 1984

3 X 5 . . . . .15.00

8 X 10 Photo 50.00

Canceled Check 100.00

Gold HOF Signed Postcard 30.00

Perez-Steele Signed Postcard . . .300.00

Single Signed Ball 250.00

Kelly, Mike "King"-(1945) d. 1894

3 X 5 .2000.00

Signed Document 5000.00

Killebrew, Harmon-(1984)

3 X 5 . . . . .8.00

8 X 10 Photo 20.00

Gold HOF Signed Postcard 15.00

Perez-Steele Signed Postcard 20.00

Signed Bat 75.00

Single Signed Ball 35.00

Kiner, Ralph-(1975)

3 X 5 . . . . .5.00

8 X 10 Photo 15.00

Canceled Check 25.00

Gold HOF Signed Postcard 10.00

Perez-Steele Signed Postcard 15.00

Signed Bat 60.00

Single Signed Ball 25.00

Klein, Chuck-(1980) d. 1958

3 X 5 .250.00

8 X 10 Photo 750.00

Single Signed Ball 2500.00

Klem, Bill-(1953) d. 1951

3 X 5 .300.00

8 X 10 Photo 750.00

Single Signed Ball 2500.00

Kluszewski, Ted d. 1988

3 X 5 . . . . .20.00

8 X 10 Photo 50.00

Canceled Check 100.00

Single Signed Ball 150.00

Koufax, Sandy-(1972)

3 X 5 . . . . .15.00

8 X 10 Photo 40.00

Gold HOF Signed Postcard 50.00

Perez-Steele Signed Postcard 60.00

Signed Bat 100.00

Single Signed Ball 75.00

Lajoie, Nap-(1937) d. 1959

3 X 5 .300.00

8 X 10 Photo 1200.00

B&W HOF Signed Postcard 750.00

Single Signed Ball 4000.00

MICKEY MANTLE

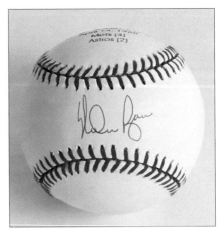

HANK GREENBERG

NOLAN RYAN

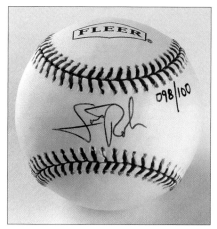

SCOTT ROLEN

TONY GWYNN

ROGER CLEMENS

JESSE HAINES

Landis, Kenesaw-(1939) d. 1944

3 X 5 . . . . .250.00

8 X 10 Photo 750.00

Single Signed Ball 3500.00

Lazzeri, Tony-(1991) d. 1946

3 X 5 . . . . .350.00

8 X 10 Photo 850.00

Single Signed Ball 3500.00

Lemon, Bob-(1976)

3 X 5 . . . . .5.00

8 X 10 Photo 12.00

Gold HOF Signed Postcard 7.00

Perez-Steele Signed Postcard 15.00

Single Signed Ball 25.00

Leonard, Buck-(1972) d. 1997

3 X 5 . . . . .15.00

8 X 10 Photo 30.00

Canceled Check 20.00

Gold HOF Signed Postcard 20.00

Perez-Steele Signed Postcard 35.00

Single Signed Ball 75.00

Lindstrom, Fred-(1976) d. 1981

3 X 5 . . . . .20.00

8 X 10 Photo 100.00

Gold HOF Signed Postcard 50.00

Single Signed Ball 500.00

Lloyd, John Henry-(1977) d. 1964

3 X 5 . . . . .750.00

8 X 10 Photo 2500.00

Single Signed Ball 6000.00

Lombardi, Ernie-(1986) d. 1977

3 X 5 . . . . .50.00

8 X 10 Photo 150.00

Single Signed Ball 1000.00

Lopez, Al-(1977)

3 X 5 . . . . .15.00

8 X 10 Photo 40.00

Gold HOF Signed Postcard 30.00

Perez-Steele Signed Postcard 75.00

Signed Bat 175.00

Single Signed Ball 125.00

Lyons, Ted-(1955) d. 1986

3 X 5 . . . . .20.00

8 X 10 Photo 75.00

B&W HOF Signed Postcard 35.00

Canceled Check 60.00

Gold HOF Signed Postcard 40.00

Perez-Steele Signed Postcard . . .250.00

Single Signed Ball 350.00

Mack, Connie-(1937) d. 1956

3 X 5 . . . . .150.00

8 X 10 Photo 350.00

B&W HOF Signed Postcard 750.00

Single Signed Ball 2500.00

MacPhail, Larry-(1978) d. 1975

3 X 5 . . . . .100.00

8 X 10 Photo 250.00

Single Signed Ball 1500.00

Maglie, Sal d. 1992

3 X 5 . . . . .25.00

8 X 10 Photo 50.00

Canceled Check 60.00

Single Signed Ball 250.00

Mantle, Mickey-(1974) d. 1995

3 X 5 . . . . .50.00

8 X 10 Photo 125.00

Gold HOF Signed Postcard 150.00

Perez-Steele Signed Postcard . . .250.00

Signed Bat 2000.00

Single Signed Ball 225.00

Manush, Heinie-(1964) d. 1971

3 X 5 . . . . .50.00

8 X 10 Photo 200.00

Canceled Check 400.00

Gold HOF Signed Postcard 200.00

Single Signed Ball 1500.00

Maranville, Rabbit-(1954) d. 1954

3 X 5 .200.00

8 X 10 Photo 500.00

B&W HOF Signed Postcard 750.00

Single Signed Ball 2000.00

Marichal, Juan-(1983)

3 X 5 . . . . .5.00

8 X 10 Photo 20.00

Gold HOF Signed Postcard 10.00

Perez-Steele Signed Postcard 10.00

Signed Bat 50.00

Single Signed Ball 30.00

Maris, Roger d. 1985

3 X 5 .175.00

8 X 10 Photo 500.00

Single Signed Ball 1200.00

Marquard, Rube-(1971) d. 1980

3 X 5 . . . . .40.00

8 X 10 Photo 100.00

Gold HOF Signed Postcard 40.00

Single Signed Ball 750.00

Martin, Billy d. 1989

3 X 5 . . . . .15.00

8 X 10 Photo 50.00

Single Signed Ball 200.00

Martin, Pepper d. 1965

3 X 5 . . . . .75.00

8 X 10 Photo 250.00

Single Signed Ball 850.00

Mathews, Eddie-(1978)

3 X 5 . . . . .8.00

8 X 10 Photo 20.00

Gold HOF Signed Postcard 10.00

Perez-Steele Signed Postcard 15.00

Signed Bat 100.00

Single Signed Ball 30.00

Mathewson, Christy-(1936) d. 1925

3 X 5 . . . . .1200.00

8 X 10 Photo 3500.00

Single Signed Ball 10000.00

Mattingly, Don

3 X 5 . . . . .12.00

8 X 10 Photo 30.00

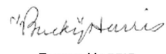

BUCKY HARRIS

STEVE CARLTON

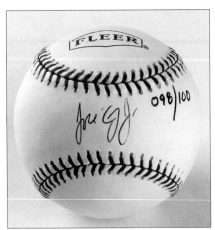

JOSE CRUZ JR.

ROGER CLEMENS

Signed Bat 175.00

Single Signed Ball 50.00

Mays, Willie-(1979)

3 X 5 . . . . .20.00

8 X 10 Photo 35.00

Gold HOF Signed Postcard 30.00

Perez-Steele Signed Postcard 50.00

Signed Bat 150.00

Single Signed Ball 50.00

McCarthy, Joe-(1957) d. 1978

3 X 5 . . . . .40.00

8 X 10 Photo 150.00

B&W HOF Signed Postcard 100.00

Gold HOF Signed Postcard 75.00

Single Signed Ball 1200.00

McCarthy, Tom-(1946) d. 1922

3 X 5 .1200.00

8 X 10 Photo 4000.00

McCovey, Willie-(1986)

3 X 5 . . . . .8.00

8 X 10 Photo 20.00

Canceled Check 40.00

Gold HOF Signed Postcard 15.00

Perez-Steele Signed Postcard 15.00

Signed Bat 60.00

Single Signed Ball 40.00

McGinnity, Joe-(1946) d. 1929

3 X 5 .1000.00

Signed Document 4500.00

Single Signed Ball 18000.00

McGowan, Bill-(1992) d. 1954

3 X 5 . . . . .350.00

8 X 10 Photo 1200.00

Single Signed Ball 4000.00

McGraw, John-(1937) d. 1934

3 X 5 . . . . .650.00

8 X 10 Photo 2000.00

Single Signed Ball 6000.00

McKechnie, Bill-(1962) d. 1965

3 X 5 . . . . .125.00

8 X 10 Photo 450.00

B&W HOF Signed Postcard 400.00

Single Signed Ball 3000.00

Medwick, Joe-(1968) d. 1975

3 X 5 . . . . .40.00

8 X 10 Photo 150.00

Gold HOF Signed Postcard 150.00

Single Signed Ball 750.00

Mize, Johnny-(1981) d. 1993

3 X 5 . . . . .10.00

8 X 10 Photo 25.00

Gold HOF Signed Postcard 15.00

Perez-Steele Signed Postcard 25.00

Signed Bat 150.00

Single Signed Ball 75.00

Morgan, Joe-(1990)

3 X 5 . . . . .8.00

8 X 10 Photo 15.00

Gold HOF Signed Postcard 15.00

Perez-Steele Signed Postcard 20.00

MONTE IRVIN

SANDY KOUFAX

Signed Bat 150.00

Single Signed Ball 35.00

8 X 10 Photo 200.00

Single Signed Ball 1500.00

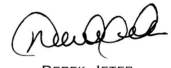

DEREK JETER

Munson, Thurman d. 1979

3 X 5 . . . . .175.00

8 X 10 Photo 400.00

Canceled Check 600.00

Single Signed Ball 1500.00

Musial, Stan-(1969)

3 X 5 .15.00

8 X 10 Photo 25.00

Canceled Check 100.00

Gold HOF Signed Postcard 25.00

Perez-Steele Signed Postcard 50.00

Signed Bat 225.00

Single Signed Ball 50.00

Newhouser, Hal-(1992)

3 X 5 . . . . .5.00

8 X 10 Photo 15.00

Canceled Check 35.00

Gold HOF Signed Postcard 7.00

Perez-Steele Signed Postcard 25.00

Signed Bat 60.00

Single Signed Ball 30.00

Nichols, Kid-(1949) d. 1953

3 X 5 . . . . .300.00

8 X 10 Photo 600.00

B&W HOF Signed Postcard . . .1500.00

Single Signed Ball 7000.00

O'Doul, Lefty d. 1969

3 X 5 .75.00

O'Rourke, Jim-(1945) d. 1914

3 X 5 . . . . .1200.00

Signed Document 3500.00

Ott, Mel-(1951) d. 1958

3 X 5 . . . . .250.00

8 X 10 Photo 750.00

B&W HOF Signed Postcard 700.00

Canceled Check 350.00

Single Signed Ball 3500.00

Paige, Satchel-(1971) d. 1982

3 X 5 .75.00

8 X 10 Photo 275.00

Gold HOF Signed Postcard 175.00

Single Signed Ball 1500.00

Palmer, Jim-(1990)

3 X 5 . . . . .5.00

8 X 10 Photo 20.00

Gold HOF Signed Postcard 15.00

Perez-Steele Signed Postcard 20.00

Signed Bat 60.00

Single Signed Ball 30.00

Pennock, Herb-(1948) d. 1948

3 X 5 . . . . .200.00

8 X 10 Photo 600.00

Canceled Check 1200.00

Single Signed Ball 3000.00

Perry, Gaylord-(1991)

3 X 5 . . . . .5.00

BABE RUTH

CHIPPER JONES

TED KLUSZEWSKI

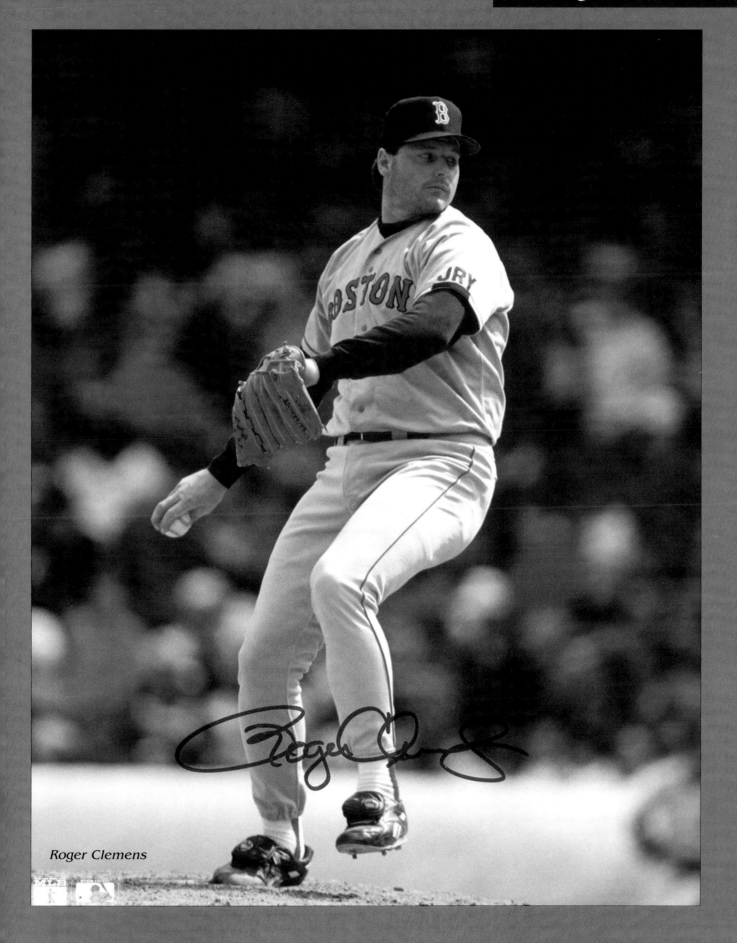

Roger Clemens

8 X 10 Photo 15.00

Canceled Check 25.00

Gold HOF Signed Postcard 7.00

Perez-Steele Signed Postcard 15.00

Signed Bat 50.00

Single Signed Ball 25.00

Plank, Eddie-(1946) d. 1926

3 X 5 . . . . .1000.00

8 X 10 Photo 3500.00

Single Signed Ball 9000.00

Puckett, Kirby

3 X 5 . . . . .10.00

8 X 10 Photo 30.00

Signed Bat 150.00

Single Signed Ball 50.00

Radbourne, Hoss-(1939) d. 1897

3 X 5 . . . . .1500.00

Signed Document 4000.00

Reese, Pee Wee-(1984)

3 X 5 . . . . .10.00

8 X 10 Photo 30.00

Gold HOF Signed Postcard 30.00

Perez-Steele Signed Postcard 25.00

Signed Bat 150.00

Single Signed Ball 75.00

Rice, Sam-(1963) d. 1974

3 X 5 . . . . .40.00

8 X 10 Photo 200.00

B&W HOF Signed Postcard 125.00

Gold HOF Signed Postcard 150.00

Single Signed Ball 1500.00

Rickey, Branch-(1967) d. 1965

3 X 5 . . . . .150.00

8 X 10 Photo 400.00

Canceled Check 800.00

Single Signed Ball 2000.00

Rixey, Eppa-(1963) d. 1963

3 X 5 . . . . .150.00

8 X 10 Photo 500.00

Canceled Check 150.00

Single Signed Ball 2500.00

Rizzuto, Phil-(1994)

3 X 5 .8.00

8 X 10 Photo 15.00

Gold HOF Signed Postcard 20.00

Perez-Steele Signed Postcard 25.00

Signed Bat 125.00

Single Signed Ball 30.00

Roberts, Robin-(1976)

3 X 5 .5.00

8 X 10 Photo 12.00

Gold HOF Signed Postcard 7.00

Perez-Steele Signed Postcard 15.00

Signed Bat 75.00

Single Signed Ball 30.00

Robinson, Brooks-(1983)

3 X 5 .5.00

8 X 10 Photo 20.00

Canceled Check 25.00

Gold HOF Signed Postcard 10.00

WILLIE MAYS

NAP LAJOIE

NOMAR GARCIAPARRA

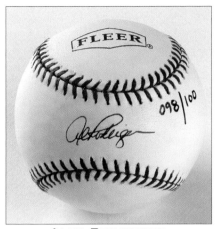

ALEX RODRIGUEZ

BUCK LEONARD

OZZIE SMITH

TED LYONS

Perez-Steele Signed Postcard 15.00

Signed Bat 60.00

Single Signed Ball 30.00

Robinson, Frank-(1982)

3 X 5 . . . . .10.00

8 X 10 Photo 25.00

Gold HOF Signed Postcard 15.00

Perez-Steele Signed Postcard 15.00

Signed Bat 175.00

Single Signed Ball 35.00

Robinson, Jackie-(1962) d. 1972

3 X 5 . . . . .250.00

8 X 10 Photo 600.00

B&W HOF Signed Postcard 800.00

Canceled Check 500.00

Gold HOF Signed Postcard 350.00

Single Signed Ball 4000.00

Robinson, Wilbert-(1945) d. 1934

3 X 5 . . . . .750.00

8 X 10 Photo 2000.00

Single Signed Ball 8500.00

Rose, Pete

3 X 5 . . . . .10.00

8 X 10 Photo 20.00

Signed Bat 100.00

Single Signed Ball 40.00

Roush, Edd-(1962) d. 1988

3 X 5 . . . . .12.00

8 X 10 Photo 40.00

B&W HOF Signed Postcard 40.00

Gold HOF Signed Postcard 25.00

Perez-Steele Signed Postcard 75.00

Single Signed Ball 300.00

Ruffing, Red-(1967) d. 1986

3 X 5 . . . . .25.00

8 X 10 Photo 100.00

Gold HOF Signed Postcard 75.00

Single Signed Ball 500.00

Rusie, Amos-(1977) d. 1942

3 X 5 . . . . .700.00

8 X 10 Photo 2000.00

Single Signed Ball 5000.00

Ruth, Babe-(1936) d. 1948

3 X 5 . . . . .750.00

8 X 10 Photo 2500.00

Canceled Check 1600.00

Single Signed Ball 5500.00

Ryan, Nolan

3 X 5 . . . . .15.00

8 X 10 Photo 30.00

Signed Bat 175.00

Single Signed Ball 50.00

Schalk, Ray-(1955) d. 1970

3 X 5 . . . . .50.00

8 X 10 Photo 150.00

B&W HOF Signed Postcard 275.00

Gold HOF Signed Postcard 450.00

Single Signed Ball 1200.00

Schmidt, Mike-(1995)

3 X 5 . . . . .10.00

8 X 10 Photo 25.00

Gold HOF Signed Postcard 50.00

Perez-Steele Signed Postcard 60.00

Signed Bat 150.00

Single Signed Ball 60.00

Schoendienst, Red-(1989)

3 X 5 . . . . .5.00

8 X 10 Photo 15.00

Gold HOF Signed Postcard 10.00

Perez-Steele Signed Postcard 15.00

Signed Bat 75.00

Single Signed Ball 25.00

Seaver, Tom-(1992)

3 X 5 . . . . .8.00

8 X 10 Photo 20.00

Gold HOF Signed Postcard 20.00

Perez-Steele Signed Postcard 40.00

Signed Bat 100.00

Single Signed Ball 50.00

Sewell, Joe-(1977) d. 1990

3 X 5 . . . . .15.00

8 X 10 Photo 40.00

Canceled Check 25.00

Gold HOF Signed Postcard 20.00

Perez-Steele Signed Postcard 50.00

Single Signed Ball 125.00

Simmons, Al-(1953) d. 1956

3 X 5 .200.00

8 X 10 Photo 500.00

B&W HOF Signed Postcard 600.00

Canceled Check 175.00

Single Signed Ball 2500.00

Sisler, George-(1939) d. 1973

3 X 5 . . . . .50.00

8 X 10 Photo 150.00

B&W HOF Signed Postcard 150.00

Gold HOF Signed Postcard 150.00

Single Signed Ball 1500.00

Slaughter Enos-(1985)

3 X 5 . . . . .5.00

8 X 10 Photo 15.00

Canceled Check 35.00

Gold HOF Signed Postcard 7.00

Perez-Steele Signed Postcard 15.00

Signed Bat 75.00

Single Signed Ball 25.00

Smith, Ozzie

3 X 5 .10.00

8 X 10 Photo 25.00

Signed Bat 100.00

Single Signed Ball 40.00

Snider, Duke-(1980)

3 X 5 .10.00

8 X 10 Photo 20.00

Canceled Check 40.00

Gold HOF Signed Postcard 15.00

Perez-Steele Signed Postcard 25.00

Signed Bat 125.00

Single Signed Ball 35.00

Spahn, Warren-(1973)

3 X 5 . . . . .8.00

CONNIE MACK

ROGER MARIS

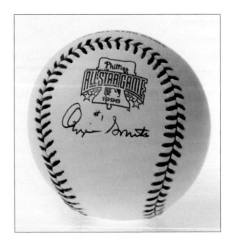

OZZIE SMITH

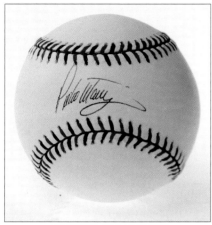

PEDRO MARTINEZ

MICKEY MANTLE

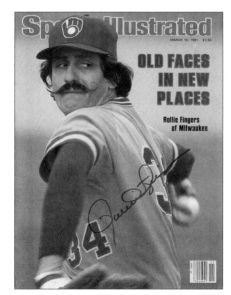

ROLLIE FINGERS

8 X 10 Photo 20.00

Canceled Check 15.00

Gold HOF Signed Postcard 10.00

Perez-Steele Signed Postcard 20.00

Signed Bat 75.00

Single Signed Ball 30.00

Spalding, Al-(1939) d. 1915

3 X 5 . . . . .1000.00

Signed Document 3000.00

Speaker, Tris-(1937) d. 1958

3 X 5 .300.00

8 X 10 Photo 750.00

B&W HOF Signed Postcard 800.00

Single Signed Ball 3500.00

Stargell, Willie-(1988)

3 X 5 . . . . .5.00

8 X 10 Photo 20.00

Gold HOF Signed Postcard 7.00

Perez-Steele Signed Postcard 15.00

Signed Bat 100.00

Single Signed Ball 25.00

Stengel, Casey-(1966) d. 1975

3 X 5 .60.00

8 X 10 Photo 200.00

Gold HOF Signed Postcard 150.00

Single Signed Ball 1000.00

Sutton Don-(1998)

3 X 5 . . . . .5.00

8 X 10 Photo 15.00

Single Signed Ball 30.00

Terry, Bill-(1954) d. 1989

3 X 5 .15.00

8 X 10 Photo 40.00

B&W HOF Signed Postcard 40.00

Canceled Check 60.00

Gold HOF Signed Postcard 25.00

Perez-Steele Signed Postcard 75.00

Single Signed Ball 300.00

Thompson, Sam-(1974) d. 1922

3 X 5 . . . . .1500.00

Signed Document 4000.00

Thomson, Bobby

3 X 5 . . . . .5.00

8 X 10 Photo 15.00

Canceled Check 30.00

Signed Bat 60.00

Single Signed Ball 35.00

Tinker, Joe-(1946) d. 1948

3 X 5 .450.00

8 X 10 Photo 1200.00

Single Signed Ball 4000.00

Traynor, Pie-(1948) d. 1972

3 X 5 .100.00

8 X 10 Photo 400.00

B&W HOF Signed Postcard 300.00

Gold HOF Signed Postcard 500.00

Single Signed Ball 1800.00

Vance, Dazzy-(1955) d. 1961

3 X 5 .200.00

8 X 10 Photo 500.00

Single Signed Ball 2000.00

VanderMeer, Johnny d. 1997

3 X 5 ....10.00

8 X 10 Photo 20.00

Canceled Check 30.00

Single Signed Ball 40.00

Vaughan, Arky-(1985) d. 1952

3 X 5 ....300.00

8 X 10 Photo 600.00

Single Signed Ball 3000.00

Veeck, Bill-(1991) d. 1987

3 X 5 ....12.00

8 X 10 Photo 50.00

Canceled Check 100.00

Single Signed Ball 750.00

Waddell, Rube-(1946) d. 1914

3 X 5 ....1250.00

Signed Document 4000.00

Wagner, Honus-(1936) d. 1955

3 X 5 ....350.00

8 X 10 Photo 1000.00

Canceled Check 2000.00

Single Signed Ball 4000.00

Wallace, Bobby-(1953) d. 1960

3 X 5 ....300.00

8 X 10 Photo 1200.00

B&W HOF Signed Postcard ...1500.00

Single Signed Ball 3000.00

Walsh, Ed-(1946) d. 1959

3 X 5 ....250.00

8 X 10 Photo 750.00

B&W HOF Signed Postcard 400.00

Single Signed Ball 3500.00

Waner, Lloyd-(1967) d. 1982

3 X 5 ....20.00

8 X 10 Photo 75.00

Gold HOF Signed Postcard 30.00

Perez-Steele Signed Postcard ..3000.00

Single Signed Ball 500.00

Waner, Paul-(1952) d. 1965

3 X 5 ....150.00

8 X 10 Photo 300.00

B&W HOF Signed Postcard 350.00

Single Signed Ball 2000.00

Ward, John-(1964) d. 1925

3 X 5 ....2000.00

Signed Document 4000.00

Weaver, Earl (1996)

3 X 5 ....5.00

8 X 10 Photo 20.00

Gold HOF Signed Postcard 15.00

Signed Bat 75.00

Single Signed Ball 30.00

Welch, Mickey-(1973) d. 1941

3 X 5 ....1200.00

8 X 10 Photo 4000.00

Single Signed Ball 20000.00

AL KALINE

ROGER MARIS

ROGER CLEMENS

JEFF BAGWELL

Joe McCarthy

JOE McCARTHY

BOB LEMON

Wheat, Zack-(1959) d. 1972

3 X 5	.50.00
8 X 10 Photo	.150.00
B&W HOF Signed Postcard	.250.00
Canceled Check	.650.00
Gold HOF Signed Postcard	.350.00
Single Signed Ball	.2000.00

Wilhelm, Hoyt-(1985)

3 X 5	.5.00
8 X 10 Photo	.15.00
Canceled Check	.25.00
Gold HOF Signed Postcard	.7.00
Perez-Steele Signed Postcard	.10.00
Signed Bat	.50.00
Single Signed Ball	.25.00

Williams, Billy-(1987)

3 X 5	.5.00
8 X 10 Photo	.12.00
Gold HOF Signed Postcard	.7.00
Perez-Steele Signed Postcard	.10.00
Signed Bat	.75.00
Single Signed Ball	.25.00

Williams, Ted-(1966)

3 X 5	.50.00
8 X 10 Photo	.150.00
Gold HOF Signed Postcard	.125.00
Perez-Steele Signed Postcard	.200.00
Signed Bat	.1500.00
Single Signed Ball	.200.00

Willis, Vic-(1995) d. 1947

3 X 5	.1000.00
Signed Document	.4000.00

Wilson, Hack-(1979) d. 1948

3 X 5	.400.00
8 X 10 Photo	.1000.00
Canceled Check	.650.00
Single Signed Ball	.4500.00

Winfield, Dave

3 X 5	.8.00
8 X 10 Photo	.20.00
Signed Bat	.100.00
Single Signed Ball	.50.00

Wood, Joe d. 1985

3 X 5	.20.00
8 X 10 Photo	.100.00
Canceled Check	.30.00
Single Signed Ball	.600.00

Wright, George-(1937) d. 1937

3 X 5	.700.00
8 X 10 Photo	.2500.00
Single Signed Ball	.7500.00

Wright, Harry-(1953) d. 1895

3 X 5	.1500.00
Signed Document	.5000.00

Wynn, Early-(1972)

3 X 5	.8.00
8 X 10 Photo	.20.00
Canceled Check	.35.00
Gold HOF Signed Postcard	.10.00
Perez-Steele Signed Postcard	.20.00
Signed Bat	.100.00
Single Signed Ball	.40.00

Yastrzemski, Carl-(1989)

3 X 5	10.00
8 X 10 Photo	30.00
Gold HOF Signed Postcard	25.00
Perez-Steele Signed Postcard	25.00
Signed Bat	175.00
Single Signed Ball	60.00

Young, Cy-(1937) d. 1955

3 X 5	350.00
8 X 10 Photo	1250.00
B&W HOF Signed Postcard	1000.00
Single Signed Ball	5000.00

Youngs, Ross-(1972) d. 1927

3 X 5	700.00
Signed Document	2500.00

Yount, Robin

3 X 5	10.00
8 X 10 Photo	25.00
Signed Bat	100.00
Single Signed Ball	40.00

Active Players

Alomar, Roberto

8 X 10 Photo	15.00
Authentic Jersey	200.00
Signed Card	8.00
Signed Bat	70.00
Signed Cap	50.00
Signed Helmet	85.00
Single Signed Ball	30.00

Alomar, Sandy

8 X 10 Photo	15.00
Authentic Jersey	175.00
Signed Card	7.00
Signed Bat	65.00
Signed Cap	45.00
Signed Helmet	75.00
Single Signed Ball	25.00

Alou, Moises

8 X 10 Photo	15.00
Authentic Jersey	175.00
Signed Card	6.00
Signed Bat	60.00
Signed Cap	40.00
Signed Helmet	75.00
Single Signed Ball	25.00

Bagwell, Jeff

8 X 10 Photo	25.00
Authentic Jersey	240.00
Signed Card	15.00
Signed Bat	100.00
Signed Cap	65.00
Signed Helmet	110.00
Single Signed Ball	40.00

Belle, Albert

8 X 10 Photo	30.00
Authentic Jersey	300.00
Signed Card	20.00
Signed Bat	150.00
Signed Cap	80.00
Signed Helmet	150.00
Single Signed Ball	50.00

MARK McGWIRE

CAL RIPKEN JR.

STAN MUSIAL

YOGI BERRA

DANTE BICHETTE

Mel Ott

MEL OTT

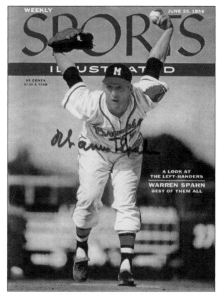

WARREN SPAHN

Bichette, Dante

8 X 10 Photo	18.00
Authentic Jersey	200.00
Signed Card	8.00
Signed Bat	70.00
Signed Cap	50.00
Signed Helmet	85.00
Single Signed Ball	25.00

Biggio, Craig

8 X 10 Photo	18.00
Authentic Jersey	200.00
Signed Card	8.00
Signed Bat	70.00
Signed Cap	50.00
Signed Helmet	85.00
Single Signed Ball	25.00

Boggs, Wade

8 X 10 Photo	20.00
Authentic Jersey	200.00
Signed Card	10.00
Signed Bat	75.00
Signed Cap	50.00
Signed Helmet	90.00
Single Signed Ball	35.00

Bonds, Barry

8 X 10 Photo	25.00
Authentic Jersey	225.00
Signed Card	15.00
Signed Bat	100.00
Signed Cap	60.00
Signed Helmet	100.00
Single Signed Ball	45.00

Bonilla, Bobby

8 X 10 Photo	15.00
Authentic Jersey	175.00
Signed Card	7.00
Signed Bat	60.00
Signed Cap	40.00
Signed Helmet	75.00
Single Signed Ball	20.00

Brown, Kevin

8 X 10 Photo	12.00
Authentic Jersey	180.00
Signed Card	6.00
Signed Bat	60.00
Signed Cap	40.00
Signed Helmet	75.00
Single Signed Ball	20.00

Buhner, Jay

8 X 10 Photo	15.00
Authentic Jersey	200.00
Signed Card	8.00
Signed Bat	70.00
Signed Cap	50.00
Signed Helmet	75.00
Single Signed Ball	25.00

Caminiti, Ken

8 X 10 Photo	15.00
Authentic Jersey	175.00
Signed Card	7.00
Signed Bat	65.00
Signed Cap	45.00
Signed Helmet	75.00
Single Signed Ball	25.00

BASEBALL PRICE GUIDE

Canseco, Jose

8 X 10 Photo	18.00
Authentic Jersey	200.00
Signed Card	8.00
Signed Bat	70.00
Signed Cap	50.00
Signed Helmet	85.00
Single Signed Ball	30.00

Clemens, Roger

8 X 10 Photo	30.00
Authentic Jersey	300.00
Signed Card	20.00
Signed Bat	130.00
Signed Cap	80.00
Signed Helmet	150.00
Single Signed Ball	50.00

JIM PALMER

Carter, Joe

8 X 10 Photo	18.00
Authentic Jersey	200.00
Signed Card	8.00
Signed Bat	70.00
Signed Cap	50.00
Signed Helmet	85.00
Single Signed Ball	30.00

Cone, David

8 X 10 Photo	20.00
Authentic Jersey	200.00
Signed Card	10.00
Signed Bat	70.00
Signed Cap	50.00
Signed Helmet	75.00
Single Signed Ball	30.00

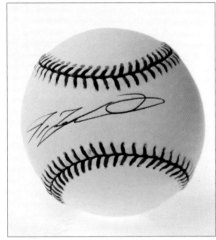

IVAN RODRIGUEZ

Castilla, Vinny

8 X 10 Photo	15.00
Authentic Jersey	180.00
Signed Card	6.00
Signed Bat	60.00
Signed Cap	40.00
Signed Helmet	75.00
Single Signed Ball	25.00

Cruz Jr., Jose

8 X 10 Photo	15.00
Authentic Jersey	175.00
Signed Card	6.00
Signed Bat	60.00
Signed Cap	40.00
Signed Helmet	75.00
Single Signed Ball	25.00

PHIL RIZZUTO

Clark, Will

8 X 10 Photo	18.00
Authentic Jersey	200.00
Signed Card	8.00
Signed Bat	70.00
Signed Cap	50.00
Signed Helmet	85.00
Single Signed Ball	25.00

Erstad, Darin

8 X 10 Photo	18.00
Authentic Jersey	200.00
Signed Card	7.00
Signed Bat	75.00
Signed Cap	45.00
Signed Helmet	80.00
Single Signed Ball	25.00

PEE WEE REESE

Joe DiMaggio

FIFTEEN CENTS

July 13, 1936

TIME

The Weekly Newsmagazine

Wide World

Volume XXVIII

YANKEE DI MAGGIO

Age, 21; batting average, .350; price, $75,000.
(See SPORT)

Number 2

Fielder, Cecil

8 X 10 Photo	15.00
Authentic Jersey	175.00
Signed Card	7.00
Signed Bat	65.00
Signed Cap	45.00
Signed Helmet	75.00
Single Signed Ball	25.00

Galarraga, Andres

8 X 10 Photo	20.00
Authentic Jersey	220.00
Signed Card	12.00
Signed Bat	90.00
Signed Cap	60.00
Signed Helmet	100.00
Single Signed Ball	35.00

Garciaparra, Nomar

8 X 10 Photo	25.00
Authentic Jersey	250.00
Signed Card	15.00
Signed Bat	100.00
Signed Cap	75.00
Signed Helmet	110.00
Single Signed Ball	40.00

Glavine, Tom

8 X 10 Photo	20.00
Authentic Jersey	200.00
Signed Card	10.00
Signed Bat	75.00
Signed Cap	55.00
Signed Helmet	90.00
Single Signed Ball	35.00

Gonzalez, Juan

8 X 10 Photo	20.00
Authentic Jersey	225.00
Signed Card	12.00
Signed Bat	125.00
Signed Cap	60.00
Signed Helmet	100.00
Single Signed Ball	35.00

Grace, Mark

8 X 10 Photo	18.00
Authentic Jersey	200.00
Signed Card	8.00
Signed Bat	70.00
Signed Cap	50.00
Signed Helmet	85.00
Single Signed Ball	25.00

Greer, Rusty

8 X 10 Photo	15.00
Authentic Jersey	175.00
Signed Card	6.00
Signed Bat	60.00
Signed Cap	40.00
Signed Helmet	75.00
Single Signed Ball	20.00

Griffey Jr., Ken

8 X 10 Photo	40.00
Authentic Jersey	350.00
Signed Card	25.00
Signed Bat	150.00
Signed Cap	100.00
Signed Helmet	175.00
Single Signed Ball	60.00

REGGIE JACKSON

CAL RIPKEN JR.

STEVE CARLTON

ROLLIE FINGERS

DAVE WINFIELD

KEN GRIFFEY JR.

ALEX RODRIGUEZ

Guerrero, Vladimir

8 X 10 Photo	15.00
Authentic Jersey	180.00
Signed Card	6.00
Signed Bat	60.00
Signed Cap	40.00
Signed Helmet	75.00
Single Signed Ball	25.00

Guillen, Jose

8 X 10 Photo	15.00
Authentic Jersey	180.00
Signed Card	6.00
Signed Bat	60.00
Signed Cap	40.00
Signed Helmet	75.00
Single Signed Ball	20.00

Gwynn, Tony

8 X 10 Photo	25.00
Authentic Jersey	260.00
Signed Card	15.00
Signed Bat	110.00
Signed Cap	75.00
Signed Helmet	125.00
Single Signed Ball	45.00

Henderson, Rickey

8 X 10 Photo	25.00
Authentic Jersey	225.00
Signed Card	15.00
Signed Bat	100.00
Signed Cap	65.00
Signed Helmet	110.00
Single Signed Ball	50.00

Hernandez, Livan

8 X 10 Photo	15.00
Authentic Jersey	175.00
Signed Card	6.00
Signed Bat	60.00
Signed Cap	40.00
Signed Helmet	75.00
Single Signed Ball	20.00

Hundley, Todd

8 X 10 Photo	15.00
Authentic Jersey	175.00
Signed Card	6.00
Signed Bat	60.00
Signed Cap	40.00
Signed Helmet	75.00
Single Signed Ball	20.00

Hunter, Brian

8 X 10 Photo	15.00
Authentic Jersey	175.00
Signed Card	6.00
Signed Bat	60.00
Signed Cap	40.00
Signed Helmet	75.00
Single Signed Ball	20.00

Jeter, Derek

8 X 10 Photo	30.00
Authentic Jersey	300.00
Signed Card	20.00
Signed Bat	130.00
Signed Cap	80.00
Signed Helmet	150.00
Single Signed Ball	50.00

BASEBALL PRICE GUIDE

Johnson, Charles

8 X 10 Photo	15.00
Authentic Jersey	175.00
Signed Card	6.00
Signed Bat	60.00
Signed Cap	40.00
Signed Helmet	75.00
Single Signed Ball	20.00

Johnson, Randy

8 X 10 Photo	30.00
Authentic Jersey	300.00
Signed Card	20.00
Signed Bat	130.00
Signed Cap	80.00
Signed Helmet	150.00
Single Signed Ball	50.00

Jones, Andruw

8 X 10 Photo	20.00
Authentic Jersey	200.00
Signed Card	10.00
Signed Bat	75.00
Signed Cap	55.00
Signed Helmet	100.00
Single Signed Ball	35.00

Jones, Chipper

8 X 10 Photo	30.00
Authentic Jersey	260.00
Signed Card	15.00
Signed Bat	110.00
Signed Cap	75.00
Signed Helmet	125.00
Single Signed Ball	50.00

Justice, David

8 X 10 Photo	20.00
Authentic Jersey	200.00
Signed Card	12.00
Signed Bat	90.00
Signed Cap	60.00
Signed Helmet	100.00
Single Signed Ball	30.00

Karros, Eric

8 X 10 Photo	15.00
Authentic Jersey	175.00
Signed Card	6.00
Signed Bat	60.00
Signed Cap	40.00
Signed Helmet	75.00
Single Signed Ball	20.00

Klesko, Ryan

8 X 10 Photo	15.00
Authentic Jersey	200.00
Signed Card	7.00
Signed Bat	65.00
Signed Cap	45.00
Signed Helmet	80.00
Single Signed Ball	25.00

Knoblauch, Chuck

8 X 10 Photo	20.00
Authentic Jersey	200.00
Signed Card	10.00
Signed Bat	75.00
Signed Cap	50.00
Signed Helmet	75.00
Single Signed Ball	30.00

HANK AARON

IVAN RODRIGUEZ

BROOKS ROBINSON

JUAN GONZALEZ

Red Ruffing

RED RUFFING

HIDEO NOMO

Larkin, Barry

8 X 10 Photo	18.00
Authentic Jersey	200.00
Signed Card	8.00
Signed Bat	70.00
Signed Cap	50.00
Signed Helmet	85.00
Single Signed Ball	25.00

Lofton, Kenny

8 X 10 Photo	20.00
Authentic Jersey	200.00
Signed Card	10.00
Signed Bat	75.00
Signed Cap	50.00
Signed Helmet	90.00
Single Signed Ball	35.00

Lopez, Javier

8 X 10 Photo	15.00
Authentic Jersey	175.00
Signed Card	7.00
Signed Bat	65.00
Signed Cap	45.00
Signed Helmet	75.00
Single Signed Ball	25.00

Maddux, Greg

8 X 10 Photo	40.00
Authentic Jersey	350.00
Signed Card	25.00
Signed Bat	150.00
Signed Cap	100.00
Signed Helmet	170.00
Single Signed Ball	65.00

Martinez, Edgar

8 X 10 Photo	18.00
Authentic Jersey	200.00
Signed Card	8.00
Signed Bat	70.00
Signed Cap	50.00
Signed Helmet	85.00
Single Signed Ball	25.00

Martinez, Pedro

8 X 10 Photo	20.00
Authentic Jersey	200.00
Signed Card	10.00
Signed Bat	77.00
Signed Cap	50.00
Signed Helmet	85.00
Single Signed Ball	40.00

Martinez, Tino

8 X 10 Photo	20.00
Authentic Jersey	220.00
Signed Card	12.00
Signed Bat	90.00
Signed Cap	60.00
Signed Helmet	100.00
Single Signed Ball	40.00

McGriff, Fred

8 X 10 Photo	25.00
Authentic Jersey	225.00
Signed Card	15.00
Signed Bat	100.00
Signed Cap	65.00
Signed Helmet	100.00
Single Signed Ball	40.00

McGwire, Mark

* Mark McGwire doesn't usually sign current NL baseballs on the sweet spot. Thus the NL baseball price is listed with autograph not on the sweet spot. A baseball that is signed on the sweet spot of an NL baseball would command a premium of up to 50%. Since McGwire doesn't currently sign at shows or participate in private signings (besides the occasional charity event) authenticating his items is problematic.

Signed AL Baseball 150.00

Signed NL Baseball 200.00

8 X 10 Photo AL 125.00

8 X 10 Photo NL 150.00

Signed Card 60.00

Signed Bat 350.00

Signed Cap 175.00

Authentic Jersey 500.00

Signed Helmet 250.00

Molitor, Paul

8 X 10 Photo 25.00

Authentic Jersey 225.00

Signed Card 15.00

Signed Bat 100.00

Signed Cap 65.00

Signed Helmet 100.00

Single Signed Ball 40.00

Mondesi, Raul

8 X 10 Photo 20.00

Authentic Jersey 200.00

Signed Card 10.00

Signed Bat 75.00

Signed Cap 55.00

Signed Helmet 90.00

Single Signed Ball 30.00

Mussina, Mike

8 X 10 Photo 20.00

Authentic Jersey 220.00

Signed Card 12.00

Signed Bat 90.00

Signed Cap 60.00

Signed Helmet 100.00

Single Signed Ball 35.00

Nomo, Hideo

8 X 10 Photo 25.00

Authentic Jersey 275.00

Signed Card 15.00

Signed Bat 125.00

Signed Cap 75.00

Signed Helmet 125.00

Single Signed Ball 45.00

Palmeiro, Rafael

8 X 10 Photo 15.00

Authentic Jersey 175.00

Signed Card 7.00

Signed Bat 65.00

Signed Cap 45.00

Signed Helmet 75.00

Single Signed Ball 25.00

Pettitte, Andy

8 X 10 Photo 20.00

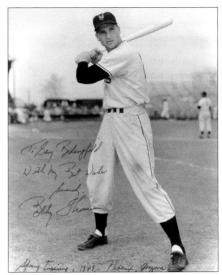

BOBBY THOMSON

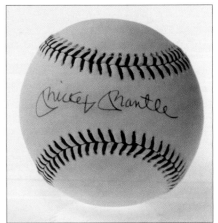

BABE RUTH

MICKEY MANTLE

TOM SEAVER

CHUCK KNOBLAUCH

ENOS SLAUGHTER

FRANK THOMAS

SAMMY SOSA

Authentic Jersey	220.00
Signed Card	12.00
Signed Bat	90.00
Signed Cap	60.00
Signed Helmet	100.00
Single Signed Ball	40.00

Piazza, Mike

8 X 10 Photo	35.00
Authentic Jersey	325.00
Signed Card	20.00
Signed Bat	140.00
Signed Cap	90.00
Signed Helmet	160.00
Single Signed Ball	55.00

Ramirez, Manny

8 X 10 Photo	18.00
Authentic Jersey	200.00
Signed Card	8.00
Signed Bat	70.00
Signed Cap	50.00
Signed Helmet	85.00
Single Signed Ball	30.00

Ripken Jr., Cal

8 X 10 Photo	45.00
Authentic Jersey	400.00
Signed Card	28.00
Signed Bat	175.00
Signed Cap	120.00
Signed Helmet	200.00
Single Signed Ball	70.00

Rodriguez, Alex

8 X 10 Photo	30.00

Authentic Jersey	275.00
Signed Card	18.00
Signed Bat	125.00
Signed Cap	75.00
Signed Helmet	150.00
Single Signed Ball	60.00

Rodriguez, Ivan

8 X 10 Photo	25.00
Authentic Jersey	220.00
Signed Card	12.00
Signed Bat	90.00
Signed Cap	60.00
Signed Helmet	100.00
Single Signed Ball	35.00

Rolen, Scott

8 X 10 Photo	15.00
Authentic Jersey	175.00
Signed Card	7.00
Signed Bat	65.00
Signed Cap	45.00
Signed Helmet	75.00
Single Signed Ball	25.00

Salmon, Tim

8 X 10 Photo	15.00
Authentic Jersey	175.00
Signed Card	7.00
Signed Bat	65.00
Signed Cap	45.00
Signed Helmet	75.00
Single Signed Ball	25.00

Smoltz, John

8 X 10 Photo	15.00

Authentic Jersey 175.00

Signed Card 7.00

Signed Bat 65.00

Signed Cap 45.00

Signed Helmet 50.00

Single Signed Ball 25.00

Sosa, Sammy

8 X 10 Photo 75.00

Authentic Jersey 350.00

Signed Card 50.00

Signed Bat 250.00

Signed Cap 150.00

Signed Helmet 200.00

Single Signed Ball 125.00

Thomas, Frank

8 X 10 Photo 40.00

Authentic Jersey 350.00

Signed Card 25.00

Signed Bat 150.00

Signed Cap 100.00

Signed Helmet 150.00

Single Signed Ball 60.00

Thome, Jim

8 X 10 Photo 20.00

Authentic Jersey 200.00

Signed Card 10.00

Signed Bat 75.00

Signed Cap 50.00

Signed Helmet 75.00

Single Signed Ball 30.00

Vaughn, Mo

8 X 10 Photo 20.00

Authentic Jersey 300.00

Signed Bat 75.00

Signed Cap 60.00

Signed Helmet 100.00

Single Signed Ball 35.00

Walker, Larry

8 X 10 Photo 20.00

Authentic Jersey 200.00

Signed Card 15.00

Signed Bat 90.00

Signed Cap 60.00

Signed Helmet 100.00

Single Signed Ball 35.00

Williams, Bernie

8 X 10 Photo 25.00

Authentic Jersey 250.00

Signed Card 12.00

Signed Bat 100.00

Signed Cap 75.00

Signed Helmet 125.00

Single Signed Ball 40.00

Wood, Kerry

8 X 10 Photo 20.00

Authentic Jersey 200.00

Signed Card 10.00

Signed Bat 100.00

Signed Cap 60.00

Signed Helmet 100.00

Single Signed Ball 35.00

CASEY STENGEL

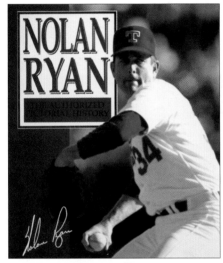

NOLAN RYAN

KERRY WOOD

LLOYD WANER

Gary.
Best of Luck Always
Pee Wee Reese

Pee Wee Reese

Wilt Chamberlain

COLLECTING BASKETBALL AUTOGRAPHS

O f the four major team sports, basketball superstar autographs are the most difficult to obtain.

I believe this is directly related to the players' recognition factor. Top athletes from other sports may have just as recognizable faces, but (with the exception of baseball pitcher Randy Johnson) they don't stand head and shoulders above a crowd. Ken Griffey Jr. can hide, but Shaquille O'Neal?

On the flip side, because basketball is a relatively young sport compared to the other three, you don't face much of a problem with numerous prominent players from the past having passed away. In fact, when the NBA named its 50 Greatest Players at the league's 50th anniversary celebration in Cleveland, only one member (Pistol Pete Maravich) was deceased.

That means you can obtain almost every great NBA player's signature in person, at shows, or via mail order private signings —

even Bill Russell's — if you are willing to pay the price.

Speaking of price, since market value is determined by supply and demand, the scarcity of hoops star signatures naturally means that they command a premium over those of other sports. While signed 8 x 10s of the top recent or current stars in other sports almost never command $50 or more, basketball has several, including: Kareem Abdul-

Kareem Abdul-Jabbar

BY THEO CHEN

Jabbar, Larry Bird, Grant Hill, Magic Johnson, Shaquille O'Neal and Dennis Rodman.

Of course, the value of Michael Jordan's autograph, the closest thing to a Babe Ruth of this generation, is as valuable as any living athlete's signature. It also probably is the most forged signature of any person who has ever lived. Since 1994, Jordan has signed under the restrictions of an exclusive Upper Deck Authenticated contract. As with all UDA items, Jordan's signature is guaranteed by matching numbered holograms on the item and certificate of authenticity.

In the past few years, UDA Jordan items have skyrocketed in value due to three main factors: increase in demand; increase in forgeries; and UDA price increases. Currently, UDA

Michael Jordan

Jordan basketballs and framed 16 x 20s command $800-$1,000, with jerseys bringing a couple hundred more.

Jordan occasionally signs a few free autographs at charity golf tournaments or team hotels, but buyers should always beware of forgeries.

The most notorious non-signer in the sports world is from the basketball world. Former Celtics great Bill Russell is so anti-autograph that he doesn't even sign his own checks or credit card slips. As legend has it, during the 1960s Russell was approached for a signature in a public rest room, and the incident so disgusted him that he vowed never to sign again.

Russell for the most part kept to his word, then eventually caved in to cash in. At his first sign-for-dough event, the price per autograph exceeded $300 and has dropped only slightly since then. Unfortunately for bas-

Alonzo Mourning

ketball fans, while Russell is the toughest of the tough, this sport has many superstars past and present whose signatures are nearly as challenging to obtain.

Again, the recognition factor comes into play, as most big name seven-footers are notoriously reluctant signers. This includes Russell, Wilt

Chamberlain, Abdul-Jabbar, Patrick Ewing and Shaquille O'Neal. Ewing is doing his best to top Russell for difficulty in the modern era.

Among the few exceptions to this seven-footer rule are active stars Dikembe Mutombo and David Robinson, and current broadcaster Bill Walton. I once saw Mutombo at the San Antonio airport after the 1996 NBA All-Star Game. He had just checked his luggage and was on his way to catch his flight. As a handful of autograph hounds gathered around him in the terminal, he looked down and said simply, "Walk with me!" as he headed to his gate.

Once he got to the security checkpoint, he announced, "I hate to fly commercial! The airport is the worst place for an autograph session!"

Then he started to sign. After he signed for me, I followed

Dennis Rodman

him through the terminal to his gate. I seldom ask a player for his autograph twice in a row, but I had never gotten him before, and I really needed him on another item.

Once Dikembe arrived at his gate and sat down to wait for boarding, he started signing again. I waited in the small line that had formed. Once he got to me, he said, "I already signed for you!" I started to mumble my excuse for daring to bother him again, but Mutombo interrupted me. "I do not want to hear your explanation!" he barked — but signed for me anyway. As I walked off I was barely able to stop from bursting out laughing at his remark.

Walton is almost in a class by himself. Once he spotted a few of us waiting for him, and shouted, "Hey, how are you doing, guys? I'll be right back . . . you guys got good pens?" Sure enough, Bill came right back and

Bob Cousy

signed everything each of us had for him.

Unfortunately for collectors, most hoops superstars — especially from recent years —

are more likely to behave like Russell than Walton when asked for an autograph. So if you want to own them, get out your wallet, and watch out for fakes. ▪

Stephon Marbury

ALLEN IVERSON

KAREEM ABDUL-JABBAR

Retired Players

Archibald, Nate-(1991)

3 X 5 . . . . .5.00

8 X 10 . . . . .15.00

Single Signed Ball 100.00

Arizin, Paul-(1977)

3 X 5 . . . . .8.00

8 X 10 . . . . .20.00

Single Signed Ball 125.00

Barry, Rick-(1987)

3 X 5 . . . . .8.00

8 X 10 . . . . .20.00

Single Signed Ball 125.00

Baylor, Elgin-(1976)

3 X 5 . . . . .8.00

8 X 10 . . . . .20.00

Single Signed Ball 125.00

Bellamy, Walt-(1993)

3 X 5 . . . . .5.00

8 X 10 . . . . .15.00

Single Signed Ball 100.00

Belov, Sergei-(1992)

3 X 5 . . . . .8.00

8 X 10 . . . . .15.00

Single Signed Ball 100.00

Bing, Dave-(1990)

3 X 5 . . . . .8.00

8 X 10 . . . . .20.00

Single Signed Ball 100.00

Bird, Larry

3 X 5 . . . . .15.00

8 X 10 . . . . .50.00

Single Signed Ball 175.00

Blazejowski, Carol-(1994)

3 X 5 . . . . .5.00

8 X 10 . . . . .15.00

Bradley, Bill-(1982)

3 X 5 . . . . .15.00

8 X 10 . . . . .40.00

Single Signed Ball 200.00

Chamberlain, Wilt-(1978)

3 X 5 . . . . .30.00

8 X 10 . . . . .75.00

Single Signed Ball 250.00

Cousy, Bob-(1970)

3 X 5 . . . . .10.00

8 X 10 . . . . .30.00

Single Signed Ball 125.00

Cunningham, Billy-(1986)

3 X 5 . . . . .8.00

8 X 10 . . . . .20.00

Single Signed Ball 100.00

Davies, Bob-(1969) d. 1990

3 X 5 . . . . .15.00

8 X 10 . . . . .40.00

Single Signed Ball 250.00

DeBusschere, Dave-(1982)

3 X 5 . . . . .8.00

8 X 10 . . . . .20.00

Single Signed Ball 125.00

Erving, Julius-(1993)

3 X 5 . . . . .15.00

8 X 10 . . . . .50.00

Single Signed Ball 200.00

Frazier, Walt-(1987)

3 X 5 . . . . .8.00

8 X 10 . . . . .15.00

Single Signed Ball 100.00

Fulks, Joe-(1977) d. 1976

3 X 5 . . . . .30.00

8 X 10 . . . . .100.00

Gola, Tom-(1975)

3 X 5 . . . . .8.00

8 X 10 . . . . .20.00

Single Signed Ball 100.00

Greer, Hal-(1981)

3 X 5 . . . . .5.00

8 X 10 . . . . .15.00

Single Signed Ball 75.00

Hagan, Cliff-(1977)

3 X 5 . . . . .8.00

8 X 10 . . . . .20.00

Single Signed Ball 100.00

Havlicek, John-(1983)

3 X 5 . . . . .10.00

8 X 10 . . . . .25.00

Single Signed Ball 150.00

Hawkins, Connie-(1992)

3 X 5 . . . . .5.00

8 X 10 . . . . .15.00

Single Signed Ball 100.00

Hayes, Elvin-(1990)

3 X 5 . . . . .5.00

8 X 10 . . . . .15.00

Single Signed Ball 100.00

Heinsohn, Tom-(1986)

3 X 5 . . . . .10.00

8 X 10 . . . . .25.00

Single Signed Ball 150.00

Holman, Nat-(1964) d,

3 X 5 . . . . .10.00

8 X 10 . . . . .25.00

Single Signed Ball 250.00

Iba, Henry-(1968) d. 1993

3 X 5 . . . . .20.00

8 X 10 . . . . .50.00

Single Signed Ball 350.00

Issel, Dan-(1993)

3 X 5 . . . . .8.00

8 X 10 . . . . .20.00

Single Signed Ball 100.00

Jabbar, Kareem Abdul-(1995)

8 X 10 . . . . .40.00

Single Signed Ball 150.00

Jeannette, Buddy-(1994)

3 X 5 . . . . .5.00

RICK BARRY

CHARLES BARKLEY

ANFERNEE HARDAWAY

8 X 10 . . . . .15.00

Single Signed Ball 100.00

CHRIS MULLIN

Johnson, Magic

3 X 5 . . . . .15.00

8 X 10 . . . . .50.00

Single Signed Ball 175.00

Jones, K.C.-(1989)

3 X 5 . . . . .5.00

8 X 10 . . . . .15.00

Single Signed Ball 100.00

Jones, Sam-(1983)

3 X 5 . . . . .8.00

8 X 10 . . . . .20.00

Single Signed Ball 150.00

BILL BRADLEY

Lanier, Bob-(1992)

3 X 5 . . . . .5.00

8 X 10 . . . . .15.00

Single Signed Ball 75.00

Lovellette, Clyde-(1988)

3 X 5 . . . . .5.00

8 X 10 . . . . .15.00

Single Signed Ball 75.00

WILT CHAMBERLAIN

Lucas, Jerry-(1979)

3 X 5 . . . . .5.00

8 X 10 . . . . .15.00

Single Signed Ball 100.00

Macauley, Ed-(1960)

3 X 5 . . . . .8.00

8 X 10 . . . . .15.00

Single Signed Ball 125.00

Maravich, Pete-(1987) d. 1988

3 X 5 .125.00

8 X 10 . . . . .300.00

Single Signed Ball 800.00

Martin, Slater-(1981)

3 X 5 . . . . .8.00

8 X 10 . . . . .20.00

Single Signed Ball 125.00

McGuire, Dick-(1993)

3 X 5 . . . . .5.00

8 X 10 . . . . .15.00

Single Signed Ball 100.00

Mikan, George-(1959)

3 X 5 .12.00

8 X 10 . . . . .30.00

Single Signed Ball 150.00

Mikkelsen, Vern-(1995)

3 X 5 . . . . .5.00

8 X 10 . . . . .15.00

Single Signed Ball 75.00

Miller, Cheryl-(1995)

3 X 5 . . . . .5.00

8 X 10 . . . . .15.00

Single Signed Ball 75.00

Monroe, Earl-(1990)

3 X 5 . . . . .5.00

8 X 10 . . . . .15.00

Single Signed Ball 100.00

Murphy, Calvin-(1993)

3 X 5 . . . . .5.00

8 X 10 . . . . .15.00

Single Signed Ball 100.00

Murphy, Stretch-(1960) d. 1992

3 X 5 . . . . .10.00

8 X 10 . . . . .25.00

Single Signed Ball 250.00

Pettit, Bob-(1970)

3 X 5 . . . . .8.00

8 X 10 . . . . .20.00

Single Signed Ball 150.00

Phillip, Andy-(1961)

3 X 5 . . . . .10.00

8 X 10 . . . . .20.00

Single Signed Ball 150.00

Pollard, Jim-(1977) d. 1993

3 X 5 . . . . .25.00

8 X 10 . . . . .50.00

Single Signed Ball 250.00

Ramsey, Frank-(1981)

3 X 5 . . . . .5.00

8 X 10 . . . . .20.00

Single Signed Ball 100.00

Reed, Willis-(1981)

3 X 5 . . . . .5.00

8 X 10 . . . . .15.00

Single Signed Ball 100.00

Robertson, Oscar-(1979)

3 X 5 . . . . .20.00

8 X 10 . . . . .40.00

Single Signed Ball 175.00

Russell, Bill-(1974)

3 X 5 . . . . .100.00

8 X 10 .200.00

Single Signed Ball 600.00

Schayes, Dolph-(1972)

3 X 5 . . . . .8.00

8 X 10 . . . . .20.00

Single Signed Ball 150.00

Sharman, Bill-(1975)

3 X 5 . . . . .8.00

8 X 10 . . . . .20.00

Single Signed Ball 125.00

Thomas, Isiah

3 X 5 . . . . .8.00

8 X 10 . . . . .20.00

Single Signed Ball 100.00

Thurmond, Nate-(1984)

3 X 5 . . . . .5.00

8 X 10 . . . . .15.00

Single Signed Ball 100.00

Twyman, Jack-(1982)

3 X 5 . . . . .5.00

BOB COUSY

JERRY STACKHOUSE

MIKE KRZYZEWSKI, MOOKIE
BLAYLOCK, JOHN STARKS

GEORGE GERVIN

OSCAR ROBERTSON

8 X 10 . . . . .15.00

Single Signed Ball 75.00

Unseld, Wes-(1988)

3 X 5 . . . . .5.00

8 X 10 . . . . .15.00

Single Signed Ball 75.00

Walton, Bill-(1993)

3 X 5 . . . . .8.00

8 X 10 . . . . .20.00

Single Signed Ball 100.00

West, Jerry-(1979)

3 X 5 . . . . .12.00

8 X 10 . . . . .35.00

Single Signed Ball 150.00

Wilkens, Lenny-(1989)

3 X 5 . . . . .5.00

8 X 10 . . . . .15.00

Single Signed Ball 75.00

Wooden, John-(1960)

3 X 5 . . . . .10.00

8 X 10 . . . . .30.00

Single Signed Ball 125.00

Worthy, James

3 X 5 . . . . .8.00

8 X 10 . . . . .20.00

Single Signed Ball 75.00

Active Players

Abdur-Rahim, Shareef

8 X 10 Photo 20.00

Authentic Jersey 175.00

Game Ball 120.00

I/O Ball .65.00

Mini Ball 50.00

Replica Jersey 90.00

Signed Card 10.00

Allen, Ray

8 X 10 Photo 15.00

Game Ball 90.00

I/O Ball .50.00

Mini Ball 35.00

Replica Jersey 70.00

Signed Card 6.00

Anderson, Kenny

8 X 10 Photo 15.00

Game Ball 90.00

I/O Ball .50.00

Mini Ball 35.00

Replica Jersey 70.00

Signed Card 6.00

Baker, Vin

8 X 10 Photo 15.00

Game Ball 100.00

I/O Ball .60.00

Mini Ball 40.00

Replica Jersey 75.00

Signed Card 7.00

Barkley, Charles

8 X 10 Photo 40.00

Authentic Jersey 300.00

Game Ball 225.00

I/O Ball 125.00

Mini Ball 100.00

Replica Jersey 175.00

Signed Card 25.00

Blaylock, Mookie

8 X 10 Photo 12.00

Game Ball 75.00

I/O Ball 45.00

Mini Ball 30.00

Replica Jersey 65.00

Signed Card 5.00

Bryant, Kobe

8 X 10 Photo 30.00

Authentic Jersey 275.00

Game Ball 200.00

I/O Ball 110.00

Mini Ball 90.00

Replica Jersey 160.00

Signed Card 20.00

Camby, Marcus

8 X 10 Photo 15.00

Game Ball 90.00

I/O Ball 50.00

Mini Ball 35.00

Replica Jersey 70.00

Signed Card 6.00

Cassell, Sam

8 X 10 Photo 12.00

Game Ball 80.00

I/O Ball 45.00

Mini Ball 30.00

Replica Jersey 65.00

Signed Card 5.00

Drexler, Clyde

8 X 10 Photo 30.00

Authentic Jersey 240.00

Game Ball 175.00

I/O Ball 90.00

Mini Ball 75.00

Replica Jersey 135.00

Signed Card 18.00

Dumars, Joe

8 X 10 Photo 20.00

Authentic Jersey 180.00

Game Ball 120.00

I/O Ball 65.00

Mini Ball 50.00

Replica Jersey 90.00

Signed Card 10.00

Duncan, Tim

8 X 10 Photo 20.00

Authentic Jersey 180.00

Game Ball 120.00

I/O Ball 65.00

Mini Ball 50.00

Replica Jersey 90.00

Signed Card 12.00

Ewing, Patrick

8 X 10 Photo 40.00

Authentic Jersey 300.00

Game Ball 225.00

I/O Ball 125.00

PENNY HARDAWAY

JOHN HAVLICEK

KENNY ANDERSON

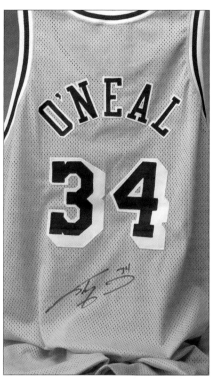

SHAQUILLE O'NEAL

CONNIE HAWKINS

MICHAEL JORDAN

Mini Ball 100.00

Replica Jersey 175.00

Signed Card 25.00

Garnett, Kevin

8 X 10 Photo 30.00

Authentic Jersey 240.00

Game Ball 175.00

I/O Ball 90.00

Mini Ball 75.00

Replica Jersey 135.00

Signed Card 18.00

Gill, Kendall

8 X 10 Photo 12.00

Game Ball 80.00

I/O Ball 45.00

Mini Ball 30.00

Replica Jersey 65.00

Signed Card 5.00

Grant, Brian

8 X 10 Photo 12.00

Game Ball 80.00

I/O Ball 45.00

Mini Ball 30.00

Replica Jersey 65.00

Signed Card 5.00

Gugliotta, Tom

8 X 10 Photo 15.00

Game Ball 90.00

I/O Ball 50.00

Mini Ball 35.00

Replica Jersey 70.00

Signed Card 6.00

Hardaway, Anfernee

8 X 10 Photo 40.00

Authentic Jersey 300.00

Game Ball 225.00

I/O Ball 125.00

Mini Ball 100.00

Replica Jersey 175.00

Signed Card 25.00

Hardaway, Tim

8 X 10 Photo 15.00

Game Ball 100.00

Ball .55.00

Mini Ball 40.00

Replica Jersey 75.00

Signed Card 7.00

Hill, Grant

8 X 10 Photo 40.00

Authentic Jersey 300.00

Wilson Ball 200.00

Mini Ball 100.00

Replica Jersey 175.00

Signed Card 30.00

Howard, Juwan

8 X 10 Photo 20.00

Authentic Jersey 160.00

Game Ball 110.00

I/O Ball 60.00

Mini Ball 45.00

Replica Jersey 80.00

Signed Card 10.00

Iverson, Allen

8 X 10 Photo	25.00
Authentic Jersey	220.00
Game Ball	160.00
I/O Ball	85.00
Mini Ball	70.00
Replica Jersey	120.00
Signed Card	15.00

Jackson, Jim

8 X 10 Photo	10.00
Game Ball	75.00
I/O Ball	40.00
Mini Ball	25.00
Replica Jersey	60.00
Signed Card	5.00

Johnson, Kevin

8 X 10 Photo	20.00
Authentic Jersey	200.00
Game Ball	140.00
I/O Ball	75.00
Mini Ball	60.00
Replica Jersey	100.00
Signed Card	12.00

Johnson, Larry

8 X 10 Photo	15.00
Game Ball	100.00
I/O Ball	55.00
Mini Ball	40.00
Replica Jersey	75.00
Signed Card	7.00

Jones, Eddie

8 X 10 Photo	18.00

Authentic Jersey	160.00
Game Ball	110.00
I/O Ball	60.00
Mini Ball	45.00
Replica Jersey	80.00
Signed Card	8.00

Jordan, Michael

8 X 10 Photo	150.00
Authentic Jersey	550.00
Game Ball	400.00
I/O Ball	275.00
Mini Ball	200.00
Replica Jersey	325.00
Signed Card	60.00

Kemp, Shawn

8 X 10 Photo	15.00
Authentic Jersey	160.00
Game Ball	100.00
I/O Ball	60.00
Mini Ball	45.00
Replica Jersey	75.00
Signed Card	8.00

Kidd, Jason

8 X 10 Photo	20.00
Authentic Jersey	180.00
Game Ball	120.00
I/O Ball	65.00
Mini Ball	50.00
Replica Jersey	90.00
Signed Card	10.00

Kittles, Kerry

8 X 10 Photo	15.00

GEORGE MIKAN

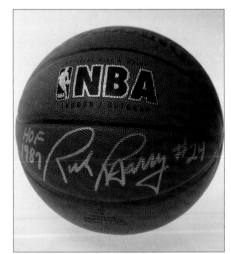

RICK BARRY

Pete Maravich

Game Ball 100.00

I/O Ball 50.00

Mini Ball 30.00

Replica Jersey 75.00

Signed Card 6.00

Knight, Brevin

8 X 10 Photo 12.00

Game Ball 80.00

I/O Ball 45.00

Mini Ball 30.00

Replica Jersey 65.00

Signed Card 5.00

Kukoc, Toni

8 X 10 Photo 20.00

Authentic Jersey 160.00

Game Ball 110.00

I/O Ball 60.00

Mini Ball 45.00

Replica Jersey 80.00

Signed Card 10.00

Laettner, Christian

8 X 10 Photo 12.00

Game Ball 80.00

I/O Ball 45.00

Mini Ball 30.00

Replica Jersey 65.00

Signed Card 5.00

Malone, Karl

8 X 10 Photo 30.00

Authentic Jersey 275.00

Game Ball 200.00

I/O Ball 110.00

Mini Ball 90.00

Replica Jersey 160.00

Signed Card 20.00

Marbury, Stephon

8 X 10 Photo 25.00

Authentic Jersey 220.00

Game Ball 160.00

I/O Ball 85.00

Mini Ball 70.00

Replica Jersey 120.00

Signed Card 15.00

Mashburn, Jamal

8 X 10 Photo 12.00

Game Ball 80.00

I/O Ball 45.00

Mini Ball 30.00

Replica Jersey 65.00

Signed Card 5.00

Mason, Anthony

8 X 10 Photo 12.00

Game Ball 80.00

I/O Ball 45.00

Mini Ball 30.00

Replica Jersey 65.00

Signed Card 5.00

McDyess, Antonio

8 X 10 Photo 18.00

Authentic Jersey 160.00

Game Ball 110.00

I/O Ball 60.00

ALONZO MOURNING

SHAWN KEMP

THE DREAM TEAM

BOB NETOLICKY

Bob Pettit

BOB PETTIT

Mini Ball 45.00

Replica Jersey 80.00

Signed Card 8.00

Mercer, Ron

8 X 10 Photo 12.00

Game Ball 80.00

I/O Ball .45.00

Mini Ball 30.00

Replica Jersey 65.00

Signed Card 5.00

Miller, Reggie

8 X 10 Photo 25.00

Authentic Jersey 220.00

Game Ball 160.00

I/O Ball .85.00

Mini Ball 70.00

Replica Jersey 120.00

Signed Card 15.00

Mourning, Alonzo

8 X 10 Photo 20.00

Authentic Jersey 200.00

Game Ball 140.00

I/O Ball .75.00

Mini Ball 60.00

Replica Jersey 100.00

Signed Card 12.00

Mullin, Chris

8 X 10 Photo 20.00

Authentic Jersey 175.00

Game Ball 120.00

I/O Ball .65.00

Mini Ball 50.00

Replica Jersey 90.00

Signed Card 10.00

Mutombo, Dikembe

8 X 10 Photo 20.00

Authentic Jersey 175.00

Game Ball 120.00

I/O Ball .65.00

Mini Ball 50.00

Replica Jersey 90.00

Signed Card 10.00

O'Neal, Shaquille

8 X 10 Photo 40.00

Authentic Jersey 300.00

Game Ball 225.00

I/O Ball 125.00

Mini Ball 100.00

Replica Jersey 175.00

Signed Card 25.00

Olajuwon, Hakeem

8 X 10 Photo 30.00

Authentic Jersey 275.00

Game Ball 200.00

I/O Ball 110.00

Mini Ball 90.00

Replica Jersey 160.00

Signed Card 20.00

Payton, Gary

8 X 10 Photo 18.00

Authentic Jersey 160.00

Game Ball 110.00

I/O Ball .60.00

Mini Ball 45.00

Replica Jersey 80.00

Signed Card 8.00

Pippen, Scottie

8 X 10 Photo 60.00

Authentic Jersey 275.00

Game Ball 200.00

I/O Ball 110.00

Mini Ball 100.00

Replica Jersey 175.00

Signed Card 25.00

Reeves, Bryant

8 X 10 Photo 12.00

Game Ball 80.00

I/O Ball 45.00

Mini Ball 30.00

Replica Jersey 65.00

Signed Card 5.00

Rice, Glen

8 X 10 Photo 18.00

Authentic Jersey 160.00

Game Ball 110.00

I/O Ball 60.00

Mini Ball 45.00

Replica Jersey 80.00

Signed Card 8.00

Richmond, Mitch

8 X 10 Photo 18.00

Authentic Jersey 160.00

Game Ball 110.00

I/O Ball .60.00

Mini Ball 45.00

Replica Jersey 80.00

Signed Card 8.00

Rider, Isaiah

8 X 10 Photo 12.00

Game Ball 80.00

I/O Ball 45.00

Mini Ball 30.00

Replica Jersey 65.00

Signed Card 5.00

Robinson, David

8 X 10 Photo 30.00

Authentic Jersey 240.00

Game Ball 175.00

I/O Ball 90.00

Mini Ball 75.00

Replica Jersey 135.00

Signed Card 18.00

Robinson, Glen

8 X 10 Photo 20.00

Authentic Jersey 180.00

Game Ball 120.00

I/O Ball .65.00

Mini Ball 50.00

Replica Jersey 90.00

Signed Card 10.00

Rodman, Dennis

8 X 10 Photo 40.00

Authentic Jersey 300.00

Game Ball 225.00

MICHAEL JORDAN

WILLIS REED

OSCAR ROBERTSON

I/O Ball .125.00

Mini Ball 100.00

Replica Jersey 175.00

Signed Card 25.00

Sabonis Arvydas

8 X 10 Photo 12.00

Game Ball 80.00

I/O Ball .45.00

Mini Ball 30.00

Replica Jersey 65.00

Signed Card 5.00

Schrempf, Detlef

8 X 10 Photo 12.00

Game Ball 80.00

I/O Ball .45.00

Mini Ball 30.00

Replica Jersey 65.00

Signed Card 5.00

Smith, Joe

8 X 10 Photo 18.00

Authentic Jersey 160.00

Game Ball 110.00

I/O Ball .60.00

Mini Ball 45.00

Replica Jersey 80.00

Signed Card 8.00

Smits, Rik

8 X 10 Photo 12.00

Game Ball 80.00

I/O Ball .45.00

Mini Ball 30.00

DOLPH SCHAYES

MICHAEL JORDAN

Replica Jersey 65.00

Signed Card 5.00

Sprewell, Latrell

8 X 10 Photo 15.00

Game Ball 100.00

I/O Ball .55.00

Mini Ball 40.00

Replica Jersey 75.00

Signed Card 7.00

Stackhouse, Jerry

8 X 10 Photo 18.00

Authentic Jersey 160.00

Game Ball 110.00

I/O Ball .60.00

Mini Ball 45.00

Replica Jersey 80.00

Signed Card 8.00

Starks, John

8 X 10 Photo 15.00

Authentic Jersey 150.00

Game Ball 100.00

I/O Ball .50.00

Mini Ball 40.00

Replica Jersey 75.00

Signed Card 8.00

Stockton, John

8 X 10 Photo 30.00

Authentic Jersey 240.00

Game Ball 175.00

I/O Ball .90.00

Mini Ball 75.00

Replica Jersey 135.00

Signed Card 18.00

Stoudamire, Damon

8 X 10 Photo 25.00

Authentic Jersey 220.00

Game Ball 160.00

I/O Ball 85.00

Mini Ball .70.00

Replica Jersey 120.00

Signed Card 15.00

Strickland, Rod

8 X 10 Photo 12.00

Game Ball 80.00

I/O Ball 45.00

Mini Ball .30.00

Replica Jersey 65.00

Signed Card 5.00

Van Exel, Nick

8 X 10 Photo 15.00

Authentic Jersey 150.00

Game Ball 100.00

I/O Ball 50.00

Mini Ball .40.00

Replica Jersey 75.00

Signed Card 8.00

Van Horn, Keith

8 X 10 Photo 20.00

Game Ball 100.00

I/O Ball 55.00

Mini Ball .40.00

Replica Jersey 75.00

Signed Card 10.00

Walker, Antoine

8 X 10 Photo 20.00

Authentic Jersey 180.00

Game Ball 120.00

I/O Ball 65.00

Mini Ball .50.00

Replica Jersey 90.00

Signed Card 10.00

Wallace, Rasheed

8 X 10 Photo 12.00

Authentic Jersey 200.00

Game Ball 80.00

I/O Ball 45.00

Mini Ball .30.00

Replica Jersey 65.00

Signed Card 5.00

Webber, Chris

8 X 10 Photo 20.00

Game Ball 140.00

I/O Ball 75.00

Mini Ball .60.00

Replica Jersey 100.00

Signed Card 12.00

Wilkins, Dominique

8 X 10 Photo 18.00

Authentic Jersey 160.00

Game Ball 110.00

I/O Ball 60.00

Mini Ball .45.00

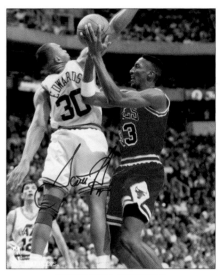

SCOTTIE PIPPEN

ALONZO MOURNING

Replica Jersey	. . . . .80.00	Game Ball	. . . . .80.00
Signed Card	. . . . .8.00	I/O Ball	. . . . .45.00
		Mini Ball	. . . . .30.00
Williams, Jayson		Replica Jersey	. . . . .65.00
8 X 10 Photo	. . . . .12.00	Signed Card	. . . . .5.00

Pete Maravich

Terrell Davis

COLLECTING FOOTBALL AUTOGRAPHS

Collecting football autographs can be difficult. It's not that the big names won't sign, because most of them will at the right time and place.

Finding the right time and place is the problem. There are so few games in a season that each one is important. Even preseason games require tremendous preparation from the coaching staff and players.

Therefore, getting autographs before or after games at the stadium is often hopeless. Most stadiums offer poor player access, if any. Team hotels used to be a prime collecting zone, but as each season passes, more hotels crack down on autograph seekers.

Even training camp is difficult, because the sites are spread all over the country with the exception of the Wisconsin "cheese league" comprising a handful of teams. Your best bet for obtaining free NFL superstar signatures is an off-season charity golf tournament, or if you can afford it, a trip to the Pro Bowl in Honolulu or the Super Bowl.

For both of the latter events, most of the sport's big names past and present show up for the game and attend various pre-game and post-game events. On Super Bowl weekend, you almost can't walk through a luxury hotel without bumping into a football celebrity.

This is definitely a good time to collect NFL signatures.

Brett Favre

BY THEO CHEN

Eventually, the NFL of the late 1990s may be regarded as a golden age for superstars.

The number of all-time greats active during this period is incredible. Troy Aikman, Terrell Davis, John Elway, Brett Favre, Dan Marino, Jerry Rice, Barry Sanders, Emmitt Smith and Steve Young are not only likely future hall of famers, but record-setting ones at that.

Look up the stats. Marino is the all-time most prolific passer. Rice is the all-time greatest receiver and has scored more touchdowns than anyone in history. Sanders, barring injury, will be the all-time greatest runner. Smith owns the record for career rushing touchdowns, and Young is the highest rated QB of all-time. Aikman, Elway, Favre and Young all have at least one Super

John Elway

Bowl title.

As far as the relative pricing for autographed memorabilia of these superstars, the market forces of demand and supply determine that. The demand, of course, is based on their relative popularity, which ebbs and flows in response to their on-field performance.

The supply, however, varies considerably from player to player depending on his signing habits and memorabilia deals he has been involved in.

Take Sanders and Smith, for example, two certain HOF running backs whose careers have been compared for an entire decade. On one hand, Sanders might be the toughest superstar signature in the NFL. He rarely does shows, and only occasionally does he do a private signing. In person? Forget it.

I ran into him at the San Antonio airport after the 1996 NBA All-Star Game. Barry's flight

Junior Seau

was cancelled, so he had a few hours to kill. He adamantly refused to sign even though all we had were index cards. Later that same year, prior to a charity basketball game in Oklahoma City, Barry sat down in the hotel lobby next to a few kids seeking 'graphs, asked them if they were getting a lot of autographs — and then turned them down cold.

Emmitt isn't exactly easy in person, either. He is very wary of people who may resell his signature, so he often turns down adults, especially if they have easily sellable items such as footballs, helmets, jerseys or mini helmets. He usually signs for kids, though.

But Emmitt signatures are relatively plentiful in the market.

Not only does he sign at shows more often than Barry, but Emmitt has his own memorabilia business that his family runs. As a result, there are authentic signed 8x10s available for $25, while a real Barry Sanders signed 8x10 would cost you double that. That gives you an idea of how important supply is to the autograph value equation.

Notice that all the house-

hold names I specifically mentioned are offensive skill position players. That's more than a trend; it's more of an axiom really, and it applies both to football cards and football autographs. Collectors simply aren't very interested in defensive standouts.

In fact, about the only recent defensive players whose autographs are in strong demand are Deion Sanders and Reggie

Emmitt Smith

White. Despite the fact that Deion and Reggie both are notoriously reluctant signers, their autographs still are a notch below the offensive stars in terms of market value.

As far as players from the past, it's interesting that in football, even the biggest names don't command more dollars than today's stars. In baseball, legends such as Joe DiMaggio, Mickey Mantle and Ted Williams were always larger than life. But in football, the equivalents of Jim Brown, Joe Namath and Johnny Unitas don't command nearly as much attention.

To a collector with a sense of history, that should signal an opportunity. And don't forget more recent retirees such as Terry Bradshaw, Joe Montana, Roger Staubach or Walter Payton — their signed memorabilia still is very affordable. ▪

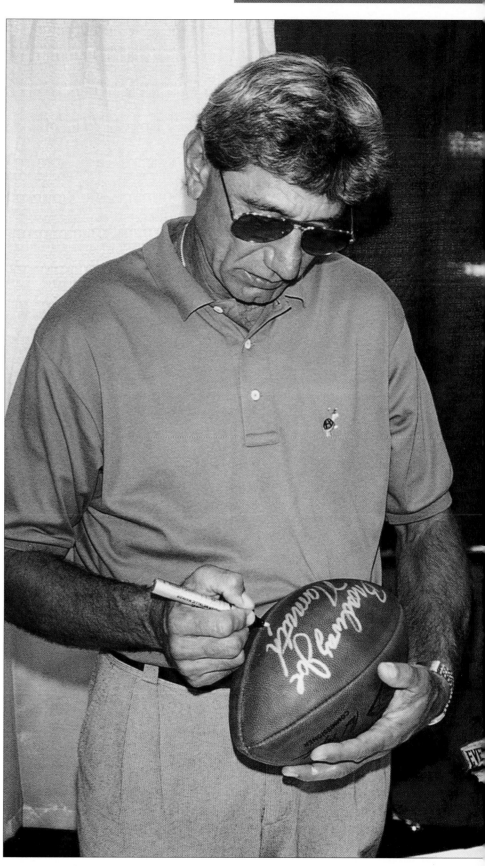

Joe Namath

Autographs

TROY AIKMAN

EMMITT SMITH

LANCE ALWORTH

Peyton Manning

Retired Players

Adderley, Herb-(1980)

3 X 5	.5.00
8 X 10 Photo	.15.00
Mini Helmet	.50.00
Signed Goal Line Art	.15.00
Single Signed Ball	.75.00

Alworth, Lance-(1978)

3 X 5	.8.00
8 X 10 Photo	.20.00
Mini Helmet	.50.00
Signed Goal Line Art	.25.00
Single Signed Ball	.100.00

Ameche, Alan d. 1988

3 X 5	.50.00
8 X 10 Photo	.150.00

Badgro, Red-(1981) d. 1998

3 X 5	.5.00
8 X 10 Photo	.15.00
Mini Helmet	.50.00
Signed Goal Line Art	.15.00
Single Signed Ball	.75.00

Barney, Lem-(1992)

3 X 5	.5.00
8 X 10 Photo	.15.00
Mini Helmet	.50.00
Signed Goal Line Art	.15.00
Single Signed Ball	.75.00

Battles, Cliff-(1968) d. 1981

3 X 5	.75.00
8 X 10 Photo	.200.00
Single Signed Ball	.350.00

Baugh, Sammy-(1963)

3 X 5	.25.00
8 X 10 Photo	.75.00
Mini Helmet	.100.00
Signed Goal Line Art	.50.00
Single Signed Ball	.300.00

Bednarik, Chuck-(1967)

3 X 5	.10.00
8 X 10 Photo	.20.00
Canceled Check	.15.00
Mini Helmet	.50.00
Signed Goal Line Art	.20.00
Single Signed Ball	.125.00

Bell, Bert-(1963) d. 1959

3 X 5	.75.00
8 X 10 Photo	.350.00

Bell, Bobby-(1983)

3 X 5	.5.00
8 X 10 Photo	.15.00
Mini Helmet	.50.00
Signed Goal Line Art	.20.00
Single Signed Ball	.75.00

Berry, Raymond-(1973)

3 X 5	.5.00
8 X 10 Photo	.15.00
Mini Helmet	.50.00

Signed Goal Line Art 20.00

Single Signed Ball 100.00

Biletnikoff, Fred-(1988)

3 X 5 . . . . .5.00

8 X 10 Photo 15.00

Mini Helmet 60.00

Signed Goal Line Art 15.00

Single Signed Ball 100.00

Blanda, George-(1981)

3 X 5 . . . . .5.00

8 X 10 Photo 15.00

Mini Helmet 60.00

Signed Goal Line Art 20.00

Single Signed Ball 125.00

Blount, Mel-(1989)

3 X 5 . . . . .5.00

8 X 10 Photo 15.00

Mini Helmet 50.00

Signed Goal Line Art 15.00

Single Signed Ball 75.00

Bradshaw, Terry-(1989)

3 X 5 . . . . .10.00

8 X 10 Photo 30.00

Mini Helmet 100.00

Signed Goal Line Art 30.00

Single Signed Ball 150.00

Brown, Jim-(1971)

3 X 5 . . . . .10.00

8 X 10 Photo 30.00

Mini Helmet 100.00

Signed Goal Line Art 30.00

Single Signed Ball 150.00

Brown, Paul-(1967) d. 1991

3 X 5 . . . . .20.00

8 X 10 Photo 40.00

Signed Goal Line Art 125.00

Single Signed Ball 350.00

Brown, Roosevelt-(1975)

3 X 5 . . . . .5.00

8 X 10 Photo 15.00

Mini Helmet 50.00

Signed Goal Line Art 20.00

Single Signed Ball 100.00

Brown, Willie-(1984)

3 X 5 . . . . .5.00

8 X 10 Photo 15.00

Canceled Check 15.00

Mini Helmet 50.00

Signed Goal Line Art 15.00

Single Signed Ball 75.00

Buchanan, Buck-(1990) d. 1992

3 X 5 . . . . .15.00

8 X 10 Photo 50.00

Signed Goal Line Art 50.00

Single Signed Ball 250.00

Butkus, Dick-(1979)

3 X 5 . . . . .10.00

8 X 10 Photo 20.00

Mini Helmet 75.00

Signed Goal Line Art 25.00

Single Signed Ball 125.00

JAMAL ANDERSON

RED BADGRO

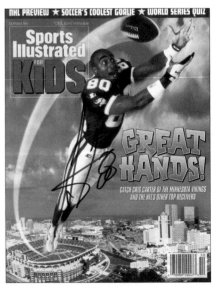

CRIS CARTER

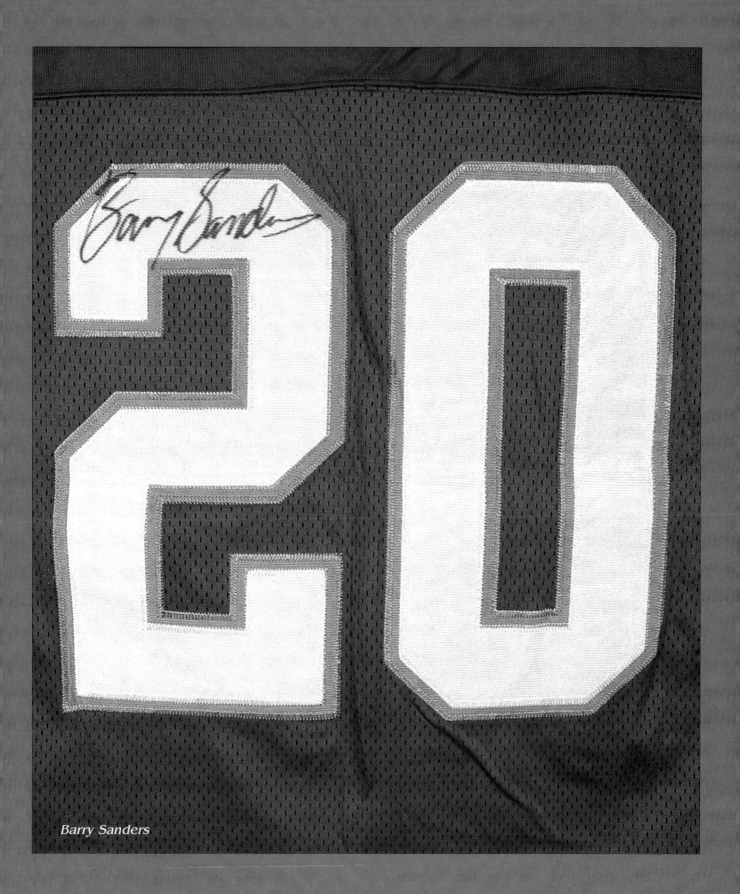

Barry Sanders

Campbell, Earl-(1991)

3 X 5 . . . . .5.00

8 X 10 Photo 15.00

Mini Helmet 60.00

Signed Goal Line Art 20.00

Single Signed Ball 125.00

Canadeo, Tony-(1974)

3 X 5 . . . . .5.00

8 X 10 Photo 15.00

Canceled Check 20.00

Mini Helmet 50.00

Signed Goal Line Art 15.00

Chamberlin, Guy-(1965) d. 1967

3 X 5 . . . . .50.00

8 X 10 Photo 150.00

Christiansen, Jack-(1970) d. 1986

3 X 5 . . . . .50.00

8 X 10 Photo 150.00

Clark, Dutch-(1963) d. 1978

3 X 5 . . . . .40.00

8 X 10 Photo 175.00

Connor, George-(1975)

3 X 5 . . . . .5.00

8 X 10 Photo 15.00

Signed Goal Line Art 15.00

Single Signed Ball 75.00

Creekmur, Lou-(1996)

3 X 5 . . . . .5.00

8 X 10 Photo 15.00

Mini Helmet 50.00

Signed Goal Line Art 15.00

Single Signed Ball 75.00

Csonka, Larry-(1987)

3 X 5 . . . . .8.00

8 X 10 Photo 20.00

Mini Helmet 75.00

Signed Goal Line Art 30.00

Single Signed Ball 125.00

Davis, Al-(1992)

3 X 5 . . . . .25.00

8 X 10 Photo 60.00

Signed Goal Line Art 100.00

Single Signed Ball 150.00

Davis, Willie-(1981)

3 X 5 . . . . .5.00

8 X 10 Photo 15.00

Mini Helmet 60.00

Signed Goal Line Art 15.00

Single Signed Ball 75.00

Dawson, Len-(1987)

3 X 5 . . . . .8.00

8 X 10 Photo 20.00

Mini Helmet 75.00

Signed Goal Line Art 30.00

Single Signed Ball 125.00

Dierdorf, Dan-(1996)

3 X 5 . . . . .5.00

8 X 10 Photo 15.00

Mini Helmet 50.00

JERRY RICE

SAMMY BAUGH

RAYMOND BERRY

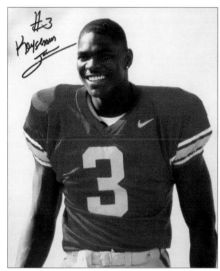

FRED BILENTNIKOFF

KEYSHAWN JOHNSON

Signed Goal Line Art 15.00

Single Signed Ball 75.00

Ditka, Mike-(1988)

3 X 5 . . . . .8.00

8 X 10 Photo 20.00

Mini Helmet 60.00

Signed Goal Line Art 25.00

Single Signed Ball 125.00

Donovan, Art-(1968)

3 X 5 . . . . .8.00

8 X 10 Photo 15.00

Mini Helmet 50.00

Signed Goal Line Art 15.00

Single Signed Ball 125.00

Dorsett, Tony-(1994)

3 X 5 . . . . .5.00

8 X 10 Photo 20.00

Mini Helmet 60.00

Signed Goal Line Art 35.00

Single Signed Ball 100.00

Dudley, Bill-(1966)

3 X 5 . . . . .5.00

8 X 10 Photo 15.00

Mini Helmet 50.00

Signed Goal Line Art 15.00

Single Signed Ball 75.00

Edwards, Turk-(1969) d. 1973

3 X 5 . . . . .125.00

8 X 10 Photo 300.00

Fears, Tom-(1970)

3 X 5 . . . . .5.00

8 X 10 Photo 15.00

Mini Helmet 50.00

Signed Goal Line Art 15.00

Single Signed Ball 100.00

Finks, Jim-(1995) d. 1994

3 X 5 . . . . .25.00

8 X 10 Photo 125.00

Flaherty, Ray-(1976) d. 1995

3 X 5 . . . . .20.00

8 X 10 Photo 50.00

Signed Goal Line Art 35.00

Single Signed Ball 200.00

Ford, Len-(1976) d. 1972

3 X 5 . . . . .200.00

8 X 10 Photo 500.00

Fortmann, Dan-(1965) d. 1995

3 X 5 . . . . .30.00

8 X 10 Photo 60.00

Signed Goal Line Art 50.00

Single Signed Ball 200.00

Fouts, Dan-(1993)

3 X 5 . . . . .8.00

8 X 10 Photo 20.00

Mini Helmet 60.00

Signed Goal Line Art 25.00

Single Signed Ball 100.00

Gatski, Frank-(1985)

3 X 5 . . . . .5.00

8 X 10 Photo 15.00

Mini Helmet 50.00

Signed Goal Line Art 15.00

Single Signed Ball 75.00

George, Bill-(1974) d. 1982

3 X 5 . . . . .75.00

8 X 10 Photo 150.00

Gibbs, Joe-(1996)

3 X 5 . . . . .5.00

8 X 10 Photo 15.00

Signed Goal Line Art 15.00

Single Signed Ball 75.00

Gifford, Frank-(1977)

3 X 5 . . . . .8.00

8 X 10 Photo 20.00

Mini Helmet 60.00

Signed Goal Line Art 25.00

Single Signed Ball 125.00

Gillman, Sid-(1983)

3 X 5 . . . . .5.00

8 X 10 Photo 15.00

Mini Helmet 50.00

Signed Goal Line Art 15.00

Single Signed Ball 75.00

Graham, Otto-(1965)

3 X 5 . . . . .10.00

8 X 10 Photo 25.00

Mini Helmet 60.00

Signed Goal Line Art 25.00

Single Signed Ball 150.00

Grange, Red-(1963) d. 1991

3 X 5 . . . . .60.00

8 X 10 Photo 150.00

Signed Goal Line Art 125.00

Single Signed Ball 750.00

Grant, Bud-(1994)

3 X 5 . . . . .5.00

8 X 10 Photo 20.00

Signed Goal Line Art 20.00

Greene, Joe-(1987)

3 X 5 . . . . .10.00

8 X 10 Photo 25.00

Mini Helmet 60.00

Signed Goal Line Art 25.00

Single Signed Ball 125.00

Gregg, Forrest-(1977)

3 X 5 . . . . .5.00

8 X 10 Photo 15.00

Mini Helmet 50.00

Signed Goal Line Art 15.00

Single Signed Ball 75.00

Griese, Bob-(1990)

3 X 5 . . . . .10.00

8 X 10 Photo 20.00

Mini Helmet 75.00

Signed Goal Line Art 25.00

Single Signed Ball 125.00

BUCK BUCHANAN

DICK BUTKUS

EARL CAMPBELL

CRIS CARTER

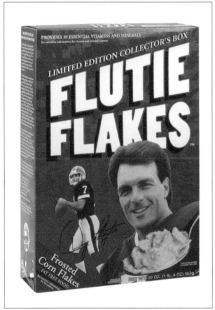

DOUG FLUTIE

Groza, Lou-(1974)

3 X 5 . . . . .8.00

8 X 10 Photo 20.00

Mini Helmet 25.00

Signed Goal Line Art 15.00

Single Signed Ball 100.00

Halas, George-(1963) d. 1983

3 X 5 . . . . .60.00

8 X 10 Photo 150.00

Single Signed Ball 800.00

Ham, Jack-(1988)

3 X 5 . . . . .5.00

8 X 10 Photo 15.00

Mini Helmet 50.00

Signed Goal Line Art 20.00

Single Signed Ball 75.00

Hannah, John-(1991)

3 X 5 . . . . .5.00

8 X 10 Photo 15.00

Mini Helmet 50.00

Signed Goal Line Art 20.00

Single Signed Ball 75.00

Harris, Franco-(1990)

3 X 5 . . . . .8.00

8 X 10 Photo 20.00

Mini Helmet 75.00

Signed Goal Line Art 20.00

Single Signed Ball 125.00

Hein, Mel-(1963) d. 1992

3 X 5 . . . . .20.00

8 X 10 Photo 75.00

Signed Goal Line Art 150.00

Single Signed Ball 200.00

Hendricks, Ted-(1990)

3 X 5 . . . . .5.00

8 X 10 Photo 15.00

Mini Helmet 50.00

Signed Goal Line Art 25.00

Single Signed Ball 75.00

Henry, Pete-(1963) d. 1952

3 X 5 . . . . .150.00

Canceled Check 500.00

Hirsch, Elroy-(1968)

3 X 5 . . . . .8.00

8 X 10 Photo 20.00

Signed Goal Line Art 20.00

Single Signed Ball 125.00

Hornung, Paul-(1986)

3 X 5 . . . . .10.00

8 X 10 Photo 25.00

Mini Helmet 60.00

Signed Goal Line Art 20.00

Single Signed Ball 125.00

Houston, Ken-(1986)

3 X 5 . . . . .5.00

8 X 10 Photo 15.00

Mini Helmet 50.00

Signed Goal Line Art 15.00

Single Signed Ball 75.00

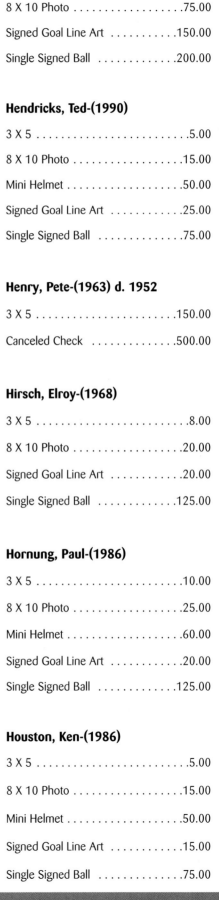

Hubbard, Cal-(1963) d. 1977

3 X 5 . . . . .60.00

8 X 10 Photo (Football) 200.00

Huff, Sam-(1982)

3 X 5 . . . . .8.00

8 X 10 Photo 20.00

Mini Helmet 50.00

Signed Goal Line Art 20.00

Single Signed Ball 100.00

Hutson, Don-(1963) d. 1997

3 X 5 . . . . .12.00

8 X 10 Photo 50.00

Mini Helmet 75.00

Signed Goal Line Art 50.00

Single Signed Ball 175.00

Johnson, Jimmy (DB)-(1994)

3 X 5 . . . . .5.00

8 X 10 Photo 15.00

Mini Helmet 50.00

Signed Goal Line Art 15.00

Single Signed Ball 75.00

Johnson, John Henry-(1987)

3 X 5 . . . . .5.00

8 X 10 Photo 15.00

Mini Helmet 50.00

Signed Goal Line Art 15.00

Single Signed Ball 75.00

Joiner, Charlie-(1996)

3 X 5 . . . . .5.00

8 X 10 Photo 15.00

Mini Helmet 50.00

Signed Goal Line Art 20.00

Single Signed Ball 75.00

Jones, Deacon-(1980)

3 X 5 . . . . .5.00

8 X 10 Photo 15.00

Mini Helmet 50.00

Signed Goal Line Art 20.00

Single Signed Ball 100.00

Jones, Stan-(1991)

3 X 5 . . . . .5.00

8 X 10 Photo 15.00

Mini Helmet 50.00

Signed Goal Line Art 15.00

Single Signed Ball 75.00

Jordan, Henry-(1995) d. 1977

3 X 5 . . . . .200.00

8 X 10 Photo 400.00

Jurgensen, Sonny-(1983)

3 X 5 . . . . .8.00

8 X 10 Photo 20.00

Mini Helmet 60.00

Signed Goal Line Art 20.00

Single Signed Ball 100.00

Karras, Alex

3 X 5 . . . . .5.00

8 X 10 Photo 15.00

Single Signed Ball 75.00

Kelly, Jim

3 X 5 . . . . .10.00

LARRY CSONKA

MARK BRUNELL

TERRELL DAVIS

Joe Namath

8 X 10 Photo 25.00

Mini Helmet 100.00

Single Signed Ball 125.00

Kelly, Leroy-(1994)

3 X 5 .5.00

8 X 10 Photo 15.00

Mini Helmet 50.00

Signed Goal Line Art 20.00

Single Signed Ball 75.00

Kemp, Jack

3 X 5 .10.00

8 X 10 Photo 25.00

Single Signed Ball 100.00

Lambert, Jack-(1990)

3 X 5 .10.00

8 X 10 Photo 25.00

Mini Helmet 75.00

Signed Goal Line Art 25.00

Single Signed Ball 125.00

Landry, Tom-(1990)

3 X 5 .5.00

8 X 10 Photo 15.00

Signed Goal Line Art 20.00

Single Signed Ball 100.00

Lane, Dick-(1974)

3 X 5 .8.00

8 X 10 Photo 20.00

Signed Goal Line Art 15.00

Single Signed Ball 100.00

Langer, Jim-(1987)

3 X 5 .5.00

8 X 10 Photo 15.00

Mini Helmet 50.00

Signed Goal Line Art 15.00

Single Signed Ball 75.00

Lanier, Willie-(1986)

3 X 5 .5.00

8 X 10 Photo 15.00

Mini Helmet 75.00

Signed Goal Line Art 20.00

Single Signed Ball 75.00

Largent, Steve-(1995)

3 X 5 .8.00

8 X 10 Photo 20.00

Mini Helmet 60.00

Signed Goal Line Art 25.00

Single Signed Ball 125.00

Lary, Yale-(1979)

3 X 5 .5.00

8 X 10 Photo 15.00

Canceled Check 20.00

Mini Helmet 50.00

Signed Goal Line Art 15.00

Single Signed Ball 75.00

Lavelli, Dante-(1975)

3 X 5 .5.00

8 X 10 Photo 15.00

Mini Helmet 50.00

Signed Goal Line Art 15.00

Single Signed Ball 75.00

LEN DAWSON

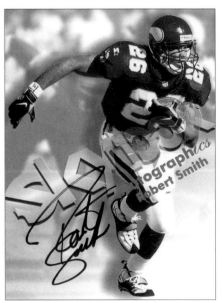

COREY DILLON

ROBERT SMITH

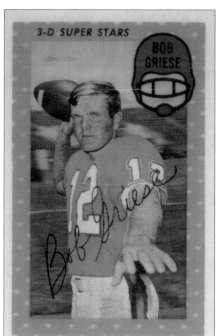

ART DONOVAN

BOB GRIESE

WARRICK DUNN

Layne, Bobby-(1967) d. 1986

3 X 5 . . . . .60.00

8 X 10 Photo 150.00

Single Signed Ball 750.00

Lilly, Bob-(1980)

3 X 5 . . . . .8.00

8 X 10 Photo 20.00

Mini Helmet 50.00

Signed Goal Line Art 15.00

Single Signed Ball 100.00

Little, Larry-(1993)

3 X 5 . . . . .5.00

8 X 10 Photo 15.00

Mini Helmet 50.00

Signed Goal Line Art 15.00

Single Signed Ball 75.00

Lombardi, Vince-(1971) d. 1970

3 X 5 . . . . .175.00

8 X 10 Photo 400.00

Canceled Check 275.00

Lott, Ronnie

3 X 5 . . . . .6.00

8 X 10 Photo 20.00

Mini Helmet 75.00

Single Signed Ball 100.00

Luckman, Sid-(1965) d. 1998

3 X 5 . . . . .10.00

8 X 10 Photo 25.00

Mini Helmet 60.00

Signed Goal Line Art 25.00

Single Signed Ball 150.00

Mackey, John-(1992)

3 X 5 . . . . .5.00

8 X 10 Photo 15.00

Mini Helmet 50.00

Signed Goal Line Art 15.00

Single Signed Ball 75.00

Marchetti, Gino-(1972)

3 X 5 . . . . .5.00

8 X 10 Photo 15.00

Mini Helmet 50.00

Signed Goal Line Art 20.00

Single Signed Ball 75.00

Matson, Ollie-(1972)

3 X 5 . . . . .8.00

8 X 10 Photo 20.00

Mini Helmet 50.00

Signed Goal Line Art 20.00

Single Signed Ball 125.00

Maynard, Don-(1987)

3 X 5 . . . . .5.00

8 X 10 Photo 15.00

Mini Helmet 50.00

Signed Goal Line Art 15.00

Single Signed Ball 75.00

McAfee, George-(1966)

3 X 5 . . . . .5.00

8 X 10 Photo 15.00

Mini Helmet 50.00

Signed Goal Line Art 15.00

Single Signed Ball 75.00

McCormack, Mike-(1984)

3 X 5 . . . . .5.00

8 X 10 Photo 15.00

Mini Helmet 50.00

Signed Goal Line Art 15.00

Single Signed Ball 75.00

McElhenny, Hugh-(1970)

3 X 5 . . . . .8.00

8 X 10 Photo 20.00

Mini Helmet 60.00

Signed Goal Line Art 20.00

Single Signed Ball 125.00

McNally, Johnny-(1963) d. 1985

3 X 5 . . . . .25.00

8 X 10 Photo 150.00

Michalske, Mike-(1964) d. 1983

3 X 5 . . . . .50.00

8 X 10 Photo 150.00

Millner, Wayne-(1968) d. 1976

3 X 5 . . . . .50.00

8 X 10 Photo 250.00

Mitchell, Bobby-(1983)

3 X 5 . . . . .5.00

8 X 10 Photo 15.00

Mini Helmet 50.00

Signed Goal Line Art 15.00

Single Signed Ball 75.00

Mix, Ron-(1979)

3 X 5 . . . . .5.00

8 X 10 Photo 15.00

Mini Helmet 50.00

Signed Goal Line Art 25.00

Single Signed Ball 75.00

Monk, Art

3 X 5 . . . . .8.00

8 X 10 Photo 20.00

Mini Helmet 75.00

Single Signed Ball 125.00

Montana, Joe

3 X 5 . . . . .12.00

8 X 10 Photo 30.00

Mini Helmet 125.00

Single Signed Ball 175.00

Moore, Lenny-(1975)

3 X 5 . . . . .8.00

8 X 10 Photo 20.00

Canceled Check 25.00

Mini Helmet 50.00

Signed Goal Line Art 20.00

Single Signed Ball 100.00

Motley, Marion-(1968)

3 X 5 . . . . .8.00

8 X 10 Photo 20.00

Mini Helmet 50.00

Signed Goal Line Art 20.00

Single Signed Ball 100.00

Musso, George-(1982)

3 X 5 . . . . .8.00

JOHN ELWAY

JAMAL ANDERSON

BRETT FAVRE

Steve Young

8 X 10 Photo 20.00

Mini Helmet 50.00

Signed Goal Line Art 15.00

Single Signed Ball 100.00

Nagurski, Bronko-(1963) d. 1990

3 X 5 . . . . .50.00

8 X 10 Photo 150.00

Canceled Check 150.00

Single Signed Ball 400.00

Namath, Joe-(1985)

3 X 5 . . . . .20.00

8 X 10 Photo 50.00

Mini Helmet 125.00

Signed Goal Line Art 50.00

Single Signed Ball 175.00

Nevers, Ernie-(1963) d. 1976

3 X 5 . . . . .60.00

8 X 10 Photo 150.00

Single Signed Ball 500.00

Nitschke, Ray-(1978) d. 1998

3 X 5 . . . . .5.00

8 X 10 Photo 15.00

Mini Helmet 50.00

Signed Goal Line Art 20.00

Single Signed Ball 75.00

Noll, Chuck-(1993)

3 X 5 . . . . .5.00

8 X 10 Photo 15.00

Signed Goal Line Art 20.00

Single Signed Ball 100.00

Nomellini, Leo-(1969)

3 X 5 . . . . .5.00

8 X 10 Photo 15.00

Mini Helmet 50.00

Signed Goal Line Art 15.00

Single Signed Ball 100.00

Olsen, Merlin-(1982)

3 X 5 . . . . .8.00

8 X 10 Photo 20.00

Mini Helmet 60.00

Signed Goal Line Art 20.00

Single Signed Ball 100.00

Otto, Jim-(1980)

3 X 5 . . . . .5.00

8 X 10 Photo 15.00

Mini Helmet 50.00

Signed Goal Line Art 15.00

Single Signed Ball 100.00

Page, Alan-(1988)

3 X 5 . . . . .10.00

8 X 10 Photo 25.00

Mini Helmet 60.00

Signed Goal Line Art 25.00

Single Signed Ball 125.00

Parker, Clarence-(1972)

3 X 5 . . . . .5.00

8 X 10 Photo 15.00

Single Signed Ball 150.00

Parker, Jim-(1973)

3 X 5 . . . . .5.00

JAKE PLUMMER

ANTONIO FREEMAN

MARSHALL FAULK

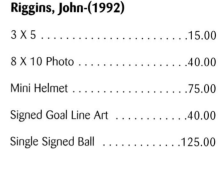

JERRY RICE

8 X 10 Photo 15.00

Mini Helmet 50.00

Signed Goal Line Art 15.00

Single Signed Ball 75.00

Payton, Walter-(1993)

3 X 5 . . . . .15.00

8 X 10 Photo 40.00

Mini Helmet 100.00

Signed Goal Line Art 40.00

Single Signed Ball 150.00

Perry, Joe-(1969)

3 X 5 . . . . .5.00

8 X 10 Photo 15.00

Mini Helmet 50.00

Signed Goal Line Art 15.00

Single Signed Ball 75.00

Piccolo, Brian d. 1970

3 X 5 . . . . .150.00

Pihos, Pete-(1970)

3 X 5 . . . . .5.00

8 X 10 Photo 15.00

Mini Helmet 50.00

Signed Goal Line Art 15.00

Single Signed Ball 75.00

Renfro, Mel-(1996)

3 X 5 . . . . .5.00

8 X 10 Photo 15.00

Mini Helmet 50.00

Signed Goal Line Art 15.00

Single Signed Ball 75.00

Riggins, John-(1992)

3 X 5 . . . . .15.00

8 X 10 Photo 40.00

Mini Helmet 75.00

Signed Goal Line Art 40.00

Single Signed Ball 125.00

Ringo, Jim-(1981)

3 X 5 . . . . .5.00

8 X 10 Photo 15.00

Mini Helmet 50.00

Signed Goal Line Art 15.00

Single Signed Ball 100.00

Robustelli, Andy-(1971)

3 X 5 . . . . .5.00

8 X 10 Photo 15.00

Mini Helmet 50.00

Signed Goal Line Art 15.00

Single Signed Ball 75.00

Rockne, Knute- d. 1931

3 X 5 . . . . .400.00

8 X 10 Photo 1500.00

Rooney, Art-(1964) d. 1988

3 X 5 . . . . .30.00

8 X 10 Photo 100.00

Rozelle, Pete-(1985) d. 1996

3 X 5 . . . . .15.00

8 X 10 Photo 40.00

Signed Goal Line Art 60.00

Single Signed Ball 175.00

JOEY GALLOWAY

Sayers, Gale-(1977)

3 X 5 . . . . .8.00

8 X 10 Photo 20.00

Mini Helmet 75.00

Signed Goal Line Art 20.00

Single Signed Ball 125.00

Schmidt, Joe-(1973)

3 X 5 . . . . .5.00

8 X 10 Photo 15.00

Mini Helmet 50.00

Signed Goal Line Art 15.00

Single Signed Ball 75.00

Selmon, Lee Roy-(1995)

3 X 5 . . . . .5.00

8 X 10 Photo 15.00

Mini Helmet 50.00

Signed Goal Line Art 15.00

Single Signed Ball 75.00

Shell, Art-(1989)

3 X 5 . . . . .8.00

8 X 10 Photo 20.00

Mini Helmet 50.00

Signed Goal Line Art 20.00

Single Signed Ball 100.00

Simms, Phil

3 X 5 . . . . .8.00

8 X 10 Photo 20.00

Mini Helmet 75.00

Single Signed Ball 125.00

Simpson, O.J.-(1985)

3 X 5 . . . . .15.00

8 X 10 Photo 35.00

Mini Helmet 75.00

Signed Goal Line Art 40.00

Single Signed Ball 175.00

Singletary, Mike-(1998)

3 X 5 . . . . .8.00

8 X 10 Photo 20.00

Mini Helmet 75.00

Single Signed Ball 125.00

Smith, Jackie-(1994)

3 X 5 . . . . .5.00

8 X 10 Photo 15.00

Mini Helmet 50.00

Signed Goal Line Art 20.00

Single Signed Ball 75.00

St. Clair, Bob-(1990)

3 X 5 . . . . .5.00

8 X 10 Photo 15.00

Mini Helmet 50.00

Signed Goal Line Art 15.00

Single Signed Ball 75.00

Starr, Bart-(1977)

3 X 5 . . . . .8.00

8 X 10 Photo 20.00

Mini Helmet 100.00

Signed Goal Line Art 25.00

Single Signed Ball 125.00

Staubach, Roger-(1985)

3 X 5 . . . . .10.00

8 X 10 Photo 35.00

GARRISON HEARST

RANDALL HILL

PAUL HORNUNG

CAL HUBBARD

DEACON JONES

JERRY RICE

Mini Helmet 100.00

Signed Goal Line Art 35.00

Single Signed Ball 150.00

Stautner, Ernie-(1969)

3 X 5 . . . . .5.00

8 X 10 Photo 15.00

Mini Helmet 50.00

Signed Goal Line Art 15.00

Single Signed Ball 100.00

Stenerud, Jan-(1991)

3 X 5 . . . . .5.00

8 X 10 Photo 15.00

Mini Helmet 50.00

Signed Goal Line Art 15.00

Single Signed Ball 75.00

Strong, Ken-(1967) d. 1979

3 X 5 . . . . .50.00

8 X 10 Photo 150.00

Canceled Check 100.00

Stydahar, Joe-(1967) d. 1977

3 X 5 . . . . .50.00

8 X 10 Photo 150.00

Tarkenton, Fran-(1986)

3 X 5 . . . . .10.00

8 X 10 Photo 30.00

Mini Helmet 100.00

Signed Goal Line Art 40.00

Single Signed Ball 150.00

Taylor, Charley-(1984)

3 X 5 . . . . .8.00

8 X 10 Photo 20.00

Mini Helmet 60.00

Signed Goal Line Art 20.00

Single Signed Ball 100.00

Taylor, Jim-(1976)

3 X 5 . . . . .8.00

8 X 10 Photo 20.00

Mini Helmet 50.00

Signed Goal Line Art 20.00

Single Signed Ball 100.00

Taylor, Lawrence

3 X 5 . . . . .8.00

8 X 10 Photo 20.00

Mini Helmet 75.00

Single Signed Ball 125.00

Thorpe, Jim-(1963) d. 1953

3 X 5 . . . . .450.00

8 X 10 Photo 1250.00

Tittle, Y.A.-(1971)

3 X 5 . . . . .8.00

8 X 10 Photo 20.00

Mini Helmet 60.00

Signed Goal Line Art 20.00

Single Signed Ball 125.00

Trafton, George-(1964) d. 1971

3 X 5 . . . . .75.00

8 X 10 Photo 300.00

Canceled Check 150.00

Trippi, Charley-(1968)

3 X 5 . . . . .5.00

8 X 10 Photo 15.00

Canceled Check 20.00

Mini Helmet 50.00

Signed Goal Line Art 15.00

Single Signed Ball 100.00

Tunnell, Emlen-(1967) d. 1975

3 X 5 . . . . .50.00

8 X 10 Photo 150.00

Turner, Clyde-(1966)

3 X 5 . . . . .8.00

8 X 10 Photo 20.00

Canceled Check 15.00

Signed Goal Line Art 20.00

Unitas, Johnny-(1979)

3 X 5 . . . . .12.00

8 X 10 Photo 35.00

Mini Helmet 100.00

Signed Goal Line Art 60.00

Single Signed Ball 150.00

Upshaw, Gene-(1987)

3 X 5 . . . . .5.00

8 X 10 Photo 15.00

Mini Helmet 50.00

Signed Goal Line Art 15.00

Single Signed Ball 75.00

Van Brocklin, Norm-(1971) d. 1983

3 X 5 . . . . .60.00

8 X 10 Photo 150.00

Single Signed Ball 400.00

Van Buren, Steve-(1965)

3 X 5 . . . . .8.00

8 X 10 Photo 20.00

Mini Helmet 50.00

Signed Goal Line Art 15.00

Single Signed Ball 125.00

Walker, Doak-(1986) d. 1998

3 X 5 . . . . .15.00

8 X 10 Photo 35.00

Mini Helmet 100.00

Signed Goal Line Art 50.00

Single Signed Ball 150.00

Warfield, Paul-(1983)

3 X 5 . . . . .5.00

8 X 10 Photo 15.00

Mini Helmet 50.00

Signed Goal Line Art 15.00

Single Signed Ball 75.00

Waterfield, Bob-(1965) d. 1983

3 X 5 . . . . .60.00

8 X 10 Photo 150.00

Single Signed Ball 350.00

Weinmeister, Arnie-(1984)

3 X 5 . . . . .5.00

8 X 10 Photo 15.00

Mini Helmet 50.00

Signed Goal Line Art 20.00

Single Signed Ball 75.00

White, Randy-(1994)

3 X 5 . . . . .5.00

KEYSHAWN JOHNSON

DICK LANE

WILLIE LANIER

8 X 10 Photo 15.00

Mini Helmet 50.00

Signed Goal Line Art 25.00

Single Signed Ball 75.00

RONNIE LOTT

OLLIE MATSON

Willis, Bill-(1977)

3 X 5 . . . . .5.00

8 X 10 Photo 15.00

Mini Helmet 50.00

Signed Goal Line Art 15.00

Single Signed Ball 75.00

Wilson, Larry-(1978)

3 X 5 . . . . .8.00

8 X 10 Photo 15.00

Mini Helmet 50.00

Signed Goal Line Art 15.00

Single Signed Ball 100.00

Winslow, Kellen-(1995)

3 X 5 . . . . .5.00

8 X 10 Photo 15.00

Mini Helmet 50.00

Signed Goal Line Art 15.00

Single Signed Ball 75.00

Wojciechowicz, Alex-(1968) d. 1992

3 X 5 . . . . .15.00

8 X 10 Photo 40.00

Mini Helmet 50.00

Signed Goal Line Art 1000.00

Wood, Willie-(1989)

3 X 5 . . . . .5.00

8 X 10 Photo 15.00

Mini Helmet 60.00

Signed Goal Line Art 15.00

Single Signed Ball 75.00

Active Players

Abdul-Jabbar, Karim

8 X 10 Photo 15.00

Authentic Jersey 140.00

Authentic Mini Helmet 70.00

Game Ball 90.00

Replica Jersey 80.00

Replica Mini Helmet 55.00

Signed Card 7.00

Aikman, Troy

8 X 10 Photo 35.00

Authentic Jersey 260.00

Replica Mini Helmet 140.00

Game Ball 190.00

Replica Jersey 160.00

Replica Mini Helmet 120.00

Signed Card 20.00

Allen, Marcus

8 X 10 Photo 25.00

Authentic Jersey 185.00

Authentic Mini Helmet 100.00

Game Ball 135.00

Replica Jersey 110.00

Replica Mini Helmet 80.00

Signed Card 15.00

Allen, Terry

8 X 10 Photo 15.00

Authentic Jersey 140.00	Authentic Jersey 140.00
Authentic Mini Helmet 70.00	Authentic Mini Helmet 70.00
Game Ball 90.00	Game Ball 90.00
Replica Jersey 80.00	Replica Jersey 80.00
Replica Mini Helmet 55.00	Replica Mini Helmet 55.00
Signed Card 7.00	Signed Card 7.00

JOE MONTANA

Alstott, Mike

8 X 10 Photo 18.00
Authentic Jersey 150.00
Authentic Mini Helmet 75.00
Game Ball 100.00
Replica Jersey 85.00
Replica Mini Helmet 60.00
Signed Card 8.00

Bledsoe, Drew

8 X 10 Photo 30.00
Authentic Jersey 230.00
Authentic Mini Helmet 120.00
Game Ball 165.00
Replica Jersey 140.00
Replica Mini Helmet 100.00
Signed Card 18.00

BRONKO NAGURSKI

Anderson, Jamal

8 X 10 Photo 15.00
Authentic Jersey 140.00
Authentic Mini Helmet 70.00
Game Ball 90.00
Replica Jersey 80.00
Replica Mini Helmet 55.00
Signed Card 7.00

Brooks, Robert

8 X 10 Photo 18.00
Authentic Jersey 150.00
Authentic Mini Helmet 75.00
Game Ball 100.00
Replica Jersey 85.00
Replica Mini Helmet 60.00
Signed Card 8.00

Bettis, Jerome

8 X 10 Photo 20.00
Authentic Jersey 160.00
Authentic Mini Helmet 80.00
Game Ball 110.00
Replica Jersey 90.00
Replica Mini Helmet 65.00
Signed Card 10.00

Brown, Tim

8 X 10 Photo 20.00
Authentic Jersey 170.00
Authentic Mini Helmet 85.00
Game Ball 120.00
Replica Jersey 100.00
Replica Mini Helmet 70.00
Signed Card 12.00

JOE NAMATH

Blake, Jeff

8 X 10 Photo 15.00

Bruce, Isaac

8 X 10 Photo 15.00

Authentic Jersey 140.00

Authentic Mini Helmet 70.00

Game Ball 90.00

Replica Jersey 80.00

Replica Mini Helmet 55.00

Signed Card 7.00

Authentic Jersey 150.00

Authentic Mini Helmet 75.00

Game Ball 100.00

Replica Jersey 85.00

Replica Mini Helmet 60.00

Signed Card 8.00

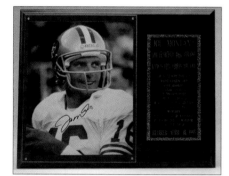

JOE MONTANA

Brunell, Mark

8 X 10 Photo 20.00

Authentic Jersey 170.00

Authentic Mini Helmet 85.00

Game Ball 120.00

Replica Jersey 100.00

Replica Mini Helmet 70.00

Signed Card 12.00

Cunningham, Randall

8 X 10 Photo 15.00

Authentic Jersey 140.00

Authentic Mini Helmet 70.00

Game Ball 90.00

Replica Jersey 80.00

Replica Mini Helmet 55.00

Signed Card 7.00

Carter, Cris

8 X 10 Photo 20.00

Authentic Jersey 170.00

Authentic Mini Helmet 85.00

Game Ball 120.00

Replica Jersey 100.00

Replica Mini Helmet 70.00

Signed Card 12.00

Davis, Terrell

8 X 10 Photo 30.00

Authentic Jersey 230.00

Authentic Mini Helmet 120.00

Game Ball 165.00

Replica Jersey 140.00

Replica Mini Helmet 100.00

Signed Card 18.00

Ernie Nevers

ERNIE NEVERS

Coates, Ben

8 X 10 Photo 15.00

Authentic Jersey 140.00

Authentic Mini Helmet 70.00

Game Ball 90.00

Replica Jersey 80.00

Replica Mini Helmet 55.00

Signed Card 7.00

Dilfer, Trent

8 X 10 Photo 15.00

Authentic Jersey 140.00

Authentic Mini Helmet 70.00

Game Ball 90.00

Replica Jersey 80.00

Replica Mini Helmet 55.00

Signed Card 7.00

Collins, Kerry

8 X 10 Photo 18.00

Dillon, Corey

8 X 10 Photo 15.00

FOOTBALL PRICE GUIDE

Authentic Jersey 140.00

Authentic Mini Helmet 70.00

Game Ball 90.00

Replica Jersey 80.00

Replica Mini Helmet 55.00

Signed Card 7.00

Authentic Jersey 280.00

Authentic Mini Helmet 150.00

Game Ball 200.00

Replica Jersey 175.00

Replica Mini Helmet 125.00

Signed Card 25.00

KEN NORTON JR.

Dunn, Warrick

8 X 10 Photo 20.00

Authentic Jersey 160.00

Authentic Mini Helmet 80.00

Game Ball 110.00

Replica Jersey 90.00

Replica Mini Helmet 65.00

Signed Card 10.00

Freeman, Antonio

8 X 10 Photo 18.00

Authentic Jersey 150.00

Authentic Mini Helmet 75.00

Game Ball 100.00

Replica Jersey 85.00

Replica Mini Helmet 60.00

Signed Card 8.00

MERLIN OLSEN

Elway, John

8 X 10 Photo 35.00

Authentic Jersey 260.00

Authentic Mini Helmet 140.00

Game Ball 200.00

Replica Jersey 160.00

Replica Mini Helmet 120.00

Signed Card 20.00

Fryar, Irving

8 X 10 Photo 15.00

Authentic Jersey 140.00

Authentic Mini Helmet 70.00

Game Ball 90.00

Replica Jersey 80.00

Replica Mini Helmet 55.00

Signed Card 7.00

JEROME BETTIS

Faulk, Marshall

8 X 10 Photo 18.00

Authentic Jersey 150.00

Authentic Mini Helmet 75.00

Game Ball 100.00

Replica Jersey 85.00

Replica Mini Helmet 60.00

Signed Card 8.00

Galloway, Joey

8 X 10 Photo 20.00

Authentic Jersey 160.00

Authentic Mini Helmet 80.00

Game Ball 110.00

Replica Jersey 90.00

Replica Mini Helmet 65.00

Signed Card 10.00

CLARENCE PARKER

Favre, Brett

8 X 10 Photo 40.00

George, Eddie

8 X 10 Photo 20.00

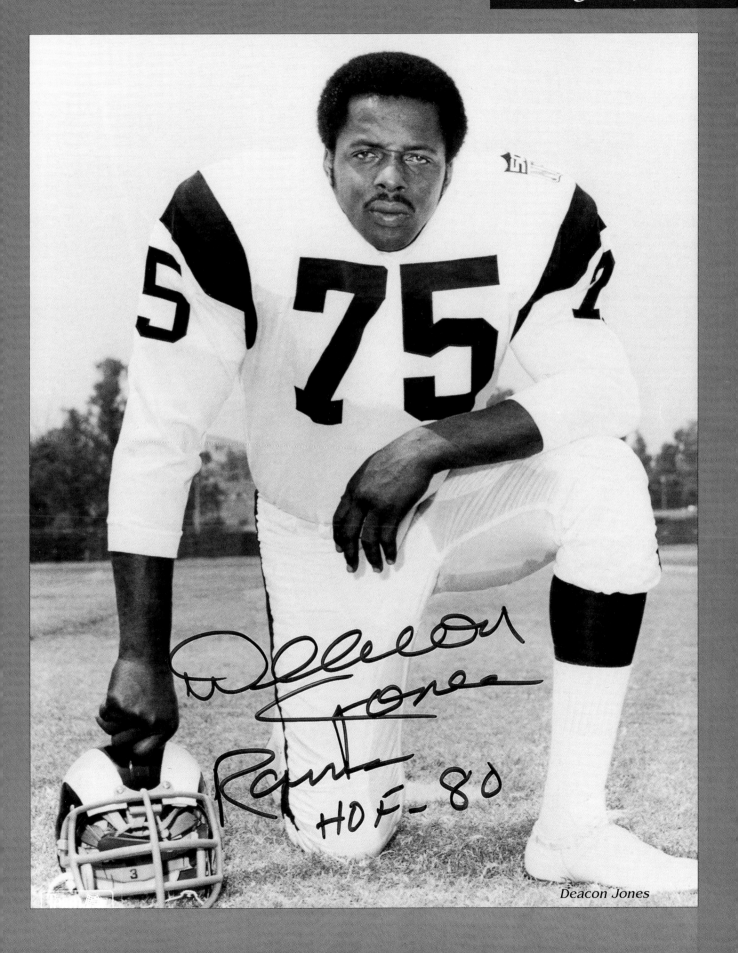

Deacon Jones

Authentic Jersey 170.00	Authentic Jersey 140.00
Authentic Mini Helmet 85.00	Authentic Mini Helmet 70.00
Game Ball 120.00	Game Ball 90.00
Replica Jersey 100.00	Replica Jersey 80.00
Replica Mini Helmet 70.00	Replica Mini Helmet 55.00
Signed Card 12.00	Signed Card 7.00

JAKE PLUMMER

George, Jeff

8 X 10 Photo 15.00
Authentic Jersey 140.00
Authentic Mini Helmet 70.00
Game Ball 90.00
Replica Jersey 80.00
Replica Mini Helmet 55.00
Signed Card 7.00

Harris, Raymont

8 X 10 Photo 15.00
Authentic Jersey 140.00
Authentic Mini Helmet 70.00
Game Ball 90.00
Replica Jersey 80.00
Replica Mini Helmet 55.00
Signed Card 7.00

O.J. SIMPSON

Glenn, Terry

8 X 10 Photo 18.00
Authentic Jersey 150.00
Authentic Mini Helmet 75.00
Game Ball 100.00
Replica Jersey 85.00
Replica Mini Helmet 60.00
Signed Card 8.00

Hearst, Garrison

8 X 10 Photo 15.00
Authentic Jersey 140.00
Authentic Mini Helmet 70.00
Game Ball 90.00
Replica Jersey 80.00
Replica Mini Helmet 55.00
Signed Card 7.00

Grbac, Elvis

8 X 10 Photo 15.00
Authentic Jersey 140.00
Authentic Mini Helmet 70.00
Game Ball 90.00
Replica Jersey 80.00
Replica Mini Helmet 50.00
Signed Card 7.00

Johnson, Brad

8 X 10 Photo 15.00
Authentic Jersey 140.00
Authentic Mini Helmet 70.00
Game Ball 90.00
Replica Jersey 80.00
Replica Mini Helmet 55.00
Signed Card 7.00

JERRY RICE

Greene, Kevin

8 X 10 Photo 15.00

Johnson, Keyshawn

8 X 10 Photo 18.00

ANDRE REED

Authentic Jersey	150.00
Authentic Mini Helmet	75.00
Game Ball	100.00
Replica Jersey	85.00
Replica Mini Helmet	60.00
Signed Card	8.00

BARRY SANDERS

Authentic Jersey	150.00
Authentic Mini Helmet	75.00
Game Ball	100.00
Replica Jersey	85.00
Replica Mini Helmet	60.00
Signed Card	8.00

Johnston, Daryl

8 X 10 Photo	15.00
Authentic Jersey	140.00
Authentic Mini Helmet	70.00
Game Ball	90.00
Replica Jersey	80.00
Replica Mini Helmet	55.00
Signed Card	7.00

Lloyd, Greg

8 X 10 Photo	18.00
Authentic Jersey	150.00
Authentic Mini Helmet	75.00
Game Ball	100.00
Replica Jersey	85.00
Replica Mini Helmet	60.00
Signed Card	8.00

MIKE SINGLETARY

Kaufman, Napolean

8 X 10 Photo	20.00
Authentic Jersey	160.00
Authentic Mini Helmet	80.00
Game Ball	110.00
Replica Jersey	90.00
Replica Mini Helmet	65.00
Signed Card	10.00

Manning, Peyton

8 X 10 Photo	30.00
Authentic Jersey	200.00
Authentic Mini Helmet	100.00
Game Ball	125.00
Replica Jersey	100.00
Replica Mini Helmet	75.00
Signed Card	15.00

Leaf, Ryan

8 X 10 Photo	30.00
Authentic Jersey	200.00
Authentic Mini Helmet	100.00
Game Ball	125.00
Replica Jersey	100.00
Replica Mini Helmet	75.00
Signed Card	15.00

Marino, Dan

8 X 10 Photo	35.00
Authentic Jersey	260.00
Authentic Mini Helmet	140.00
Game Ball	190.00
Replica Jersey	160.00
Replica Mini Helmet	120.00
Signed Card	20.00

BART STARR

Levens, Dorsey

8 X 10 Photo	18.00

Martin, Curtis

8 X 10 Photo	18.00

Authentic Jersey 150.00

Authentic Mini Helmet 75.00

Game Ball 100.00

Replica Jersey 85.00

Replica Mini Helmet 60.00

Signed Card 8.00

McCardell, Keenan

8 X 10 Photo 15.00

Authentic Jersey 140.00

Authentic Mini Helmet 70.00

Game Ball 90.00

Replica Jersey 80.00

Replica Mini Helmet 55.00

Signed Card 7.00

McNair, Steve

8 X 10 Photo 15.00

Authentic Jersey 140.00

Authentic Mini Helmet 70.00

Game Ball 90.00

Replica Jersey 80.00

Replica Mini Helmet 55.00

Signed Card 7.00

Means, Natrone

8 X 10 Photo 18.00

Authentic Jersey 150.00

Authentic Mini Helmet 75.00

Game Ball 100.00

Replica Jersey 85.00

Replica Mini Helmet 60.00

Signed Card 8.00

Moon, Warren

8 X 10 Photo 25.00

Authentic Jersey 185.00

Authentic Mini Helmet 100.00

Game Ball 135.00

Replica Jersey 110.00

Replica Mini Helmet 80.00

Signed Card 15.00

Moore, Herman

8 X 10 Photo 20.00

Authentic Jersey 160.00

Authentic Mini Helmet 80.00

Game Ball 110.00

Replica Jersey 90.00

Replica Mini Helmet 65.00

Signed Card 10.00

Moss, Randy

8 X 10 Photo 30.00

Authentic Jersey 200.00

Authentic Mini Helmet 100.00

Game Ball 125.00

Replica Jersey 100.00

Replica Mini Helmet 75.00

Signed Card 15.00

Murrell, Adrian

8 X 10 Photo 15.00

Authentic Jersey 140.00

Authentic Mini Helmet 70.00

Game Ball 90.00

Replica Jersey 80.00

Replica Mini Helmet 55.00

Signed Card 7.00

Norton Jr., Ken

8 X 10 Photo 15.00

ROGER STAUBACH

JAN STENERUD

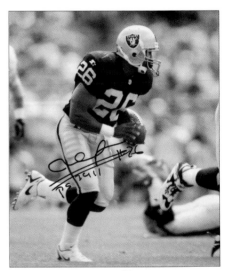

NAPOLEON KAUFMAN

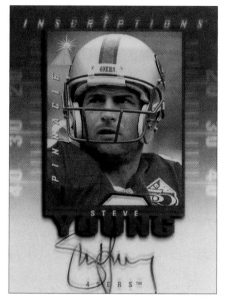

STEVE YOUNG

FRAN TARKENTON

CHARLEY TAYLOR

Authentic Jersey 140.00

Authentic Mini Helmet 70.00

Game Ball 90.00

Replica Jersey 80.00

Replica Mini Helmet 55.00

Signed Card 7.00

Owens, Terrell

8 X 10 Photo 15.00

Authentic Jersey 140.00

Authentic Mini Helmet 70.00

Game Ball 90.00

Replica Jersey 80.00

Replica Mini Helmet 55.00

Signed Card 7.00

Pickens, Carl

8 X 10 Photo 18.00

Authentic Jersey 150.00

Authentic Mini Helmet 75.00

Game Ball 100.00

Replica Jersey 85.00

Replica Mini Helmet 60.00

Signed Card 8.00

Reed, Andre

8 X 10 Photo 15.00

Authentic Jersey 140.00

Authentic Mini Helmet 70.00

Game Ball 90.00

Replica Jersey 80.00

Replica Mini Helmet 55.00

Signed Card 7.00

Reed, Jake

8 X 10 Photo 15.00

Authentic Jersey 140.00

Authentic Mini Helmet 70.00

Game Ball 90.00

Replica Jersey 80.00

Replica Mini Helmet 55.00

Signed Card 7.00

Rice, Jerry

8 X 10 Photo 30.00

Authentic Jersey 250.00

Authentic Mini Helmet 130.00

Game Ball 180.00

Replica Jersey 150.00

Replica Mini Helmet 110.00

Signed Card 20.00

Rison, Andre

8 X 10 Photo 15.00

Authentic Jersey 140.00

Authentic Mini Helmet 70.00

Game Ball 90.00

Replica Jersey 80.00

Replica Mini Helmet 55.00

Signed Card 7.00

Sanders, Barry

8 X 10 Photo 50.00

Authentic Jersey 280.00

Authentic Mini Helmet 150.00

Game Ball 200.00

Replica Jersey 175.00

Replica Mini Helmet 150.00

Signed Card 25.00

FOOTBALL PRICE GUIDE

Sanders, Deion

8 X 10 Photo	30.00
Authentic Jersey	230.00
Authentic Mini Helmet	120.00
Game Ball	165.00
Replica Jersey	140.00
Replica Mini Helmet	100.00
Signed Card	18.00

Seau, Junior

8 X 10 Photo	20.00
Authentic Jersey	160.00
Authentic Mini Helmet	80.00
Game Ball	110.00
Replica Jersey	90.00
Replica Mini Helmet	65.00
Signed Card	10.00

Sharpe, Shannon

8 X 10 Photo	20.00
Authentic Jersey	160.00
Authentic Mini Helmet	80.00
Game Ball	110.00
Replica Jersey	90.00
Replica Mini Helmet	65.00
Signed Card	10.00

Smith, Antowain

8 X 10 Photo	15.00
Authentic Jersey	140.00
Authentic Mini Helmet	70.00
Game Ball	90.00
Replica Jersey	80.00
Replica Mini Helmet	55.00
Signed Card	7.00

Smith, Bruce

8 X 10 Photo	20.00
Authentic Jersey	170.00
Authentic Mini Helmet	75.00
Game Ball	120.00
Replica Jersey	100.00
Replica Mini Helmet	70.00
Signed Card	12.00

Smith, Emmitt

8 X 10 Photo	35.00
Authentic Jersey	260.00
Authentic Mini Helmet	140.00
Game Ball	190.00
Replica Jersey	160.00
Replica Mini Helmet	120.00
Signed Card	20.00

Smith, Jimmy

8 X 10 Photo	15.00
Authentic Jersey	140.00
Authentic Mini Helmet	70.00
Game Ball	90.00
Replica Jersey	80.00
Replica Mini Helmet	55.00
Signed Card	7.00

Smith, Neil

8 X 10 Photo	15.00
Authentic Jersey	140.00
Authentic Mini Helmet	70.00
Game Ball	90.00
Replica Jersey	80.00
Replica Mini Helmet	55.00
Signed Card	7.00

TERRY ALLEN

THURMAN THOMAS

RANDY WHITE

WARREN MOON

JERRY RICE

Smith, Robert

8 X 10 Photo	15.00
Authentic Jersey	140.00
Authentic Mini Helmet	70.00
Game Ball	90.00
Replica Jersey	80.00
Replica Mini Helmet	55.00
Signed Card	7.00

Stewart, Kordell

8 X 10 Photo	20.00
Authentic Jersey	170.00
Authentic Mini Helmet	85.00
Game Ball	120.00
Replica Jersey	100.00
Replica Mini Helmet	70.00
Signed Card	12.00

Stubblefield, Dana

8 X 10 Photo	15.00
Authentic Jersey	140.00
Authentic Mini Helmet	70.00
Game Ball	90.00
Replica Jersey	80.00
Replica Mini Helmet	55.00
Signed Card	7.00

Testaverde, Vinny

8 X 10 Photo	18.00
Authentic Jersey	150.00
Authentic Mini Helmet	75.00
Game Ball	100.00
Replica Jersey	85.00
Replica Mini Helmet	60.00
Signed Card	8.00

Thigpen, Yancy

8 X 10 Photo	15.00
Authentic Jersey	140.00
Authentic Mini Helmet	70.00
Game Ball	90.00
Replica Jersey	80.00
Replica Mini Helmet	55.00
Signed Card	7.00

Thomas, Derrick

8 X 10 Photo	15.00
Authentic Jersey	140.00
Authentic Mini Helmet	70.00
Game Ball	90.00
Replica Jersey	80.00
Replica Mini Helmet	55.00
Signed Card	7.00

Thomas, Thurman

8 X 10 Photo	20.00
Authentic Jersey	170.00
Authentic Mini Helmet	85.00
Game Ball	120.00
Replica Jersey	100.00
Replica Mini Helmet	70.00
Signed Card	12.00

Walker, Herschel

8 X 10 Photo	18.00
Authentic Jersey	150.00
Authentic Mini Helmet	75.00
Game Ball	100.00
Replica Jersey	85.00
Replica Mini Helmet	60.00
Signed Card	8.00

FOOTBALL PRICE GUIDE

Warren, Chris

8 X 10 Photo	15.00
Authentic Jersey	140.00
Authentic Mini Helmet	70.00
Game Ball	90.00
Replica Jersey	80.00
Replica Mini Helmet	55.00
Signed Card	7.00

Watters, Ricky

8 X 10 Photo	20.00
Authentic Jersey	160.00
Authentic Mini Helmet	80.00
Game Ball	110.00
Replica Jersey	90.00
Replica Mini Helmet	65.00
Signed Card	10.00

White, Reggie

8 X 10 Photo	30.00
Authentic Jersey	230.00
Authentic Mini Helmet	120.00
Game Ball	165.00
Replica Jersey	140.00
Replica Mini Helmet	100.00
Signed Card	18.00

Woodson, Rod

8 X 10 Photo	20.00
Authentic Jersey	170.00
Authentic Mini Helmet	85.00
Game Ball	120.00
Replica Jersey	100.00
Replica Mini Helmet	70.00
Signed Card	12.00

Young, Steve

8 X 10 Photo	30.00
Authentic Jersey	230.00
Authentic Mini Helmet	120.00
Game Ball	150.00
Replica Jersey	140.00
Replica Mini Helmet	100.00
Signed Card	15.00

STEVE YOUNG

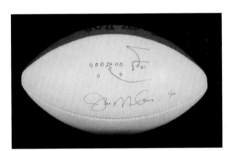

JOE MONTANA

Dan Marino

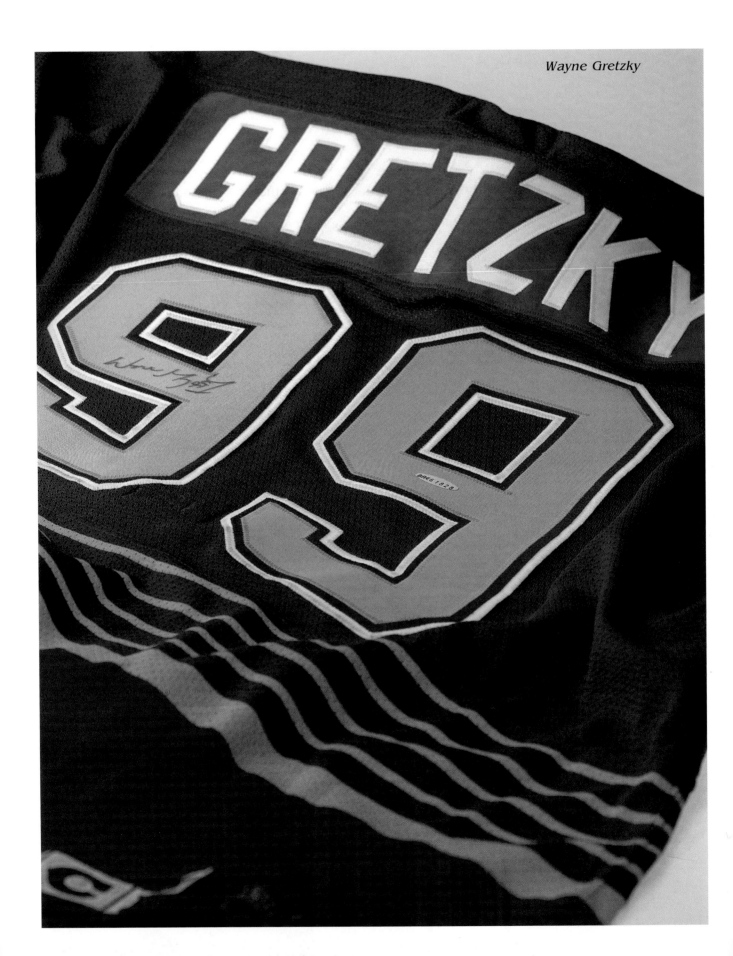

COLLECTING HOCKEY AUTOGRAPHS

It's been said before, but with new evidence each month, it bears repeating: Hockey players easily are the most accessible and accommodating of professional athletes and most willing to sign autographs. Indeed, in-person experiences with the lords of the boards continue to be most rewarding.

Specifically, young players have proven to be the most fan-friendly. I've had multiple reports of good experiences with Mark Parrish, a hot youngster from the Florida Panthers, and Manny Malhotra of the New York Rangers. Being so new to the NHL, it can sometimes be a problem finding something personal for both of them to sign. Their early success demonstrates the value in bringing several team logo pucks or similar items whenever you head out on the hunt.

Young New Jersey Devils forwards Patrick Elias and Brendan Morrison also have been exceptionally gracious in person, to the point of signing multiple autographs. Although their penmanship leaves a little to be desired, you've got to love their willingness to take care of collectors.

Devils' teammate Martin Brodeur had another solid season in 1998-99, and fans are benefiting as much as the Devils. More than a few fans have gotten multiple autographs, but the quality of his signature deteriorates noticeably when you ask for

Patrick Roy

BY DAVE SLIEPKA

more than one. Most multiple examples I've seen this season are little more than "Mtn Br 30." So would you prefer quantity or quality? Address your request accordingly.

Also from the Devils' front comes the good news that Slava Fetisov is again signing. After two years of nearly consistent refusals as a member of the Red Wings, "Papa" has been going out of his way to take care of collectors. One report even had him coming off the team bus to have his picture taken with an adoring fan.

Given the tough year Colorado's Patrick Roy is enduring, common sense should tell you he's not going to be an easy

Tom Barrasso

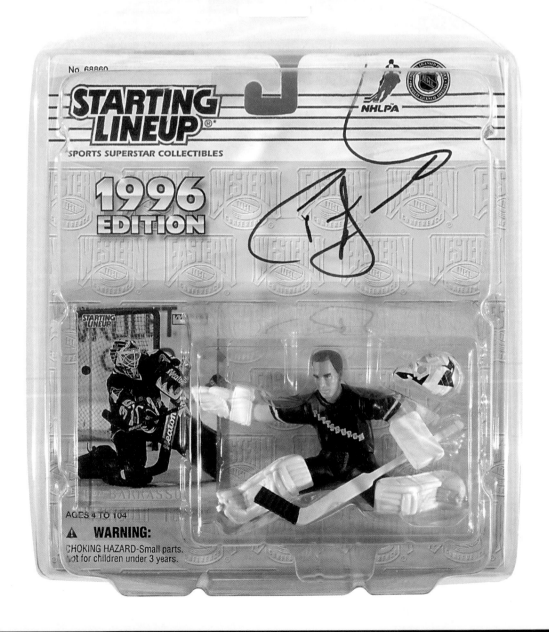

Tom Barrasso

autograph. Reports confirm Roy has become extremely tough, with many stops yielding no autographs whatsoever. It's worth remembering that when a player is having a rough season, it's probably best to stay out of his way. Badgering a player at a low point may spoil his feelings toward autograph seekers when he finally does turn things around.

Even though the Capitals aren't enjoying the kind of success that led them to the Stanley

Cup Finals last season, it hasn't turned the players into grouches quite yet. Olaf Kolzig seems to be enjoying the fan attention after years as an unknown backup.

Superstars Peter Bondra and Adam Oates continue to sign for everyone in sight, but don't get greedy. Upon exiting his Dallas hotel in November, Peter announced to the waiting crowd, "Just one per, guys." Even those who tried a sob story to get two were turned down. "Did you get one?" Bondra asked. "OK. We're all even then."

Oates gives a very legible signature, and obviously takes the time to properly place it on the item (ah, if only all players were like him). The quality of his penmanship is matched only by his memory. People who tried to "double-up" by asking him

Paul Coffey

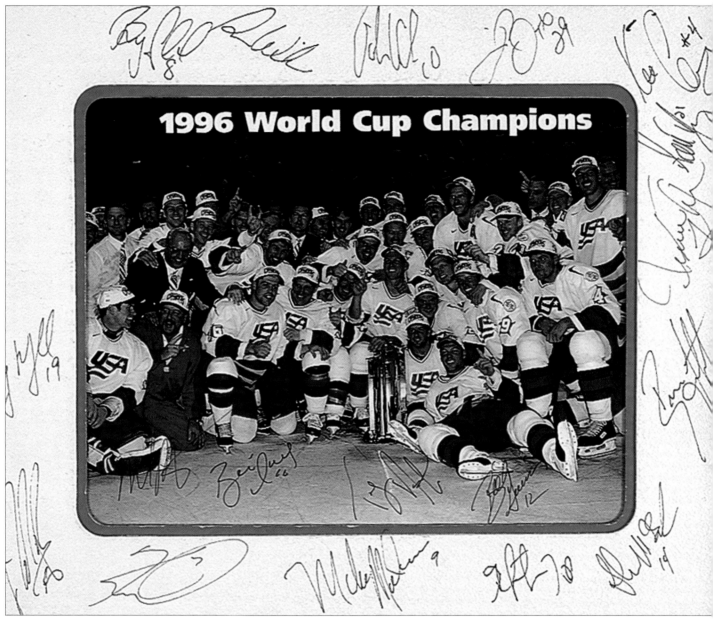

Team USA

before and after practice were quickly shot down.

Caps teammate Joe Reekie may not top many want lists, but you've got to love his attitude. Emerging from the hotel with Oates and Bondra, he watched unmolested as the mob converged on his star teammates. Finally, Reekie jokingly pleaded, "Doesn't anyone have a card of me?" Steve Konowalchuk pointed out that I did. After signing, he mumbled, "Thirteen years in this league and only one card! That's what I get for hanging out with stars like Oates and Juneau!" ▪

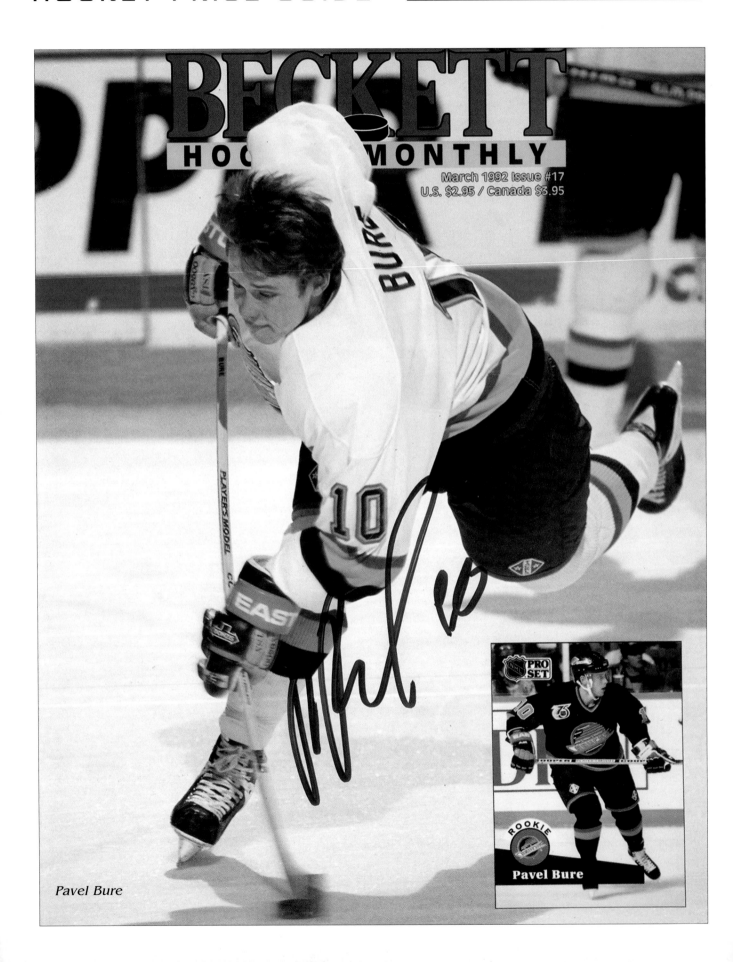

Pavel Bure

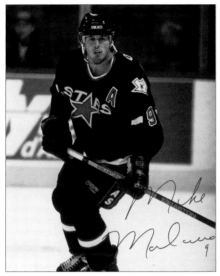

MIKE MODANO

SID ABEL

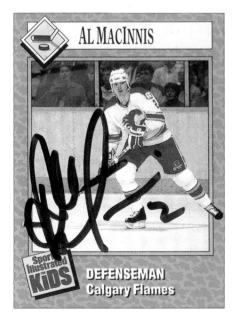

AL MACINNIS

Autographs

Retired Players

Abel, Sid-(1969)

3 X 5 . . . . .5.00

8 X 10 Photo 15.00

Single Signed Puck 30.00

Apps Sr., Syl-(1961)

3 X 5 . . . . .15.00

8 X 10 Photo 35.00

Single Signed Puck 50.00

Armstrong, George-(1975)

3 X 5 . . . . .15.00

8 X 10 Photo 35.00

Single Signed Puck 50.00

Bailey, Ace-(1975) d. 1992

3 X 5 . . . . .50.00

8 X 10 Photo 125.00

Single Signed Puck 200.00

Barber, Bill-(1990)

3 X 5 . . . . .5.00

8 X 10 Photo 15.00

Single Signed Puck 20.00

Barry, Marty-(1965) d. 1969

3 X 5 . . . . .75.00

8 X 10 Photo 200.00

Bathgate, Andy-(1978)

3 X 5 . . . . .5.00

8 X 10 Photo 15.00

Single Signed Puck 20.00

Bauer, Bobby-(1996) d. 1964

3 X 5 . . . . .100.00

8 X 10 Photo 250.00

Beliveau, Jean-(1972)

3 X 5 . . . . .10.00

8 X 10 Photo 20.00

Single Signed Puck 30.00

Benedict, Clint-(1965) d. 1976

3 X 5 . . . . .50.00

8 X 10 Photo 150.00

Bentley, Doug-(1964) d. 1972

3 X 5 . . . . .50.00

8 X 10 Photo 175.00

Bentley, Max-(1966) d. 1984

3 X 5 . . . . .30.00

8 X 10 Photo 125.00

Blake, Toe-(1966) d. 1995

3 X 5 . . . . .25.00

8 X 10 Photo 100.00

Single Signed Puck 150.00

Boivin, Leo-(1986)

3 X 5 . . . . .5.00

8 X 10 Photo 15.00

Single Signed Puck 25.00

Bossy, Mike-(1991)

3 X 5 . . . . .5.00

8 X 10 Photo 15.00

Single Signed Puck 25.00

Bouchard, Butch-(1966)

3 X 5 . . . . .20.00

8 X 10 Photo 35.00

Single Signed Puck 75.00

Boucher, Frank-(1958) d. 1977

3 X 5 . . . . .100.00

8 X 10 Photo 250.00

Boucher, George-(1960) d. 1960

3 X 5 . . . . .50.00

8 X 10 Photo 150.00

Bower, Johnny-(1976)

3 X 5 . . . . .5.00

8 X 10 Photo 15.00

Single Signed Puck 25.00

Brimsek, Frank-(1966)

3 X 5 . . . . .10.00

8 X 10 Photo 30.00

Single Signed Puck 50.00

Broadbent, Punch-(1962) d. 1971

3 X 5 . . . . .75.00

8 X 10 Photo 200.00

Broda, Turk-(1967) d. 1972

3 X 5 . . . . .75.00

8 X 10 Photo 200.00

Bucyk, John-(1981)

3 X 5 . . . . .10.00

8 X 10 Photo 20.00

Single Signed Puck 30.00

Burch, Billy-(1974) d. 1950

3 X 5 . . . . .100.00

8 X 10 Photo 250.00

Cameron, Harry-(1962) d. 1953

3 X 5 . . . . .100.00

8 X 10 Photo 300.00

Cheevers, Gerry-(1985)

3 X 5 . . . . .5.00

8 X 10 Photo 15.00

Single Signed Puck 25.00

Clancy, King-(1958) d. 1986

3 X 5 . . . . .50.00

8 X 10 Photo 100.00

Single Signed Puck 175.00

Clapper, Dit-(1947) d. 1978

3 X 5 . . . . .50.00

8 X 10 Photo 150.00

Clarke, Bobby-(1987)

3 X 5 . . . . .5.00

8 X 10 Photo 15.00

Single Signed Puck 25.00

Cleghorn, Sprague-(1958) d. 1956

3 X 5 . . . . .100.00

8 X 10 Photo 250.00

Colville, Neil-(1967) d. 1987

3 X 5 . . . . .40.00

8 X 10 Photo 100.00

MARIO LEMIEUX

TEEMU SELANNE

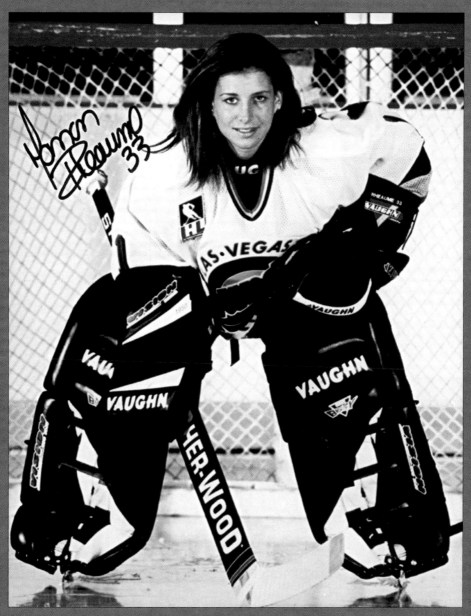

Manon Rheaume

Conacher, Charlie-(1961) d. 1967

3 X 5 . . . . .75.00

8 X 10 Photo 200.00

Cook, Bill-(1952) d. 1986

3 X 5 . . . . .40.00

8 X 10 Photo 100.00

Coulter, Art-(1974)

3 X 5 . . . . .15.00

8 X 10 Photo 40.00

Cournoyer, Yvan-(1982)

3 X 5 . . . . .5.00

8 X 10 Photo 15.00

Single Signed Puck 20.00

Cowley, Bill-(1968) d. 1993

3 X 5 . . . . .40.00

8 X 10 Photo 100.00

Single Signed Puck 150.00

Crawford, Rusty-(1962) d. 1971

3 X 5 . . . . .50.00

Day, Hap-(1961) d. 1990

3 X 5 . . . . .40.00

8 X 10 Photo 125.00

Delvecchio, Alex-(1977)

3 X 5 . . . . .5.00

8 X 10 Photo 15.00

Single Signed Puck 20.00

Denneny, Cy-(1959) d. 1970

3 X 5 . . . . .75.00

8 X 10 Photo 200.00

Dionne, Marcel-(1992)

3 X 5 . . . . .5.00

8 X 10 Photo 15.00

Single Signed Puck 20.00

Drillon, Gordie-(1975) d. 1986

3 X 5 . . . . .25.00

8 X 10 Photo 100.00

Dumart, Woody-(1992)

3 X 5 . . . . .5.00

8 X 10 Photo 15.00

Single Signed Puck 25.00

Durnan, Bill-(1964) d. 1972

3 X 5 . . . . .75.00

8 X 10 Photo 200.00

Dutton, Red-(1958) d. 1987

3 X 5 . . . . .40.00

8 X 10 Photo 100.00

Dye, Babe-(1970) d. 1962

3 X 5 . . . . .100.00

8 X 10 Photo 250.00

Esposito, Phil-(1984)

3 X 5 . . . . .5.00

8 X 10 Photo 15.00

Single Signed Puck 25.00

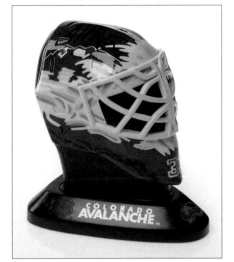

PATRICK ROY

JEAN BELIVEAU

JOHN BUCYK

Esposito, Tony-(1988)

3 X 5 . . . . .8.00

8 X 10 Photo 20.00

Single Signed Puck 30.00

Flaman, Fern-(1990)

3 X 5 . . . . .5.00

8 X 10 Photo 15.00

Single Signed Puck 20.00

Foyston, Frank-(1958) d. 1966

3 X 5 . . . . .50.00

8 X 10 Photo 150.00

Frederickson, Frank-(1958) d. 1979

3 X 5 . . . . .50.00

8 X 10 Photo 175.00

Gadsby, Bill-(1970)

3 X 5 . . . . .5.00

8 X 10 Photo 15.00

Single Signed Puck 20.00

Gainey, Bob-(1992)

3 X 5 . . . . .5.00

8 X 10 Photo 15.00

Single Signed Puck 20.00

Gardiner, Herb-(1958) d. 1972

3 X 5 . . . . .50.00

8 X 10 Photo 150.00

Geoffrion, Boom Boom-(1972)

3 X 5 . . . . .10.00

8 X 10 Photo 15.00

Single Signed Puck 30.00

Giacomin, Eddie-(1987)

3 X 5 . . . . .10.00

8 X 10 Photo 20.00

Single Signed Puck 25.00

Gilbert, Rod-(1982)

3 X 5 . . . . .5.00

8 X 10 Photo 15.00

Single Signed Puck 25.00

Goodfellow, Ebbie-(1963) d. 1985

3 X 5 . . . . .25.00

8 X 10 Photo 100.00

Hainsworth, George-(1961) d. 1950

3 X 5 . . . . .100.00

8 X 10 Photo 250.00

Hall, Glenn-(1975)

3 X 5 . . . . .5.00

8 X 10 Photo 15.00

Single Signed Puck 20.00

Harvey, Doug-(1973) d. 1989

3 X 5 . . . . .60.00

8 X 10 Photo 150.00

Single Signed Puck 200.00

Hay, George-(1958) d. 1975

3 X 5 . . . . .50.00

8 X 10 Photo 150.00

Hextall, Bryan-(1969) d. 1984

3 X 5 . . . . .20.00

8 X 10 Photo 50.00

Single Signed Puck 150.00

CHRIS CHELIOS

ED BELFOUR

Horton, Tim-(1977) d. 1974

3 X 5 . . . . .75.00

8 X 10 Photo 200.00

Howe, Gordie-(1972)

3 X 5 . . . . .10.00

8 X 10 Photo 20.00

Single Signed Puck 30.00

Howe, Syd-(1965) d. 1976

3 X 5 . . . . .60.00

8 X 10 Photo 150.00

Howell, Harry-(1979)

3 X 5 . . . . .5.00

8 X 10 Photo 15.00

Single Signed Puck 20.00

Hull, Bobby-(1983)

3 X 5 . . . . .10.00

8 X 10 Photo 20.00

Single Signed Puck 30.00

Irvin, Dick-(1958) d. 1957

3 X 5 . . . . .75.00

8 X 10 Photo 200.00

Jackson, Busher-(1971) d. 1966

3 X 5 . . . . .60.00

8 X 10 Photo 150.00

Johnson, Ching-(1958) d. 1979

3 X 5 . . . . .100.00

8 X 10 Photo 250.00

Johnson, Tom-(1970)

3 X 5 . . . . .5.00

8 X 10 Photo 15.00

Single Signed Puck 20.00

Joliat, Aurel-(1947) d. 1986

3 X 5 . . . . .100.00

8 X 10 Photo 125.00

Single Signed Puck 250.00

Keats, Duke-(1958) d. 1972

3 X 5 . . . . .75.00

8 X 10 Photo 250.00

Kelly, Red-(1969)

3 X 5 . . . . .5.00

8 X 10 Photo 15.00

Single Signed Puck 25.00

Kennedy, Teeder-(1966)

3 X 5 . . . . .10.00

8 X 10 Photo 20.00

Single Signed Puck 40.00

Keon, Dave-(1986)

3 X 5 . . . . .10.00

8 X 10 Photo 15.00

Single Signed Puck 25.00

Lach, Elmer-(1966)

3 X 5 . . . . .5.00

8 X 10 Photo 15.00

Single Signed Puck 25.00

Lafleur, Guy-(1988)

3 X 5 . . . . .8.00

MARIO LEMIEUX

ALEX DELVECCHIO

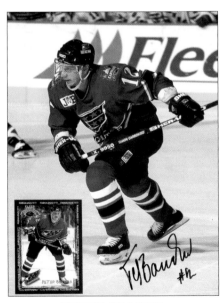

PETER BONDRA

WAYNE GRETZKY

PHIL ESPOSITO

8 X 10 Photo 20.00

Single Signed Puck 25.00

Laperriere, Jacques-(1987)

3 X 5 . . . . .5.00

8 X 10 Photo 15.00

Single Signed Puck 20.00

Lapointe, Guy-(1993)

3 X 5 . . . . .5.00

8 X 10 Photo 15.00

Single Signed Puck 20.00

Laprade, Edgar-(1993)

3 X 5 . . . . .10.00

8 X 10 Photo 20.00

Single Signed Puck 30.00

Lemaire, Jacques-(1984)

3 X 5 . . . . .5.00

8 X 10 Photo 15.00

Single Signed Puck 20.00

Lemieux, Mario

3 X 5 . . . . .15.00

8 X 10 Photo 50.00

Single Signed Puck 75.00

Lindsay, Ted-(1966)

3 X 5 . . . . .5.00

8 X 10 Photo 15.00

Single Signed Puck 25.00

Lumley, Harry-(1980) d. 1998

3 X 5 . . . . .8.00

8 X 10 Photo 20.00

Single Signed Puck 40.00

MacKay, Mickey-(1952) d. 1940

3 X 5 . . . . .100.00

8 X 10 Photo 300.00

Mahovlich, Frank-(1981)

3 X 5 . . . . .5.00

8 X 10 Photo 15.00

Single Signed Puck 20.00

Mantha, Sylvio-(1960) d. 1974

3 X 5 . . . . .50.00

8 X 10 Photo 150.00

McDonald, Lanny-(1992)

3 X 5 . . . . .5.00

8 X 10 Photo 15.00

Single Signed Puck 20.00

McNamara, George-(1958) d. 1952

3 X 5 . . . . .150.00

Mikita, Stan-(1983)

3 X 5 . . . . .10.00

8 X 10 Photo 20.00

Single Signed Puck 35.00

Moore, Dickie-(1974)

3 X 5 . . . . .5.00

8 X 10 Photo 15.00

Single Signed Puck 20.00

Morenz, Howie-(1945) d. 1937

3 X 5 . . . . .400.00

8 X 10 Photo 1200.00

Mosienko, Bill-(1965) d. 1994

3 X 5 . . . . .20.00

8 X 10 Photo 40.00

Single Signed Puck 150.00

Nighbor, Frank-(1947) d. 1966

3 X 5 . . . . .75.00

8 X 10 Photo 200.00

Noble, Reg-(1962) d. 1962

3 X 5 . . . . .75.00

8 X 10 Photo 250.00

O'Connor, Buddy-(1988) d. 1977

3 X 5 . . . . .50.00

8 X 10 Photo 150.00

Oliver, Harry-(1967) d. 1985

3 X 5 . . . . .20.00

8 X 10 Photo 150.00

Olmstead, Bert-(1985)

3 X 5 . . . . .5.00

8 X 10 Photo 15.00

Single Signed Puck 25.00

Orr, Bobby-(1979)

3 X 5 . . . . .20.00

8 X 10 Photo 75.00

Single Signed Puck 125.00

Parent, Bernie-(1984)

3 X 5 . . . . .10.00

8 X 10 Photo 20.00

Single Signed Puck 35.00

Park, Brad-(1988)

3 X 5 . . . . .5.00

8 X 10 Photo 15.00

Single Signed Puck 25.00

Perreault, Gil-(1990)

3 X 5 . . . . .5.00

8 X 10 Photo 15.00

Single Signed Puck 25.00

Pilote, Pierre-(1975)

3 X 5 . . . . .5.00

8 X 10 Photo 15.00

Single Signed Puck 20.00

Plante, Jacques-(1978) d. 1986

3 X 5 . . . . .75.00

8 X 10 Photo 200.00

Single Signed Puck 250.00

Potvin, Denis-(1991)

3 X 5 . . . . .5.00

8 X 10 Photo 15.00

Single Signed Puck 20.00

Primeau, Joe-(1963) d. 1989

3 X 5 . . . . .100.00

8 X 10 Photo 250.00

Pronovost, Marcel-(1978)

3 X 5 . . . . .5.00

8 X 10 Photo 15.00

Single Signed Puck 25.00

Pulford, Bob-(1991)

3 X 5 . . . . .5.00

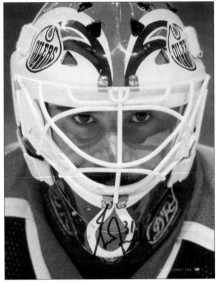

GRANT FUHR

GLENN HALL

Wayne Gretzky

8 X 10 Photo 15.00

Single Signed Puck 25.00

Pulford, Harry-(1945) d. 1940

3 X 5 . . . . .150.00

8 X 10 Photo 350.00

Quackenbush, Bill-(1976)

3 X 5 . . . . .10.00

8 X 10 Photo 20.00

Ratelle, Jean-(1985)

3 X 5 . . . . .5.00

8 X 10 Photo 15.00

Single Signed Puck 20.00

Rayner, Chuck-(1973)

3 X 5 . . . . .5.00

8 X 10 Photo 15.00

Single Signed Puck 20.00

Reardon, Ken-(1966)

3 X 5 . . . . .10.00

8 X 10 Photo 20.00

Single Signed Puck 40.00

Richard, Henri-(1979)

3 X 5 . . . . .10.00

8 X 10 Photo 20.00

Single Signed Puck 30.00

Richard, Maurice-(1961)

3 X 5 . . . . .8.00

8 X 10 Photo 15.00

Single Signed Puck 25.00

Roberts, Gordon-(1971) d. 1966

3 X 5 . . . . .50.00

8 X 10 Photo 150.00

Ross, Art-(1945) d. 1964

3 X 5 . . . . .75.00

8 X 10 Photo 250.00

Russell, Blair-(1965) d. 1961

3 X 5 . . . . .75.00

8 X 10 Photo 200.00

Russell, Ernie-(1965) d. 1963

3 X 5 . . . . .60.00

8 X 10 Photo 150.00

Ruttan, Jack-(1962) d. 1973

3 X 5 . . . . .50.00

8 X 10 Photo 125.00

Savard, Serge-(1986)

3 X 5 . . . . .5.00

8 X 10 Photo 15.00

Single Signed Puck 25.00

Sawchuk, Terry-(1971) d. 1970

3 X 5 . . . . .100.00

8 X 10 Photo 250.00

Schmidt, Milt-(1961)

3 X 5 . . . . .5.00

8 X 10 Photo 15.00

Single Signed Puck 25.00

WAYNE GRETZKY

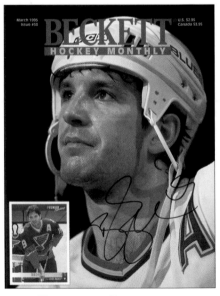

GORDIE HOWE

BRENDAN SHANAHAN

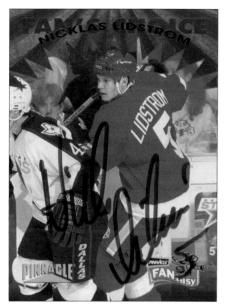

NICKLAS LIDSTROM

BOBBY HULL

MIKE MODANO

Schriner, Sweeney-(1962) d. 1990

3 X 5 . . . . .40.00

8 X 10 Photo 100.00

Seibert, Earl-(1963) d. 1990

3 X 5 . . . . .25.00

8 X 10 Photo 100.00

Shore, Eddie-(1947) d. 1985

3 X 5 . . . . .100.00

8 X 10 Photo 275.00

Shutt, Steve-(1993)

3 X 5 . . . . .5.00

8 X 10 Photo 15.00

Single Signed Puck 20.00

Simpson, Joe-(1962) d. 1973

3 X 5 . . . . .50.00

8 X 10 Photo 150.00

Sittler, Darryl-(1989)

3 X 5 . . . . .5.00

8 X 10 Photo 15.00

Single Signed Puck 25.00

Smith, Al-(1962) d. 1953

3 X 5 . . . . .100.00

8 X 10 Photo 300.00

Smith, Billy-(1993)

3 X 5 . . . . .5.00

8 X 10 Photo 15.00

Single Signed Puck 20.00

Smith, Clint-(1991)

3 X 5 . . . . .5.00

8 X 10 Photo 15.00

Single Signed Puck 25.00

Smith, Hooley-(1972) d. 1963

3 X 5 . . . . .75.00

8 X 10 Photo 200.00

Stanley, Allan-(1981)

3 X 5 . . . . .10.00

8 X 10 Photo 20.00

Single Signed Puck 30.00

Stewart, Jack-(1964) d. 1983

3 X 5 . . . . .75.00

8 X 10 Photo 100.00

Stewart, Nels-(1962) d. 1957

3 X 5 . . . . .125.00

8 X 10 Photo 250.00

Thompson, Tiny-(1959) d. 1981

3 X 5 . . . . .100.00

8 X 10 Photo 250.00

Tretiak, Vladislav-(1989)

3 X 5 . . . . .15.00

8 X 10 Photo 25.00

Single Signed Puck 40.00

Ullman, Norm-(1982)

3 X 5 . . . . .10.00

8 X 10 Photo 20.00

Single Signed Puck 30.00

Watson, Harry-(1994)

3 X 5 . . . . .10.00

8 X 10 Photo 20.00

Single Signed Puck 30.00

Weiland, Cooney-(1971) d. 1965

3 X 5 . . . . .50.00

8 X 10 Photo 175.00

Wilson, Phat-(1962) d. 1970

3 X 5 . . . . .50.00

8 X 10 Photo 200.00

Worsley, Gump-(1980)

3 X 5 . . . . .10.00

8 X 10 Photo 15.00

Single Signed Puck 25.00

Active Players

Allison, Jason

8 X 10 Photo 15.00

Authentic Jersey 200.00

Replica Jersey 100.00

Signed Card 5.00

Signed Puck 18.00

Amonte, Tony

8 X 10 Photo 12.00

Authentic Jersey 180.00

Replica Jersey 90.00

Signed Card 5.00

Signed Puck 15.00

Andreychuk, Dave

8 X 10 Photo 15.00

Authentic Jersey 200.00

Replica Jersey 100.00

Signed Card 6.00

Signed Puck 18.00

Barrasso, Tom

8 X 10 Photo 15.00

Authentic Jersey 200.00

Mini Mask 55.00

Replica Jersey 100.00

Signed Card 7.00

Signed Puck 20.00

Belfour, Ed

8 X 10 Photo 18.00

Authentic Jersey 220.00

Mini Mask 60.00

Replica Jersey 110.00

Signed Card 8.00

Signed Puck 20.00

Berard, Bryan

8 X 10 Photo 12.00

Authentic Jersey 180.00

Replica Jersey 90.00

Signed Card 5.00

Signed Puck 15.00

Bondra, Peter

8 X 10 Photo 12.00

Authentic Jersey 180.00

Replica Jersey 90.00

Signed Card 5.00

Signed Puck 15.00

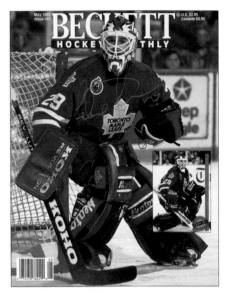

FELIX POTVIN

NIKOLAI KHABIBULIA

Wayne Gretzky

Bourque, Ray

8 X 10 Photo 20.00

Authentic Jersey 260.00

Replica Jersey 130.00

Signed Card 12.00

Signed Puck 27.00

Brodeur, Martin

8 X 10 Photo 25.00

Authentic Jersey 280.00

Mini Mask 90.00

Replica Jersey 140.00

Signed Card 15.00

Signed Puck 30.00

Bure, Pavel

8 X 10 Photo 25.00

Authentic Jersey 280.00

Mini Helmet 80.00

Mini Mask 70.00

Replica Jersey 140.00

Signed Card 15.00

Signed Puck 30.00

Chelios, Chris

8 X 10 Photo 20.00

Authentic Jersey 240.00

Replica Jersey 120.00

Signed Card 12.00

Signed Puck 25.00

Clark, Wendel

8 X 10 Photo 15.00

Authentic Jersey 200.00

Replica Jersey 100.00

Signed Card 6.00

Signed Puck 18.00

Coffey, Paul

8 X 10 Photo 20.00

Authentic Jersey 240.00

Replica Jersey 120.00

Signed Card 10.00

Signed Puck 25.00

Corson, Shayne

8 X 10 Photo 12.00

Authentic Jersey 180.00

Replica Jersey 90.00

Signed Card 5.00

Signed Puck 15.00

Dafoe, Bryon

8 X 10 Photo 12.00

Authentic Jersey 180.00

Mini Mask 50.00

Replica Jersey 90.00

Signed Card 5.00

Signed Puck 15.00

Damphousse, Vincent

8 X 10 Photo 12.00

Authentic Jersey 180.00

Replica Jersey 90.00

Signed Card 5.00

Signed Puck 15.00

Daze, Eric

8 X 10 Photo 12.00

Authentic Jersey 180.00

MARIO LEMIEUX

ELMER LACH

JAROMIR JAGR

MARIO LEMIEUX

WAYNE GRETZKY

Replica Jersey 90.00

Signed Card 5.00

Signed Puck 15.00

Domi, Tie

8 X 10 Photo 12.00

Authentic Jersey 180.00

Replica Jersey 90.00

Signed Card 5.00

Signed Puck 15.00

Duchesne, Steve

8 X 10 Photo 12.00

Authentic Jersey 180.00

Replica Jersey 90.00

Signed Card 5.00

Signed Puck 15.00

Fedorov, Sergi

8 X 10 Photo 30.00

Authentic Jersey 325.00

Mini Helmet 100.00

Mini Mask 90.00

Replica Jersey 160.00

Signed Card 18.00

Signed Puck 40.00

Fleury, Theo

8 X 10 Photo 18.00

Authentic Jersey 220.00

Replica Jersey 110.00

Signed Card 8.00

Signed Puck 20.00

Forsberg, Peter

8 X 10 Photo 30.00

Authentic Jersey 325.00

Mini Helmet 100.00

Mini Mask 90.00

Replica Jersey 160.00

Signed Card 18.00

Signed Puck 40.00

Francis, Ron

8 X 10 Photo 15.00

Authentic Jersey 200.00

Replica Jersey 100.00

Signed Card 6.00

Signed Puck 18.00

Fuhr, Grant

8 X 10 Photo 20.00

Authentic Jersey 240.00

Mini Mask 70.00

Replica Jersey 120.00

Signed Card 10.00

Signed Puck 25.00

Gartner, Mike

8 X 10 Photo 15.00

Authentic Jersey 200.00

Replica Jersey 100.00

Signed Card 6.00

Signed Puck 18.00

Gilmour, Doug

8 X 10 Photo 20.00

Authentic Jersey 240.00

Replica Jersey 120.00

Signed Card 10.00

Signed Puck 25.00

Gretzky, Wayne

8 X 10 Photo 50.00

Authentic Jersey 425.00

Mini Helmet 140.00

Mini Mask 130.00

Replica Jersey 210.00

Signed Card 30.00

Signed Puck 65.00

Hasek, Dominik

8 X 10 Photo 20.00

Authentic Jersey 260.00

Mini Mask 75.00

Replica Jersey 130.00

Signed Card 12.00

Signed Puck 27.00

Hebert, Guy

8 X 10 Photo 12.00

Authentic Jersey 180.00

Mini Mask 50.00

Replica Jersey 90.00

Signed Card 5.00

Signed Puck 15.00

Hextall, Ron

8 X 10 Photo 15.00

Authentic Jersey 200.00

Mini Mask 55.00

Replica Jersey 100.00

Signed Card 7.00

Signed Puck 20.00

Hull, Brett

8 X 10 Photo 25.00

Authentic Jersey 280.00

Mini Helmet 80.00

Mini Mask 70.00

Replica Jersey 140.00

Signed Card 15.00

Signed Puck 30.00

Iginla, Jarome

8 X 10 Photo 12.00

Authentic Jersey 180.00

Replica Jersey 90.00

Signed Card 5.00

Signed Puck 15.00

Jagr, Jaromir

8 X 10 Photo 30.00

Authentic Jersey 325.00

Mini Helmet 110.00

Mini Mask 100.00

Replica Jersey 160.00

Signed Card 20.00

Signed Puck 45.00

Joseph, Curtis

8 X 10 Photo 18.00

Authentic Jersey 220.00

Mini Mask 60.00

Replica Jersey 110.00

Signed Card 8.00

Signed Puck 20.00

Juneau, Joe

8 X 10 Photo 12.00

Authentic Jersey 180.00

Replica Jersey 90.00

TED LINDSAY

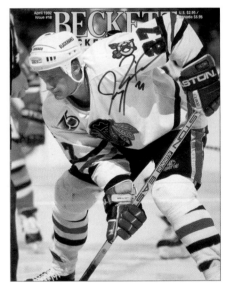

JEREMY ROENICK

JARI KURRI

Signed Card 5.00

Signed Puck 15.00

Kariya, Paul

8 X 10 Photo 30.00

Authentic Jersey 325.00

Mini Helmet 100.00

Mini Mask 90.00

Replica Jersey 160.00

Signed Card 18.00

Signed Puck 40.00

Khabibulin, Nikolai

8 X 10 Photo 15.00

Authentic Jersey 200.00

Mini Mask 55.00

Replica Jersey 100.00

Signed Card 7.00

Signed Puck 20.00

Koivu, Saku

8 X 10 Photo 18.00

Authentic Jersey 220.00

Replica Jersey 110.00

Signed Card 8.00

Signed Puck 20.00

Kolzig, Olaf

8 X 10 Photo 12.00

Authentic Jersey 180.00

Mini Mask 50.00

Replica Jersey 90.00

Signed Card 5.00

Signed Puck 15.00

Kurri, Jari

8 X 10 Photo 20.00

Authentic Jersey 240.00

Replica Jersey 120.00

Signed Card 10.00

Signed Puck 25.00

LaFontaine, Pat

8 X 10 Photo 20.00

Authentic Jersey 240.00

Replica Jersey 120.00

Signed Card 10.00

Signed Puck 25.00

LeClair, John

8 X 10 Photo 20.00

Authentic Jersey 260.00

Replica Jersey 130.00

Signed Card 12.00

Signed Puck 27.00

Leetch, Brian

8 X 10 Photo 25.00

Authentic Jersey 280.00

Mini Helmet 80.00

Mini Mask 70.00

Replica Jersey 140.00

Signed Card 15.00

Signed Puck 30.00

Lemieux, Claude

8 X 10 Photo 18.00

Authentic Jersey 220.00

Replica Jersey 110.00

Signed Card 8.00

Signed Puck 20.00

ANDY MOOG

Lidstrom, Nicklas

8 X 10 Photo	.15.00
Authentic Jersey	.190.00
Replica Jersey	.95.00
Signed Card	.6.00
Signed Puck	.18.00

Lindros, Eric

8 X 10 Photo	.40.00
Authentic Jersey	.350.00
Mini Helmet	.120.00
Mini Mask	.110.00
Replica Jersey	.175.00
Signed Card	.20.00
Signed Puck	.50.00

MacInnis, Al

8 X 10 Photo	.15.00
Authentic Jersey	.200.00
Replica Jersey	.100.00
Signed Card	.7.00
Signed Puck	.20.00

Messier, Mark

8 X 10 Photo	.55.00
Authentic Jersey	.450.00
Mini Helmet	.150.00
Mini Mask	.140.00
Replica Jersey	.225.00
Signed Card	.35.00
Signed Puck	.70.00

Modano, Mike

8 X 10 Photo	.25.00
Authentic Jersey	.260.00

Replica Jersey	.130.00
Signed Card	.15.00
Signed Puck	.30.00

Mogilny, Alexander

8 X 10 Photo	.18.00
Authentic Jersey	.220.00
Replica Jersey	.110.00
Signed Card	.8.00
Signed Puck	.20.00

Mullen, Joe

8 X 10 Photo	.12.00
Authentic Jersey	.180.00
Replica Jersey	.90.00
Signed Card	.5.00
Signed Puck	.15.00

Nicholls, Bernie

8 X 10 Photo	.12.00
Authentic Jersey	.180.00
Replica Jersey	.90.00
Signed Card	.5.00
Signed Puck	.15.00

Niedermayer, Scott

8 X 10 Photo	.12.00
Authentic Jersey	.180.00
Replica Jersey	.90.00
Signed Card	.5.00
Signed Puck	.15.00

Niewendyk, Joe

8 X 10 Photo	.12.00
Authentic Jersey	.180.00

TONY ESPOSITO

FRANK MAHOVLICH

STAN MIKITA

WAYNE GRETZKY

Replica Jersey 90.00

Signed Card 5.00

Signed Puck 15.00

Nolan, Owen

8 X 10 Photo 15.00

Authentic Jersey 200.00

Replica Jersey 100.00

Signed Card 7.00

Signed Puck 20.00

Oates, Adam

8 X 10 Photo 15.00

Authentic Jersey 200.00

Replica Jersey 100.00

Signed Card 6.00

Signed Puck 18.00

Osgood, Chris

8 X 10 Photo 20.00

Authentic Jersey 240.00

Mini Mask 70.00

Replica Jersey 120.00

Signed Card 10.00

Signed Puck 25.00

Ozolinsh, Sandis

8 X 10 Photo 12.00

Authentic Jersey 180.00

Replica Jersey 90.00

Signed Card 5.00

Signed Puck 15.00

Palffy, Zigmund

8 X 10 Photo 18.00

Authentic Jersey 220.00

Replica Jersey 110.00

Signed Card 8.00

Signed Puck 20.00

Potvin, Felix

8 X 10 Photo 20.00

Authentic Jersey 240.00

Mini Mask 70.00

Replica Jersey 120.00

Signed Card 10.00

Signed Puck 25.00

Probert, Bob

8 X 10 Photo 12.00

Authentic Jersey 180.00

Replica Jersey 90.00

Signed Card 5.00

Signed Puck 15.00

Ranford, Bill

8 X 10 Photo 12.00

Authentic Jersey 180.00

Mini Mask 50.00

Replica Jersey 90.00

Signed Card 5.00

Signed Puck 15.00

Recchi, Mark

8 X 10 Photo 15.00

Authentic Jersey 190.00

Replica Jersey 95.00

Signed Card 6.00

Signed Puck 18.00

Reichel, Robert

8 X 10 Photo 12.00

Authentic Jersey 180.00

Replica Jersey 90.00

Signed Card 5.00

Signed Puck 15.00

Renberg, Mikael

8 X 10 Photo 15.00

Authentic Jersey 200.00

Replica Jersey 100.00

Signed Card 7.00

Signed Puck 20.00

Rheaume, Manon

8 X 10 Photo 20.00

Authentic Jersey 260.00

Mini Mask 75.00

Replica Jersey 130.00

Signed Card 12.00

Signed Puck 27.00

Richter, Mike

8 X 10 Photo 25.00

Authentic Jersey 280.00

Mini Mask 90.00

Replica Jersey 140.00

Signed Card 15.00

Signed Puck 30.00

Robitaille, Luc

8 X 10 Photo 18.00

Authentic Jersey 220.00

Replica Jersey 110.00

Signed Card 8.00

Signed Puck 20.00

Roenick, Jeremy

8 X 10 Photo 20.00

Authentic Jersey 240.00

Replica Jersey 120.00

Signed Card 10.00

Signed Puck 25.00

Roy, Patrick

8 X 10 Photo 35.00

Authentic Jersey 350.00

Mini Mask 120.00

Replica Jersey 175.00

Signed Card 20.00

Signed Puck 60.00

Sakic, Joe

8 X 10 Photo 28.00

Authentic Jersey 300.00

Mini Helmet 90.00

Mini Mask 80.00

Replica Jersey 150.00

Signed Card 15.00

Signed Puck 35.00

Selanne, Teemu

8 X 10 Photo 25.00

Authentic Jersey 280.00

Mini Helmet 80.00

Mini Mask 70.00

Replica Jersey 140.00

Signed Card 15.00

Signed Puck 30.00

Shanahan, Brendan

8 X 10 Photo 25.00

TEMMU SELANNE

WENDEL CLARK

CHUCK RAYNER

Authentic Jersey 260.00

Mini Helmet 75.00

Replica Jersey 130.00

Signed Card 12.00

Signed Puck 27.00

Stevens, Scott

8 X 10 Photo 20.00

Authentic Jersey 220.00

Replica Jersey 110.00

Signed Card 8.00

Signed Puck 20.00

Stumpel, Jozef

8 X 10 Photo 18.00

Authentic Jersey 200.00

Replica Jersey 100.00

Signed Card 5.00

Signed Puck 15.00

Sundin, Mats

8 X 10 Photo 15.00

Authentic Jersey 200.00

Replica Jersey 100.00

Signed Card 6.00

Signed Puck 18.00

Thibault, Jocelyn

8 X 10 Photo 15.00

Authentic Jersey 180.00

Mini Mask 50.00

Replica Jersey 90.00

Signed Card 5.00

Signed Puck 15.00

Tkachuk, Kcith

8 X 10 Photo 12.00

Authentic Jersey 220.00

Replica Jersey 110.00

Signed Card 7.00

Signed Puck 20.00

Tocchet, Rick

8 X 10 Photo 18.00

Authentic Jersey 180.00

Replica Jersey 90.00

Signed Card 5.00

Signed Puck 15.00

Turgeon, Pierre

8 X 10 Photo 12.00

Authentic Jersey 220.00

Replica Jersey 110.00

Signed Card 8.00

Signed Puck 20.00

Vanbiesbrouck, John

8 X 10 Photo 18.00

Authentic Jersey 280.00

Mini Mask 90.00

Replica Jersey 140.00

Signed Card 15.00

Signed Puck 30.00

Vernon, Mike

8 X 10 Photo 25.00

Authentic Jersey 180.00

Mini Mask 50.00

Replica Jersey 90.00

Signed Card 5.00

Signed Puck 15.00

Weight, Doug

8 X 10 Photo 12.00

Authentic Jersey 180.00

Replica Jersey 90.00

Signed Card 5.00

Signed Puck 15.00

Yashin, Alexei

8 X 10 Photo 12.00

Authentic Jersey 180.00

Replica Jersey 90.00

Signed Card 5.00

Signed Puck 15.00

Yzerman, Steve

8 X 10 Photo 30.00

Authentic Jersey 325.00

Mini Helmet 100.00

Mini Mask 90.00

Replica Jersey 160.00

Signed Card 18.00

Signed Puck 40.00

Muhammad Ali, boxing

COLLECTING AUTOGRAPHS OF OTHER SPORTS

Announcer Michael Buffer resplendent in his trademark tuxedo steps up to the microphone and booms "LETS GET READY TO RUMMMM-BLE..." The TV cameras pan the arena and cue in on the faces of dozens of superstar celebrities in attendance. Seconds later referee Mills Lane instructs the fighters and hoarsely shouts, "Lets get it on." The bell sounds and the combatants meet in the center of the ring. Few athletic events can match boxing for sheer drama and excitement.

The watered down divisions and shameless chicanery have done little to dampen the public appetite for the sport. Many of today's stars have battled through the hype and have become household names, transcending boxing itself. Names such as George Foreman, Oscar De La Hoya, Evander Holyfield, Mike Tyson and others have left their mark on contemporary culture.

The explosion in popularity of autograph collecting in the 1980s seemed to completely exclude the sport of boxing. Autograph prices and interest in collecting skyrocketed, while boxing autographs could still be found in the "bargain basement" section of most dealers' catalogs, if at all. All of this began to change in the 1990s due in large part to the realization of what an integral role boxing had played in our culture. If autograph collecting is really about collecting the

Dale Earnhardt, auto racing

BY JIM STINSON

nostalgia of our past, then boxing seems tailor made for the scene.

Boxing was unquestionably the most popular TV sport of the 1950s. The crude camera equipment and lighting available during that time did not lend itself well to filming and broadcasting a baseball or football game with its action spread out over a large area. A boxing ring in a fixed location could be filmed and televised with relative ease even in the days before multiple camera angles, instant replay and the sky camera.

Today's broadest base of collectors, males in their 40s or 50s, were reared on those TV fights. Names such as Sugar Ray Robinson and Willie Pep became part of the sports vernacular of the day.

It seems only fitting that boxing should enjoy its popularity with today's autograph aficionados, but boxing's rich history in this country goes back much further than the 1950s.

John L. Sullivan was America's first sports superstar.

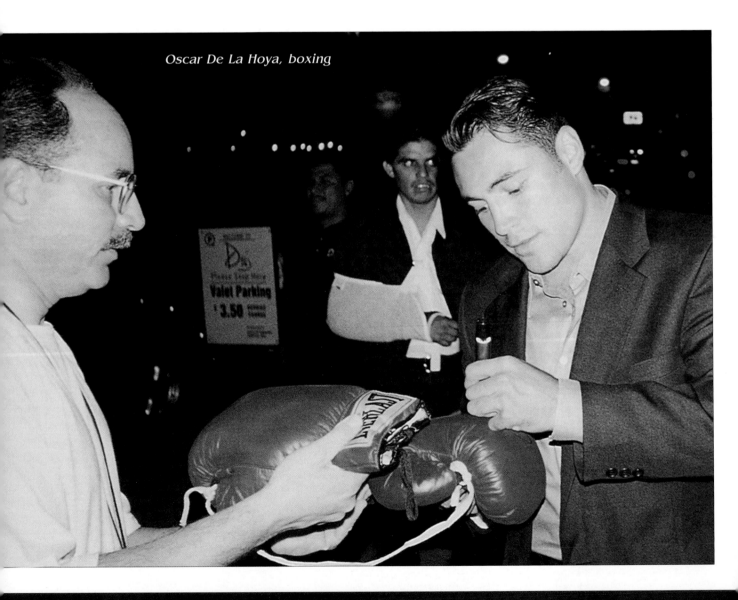

Oscar De La Hoya, boxing

Sullivan was Heavyweight champion from 1881 to 1892. The next superstar of the sporting world was also a boxer, Jack Dempsey, who held the Heavyweight crown from 1919 to 1926. Spectators often paid $50 or more for ringside seats (that's $50 in 1920s currency) and crowded stadiums with more than 100,000 strong to see Dempsey ply his craft.

In the 1930s and '40s the soft-spoken Joe Louis defended the title an unprecedented 25 times, which is still a record. While Louis entertained Heavyweight audiences, master boxer Sugar Ray Robinson held fans spellbound while he danced and slugged his way through the Welterweight and Middleweight divisions. His incomparable skills in the ring earned him the title of "Pound for Pound Greatest of All Time," and few who witnessed his pugilistic artistry would argue otherwise.

Tiger Woods, golf

In the 1960s Muhammad Ali burst on the boxing scene like a supernova. His bold predictions, his entertaining poetry and his movie star looks made Ali the most popular sports star of the '60s and '70s.

As baseball enjoyed its "Golden Age" in the 1920s and '30s with legends such as Babe Ruth, Lou Gehrig and Walter Johnson, boxing enjoyed its "Golden Age" in the 1970s. Some of the greatest champions ever to step into the squared circle held titles in many of boxing's weight classes. The Heavyweights had Muhammad Ali, Joe Frazier and George Foreman. The lighter weight classes were owned by the likes of Roberto Duran and Alexis Arguello.

By the 1980s, with the sun setting on many of the ring's greats, the sun was rising for a new crop destined to forge their own path to glory. Marvin Hagler, Sugar Ray Leonard, Thomas Hearns, Evander Holyfield and Mike Tyson needed no alphabet soup divisions to prove to the world that they were champions of the highest caliber. With today's current crop of stars such as Roy Jones and Oscar De La Hoya, boxing is likely to enjoy its popularity for years to come.

Despite the occasional black eye on boxing's image, the show will go on. And when that rare combination of combatants, with equal force of will and might challenge each other in the center of the ring, we remember why we enjoy this sport so much.

Collecting boxing autographs compared to its baseball counterpart can be a relatively inexpensive process. A good place to start might be with signed items of the stars of the 1950s through 1970s many of whom are still alive. The most popular (and expensive) area of boxing seems to be the Heavyweight champions. Autographs of John L. Sullivan, Bob Fitzsimmons and Jack Johnson though tough to find, are available from time to time and could distance you from your rent money in a hurry.

In the modem era of the division, Rocky Marciano and Sonny Liston command the highest prices. Marciano, who was the only Heavyweight champ to retire undefeated, was killed in a

Martina Hingis, tennis

plane crash in 1969 in an Iowa cornfield.

During his life he sometimes used a secretary or family member to sign autograph requests sent through the mail. Today, due his huge popularity, his signature is among the most often forged in boxing (Muhammad Ali and Mike Tyson are others).

Sonny Liston proves difficult, but for different reasons. Illiterate for most of his life, he learned to write his name shortly before winning the Heavyweight crown from Floyd Patterson in 1962. When Liston signed in person it was a slow, labored and even embarrassing process for him just to write his name, which would understandably limit the number of items he would be willing to sign.

When autograph requests arrived by mail, his wife would often sign for him. To further compound the problem, both

Pete Sampras, tennis

Liston's signature and his wife's version of his signature are very similar. The acquisition of a Liston signature should be approached with extreme caution.

Will collecting boxing autographs continue to grow in popularity? No one can say for sure, but unlike other contemporary American sports such as football and baseball, boxing is a world

sport with many champions hailing from other countries (Mexico, South America, Cuba, Puerto Rico and Europe). The apparent influx of collectors joining the fold from as far way as Australia, Japan and the United Kingdom, serves as a positive sign that boxing will experience future growth and popularity as it continues its emergence onto the hobby scene. ∎

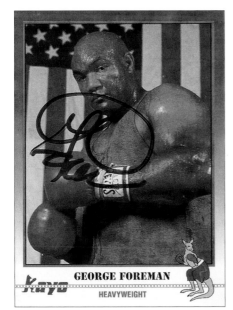

JAMES J. CORBETT

GEORGE FOREMAN

Jack Dempsey

JACK DEMPSEY

Jack Nicklaus

Boxing

Muhammad Ali
Cut	.25.00
Card	.40.00
Mag./Photo	.60.00
Glove	.150.00

Alexis Arguello
Cut	.8.00
Card	.12.00
Mag./Photo	.20.00
Glove	.75.00

Riddick Bowe
Cut	.8.00
Card	.12.00
Mag./Photo	.20.00
Glove	.75.00

Hector Camacho
Cut	.8.00
Card	.12.00
Mag./Photo	.20.00
Glove	.75.00

Michael Carbajal
Cut	.8.00
Card	.12.00
Mag./Photo	.20.00
Glove	.75.00

Primo Carnera
Cut	.175.00
Photo	.750.00

Georges Carpentier
Cut	.75.00
Photo	.250.00

Julio Cesar Chavez
Cut	.12.00
Card	.20.00
Mag./Photo	.35.00
Glove	.90.00

Cassius Clay (vintage)
Cut	.500.00
Mag./Photo	.1500.00

James J. Corbett
Cut	.250.00
Mag./Photo	.500.00
Document	.700.00

Bobby Czyz
Cut	.8.00
Card	.12.00
Mag./Photo	.20.00
Glove	.75.00

Oscar De La Hoya
Cut	.15.00
Card	.25.00
Mag./Photo	.40.00
Glove	.100.00

Jack Dempsey
Cut	.50.00
Mag./Photo	.250.00
Glove	.400.00

Buster Douglas
Cut	.8.00
Card	.12.00
Mag./Photo	.20.00
Glove	.75.00

Roberto Duran
Cut	.8.00
Card	.12.00
Mag./Photo	.20.00
Glove	.75.00

George Foreman
Cut	.12.00
Card	.20.00
Mag./Photo	.35.00
Glove	.90.00
Book	.50.00

Joe Frazier
Cut	.10.00
Card	.18.00
Mag./Photo	.30.00
Glove	.80.00

Rocky Graziano

Cut 20.00
Mag./Photo 75.00
Glove .125.00

Marvin Hagler

Cut 12.00
Card 20.00
Mag./Photo 35.00
Glove 90.00

Tommy Hearns

Cut 8.00
Card 12.00
Mag./Photo 20.00
Glove 75.00

Larry Holmes

Cut 8.00
Card 12.00
Mag./Photo 20.00
Glove 75.00

Evander Holyfield

Cut 25.00
Card 40.00
Mag./Photo 60.00
Glove .200.00

Ingemar Johansson

Cut 6.00
Photo 15.00
Glove 60.00

Jack Johnson

Cut 500.00
Photo 3500.00

Roy Jones

Cut 12.00
Card 20.00
Mag./Photo 35.00
Glove 90.00

Jake LaMotta

Cut 8.00
Card 12.00

Mag./Photo 20.00
Glove 75.00

Sugar Ray Leonard

Cut 12.00
Card 20.00
Mag./Photo 35.00
Glove 90.00

Lennox Lewis

Cut 8.00
Card 12.00
Mag./Photo 20.00
Glove 75.00

Sonny Liston

Cut 600.00
Photo 2000.00

Joe Louis

Cut 100.00
Mag./Photo 300.00
Glove .500.00

Ray Mancini

Cut 5.00
Card 8.00
Mag./Photo 18.00
Glove 60.00

Rocky Marciano

Cut 250.00
Photo .750.00

Christy Martin

Cut 5.00
Card 8.00
Mag./Photo 18.00
Glove 60.00

Archie Moore

Cut 8.00
Photo 20.00
Glove 75.00

Michael Moorer

Cut 8.00

OSCAR DE LA HOYA

GEORGE FOREMAN

Ingemar Johansson

Card .12.00
Mag./Photo 20.00
Glove .75.00

Tommy Morrison
Cut 5.00
Card 8.00
Mag./Photo 18.00
Glove .60.00

Ken Norton
Cut 8.00
Card .12.00
Mag./Photo 20.00
Glove .75.00

Floyd Patterson
Cut 8.00
Card .12.00
Mag./Photo 20.00
Glove .75.00

Willie Pep
Cut 8.00
Photo .20.00
Glove .75.00

Sugar Ray Robinson
Cut 75.00
Photo 200.00
Glove 500.00

Max Schmeling
Cut 15.00
Photo .50.00
Glove 150.00

Jack Sharkey
Cut 60.00
Photo 175.00

Earnie Shavers
Cut 5.00
Card 8.00
Mag./Photo 18.00
Glove .60.00

Leon Spinks
Cut 5.00
Card 8.00
Mag./Photo 18.00
Glove .60.00

Michael Spinks
Cut 5.00
Card 8.00
Mag./Photo 18.00
Glove .60.00

John L. Sullivan
Cut 1000.00
Photo 3500.00

James Toney
Cut 5.00
Card 8.00
Mag./Photo 18.00
Glove .60.00

Gene Tunney
Cut 75.00
Photo 250.00

Mike Tyson
Cut 25.00
Card .40.00
Mag./Photo 60.00
Glove 150.00

Jersey Joe Walcott
Cut 40.00
Photo 100.00
Glove 200.00

Pernell Whitaker
Cut 8.00
Card .12.00
Mag./Photo 20.00
Glove .75.00

Jess Willard
Cut .500.00
Photo 1500.00

LARRY HOLMES

FLOYD PATTERSON

JOHN L. SULLIVAN

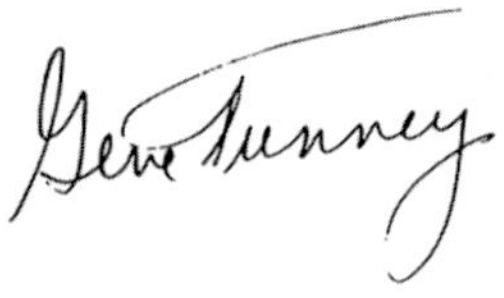

JOHN TUNNEY

NANCY KERRIGAN

PEGGY FLEMING

Figure/Speed Skating

Oksana Baiul
Cut 10.00
Mag./Photo 40.00
Book 50.00

Bonnie Blair
Cut 5.00
Card 10.00
Mag./Photo 20.00
Book 40.00

Nicole Bobek
Cut 4.00
Mag./Photo 15.00

Brian Boitano
Cut 5.00
Mag./Photo 20.00
Book 40.00

Surya Bonaly
Cut 3.00
Mag./Photo 12.00

Kurt Browning
Cut 3.00
Card 6.00
Mag./Photo 12.00

Dick Button
Cut 5.00
Card 10.00
Mag./Photo 20.00

Todd Eldredge
Cut 3.00
Mag./Photo 12.00

Peggy Fleming
Cut 8.00
Card 15.00
Mag./Photo 30.00
Book 45.00

Ekaterina Gordeeva
Cut 5.00
Mag./Photo 20.00
Book 40.00

Dorothy Hamill
Cut 8.00
Card 15.00
Mag./Photo 30.00
Book 45.00

Scott Hamilton
Cut 6.00
Card 12.00
Mag./Photo 25.00
Book 40.00

Tonya Harding
Cut 5.00
Mag./Photo 20.00

Eric Heiden
Cut 5.00
Card 10.00
Mag./Photo 20.00
Book 40.00

Sonja Henie
Cut 50.00
Mag./Photo 150.00

Dan Jansen
Cut 5.00
Card 10.00
Mag./Photo 20.00
Book 40.00

Nancy Kerrigan
Cut 8.00
Card 15.00
Mag./Photo 30.00
Book 45.00

Michelle Kwan
Cut 6.00
Mag./Photo 25.00
Book 40.00

Tara Lipinski

Cut 6.00
Mag./Photo 25.00
Book .40.00

Brian Orser

Cut 2.50
Mag./Photo 10.00

Elvis Stojko

Cut 5.00
Mag./Photo 20.00

Rosalyn Sumners

Cut 3.00
Mag./Photo 12.00

Debi Thomas

Cut 5.00
Mag./Photo 20.00

Jill Trenary

Cut 3.00
Mag./Photo 12.00

Katarina Witt

Cut 8.00
Card 15.00
Mag./Photo 30.00
Book .45.00

Paul Wylie

Cut 2.50
Mag./Photo 10.00

Kristi Yamaguchi

Cut 8.00
Card 15.00
Mag./Photo 30.00
Book .40.00

Golf

Paul Azinger

Cut 5.00
Card 8.00
Mag./Photo 18.00
Ball 25.00

Steve Ballesteros

Cut 7.00
Mag./Photo 25.00
Ball 35.00

Pat Bradley

Cut 3.00
Mag./Photo 12.00
Ball 14.00

Fred Couples

Cut 7.00
Card 12.00
Mag./Photo 25.00
Ball 35.00

Ben Crenshaw

Cut 6.00
Card 10.00
Mag./Photo 20.00
Ball 30.00

Ernie Els

Cut 7.00
Mag./Photo 25.00
Ball 35.00

Nick Faldo

Cut 10.00
Card 15.00
Mag./Photo 30.00
Ball 40.00

Ben Hogan

Cut 75.00
Photo .175.00
Ball 150.00

Hale Irwin

Cut 6.00
Mag./Photo 20.00
Ball 30.00

Bobby Jones

Cut 500.00
Photo .2000.00

BRIAN BOITANO

TIGER WOODS

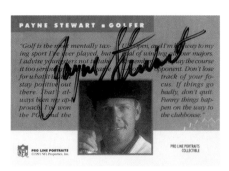

PAYNE STEWART

BANTAM BEN

BEN HOGAN

BEN HOGAN

Betsy King

Cut 3.00

Mag./Photo 12.00

Ball 18.00

Tom Kite

Cut 5.00

Card 8.00

Mag./Photo 18.00

Ball 25.00

Tom Lehman

Cut 5.00

Card 8.00

Mag./Photo 18.00

Ball 25.00

Justin Leonard

Cut 5.00

Mag./Photo 18.00

Ball 25.00

Nancy Lopez

Cut 5.00

Mag./Photo 18.00

Ball 25.00

Davis Love III

Cut 6.00

Card 10.00

Mag./Photo 20.00

Ball 30.00

Phil Mickelson

Cut 6.00

Mag./Photo 20.00

Johnny Miller

Cut 6.00

Card 20.00

Ball 30.00

Byron Nelson

Cut 15.00

Photo 40.00

Ball 60.00

Book 50.00

Jack Nicklaus

Cut 20.00

Card 30.00

Mag./Photo 50.00

Ball 60.00

Greg Norman

Cut 10.00

Card 15.00

Mag./Photo 30.00

Ball 40.00

Arnold Palmer

Cut 20.00

Card 30.00

Mag./Photo 50.00

Ball 60.00

Corey Pavin

Cut 5.00

Card 8.00

Mag./Photo 18.00

Ball 25.00

Nick Price

Cut 6.00

Card 10.00

Mag./Photo 20.00

Ball 30.00

Chi Chi Rodriguez

Cut 5.00

Mag./Photo 18.00

Ball 25.00

Gene Sarazen

Cut 10.00

Photo 25.00

Ball 40.00

Patty Sheehan

Cut 3.00

Mag./Photo 12.00

Ball 18.00

Sam Snead

Cut 10.00

Photo 25.00
Ball 40.00
Book 40.00

Annika Sorenstam

Cut 4.00
Mag./Photo 15.00
Ball 20.00

Craig Stadler

Cut 5.00
Card 8.00
Mag./Photo 18.00
Ball 25.00

Jan Stephenson

Cut 5.00
Mag./Photo 18.00
Ball 25.00

Payne Stewart

Cut 5.00
Card 8.00
Mag./Photo 18.00
Ball 25.00

Curtis Strange

Cut 7.00
Card 12.00
Mag./Photo 25.00
Ball 35.00

Lee Trevino

Cut 7.00
Card 12.00
Mag./Photo 25.00
Ball 35.00

Tom Watson

Cut 7.00
Card 12.00
Mag./Photo 25.00
Ball 35.00

Karrie Webb

Cut 3.00
Mag./Photo 12.00
Ball 18.00

Tiger Woods

Cut 30.00
Mag./Photo 75.00
Ball 90.00
Cap 100.00

Babe D. Zaharias

Cut 250.00
Photo .750.00

Gymnastics

Dominique Dawes

Cut 4.00
Card 6.00
Mag./Photo 12.00

Shannon Miller

Cut 6.00
Card 10.00
Mag./Photo 18.00

Dominique Moceanu

Cut 5.00
Card 15.00
Book 30.00

Mary Lou Retton

Cut 6.00
Card 10.00
Mag./Photo 18.00
Book 40.00

Kerri Strug

Cut 6.00
Mag./Photo 18.00
Book 30.00

Kim Zmeskal

Cut 4.00
Card 6.00
Mag./Photo 12.00

Racing

Davey Allison

Cut 15.00

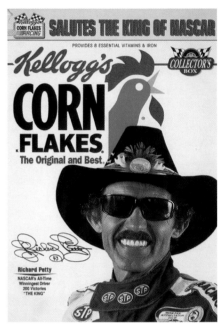

RICHARD PETTY

JEFF GORDON

MICHAEL WALTRIP

DALE JARRETT

RICHARD PETTY

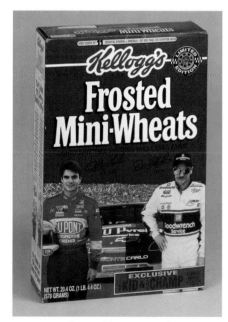

JEFF GORDON /
DALE EARNHARDT

MICHAEL WALTRIP

Card 25.00
Mag./Photo 50.00

Mario Andretti
Cut 7.00
Card 12.00
Mag./Photo 25.00

Jeff Burton
Cut 3.00
Card 6.00
Mag./Photo 12.00

Dale Earnhardt
Cut 12.00
Card 20.00
Mag./Photo 40.00

Bill Elliott
Cut 4.00
Card 8.00
Mag./Photo 15.00

John Force
Cut 6.00
Card 10.00
Mag./Photo 20.00

A.J. Foyt
Cut 6.00
Card 10.00
Mag./Photo 20.00

Jeff Gordon
Cut 12.00
Card 20.00
Mag./Photo 40.00

Ernie Irvan
Cut 4.00
Card 8.00
Mag./Photo 15.00

Dale Jarrett
Cut 4.00
Card 8.00
Mag./Photo 15.00

Bobby Labonte
Cut 3.00
Card 6.00
Mag./Photo 12.00

Terry Labonte
Cut 6.00
Card 10.00
Mag./Photo 20.00

Mark Martin
Cut 6.00
Card 10.00
Mag./Photo 20.00

Richard Petty
Cut 10.00
Card 15.00
Mag./Photo 30.00

Al Unser Jr.
Cut 6.00
Card 10.00
Mag./Photo 20.00

Rusty Wallace
Cut 6.00
Card 10.00
Mag./Photo 20.00

Swimming

Brooke Bennett
Cut 4.00
Mag./Photo 12.00

Matt Biondi
Cut 5.00
Card 8.00
Mag./Photo 15.00

Tom Dolan
Cut 4.00
Card 6.00
Mag./Photo 12.00
Wheaties Box 20.00

Janet Evans
Cut 6.00
Card .10.00
Mag./Photo 18.00

Amy Van Dyken
Cut 4.00
Mag./Photo 12.00
Wheaties Box 20.00

Tennis

Andre Agassi
Cut 10.00
Card .15.00
Mag./Photo 30.00
Ball 40.00

Arthur Ashe
Cut 25.00
Card .40.00
Mag./Photo 75.00
Ball 90.00

Tracy Austin
Cut 5.00
Card 8.00
Mag./Photo 18.00
Ball 25.00

Bjorn Borg
Cut 10.00
Card .30.00
Ball 40.00

Don Budge
Cut 6.00
Photo .20.00

Michael Chang
Cut 8.00
Card .14.00
Mag./Photo 25.00
Ball 35.00

Maureen Connolly
Cut 150.00

Photo .350.00

Jimmy Connors
Cut 8.00
Card .14.00
Mag./Photo 25.00
Ball 35.00

Margaret Court
Cut 10.00
Photo .30.00

Stefan Edberg
Cut 8.00
Card .14.00
Mag./Photo 25.00
Ball 35.00

Chris Evert
Cut 10.00
Card .15.00
Mag./Photo 30.00
Ball 40.00

Althea Gibson
Cut 15.00
Photo .50.00

Evonne Goolagong
Cut 5.00
Card 8.00
Mag./Photo 18.00
Ball 25.00

Steffi Graf
Cut 10.00
Card .15.00
Mag./Photo 30.00
Ball 40.00

Martina Hingis
Cut 10.00
Mag./Photo 30.00
Ball 40.00

Billy Jean King
Cut 8.00

OKSANA BAIUL

MATT BIONDI

MATT BIONDI

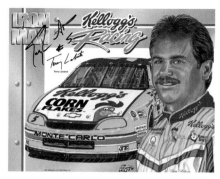

TERRY LABONTE

Card 14.00
Mag./Photo 25.00
Ball 35.00

Anna Kournikova
Cut 6.00
Mag./Photo 20.00
Ball 30.00

Rene Lacoste
Cut 8.00
Photo 25.00

Rod Laver
Cut 8.00
Card 14.00
Mag./Photo 25.00
Ball 35.00

Ivan Lendl
Cut 5.00
Card 8.00
Mag./Photo 18.00
Ball 25.00

John McEnroe
Cut 10.00
Card 15.00
Mag./Photo 30.00
Ball 40.00

STEFFI GRAF

Martina Navratilova
Cut 10.00
Card 15.00
Mag./Photo 30.00
Ball 40.00

John Newcombe
Cut 6.00
Photo 20.00
Ball 30.00

Fred Perry
Cut 8.00
Photo 25.00

Bobby Riggs
Cut 8.00

Photo 25.00

Ken Rosewall
Cut 6.00
Photo 20.00

Gabriela Sabatini
Cut 10.00
Card 15.00
Mag./Photo 30.00
Ball 40.00

Pete Sampras
Cut 10.00
Card 15.00
Mag./Photo 30.00
Ball 40.00

Monica Seles
Cut 10.00
Mag./Photo 30.00
Ball 40.00

Bill Tilden
Cut 100.00
Photo 300.00

Guillermo Vilas
Cut 6.00
Photo 20.00

Venus Williams
Cut 6.00
Mag./Photo 20.00
Ball 30.00

Helen Wills
Cut 40.00
Photo 100.00

Tony Gwynn, Alex Rodriguez, Andruw Jones, Ken Griffey Jr.

UPPER DECK AUTHENTICATED AUTOGRAPHS

Oh, you're a shrewd one all right. It took three passes on the trade-show floor, but you found the bargain ball of the day, and for 20 bucks cheaper than anywhere else. Sure, it required a little dickering, but that dealer came around soon enough. So as you turn to leave, re-pocketing your wallet that's now four twenties lighter, you glimpse that same dealer offering up a celebratory high-five. Suddenly, seemingly without reason, a seed of doubt begins to grow in the pit of your stomach.

You weren't quite sure at the show, but when you get that signed baseball home and compare it to the facsimile autograph on a baseball card, you notice some not-so-subtle differences. By now the only thing you're really sure of is that the dealer who sold it to you is long gone. Stories such as this one are told every day in this hobby, but as disheartening as it sounds, it couldn't provide a better adver-

tisement for the services of Upper Deck Authenticated.

UDA, Upper Deck's memorabilia-based sister company, has established a niche in the collectibles industry by offering autographed material of superstars such as Ken Griffey Jr., Michael Jordan, Ted Williams, Joe Montana and others. While some have criticized UDA for higher prices and saturating the market, few have criticized its famous five-step authentication process.

The Famous Five-Step Process.

1) Every athlete's signature is witnessed by a UDA representative.

2) An affirmation of the session is signed by both the athlete and the UDA representative.

3) The UDA hologram, which includes an individual serial number, is affixed to each signed piece.

4) A certificate of authenticity with a matching serialized hologram is assigned and provided to the consumer.

5) Each piece of signed memorabilia is packaged with a registration card providing the consumer with the opportunity to register the item with UDA.

The rate of autograph forgeries in the 1990s has increased at an alarming rate. Some have estimated that 60 percent to 70 percent of all autographed memorabilia is forged. Others dispute that figure, claiming the percent of forgeries is lower. But no one disputes the fact that forgeries do exist and that collectors need to take caution when buying an autograph.

While cards remain king, Upper Deck continues to increase its presence in the marketing of authenticated autographed material. While big-name players in the autograph lineup will help UDA sales, the company's No. 1 draw is already on board in the form of an unparalleled authentication system. UDA offers more than just the game's top autographs. It, along with Score Board, provide autograph collectors with something far more valuable – a safe harbor in a sea of uncertainty. ▪

BY TOL BROOME

Michael Jordan

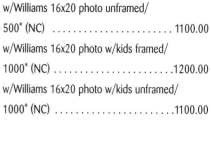

MICHAEL JORDAN

MICHAEL JORDAN

UDA Ken Griffey Jr.

1997 All-Star baseball/124 . . . . .175.00
Griffey 300 homer jersey #/28 . . . . .1800.00
8x10 horiz.photo 'sliding home' 100.00
8x10 photo 'classic shot'/327 . . . . .100.00
8x10 photo 'over the wall' 100.00
8x10 vert.photo 'sliding home' w/letter/500110.00
16x20 photo 'Classic Swing' framed/500 .250.00
AL baseball 100.00
Glove 450.00
Griffey/Buhner/A-Rod 16x20 photo/100 .450.00
Louisville Slugger black bat 450.00
Mariners alternate cap/240 . . . . .200.00
Mariners white jersey framed 700.00
Mariners white jersey unframed 500.00
Mini batting helmet 150.00
Mini glove 150.00
Shadow box mini glove and ball/500 . . . .350.00
SI Cover 'Big Numbers' 6/6/94
 framed/1000 . . . . .130.00
SI Cover 'The Natural' 5/7/90 framed 130.00
Signed Spikes #/124 . . . . .475.00
The Swing framed photos/240 . . . . .475.00
The Swing framed jersey/*240 . . . . . . .1200.00

UDA Mickey Mantle Photos

16x20 'Am Ex' photo framed (NC) 800.00
16x20 B&W photo framed/300* (NC) 800.00
16x20 B&W photo unframed/300* (NC) . .700.00
16x20 bat shave photo framed/300* (NC) 800.00
16x20 bat shave photo unframed/
300* (NC) 700.00
16x20 batting photo framed/500* (NC) . .800.00
16x20 batting photo unframed/500* (NC) .700.00
16x20 on base photo framed/500* (NC) . .800.00
16x20 on base photo unframed/500* (NC)700.00
16x20 photo first ML hit framed (NC) 800.00
16x20 photo first ML hit unframed (NC) . .700.00
16x20 portrait photo framed/500* (NC) . .800.00
16x20 portrait photo unframed/500* (NC) 700.00
16x20 w/bat 'Amer.Epic' photo
framed (NC) 800.00
w/Williams 16x20 photo framed/
500* (NC) 1200.00

w/Williams 16x20 photo unframed/
500* (NC) 1100.00
w/Williams 16x20 photo w/kids framed/
1000* (NC) 1200.00
w/Williams 16x20 photo w/kids unframed/
1000* (NC) 1100.00

UDA Mickey Mantle Other

AL baseball (NC) 350.00
'Life of a Legend' litho framed/2401* (NC) 600.00
'Life of a Legend' litho unframed/
2401* (NC) 500.00
L'ville Slugger bat w/display/1951* (NC) .4000.00
L'ville Slugger bat w/o display/1951* . . .3800.00
'No.7' AL baseball (NC) 400.00
SI Cover '1956 MVP' framed/1000 (NC) . .500.00
Yankees cap/536 (NC) 500.00
Yankees jersey unframed/1951* (NC) . . .3500.00
Yankees jersey framed/1951* (NC) 3700.00
Yankees No.7 jersey framed/536* (NC) .3700.00
Yankees No.7 jersey unframed/536* (NC)3500.00

UDA Ted Williams

'.406' AL baseball/1941 (NC) 500.00
8x10 photo All-Star HR framed (NC) 225.00
8x10 photo All-Star HR unframed (NC) . . .300.00
16x20 '41 AS game photo framed/
300* (NC) 800.00
16x20 '41 AS game photo unframed
/300* (NC) 700.00
16x20 photo 'Dugout' framed/500 (NC) . .500.00
16x20 photo 'Dugout' unframed/500 (NC) 400.00
16x20 photo 'Last at-bat' framed/500* (NC)700.00
16x20 photo 'Last at-bat' unframed/
500* (NC) 600.00
16x20 photo HR swing framed (NC) 500.00
16x20 photo HR swing unframed (NC) . . .400.00
AL baseball (NC) 350.00
All-Time Heroes 2-card set/2500 (NC) . . .150.00
Danny Day litho/416 (NC) 800.00
Career Commemorative UD sheet (NC) . . .300.00
Framed B&W 24x32 litho (NC) 350.00
L'ville Slugger bat w/display (NC) 2000.00
Red Sox jersey unframed (NC) 2200.00

Red Sox jersey framed (NC) 2400.00

SI Cover 8/1/55 framed (NC) 250.00

SI Cover 8/1/55 unframed (NC) 200.00

UD commem.sheet/521 (NC) 300.00

UDA Larry Bird Photos

8x10 Indiana St. photo framed (NC) 140.00

8x10 photo 'Takes It to the Hoop' framed .130.00

8x10 photo 'Takes It to the Hoop' unframed 80.00

16x20 photo '4:59' framed/500* 225.00

16x20 photo '4:59' unframed/500* 150.00

16x20 photo framed/500* (NC) 225.00

16x20 photo unframed/500* (NC) 150.00

16x20 practice photo framed/300* (NC) ..225.00

16x20 practice photo unframed/300* (NC)150.00

UDA Larry Bird Other

8/19/92 Boston Globe/500 (NC) 100.00

'92-93 2-card set/1000 (NC) 125.00

'92-93 Celtics jersey green framed (NC) .1100.00

'92-93 Celtics jersey green unframed (NC) 900.00

'92-93 Celtics jersey white framed (NC) ..1100.00

'92-93 Celtics jersey white unframed (NC) 900.00

'96-97 Celtics jersey green unframed 475.00

Heroes 10-card set/500 (NC) 250.00

NBA Indoor/Outdoor Basketball 175.00

Official NBA Game Basketball 200.00

'Retirement' 8 1/2x11 sheet/500 ....150.00

UDA Larry Bird/Magic Johnson

16x20 All-Star photo framed/500* (NC) ..500.00

16x20 All-Star photo unframed/500* (NC) 400.00

16x20 Bird/Jordan/Magic framed (NC) ..1800.00

16x20 Bird/Jordan/Magic no Magic

AU framed 1100.00

16x20 Bird/Jordan/Magic unframed (NC) 1700.00

16x20 Bird/Jordan/Magic no Magic

 unframed 1000.00

16x20 Dream Team photo framed/

300* (NC) 500.00

16x20 Dream Team photo unframed/

300* (NC) 400.00

16x20 joking photo framed 500.00

16x20 joking photo unframed 400.00

16x20 photo 'Classic Struggle' unframed ..325.00

16x20 photo 'Classic Struggle' framed 425.00

16x20 photo 'Finals' framed/300* 425.00

16x20 photo 'Finals' unframed/300* 325.00

16x20 retirement photo unframed/

300* (NC) 400.00

16x20 retirement photo framed/300* (NC) 500.00

'Barcelona '92' basketball/500 (NC) 600.00

Dream Team sheet framed/1992 (NC) 175.00

Dream Team sheet unframed/1992 (NC) .125.00

'MVP' NBA basketball/500 (NC) 600.00

UDA Magic Johnson

37x49 serigraph framed/750 (NC) 900.00

1992 All-Star Game Basketball/300 (NC) .600.00

'92-93 Lakers yellow jersey framed (NC) .1000.00

'92-93 Lakers yellow jersey unframed (NC)850.00

Dream Team commem.sheet framed/1992 125.00

Dream Team jersey unframed (NC) 400.00

Official NBA Game Basketball 375.00

SI Cover 'Magic's Moment' 5/26/80

 Framed 100.00

SI Cover Mich.St. 4/2/79 Framed 100.00

UDA Michael Jordan Jerseys

'92-93 Bulls Champ. jersey #23 red

unframed (NC) 2200.00

'92-93 Bulls Champ. jersey #23 white

unframed (NC) 2200.00

11/1/94 Retire.jersey unframed/111 (NC) 5500.00

'94-95 Bulls Champ. jersey #45 red

 framed (NC) 4700.00

'94-95 Bulls Champ.jersey #45 red

unframed (NC) 4500.00

'95-96 Bulls Champ. jersey #23 black

unframed (NC) 1600.00

'95-96 Bulls Champ. jersey #23 red

unframed (NC) 1600.00

'95-96 Bulls Champ. jersey #23 white

unframed (NC) 1600.00

'96-97 Bulls Champ. jersey #23 black

framed (NC) 1700.00

'96-97 Bulls Champ. jersey #23 black

unframed (NC) 1500.00

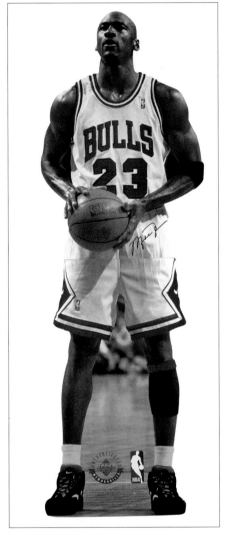

MICHAEL JORDAN

MICHAEL JORDAN

MICHAEL JORDAN

'96-97 Bulls Champ. jersey #23 red
  framed (NC) 1700.00
'96-97 Bulls Champ. jersey #23 red
  unframed (NC) 1500.00
'96-97 Bulls Champ. jersey #23 white
  framed (NC) 1700.00
'96-97 Bulls Champ. jersey #23 white
  unframed (NC) 1500.00
'97-98 Bulls Nike jersey #23 black
  unframed 1500.00
'97-98 Bulls Nike jersey #23 white
  unframed 1500.00
'97-98 Bulls Nike jersey #23 red
  unframed 1500.00
Bulls 72-10 Champ. jersey black
  framed/72 (NC) 5500.00
Birmingham Barons jersey framed/
  250* (NC) 3000.00
Birmingham Barons jersey unframed/
  250* (NC) 2800.00
Mr. June red jersey framed/423* (NC) . . .2400.00
Mr. June white jersey framed/423 (NC) . .2700.00
Retro jersey w/84-85 design framed/
  50 (NC) 6250.00
Space Jam jersey unframed/50 (NC) 4000.00

UDA Michael Jordan Photos

8x10 baseball photo framed (NC) 450.00
8x10 baseball photo unframed (NC) 400.00
8x10 photo 'first game back' unframed . . .400.00
8x10 photo 1988 Slam Dunk Contest
  framed 550.00
8x10 photo 1988 Slam Dunk Contest
  unframed 500.00
8x10 photo Jumpman unframed/500 (NC) 400.00
8x10 photo Midair Slam unframed/
  1200 (NC) 500.00
8x10 photo screaming dunk unframed/
  300 (NC) 500.00
8x10 photo UNC 17 Seconds
  unframed (NC) 500.00
8x10 photo United Center unframed 400.00
16x20 '88 Slam Dunk photo framed/
  1000* (NC) 850.00

16x20 '88 Slam Dunk photo unframed/
  1000* (NC) 800.00
16x20 photo '97 Champs framed/230 . .1000.00
16x20 photo Crying w/Trophy framed . . .850.00
16x20 photo Crying w/Trophy unframed . .800.00
16x20 photo 'flying' framed (NC) 850.00
16x20 photo 'flying' unframed (NC) 800.00
16x20 photo Golf framed/230 (NC) 1200.00
16x20 photo Jumpman framed/300 . . . .1200.00
16x20 photo Lefty Slam framed/300 . . .1200.00
16x20 photo Midair Slam framed/
  300 (NC) 1200.00
16x20 photo The Dish framed/300 . . . . .1200.00
16x20 photo UNC dunk framed (NC) 850.00
16x20 photo UNC dunk unframed (NC) . .800.00
16x20 photo UNC 17 Seconds framed/7
  50* (NC) 850.00
16x20 photo UNC 17 Seconds unframed/
  750* (NC) 800.00
'95-96 Cham.Seas. Photo Coll.Framed/
  72 (NC) 1000.00
Mr. June photo Coll. w/letter #1/423 (NC)1500.00
Mr. June photo collection w/letter #2/4231100.00

UDA Michael Jordan Other

5x7 photo w/replica floor piece/72 (NC) 1000.00
1996 SPx Record Breaker card/250 (NC) 1000.00
72-win basketball/72 (NC) 1500.00
Black baseball bat/500 (NC) 1500.00
Chicago stad.floor w/8x10 framed/
  1000 (NC) 1300.00
Danny Day litho/197 (NC) 2000.00
Hand painted basketball/200 (NC) 1600.00
'I'm Back' basketball/1995 . . . . .1300.00
Indoor/outdoor basketball (NC) 800.00
Leather 'basketball/baseball'/1000 (NC) . .700.00
Mr. June black basketball w/logo/
  423 (NC) 1500.00
Nike 'Wings' 12x36 poster framed/
  500 (NC) 800.00
'Rare Air' Auto'd Book w/linen sleeve/
  2500 (NC) 500.00
SI Cover 'Star is Born' 12/10/84
  framed (NC) 600.00

White Sox cap/250 (NC) 500.00

Wilson baseball (NC) 450.00

Wilson Jet basketball 1000.00

UDA Dan Marino Helmets

Dan the Man auth.mini helmet/343 . . . . . .225.00

Dan the Man Proline helmet/343 . . . . . . .500.00

Dolphins authentic mini helmet 200.00

Dolphins Mini Helmet (replica) 150.00

Full Size Replica Dolphins Helmet 300.00

Official Dolphins Helmet 500.00

Shadow box w/mini helmet and 5x7/500 .350.00

UDA Dan Marino Jerseys

Aqua replica jersey unframed 250.00

Dan the Man aqua jersey framed/343 . . . .650.00

Dan the Man white jersey unframed/343 .450.00

Dolphins '94 throwback jersey framed . . .450.00

Dolphins '94 throwback jersey unframed . .350.00

Dolphins aqua jersey framed 400.00

Dolphins aqua jersey unframed 300.00

Dolphins white jersey framed 400.00

Dolphins white jersey unframed 300.00

Fan collection: jersey/ball etc/75 (NC) . .1000.00

UDA Dan Marino Photos

8x10 photo 300 TD unframed 100.00

8x10 photo 343rd TD pass unframed 100.00

8x10 photo completion record/500 . . . . . .75.00

8x10 photo mud bowl unframed 100.00

8x10 photo U of Pittsburgh framed 100.00

8x10 photo U of Pittsburgh unframed 75.00

16x20 40000 yds photo framed 225.00

16x20 40000 yds photo unframed 175.00

16x20 photo framed/500* (NC) 225.00

16x20 photo unframed/500* (NC) 175.00

Dan the Man photo collection/343 . . . . . .700.00

UDA Joe Montana Helmets

Kansas City authentic mini helmet 150.00

Kansas City replica full size helmet 200.00

Kansas City replica mini helmet 125.00

Notre Dame authentic mini helmet 150.00

Notre Dame full size helmet w/display 450.00

Notre Dame replica mini helmet 125.00

Official Kansas City Helmet 350.00

Official SF Helmet 450.00

San Francisco authentic mini helmet/1995 200.00

San Francisco replica full size helmet 275.00

San Francisco replica mini helmet 150.00

Shadow box w/mini helmet and 8x10/500 300.00

Super Joe authentic mini helmet/416 . . . .200.00

Super Joe Proline full size helmet/416 . . . .450.00

UDA Joe Montana Jerseys

Kansas City '94 throwback jersey framed . .325.00

Kansas City '94 throwback jersey unframed 225.00

Kansas City red jersey framed 300.00

Kansas City red jersey unframed 200.00

Kansas City white jersey framed 300.00

Kansas City white jersey unframed 200.00

Notre Dame blue jersey framed 450.00

Notre Dame blue jersey unframed 350.00

Retirement Jersey white #/49 . . . . .900.00

Retirement Jersey red #/49 . . . . .900.00

San Francisco red jersey framed 400.00

San Francisco red jersey unframed 325.00

Super Joe red jersey framed w/Patch/416 .500.00

Super Joe white jersey unframed w/Patch/

416 . . . . .300.00

UDA Joe Montana Photos

8x10 Notre Dame photo w/letter/116 . . . .100.00

8x10 photo ND green jersey unframed 80.00

8x10 photo ND Taking Snap unframed 90.00

8x10 photo 'Super Bowl Hero' framed 125.00

8x10 photo 'Super Bowl Hero' Unframed . .80.00

8x10 photo w/letter/250 . . . . .100.00

8x10 Tunnel Walk photo unframed 80.00

8x10 warmup photo unframed 75.00

16x20 ND blue jersey photo framed 250.00

16x20 ND Taking Snap photo unframed . .150.00

16x20 photo Chiefs debut framed (NC) . . .225.00

16x20 photo Chiefs debut unframed (NC) .150.00

16x20 photo Dropping Back framed/500* 225.00

MICHAEL JORDAN

16x20 photo Dropping Back unframed/
500* 150.00

16x20 SF photo framed/500* (NC) 250.00

16x20 SF photo unframed/500* (NC) 175.00

16x20 Tunnel Walk photo framed 250.00

16x20 Tunnel Walk photo unframed 175.00

Super Joe photo collection w/letter/416 . .650.00

UDA Wayne Gretzky Jerseys

802 Commem. Kings jersey framed/
1000* 1000.00

802 Commem. Kings jersey unframed/
1000* 750.00

Blues blue jersey unframed (NC) 600.00

Blues white jersey unframed (NC) 700.00

Edmonton blue jersey unframed 500.00

Great One Edmonton white jersey/499 . . .800.00

Kings white jersey framed 650.00

Kings white jersey unframed 550.00

Olympic jersey #/99 . . . . .1200.00

Rangers third jersey unframed 600.00

Rangers white jersey unframed 500.00

Rangers white jersey framed 650.00

'Tour '94' 99ers jersey unframed/999 (NC) 750.00

UDA Wayne Gretzky Photos

8x10 Kings photo unframed 100.00

8x10 photo 802 Goal unframed 90.00

8x10 photo St. Louis First Game unframed .90.00

8x10 photo w/letter/199 . . . . .110.00

8x10 Rangers photo (3rd jersey)/250 . . . . .90.00

8x10 Rangers photo profile/200 . . . . .90.00

8x10 Rangers photo unframed/250 . . . . . .90.00

8x10 Stanley Cup photo unframed 90.00

16x20 Kings horiz.photo framed/300* (NC)200.00

16x20 Kings horiz.photo unframed/
300* (NC) 125.00

16x20 Kings ice spray photo framed/1000*200.00

16x20 Kings ice spray photo unframed/
1000* 125.00

16x20 Kings vert.photo framed/300* (NC) 200.00

16x20 Kings vert.photo unframed/
300* (NC) 125.00

16x20 Oilers photo 'Flying' framed 275.00

16x20 Oilers photo 'Flying' unframed 175.00

16x20 photo 802 Goal framed/802* (NC) .300.00

16x20 photo 802 Goal unframed/
802* (NC) 200.00

16x20 photo Rangers framed/250 . . . . . .225.00

16x20 photo Stanley Cup framed/99 . . . .250.00

Great One Photo Collection w/Letter/499 .650.00

UDA Wayne Gretzky Pucks

'97 All-Star puck/250 . . . . .160.00

801/802 Gretzky/Howe pucks
w/display (NC) 250.00

'Best Ever' Gretzky/Howe pucks w/display 200.00

Blues puck 125.00

Great One Easton blade and puck/499 . . .325.00

Kings puck 100.00

Mini shadow box w/puck and 5x7/99 . . . .400.00

Puck and blowup card framed (NC) 200.00

Rangers puck 125.00

UDA Wayne Gretzky Other

802 commemorative cap/99 (NC) 140.00

Campbell Conf. AS UD sheet/500 (NC) 65.00

Danny Day litho/880 . . . . .500.00

Easton 'Silver Tip' stick 300.00

First Kings litho w/o ticket framed/
500 (NC) 160.00

First Kings litho with ticket framed/
500 (NC) 225.00

Kings white helmet (NC) 200.00

Kings white helmet w/display (NC) 250.00

Pair of Easton gloves/350 (NC) 400.00

Rangers cap/199 . . . . .120.00

Rangers white helmet 250.00

Salvino Kings figurine/1400 (NC) 500.00

SI Great Guns cover framed 130.00

Woody Woodpecker cel framed/250* (NC) 700.00

Woody Woodpecker cel unframed/
250* (NC) 600.00

Arnold Schwarzenegger, actor

COLLECTING CELEBRITY AUTOGRAPHS

The popularity of acquiring celebrity autographs continues to grow. More people each year are discovering not only the fun to be had in this hobby, but also the value of autographs as an investment. Just take a look through a trade publication such as Autograph Collector magazine; you will see hundreds of advertisements for celebrity-autographed memorabilia, covering a wide range of prices. The value assigned to any particular item is determined by several factors:

- whether the celebrity is alive or dead;
- current popularity of this person;
- any historical significance;
- type of item (photo, contract, bank check, etc.);
- condition of item;
- rarity of this person's signature.

Of course, the old saying, "the worth of a thing is the price it will bring" certainly applies to autographed items. A collector determined to own a certain piece might be quite willing to pay more than its "book value," therefore, many dealers hold regular auction sales in order to get the maximum price for their wares. This is supply and demand in its simplest form, and many times there are bargains to be found at autograph auctions also.

So how do you get started collecting celebrity autographs? There are a few ways to go about it.

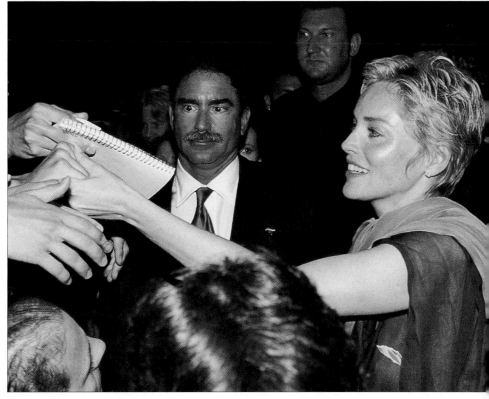

Sharon Stone, actress

BY SCOTT JOHNSON

The easiest way is to find a reputable dealer and buy your autographed items from him. This is also the most expensive method and not usually the first choice for many collectors. If the celebrity whose autograph you want is no longer alive, contacting a dealer is a good option.

Another method, and certainly the most exciting one, is to get the autograph in person directly from the celebrity. I am never in an airport without a Sharpie marker and a few 3 x 5 index cards; you never know who you might happen to see. If you live in or near a large city, I guarantee there are celebrities coming and going constantly. There are films in production, musical concerts, book signings, theatrical performances and many other events that draw famous

Paula Abdul, singer

people; you just have to be in the right place at the right time. Of course, common sense should dictate how you approach someone in public (it is rude to interrupt someone's meal in a restaurant no matter how big a fan you are).

The method I use most often is to write to the celebrity and request that he or she send me a signed photo by mail. A brief complimentary letter, accompanied by a large (9 x 12) return stamped envelope, can yield great results. Many celebrities do respond to such requests by sending an autographed 8 x 10 photo of themselves. I prefer this method because the investment is low, and the potential return is very high.

Some celebrities respond to through-the-mail requests by sending a photo with a preprinted (non-authentic) signature. When this happens to me, I send that celebrity an unsigned

Ray Liotta, actor

8 x 10 photo to sign and return; the result many times has been an authentic autograph (and it is on the photo that I chose to send). This has also worked for me when a celebrity does not respond to mail at all. I wrote to Jodie Foster several times and got nothing; I sent her a photo (a scene from her incredible movie

"Nell"), and it came back two weeks later, personally autographed to me.

Another method I like to use for difficult-to-get celebrities is to write to them when they are performing in a play. Many actors and actresses perform occasionally on Broadway, and I write care of the theater. One of my favorite actresses, Natalie Portman, is almost impossible to get by mail. She recently starred in the Broadway production "The Diary of Anne Frank," and I now have three signed photos and a signed Playbill as a result of writing to her there.

Famous people are not limited to those you see on television or in the movies. Politicians will always respond with a signed photo, though the signature is not usually authentic. A writer is usually willing to sign a copy of his or her book (Stephen King gets so many requests that he keeps track and only signs two items per person). Country music stars are also notorious for being accessible to fans, and will usually happily sign autographs by mail or in person. I love writing to cartoonists and getting an original signed sketch. I have original drawings of Dennis the Menace, Marmaduke, and several other familiar faces from the funny pages (a genuine autographed

Robert DeNiro, actor

work of art, for the cost of a postage stamp). I have also written to people who are "brief" newsmakers: I contacted the McCaugheys (the couple in Iowa who had the septuplets) when they were in the spotlight, and they both signed a newspaper article for me.

For most celebrities, popularity is not constant over a lifetime. The key is to contact the person either before he or she is immensely popular, or after the popularity has peaked. I wrote to Leonardo DiCaprio in April of 1997, and he sent me a signed photo. Now, with the success of "Titanic" propelling him to superstardom, a response by mail is not too likely (could you respond to all of your mail if you received 50,000 letters per month?). An example from the other side is Phyllis Diller. Years ago, she was seen regularly on prime-time television specials and enjoyed a very successful career as a come-

Claudia Schiffer, supermodel

dienne. Now retired, she has more free time and is happy to sign autographs for anyone who requests one.

Starting your own autograph collection is easy. Get a good list of celebrity addresses and decide which celebrities to go after first. Send out your request letters and before long you will be on your way to enjoying this great hobby. ▪

Jack Nicholson, actor

All prices are for autographed 8 x 10s.

JIMMY CARTER, POLITICIAN

SEAN CONNERY, ACTOR

Abdul, Paula 40

Abraham, F.Murray 40

Ackroyd, Dan 35

Adams, Bryan 50

Agnew, Spiro 50

Aiello, Danny 25

Alda, Alan 35

Alexander, Jason 35

Allen, Tim 40

Allen, Woody 35

Alley, Kirstie 35

Amick, Madchen 30

Anderson, Gillian 40

Anderson, Loni 25

Anderson Lee, Pamela 50

Anderson, Richard Dean 35

Andress, Ursula 40

Andrews, Julie 30

Aniston, Jennifer 40

Anwar, Gabrielle 25

Applegate, Christina 40

Archer, Anne 35

Arnold, Tom 25

Arquette, Patricia 35

Arquette, Rosanna 35

Asner, Ed 25

Assante, Armand 25

Atkins, Chet 25

Atkinson, Rowan 30

Autry, Gene 50

Aykroyd, Dan 25

Bacall, Lauren 25

Bacon, Kevin 35

Baldwin, Alec 35

Baldwin, Stephen 35

Baldwin, William 35

Bancroft, Anne 30

Banderas, Antonio 40

Banks, Tyra 35

Barr, Roseane 40

Barrymore, Drew 50

Basinger, Kim 50

Basset, Angela 40

Beatty, Ned 20

Beatty, Warren 50

Berenger, Tom 30

Bergen, Candice 35

Berkeley, Elizabeth 35

Bernard, Crystal 25

Berry, Chuck 75

Berry, Halle 35

Binoche, Juliette 30

Bisset, Jacqueline 30

Black, Clint 35

Bleeth, Yasmine 40

Bolton, Michael 50

Bono .60

Bowie, David 75

Boyle, Lara Flynn 25

Braxton, Toni 40

Bridges, Jeff 30

Brinkley, Christie 35

Broderick, Matthew 40

Bronson, Charles 25

Brooks, Garth 50

Brooks, Mel 25

Brosnan, Pierce 40

Buffet, Jimmy 40

Bullock, Sandra	.50	Cox, Courtney	.40
Burton, Tim	.40	Crawford, Cindy	.40
Bush, George	.75	Crawford, Michael	.25
Caan, James	.25	Crow, Sheryl	.40
Cage, Nicholas	.40	Cruise, Tom	.75
Cain, Dean	.40	Crystal, Billy	.30
Caine, Michael	.30	Culkin, Macauley	.30
Cameron, James	.35	Curtis, Jamie Lee	.50
Campbell, Naomi	.35	Curtis, Tony	.25
Campbell, Neve	.40	D'Errico, Donna	.30
Carey, Drew	.25	Dalton, Timothy	.40
Carey, Mariah	.60	Damon, Matt	.40
Carlisle, Belinda	.30	Dane, Taylor	.40
Carrere, Tia	.30	Danes, Claire	.40
Carrey, Jim	.40	Dangerfield, Rodney	.25
Carson, Johnny	.30	Daniels, Jeff	.35
Carter, Jimmy	.75	Danson, Ted	.25
Caruso, David	.30	Danza, Tony	.25
Carvey, Dana	.30	Davis, Geena	.35
Cates, Phoebe	.40	Degeneres, Ellen	.35
Chan, Jackie	.40	Delaney, Dana	.35
Charles, Ray	.75	DeMornay, Rebecca	.35
Chase, Chevy	.40	Dempsey, Patrick	.35
Cher	.40	DeNiro, Robert	.75
Clapton, Eric	.75	Depp, Johnny	.40
Clinton, Bill	.250	Derek, Bo	.35
Clooney, George	.40	Dern, Laura	.30
Close, Glenn	.30	DeVito, Danny	.30
Connery, Sean	.75	Diamond, Neil	.50
Connick Jr., Harry	.30	Diaz, Cameron	.40
Cooper, Alice	.50	DiCaprio, Leonardo	.50
Copperfield, David	.25	Dillon, Matt	.35
Coppola, Francis Ford	.25	Dion, Celine	.40
Cosby, Bill	.35	Doherty, Shannon	.35
Costner, Kevin	.40	Dole, Bob	.35

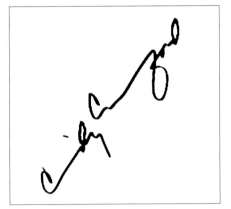

CINDY CRAWFORD,
SUPERMODEL

LEONARDO DiCAPRIO, ACTOR

Elizabeth Taylor, actor

Domino, Fats	.25	Garth, Jenny	.35
Donahue, Phil	.25	Gates, Bill	.100
Douglas, Kirk	.25	Gellar, Sarah Michelle	.50
Douglas, Michael	.50	Gere, Richard	.60
Downey, Robert Jr.	.40	Gibson, Mel	.75
Drescher, Fran	.35	Gill, Vince	.30
Dreyfuss, Richard	.35	Glenn, John	.75
Dreyfuss, Julia Louise	.35	Glover, Danny	.35
Duchovny, David	.50	Goldberg, Whoopi	.35
Duffy, Patrick	.25	Goldblum, Jeff	.35
Dunaway, Faye	.30	Gooding, Cuba Jr.	.40
Duvall, Robert	.30	Goodman, John	.35
Eastwood, Clint	.60	Gore, Al	.45
Electra, Carmen	.40	Grammer, Kelsey	.30
Elliott, Sam	.30	Grant, Hugh	.40
Estevez, Emilio	.35	Griffith, Andy	.50
Ethridge, Melissa	.50	Griffith, Melanie	.50
Fairchild, Morgan	.35	Hackman, Gene	.40
Faustino, David	.35	Hall, Anthony Michael	.35
Fawcett, Farrah	.40	Hall, Arsenio	.35
Field, Sally	.25	Hamilton, Linda	.40
Fishburne, Lawrence	.35	Hanks, Tom	.50
Fisher, Carrie	.35	Harrelson, Woody	.35
Fonda, Bridget	.40	Harris, Ed	.40
Fonda, Jane	.40	Hasselhoff, David	.35
Ford, Gerald	.50	Hatcher, Teri	.40
Ford, Harrison	.75	Hawke, Ethan	.40
Foster, Jodie	.75	Hawn, Goldie	.35
Fox, Michael J.	.40	Heston, Charlton	.20
Frakes, Johnathan	.25	Hill, Faith	.40
Fraser, Brendan	.25	Hirsch, Judd	.20
Freeman, Morgan	.35	Hoffman, Dustin	.50
Fuentes, Daisy	.40	Hogan, Paul	.25
Funicello, Annette	.50	Holly, Lauren	.35
Garcia, Andy	.35	Hope, Bob	.60

MICHAEL JACKSON, SINGER

DAVID DUCHOVNY /
GILLIAN ANDERSON, ACTORS

JENNY MCCARTHY, MODEL

CHARLIE SHEEN, ACTOR

Hopper, Dennis	.40
Howard, Ron	.35
Hunt, Helen	.50
Hunter, Holly	.40
Hunter, Rachel	.30
Hurley, Elizabeth	.35
Ireland, Kathy	.35
Ironside, Michael	.20
Jackson, Janet	.75
Jackson, Michael	.150
Jackson, Samuel L.	.40
Jaggar, Mick	.125
Jewel	.40
Joel, Billy	.50
John, Elton	.75
Jones, Catherine Zeta	.40
Jones, James Earl	.25
Jones, Jenny	.25
Jones, Tommy Lee	.40
Judd, Ashley	.40
Keaton, Diane	.40
Keaton, Michael	.35
Kelly, Gene	.75
Kidman, Nicole	.60
Kilmer, Val	.50
King, Stephen	.100
Kinnear, Greg	.35
Kissinger, Henry	.25
Kudrow, Lisa	.35
Lake, Ricki	.25
Lange, Jessica	.35
Larroquette, John	.25
Leary, Dennis	.30
LeBlanc, Matt	.40
Lee, Spike	.30

Lemmon, Jack	.25
Leno, Jay	.25
Leoni, Tea	.40
Letterman, David	.40
Liotta, Ray	.35
Lithgow, John	.25
Locklear, Heather	.40
Lopez, Jennifer	.40
Lords, Traci	.40
Loren, Sophia	.25
Loughlin, Lori	.25
Love, Courtney	.25
Lovitz, Jon	.25
Lucas, George	.50
Macdowell, Andie	.35
Macpherson, Elle	.40
Madonna	.175
Margulies, Julianna	.35
Martin, Steve	.25
McCarthy, Jenny	.40
McCartney, Paul	.200
McConaughey, Matthew	.40
McEntire, Reba	.35
McGraw, Tim	.35
McGregor, Ewan	.40
Midler, Bette	.75
Milano, Alyssa	.35
Minelli, Liza	.40
Moore, Demi	.75
Moore, Dudley	.25
Moore, Julianne	.40
Moore, Mary Tyler	.40
Morgan, Lorrie	.35
Murphy, Eddie	.40
Morissette, Alanis	.50

CELEBRITIES PRICE GUIDE

Murray, Bill	.40	Redford, Robert	.125
Myers, Mike	.40	Reeves, Keanu	.40
Neeson, Liam	.40	Reeves, Christopher	.125
Newman, Paul	.125	Reiser, Paul	.40
Newton, Wayne	.25	Reynolds, Debbie	.20
Nicholson, Jack	.40	Ricci, Christina	.35
Nicks, Stevie	.60	Roberts, Julia	.75
Nielson, Leslie	.20	Rogers, Mimi	.40
Nolin, Gena Lee	.35	Rose, Axl	.60
Nolte, Nick	.30	Russell, Kurt	.40
Norris, Chuck	.30	Russo, Rene	.40
Novak, Kim	.40	Ryan, Meg	.60
O'Donnell, Chris	.40	Ryder, Wynona	.60
Osborne, Joan	.40	Sandler, Adam	.40
Pacino, Al	.60	Sarandon, Susan	.30
Palance, Jack	.40	Schiffer, Claudia	.30
Paltrow, Gwyneth	.40	Schwarzenegger, Arnold	.75
Patric, Jason	.35	Schwimmer, David	.30
Paxton, Bill	.35	Seagal, Steven	.50
Penn, Sean	.40	Seinfeld, Jerry	.40
Perkins, Elizabeth	.25	Selleck, Tom	.30
Perry, Luke	.25	Seymour, Jane	.40
Perry, Matthew	.35	Shatner, William	.40
Pesci, Joe	.40	Sheen, Charlie	.35
Petty, Lori	.30	Sheen, Martin	.25
Pfeiffer, Michelle	.125	Shepard, Cybill	.30
Pitt, Brad	.50	Shields, Brooke	.35
Powell, Colin	.40	Shore, Pauly	.35
Presley, Lisa Marie	.40	Short, Martin	.25
Presley, Priscilla	.50	Shue, Elizabeth	.40
Pullman, Bill	.35	Silverstone, Alicia	.50
Quaid, Dennis	.35	Sinise, Gary	.25
Quaid, Randy	.35	Slater, Christian	.40
Quayle, Dan	.40	Smith, Anna Nicole	.25
Quinn, Anthony	.30	Smith, Will	.40

STEVEN SPIELBERG, DIRECTOR

CARRIE FISHER, ACTOR

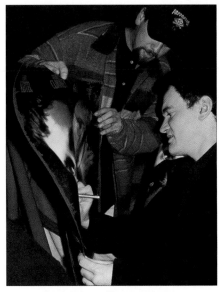

**QUENTIN TARANTINO,
DIRECTOR/ACTOR**

BILLY BOB THORNTON, ACTOR

GWYNETH PALTROW, ACTOR

Smits, Jimmy .25

Snipes, Wesley 40

Sorbo, Kevin .40

Sorvino, Mira 40

Sorvino, Paul 25

Spacey, Kevin 40

Spelling, Tori 25

Spielberg, Steven 50

Springsteen, Bruce 75

Stallone, Sylvester 75

Stefani, Gwen 50

Stern, Howard 40

Stewart, Patrick 40

Steward, Rod 40

Sting 50

Stone, Sharon 60

Streisand, Barbara 150

Sutherland, Keifer 35

Swanson, Kristy 35

Swayze, Patrick 35

Tarantino, Quentin 30

Taylor, Elizabeth 200

Thiessen, Tiffany Amber 40

Thomas, Jonathan Taylor 35

Thompson, Emma 40

Thornton, Billy Bob 35

Tillis, Pam 35

Tilly, Jennifer 40

Tilly, Meg 30

Tomei, Marisa 30

Travolta, John 40

Turner, Tina .50

Twain, Shania 40

Tyler, Liv 40

Van Damme, Jean Claude 40

Van Halen, Eddie 60

Washington, Denzel 40

Wayans, Damon 35

Wayans, Keenan Ivory 35

Westheimer, Dr Ruth 25

White, Bryan 35

Wilder, Gene 25

Williams, Robin 30

Willis, Bruce 50

Winfrey, Oprah 40

Winslet, Kate 75

Yearwood, Trisha 35

Yoakum, Dwight 30

Young, Neil .50

Young, Sean 35

Zane, Billy 35

Zellweger, Rene 40

The following price guide lists key autographed cards from various manufacturers in several sports. All prices were compiled in a joint effort by a staff of full-time expert Beckett Publications analysts and independent contributors.

Abbreviations: MT-Mint condition; NRMT- Near Mint condition; EXC-Excellent condition; VG-Very Good condition.

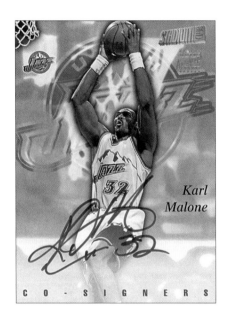

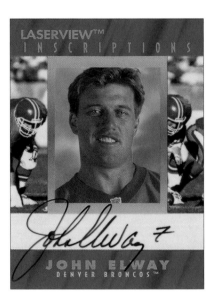

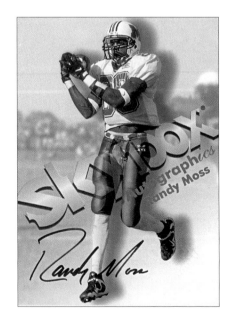

1935 Pebble Beach

COMPLETE SET (7) 2000.00

This seven-card extremely rare set features sepia tinted photos with autographs of players from the San Francisco-Oakland Bay Area Coast League minor league teams printed on postcard size cards. The set was offered on an evening sports show on radio station KYA in Oakland, sponsored by Pebble Beach clothier. The cards were issued periodically, and a collector could obtain them by sending in his name to the station when each new card was announced. The cards are unnumbered and checklisted below in alphabetical order. All cards seen in the marketplace have been signed in fountain pen ink.

	EX-MT	VG-E	GOOD
1935 Pebble Beach COMMON CARD (1-7)	100.00		
1935 Pebble Beach Leroy Anton	100.00	45.00	12.50
1935 Pebble Beach Joe DiMaggio	1500.00	700.00	190.00
1935 Pebble Beach Wee Ludolph	100.00	45.00	12.50
1935 Pebble Beach Walter Mails	100.00	45.00	12.50
1935 Pebble Beach Lefty O'Doul	250.00	110.00	31.00
1935 Pebble Beach Gabby Street	100.00	45.00	12.50
1935 Pebble Beach Oscar Vitt MG	100.00	45.00	12.50

1993 Pinnacle DiMaggio Autographs

COMPLETE SET (5) 1500.00   700.00   190.00

Joe DiMaggio personally signed a total of 9,000 cards, and one autographed card from this five-card set was randomly inserted in selected 30-card boxed 1993 Pinnacle Joe DiMaggio hobby sets. These five autographed cards are slightly smaller (narrower) than standard size and feature white-bordered black-and-white action shots from DiMaggio's career that place special emphasis on the skills that made him great. DiMaggio's signature appears below the photo within the wide white lower margin.

	MINT	NRMT	EXC
1993 Pinnacle DiMaggio Autographs COMMON CARD (1-5)	300.00	135.00	38.00
1993 Pinnacle DiMaggio Autographs Spring 1936	300.00	135.00	38.00
1993 Pinnacle DiMaggio Autographs Joltin' Joe	300.00	135.00	38.00
1993 Pinnacle DiMaggio Autographs The Streak	300.00	135.00	38.00
1993 Pinnacle DiMaggio Autographs Opening Day	300.00	135.00	38.00
1993 Pinnacle DiMaggio Autographs Ebbets Field	300.00	135.00	38.00

1994 Upper Deck All-Time Heroes Autographs

COMPLETE SET (4) 600.00   275.00   75.00

These four autograph cards were inserted one every 385 packs into the All-Time Heroes packs. Three players signed 1,000 cards while George Brett signed 2,000 cards since Nolan Ryan did not sign the 1,000 cards he had been expected to sign for this product. Each card came with a certification of authenticity on the back and could be registered with Upper Deck upon receipt.

	MINT	NRMT	EXC
1994 Upper Deck All-Time Heroes COMMON CARD	75.00	34.00	9.50
1994 Upper Deck All-Time Heroes Autographs George Brett	125.00	55.00	15.50
1994 Upper Deck All-Time Heroes Autographs Reggie Jackson	100.00	45.00	12.50
1994 Upper Deck All-Time Heroes Autographs Mickey Mantle	350.00	160.00	45.00
1994 Upper Deck All-Time Heroes Autographs Tom Seaver	75.00	34.00	9.50

1995 Upper Deck Autographs

COMPLETE SET (5) 250.00   110.00   31.00

Trade cards to redeem these autographed issues were randomly seeded into second series packs. The actual signed cards share the same front design as the basic issue 1995 Upper Deck cards. The cards were issued along with a card signed in fascimile by Brain Burr of Upper Deck along with instructions on how to register these cards.

	MINT	NRMT	EXC
1995 Upper Deck Autographs COMMON CARD	30.00	13.50	3.70
1995 Upper Deck Autographs Roger Clemens	60.00	27.00	7.50
1995 Upper Deck Autographs Reggie Jackson	40.00	18.00	5.00
1995 Upper Deck Autographs Willie Mays	100.00	45.00	12.50
1995 Upper Deck Autographs Raul Mondesi	30.00	13.50	3.70
1995 Upper Deck Autographs Frank Robinson	40.00	18.00	5.00

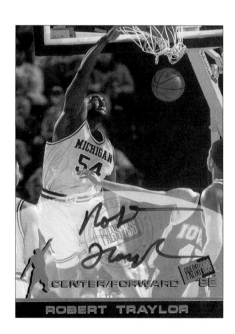

1996 Leaf Signature Autographs

COMPLETE SET (251) 2200.00   1000.00   275.00

Inserted into 1996 Leaf Signature Series first series packs, these unnumbered cards were one of the first major autograph issues featured in an MLB-licensed trading card set. First series packs contained at least one autograph, with the chance of getting more. Donruss/Leaf reports that all but 10 players in the Leaf Signature Series signed close to 5,000 total autographs (3,500 bronze, 1,000 silver, 500 gold). The 10 players who signed 1,000 (700 bronze, 200 silver, 100 gold) are: Roberto Alomar, Wade Boggs, Derek Jeter, Kenny Lofton, Paul Molitor, Raul Mondesi, Manny Ramirez, Alex Rodriguez, Frank Thomas and Mo Vaughn. It's also important to note that six additional players did not submit their cards in time to be included in first series packs. Thus, their cards were thrown into Extended series packs. Those six players are as follows: Brian L.Hunter, Carlos Delgado, Phil Plantier, Jim Thome, Terrell Wade and Ernie Young. Thome signed only silver and gold foil cards, thus the Bronze set is considered complete at 251 cards. Prices below refer exclusively to Bronze versions. Blue and black ink variations have been found for Carlos Delgado, Alex Rodriguez and Michael Tucker. No consistent premiums for these variations has been tracked. Finally, an autographed jumbo silver foil version of the Frank Thomas card was distributed to dealers in March, 1997. Dealers received either this first series or the Extended Series jumbo Thomas for every Extended Series case ordered. Each Thomas jumbo is individually serial numbered to 1,500.

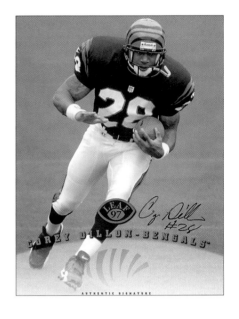

	MINT	NRMT	EXC
1996 Leaf Signature Autographs COMMON CARD (1-251)	3.00	1.35	.35
1996 Leaf Signature Autographs COMMON SILVER (1-251)	4.00	1.80	.50
1996 Leaf Signature Autographs COMMON GOLD (1-251)	5.00	2.20	.60
1996 Leaf Signature Autographs Kurt Abbott	3.00	1.35	.35
1996 Leaf Signature Autographs Juan Acevedo	3.00	1.35	.35
1996 Leaf Signature Autographs Terry Adams	3.00	1.35	.35
1996 Leaf Signature Autographs Manny Alexander	3.00	1.35	.35
1996 Leaf Signature Autographs Roberto Alomar SP	120.00	55.00	15.00
1996 Leaf Signature Autographs Moises Alou	8.00	3.60	1.00
1996 Leaf Signature Autographs Wilson Alvarez	3.00	1.35	.35
1996 Leaf Signature Autographs Garret Anderson	8.00	3.60	1.00
1996 Leaf Signature Autographs Shane Andrews	3.00	1.35	.35
1996 Leaf Signature Autographs Andy Ashby	3.00	1.35	.35
1996 Leaf Signature Autographs Pedro Astacio	3.00	1.35	.35
1996 Leaf Signature Autographs Brad Ausmus	3.00	1.35	.35
1996 Leaf Signature Autographs Bobby Ayala	3.00	1.35	.35
1996 Leaf Signature Autographs Carlos Baerga	3.00	1.35	.35
1996 Leaf Signature Autographs Harold Baines	8.00	3.60	1.00
1996 Leaf Signature Autographs Jason Bates	3.00	1.35	.35
1996 Leaf Signature Autographs Allen Battle	3.00	1.35	.35
1996 Leaf Signature Autographs Rich Becker	3.00	1.35	.35
1996 Leaf Signature Autographs David Bell	3.00	1.35	.35
1996 Leaf Signature Autographs Rafael Belliard	3.00	1.35	.35
1996 Leaf Signature Autographs Andy Benes	8.00	3.60	1.00
1996 Leaf Signature Autographs Armando Benitez	3.00	1.35	.35
1996 Leaf Signature Autographs Jason Bere	3.00	1.35	.35
1996 Leaf Signature Autographs Geronimo Berroa	3.00	1.35	.35
1996 Leaf Signature Autographs Willie Blair	3.00	1.35	.35
1996 Leaf Signature Autographs Mike Blowers	3.00	1.35	.35
1996 Leaf Signature Autographs Wade Boggs SP	200.00	90.00	25.00
1996 Leaf Signature Autographs Ricky Bones	3.00	1.35	.35
1996 Leaf Signature Autographs Mike Bordick	3.00	1.35	.35
1996 Leaf Signature Autographs Toby Borland	3.00	1.35	.35
1996 Leaf Signature Autographs Ricky Bottalico	3.00	1.35	.35
1996 Leaf Signature Autographs Darren Bragg	3.00	1.35	.35
1996 Leaf Signature Autographs Jeff Branson	3.00	1.35	.35
1996 Leaf Signature Autographs Tilson Brito	3.00	1.35	.35
1996 Leaf Signature Autographs Rico Brogna	3.00	1.35	.35
1996 Leaf Signature Autographs Scott Brosius	3.00	1.35	.35
1996 Leaf Signature Autographs Damon Buford	3.00	1.35	.35
1996 Leaf Signature Autographs Mike Busby	3.00	1.35	.35
1996 Leaf Signature Autographs Tom Candiotti	3.00	1.35	.35
1996 Leaf Signature Autographs Frank Castillo	3.00	1.35	.35
1996 Leaf Signature Autographs Andujar Cedeno	3.00	1.35	.35
1996 Leaf Signature Autographs Domingo Cedeno	3.00	1.35	.35
1996 Leaf Signature Autographs Roger Cedeno	3.00	1.35	.35
1996 Leaf Signature Autographs Norm Charlton	3.00	1.35	.35
1996 Leaf Signature Autographs Jeff Cirillo	8.00	3.60	1.00

1996 Leaf Signature Autographs Will Clark	20.00	9.00	2.50
1996 Leaf Signature Autographs Jeff Conine	8.00	3.60	1.00
1996 Leaf Signature Autographs Steve Cooke	3.00	1.35	.35
1996 Leaf Signature Autographs Joey Cora	8.00	3.60	1.00
1996 Leaf Signature Autographs Marty Cordova	8.00	3.60	1.00
1996 Leaf Signature Autographs Rheal Cormier	3.00	1.35	.35
1996 Leaf Signature Autographs Felipe Crespo	3.00	1.35	.35
1996 Leaf Signature Autographs Chad Curtis	3.00	1.35	.35
1996 Leaf Signature Autographs Johnny Damon	8.00	3.60	1.00
1996 Leaf Signature Autographs Russ Davis	3.00	1.35	.35
1996 Leaf Signature Autographs Andre Dawson	15.00	6.75	1.85
1996 Leaf Signature Autographs Carlos Delgado	8.00	3.60	1.00
1996 Leaf Signature Autographs Doug Drabek	3.00	1.35	.35
1996 Leaf Signature Autographs Darren Dreifort	3.00	1.35	.35
1996 Leaf Signature Autographs Shawon Dunston	3.00	1.35	.35
1996 Leaf Signature Autographs Ray Durham	3.00	1.35	.35
1996 Leaf Signature Autographs Jim Edmonds	15.00	6.75	1.85
1996 Leaf Signature Autographs Joey Eischen	3.00	1.35	.35
1996 Leaf Signature Autographs Jim Eisenreich	3.00	1.35	.35
1996 Leaf Signature Autographs Sal Fasano	3.00	1.35	.35
1996 Leaf Signature Autographs Jeff Fassero	3.00	1.35	.35
1996 Leaf Signature Autographs Alex Fernandez	3.00	1.35	.35
1996 Leaf Signature Autographs Darrin Fletcher	3.00	1.35	.35
1996 Leaf Signature Autographs Chad Fonville	3.00	1.35	.35
1996 Leaf Signature Autographs Kevin Foster	3.00	1.35	.35
1996 Leaf Signature Autographs John Franco	8.00	3.60	1.00
1996 Leaf Signature Autographs Julio Franco	3.00	1.35	.35
1996 Leaf Signature Autographs Marvin Freeman	3.00	1.35	.35
1996 Leaf Signature Autographs Travis Fryman	8.00	3.60	1.00
1996 Leaf Signature Autographs Gary Gaetti	3.00	1.35	.35
1996 Leaf Signature Autographs Carlos Garcia	3.00	1.35	.35
1996 Leaf Signature Autographs Jason Giambi	8.00	3.60	1.00
1996 Leaf Signature Autographs Benji Gil	3.00	1.35	.35
1996 Leaf Signature Autographs Greg Gohr	3.00	1.35	.35
1996 Leaf Signature Autographs Chris Gomez	3.00	1.35	.35
1996 Leaf Signature Autographs Leo Gomez	3.00	1.35	.35
1996 Leaf Signature Autographs Tom Goodwin	3.00	1.35	.35
1996 Leaf Signature Autographs Mike Grace	3.00	1.35	.35
1996 Leaf Signature Autographs Mike Greenwell	3.00	1.35	.35
1996 Leaf Signature Autographs Rusty Greer	12.00	5.50	1.50
1996 Leaf Signature Autographs Mark Grudzielanek	8.00	3.60	1.00
1996 Leaf Signature Autographs Mark Gubicza	3.00	1.35	.35
1996 Leaf Signature Autographs Juan Guzman	3.00	1.35	.35
1996 Leaf Signature Autographs Darryl Hamilton	3.00	1.35	.35
1996 Leaf Signature Autographs Joey Hamilton	8.00	3.60	1.00
1996 Leaf Signature Autographs Chris Hammond	3.00	1.35	.35
1996 Leaf Signature Autographs Mike Hampton	3.00	1.35	.35
1996 Leaf Signature Autographs Chris Haney	3.00	1.35	.35
1996 Leaf Signature Autographs Todd Haney	3.00	1.35	.35
1996 Leaf Signature Autographs Erik Hanson	3.00	1.35	.35
1996 Leaf Signature Autographs Pete Harnisch	3.00	1.35	.35
1996 Leaf Signature Autographs LaTroy Hawkins	3.00	1.35	.35
1996 Leaf Signature Autographs Charlie Hayes	3.00	1.35	.35
1996 Leaf Signature Autographs Jimmy Haynes	3.00	1.35	.35
1996 Leaf Signature Autographs Roberto Hernandez	3.00	1.35	.35
1996 Leaf Signature Autographs Bobby Higginson	8.00	3.60	1.00
1996 Leaf Signature Autographs Glenallen Hill	3.00	1.35	.35
1996 Leaf Signature Autographs Ken Hill	3.00	1.35	.35
1996 Leaf Signature Autographs Sterling Hitchcock	3.00	1.35	.35
1996 Leaf Signature Autographs Trevor Hoffman	3.00	1.35	.35
1996 Leaf Signature Autographs Dave Hollins	3.00	1.35	.35
1996 Leaf Signature Autographs Dwayne Hosey	3.00	1.35	.35
1996 Leaf Signature Autographs Thomas Howard	3.00	1.35	.35
1996 Leaf Signature Autographs Steve Howe	3.00	1.35	.35

1996 Leaf Signature Autographs John Hudek	3.00	1.35	.35
1996 Leaf Signature Autographs Rex Hudler	3.00	1.35	.35
1996 Leaf Signature Autographs Brian L. Hunter	8.00	3.60	1.00
1996 Leaf Signature Autographs Butch Huskey	8.00	3.60	1.00
1996 Leaf Signature Autographs Mark Hutton	3.00	1.35	.35
1996 Leaf Signature Autographs Jason Jacome	3.00	1.35	.35
1996 Leaf Signature Autographs John Jaha	3.00	1.35	.35
1996 Leaf Signature Autographs Reggie Jefferson	3.00	1.35	.35
1996 Leaf Signature Autographs Derek Jeter SP	175.00	80.00	22.00
1996 Leaf Signature Autographs Bobby Jones	3.00	1.35	.35
1996 Leaf Signature Autographs Todd Jones	3.00	1.35	.35
1996 Leaf Signature Autographs Brian Jordan	8.00	3.60	1.00
1996 Leaf Signature Autographs Kevin Jordan	3.00	1.35	.35
1996 Leaf Signature Autographs Jeff Juden	3.00	1.35	.35
1996 Leaf Signature Autographs Ron Karkovice	3.00	1.35	.35
1996 Leaf Signature Autographs Roberto Kelly	3.00	1.35	.35
1996 Leaf Signature Autographs Mark Kiefer	3.00	1.35	.35
1996 Leaf Signature Autographs Brooks Kieschnick	8.00	3.60	1.00
1996 Leaf Signature Autographs Jeff King	3.00	1.35	.35
1996 Leaf Signature Autographs Mike Lansing	3.00	1.35	.35
1996 Leaf Signature Autographs Matt Lawton	12.00	5.50	1.50
1996 Leaf Signature Autographs Al Leiter	3.00	1.35	.35
1996 Leaf Signature Autographs Mark Leiter	3.00	1.35	.35
1996 Leaf Signature Autographs Curtis Leskanic	3.00	1.35	.35
1996 Leaf Signature Autographs Darren Lewis	3.00	1.35	.35
1996 Leaf Signature Autographs Mark Lewis	3.00	1.35	.35
1996 Leaf Signature Autographs Felipe Lira	3.00	1.35	.35
1996 Leaf Signature Autographs Pat Listach	3.00	1.35	.35
1996 Leaf Signature Autographs Keith Lockhart	3.00	1.35	.35
1996 Leaf Signature Autographs Kenny Lofton SP	100.00	45.00	12.50
1996 Leaf Signature Autographs John Mabry	3.00	1.35	.35
1996 Leaf Signature Autographs Mike Macfarlane	3.00	1.35	.35
1996 Leaf Signature Autographs Kirt Manwaring	3.00	1.35	.35
1996 Leaf Signature Autographs Al Martin	3.00	1.35	.35
1996 Leaf Signature Autographs Norberto Martin	3.00	1.35	.35
1996 Leaf Signature Autographs Dennis Martinez	8.00	3.60	1.00
1996 Leaf Signature Autographs Pedro Martinez	25.00	11.00	3.10
1996 Leaf Signature Autographs Sandy Martinez	3.00	1.35	.35
1996 Leaf Signature Autographs Mike Matheny	3.00	1.35	.35
1996 Leaf Signature Autographs T.J. Mathews	3.00	1.35	.35
1996 Leaf Signature Autographs David McCarty	3.00	1.35	.35
1996 Leaf Signature Autographs Ben McDonald	3.00	1.35	.35
1996 Leaf Signature Autographs Pat Meares	3.00	1.35	.35
1996 Leaf Signature Autographs Orlando Merced	3.00	1.35	.35
1996 Leaf Signature Autographs Jose Mesa	3.00	1.35	.35
1996 Leaf Signature Autographs Matt Mieske	3.00	1.35	.35
1996 Leaf Signature Autographs Orlando Miller	3.00	1.35	.35
1996 Leaf Signature Autographs Mike Mimbs	3.00	1.35	.35
1996 Leaf Signature Autographs Paul Molitor SP	100.00	45.00	12.50
1996 Leaf Signature Autographs R.Mondesi SP Bronze	80.00	36.00	10.00
1996 Leaf Signature Autographs Jeff Montgomery	3.00	1.35	.35
1996 Leaf Signature Autographs Mickey Morandini	3.00	1.35	.35
1996 Leaf Signature Autographs Lyle Mouton	3.00	1.35	.35
1996 Leaf Signature Autographs James Mouton	3.00	1.35	.35
1996 Leaf Signature Autographs Jamie Moyer	3.00	1.35	.35
1996 Leaf Signature Autographs Rodney Myers	3.00	1.35	.35
1996 Leaf Signature Autographs Denny Neagle	12.00	5.50	1.50
1996 Leaf Signature Autographs Robb Nen	3.00	1.35	.35
1996 Leaf Signature Autographs Marc Newfield	3.00	1.35	.35
1996 Leaf Signature Autographs Dave Nilsson	3.00	1.35	.35
1996 Leaf Signature Autographs Jon Nunnally	3.00	1.35	.35
1996 Leaf Signature Autographs Chad Ogea	3.00	1.35	.35
1996 Leaf Signature Autographs Troy O'Leary	3.00	1.35	.35
1996 Leaf Signature Autographs Rey Ordonez	8.00	3.60	1.00

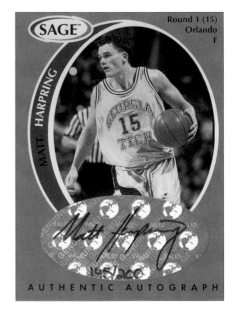

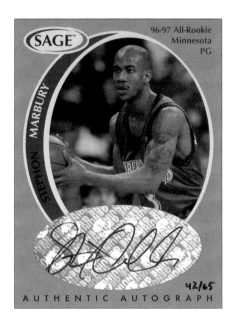

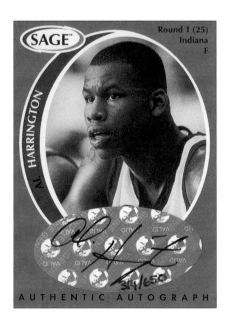

1996 Leaf Signature Autographs Jayhawk Owens	3.00	1.35	.35
1996 Leaf Signature Autographs Tom Pagnozzi	3.00	1.35	.35
1996 Leaf Signature Autographs Dean Palmer	3.00	1.35	.35
1996 Leaf Signature Autographs Roger Pavlik	3.00	1.35	.35
1996 Leaf Signature Autographs Troy Percival	3.00	1.35	.35
1996 Leaf Signature Autographs Carlos Perez	3.00	1.35	.35
1996 Leaf Signature Autographs Robert Perez	3.00	1.35	.35
1996 Leaf Signature Autographs Andy Pettitte	20.00	9.00	2.50
1996 Leaf Signature Autographs Phil Plantier	3.00	1.35	.35
1996 Leaf Signature Autographs Mike Potts	3.00	1.35	.35
1996 Leaf Signature Autographs Curtis Pride	3.00	1.35	.35
1996 Leaf Signature Autographs Ariel Prieto	3.00	1.35	.35
1996 Leaf Signature Autographs Bill Pulsipher	3.00	1.35	.35
1996 Leaf Signature Autographs Brad Radke	8.00	3.60	1.00
1996 Leaf Signature Autographs Manny Ramirez SP	50.00	22.00	6.25
1996 Leaf Signature Autographs Joe Randa	3.00	1.35	.35
1996 Leaf Signature Autographs Pat Rapp	3.00	1.35	.35
1996 Leaf Signature Autographs Bryan Rekar	3.00	1.35	.35
1996 Leaf Signature Autographs Shane Reynolds	3.00	1.35	.35
1996 Leaf Signature Autographs Arthur Rhodes	3.00	1.35	.35
1996 Leaf Signature Autographs Mariano Rivera	12.00	5.50	1.50
1996 Leaf Signature Autographs Alex Rodriguez SP	250.00	110.00	31.00
1996 Leaf Signature Autographs Frank Rodriguez	3.00	1.35	.35
1996 Leaf Signature Autographs Mel Rojas	3.00	1.35	.35
1996 Leaf Signature Autographs Ken Ryan	3.00	1.35	.35
1996 Leaf Signature Autographs Bret Saberhagen	3.00	1.35	.35
1996 Leaf Signature Autographs Tim Salmon	20.00	9.00	2.50
1996 Leaf Signature Autographs Rey Sanchez	3.00	1.35	.35
1996 Leaf Signature Autographs Scott Sanders	3.00	1.35	.35
1996 Leaf Signature Autographs Steve Scarsone	3.00	1.35	.35
1996 Leaf Signature Autographs Curt Schilling	8.00	3.60	1.00
1996 Leaf Signature Autographs Jason Schmidt	8.00	3.60	1.00
1996 Leaf Signature Autographs David Segui	3.00	1.35	.35
1996 Leaf Signature Autographs Kevin Seitzer	3.00	1.35	.35
1996 Leaf Signature Autographs Scott Servais	3.00	1.35	.35
1996 Leaf Signature Autographs Don Slaught	3.00	1.35	.35
1996 Leaf Signature Autographs Zane Smith	3.00	1.35	.35
1996 Leaf Signature Autographs Paul Sorrento	3.00	1.35	.35
1996 Leaf Signature Autographs Scott Stahoviak	3.00	1.35	.35
1996 Leaf Signature Autographs Mike Stanley	3.00	1.35	.35
1996 Leaf Signature Autographs Terry Steinbach	3.00	1.35	.35
1996 Leaf Signature Autographs Kevin Stocker	3.00	1.35	.35
1996 Leaf Signature Autographs Jeff Suppan	8.00	3.60	1.00
1996 Leaf Signature Autographs Bill Swift	3.00	1.35	.35
1996 Leaf Signature Autographs Greg Swindell	3.00	1.35	.35
1996 Leaf Signature Autographs Kevin Tapani	3.00	1.35	.35
1996 Leaf Signature Autographs Danny Tartabull	3.00	1.35	.35
1996 Leaf Signature Autographs Julian Tavarez	3.00	1.35	.35
1996 Leaf Signature Autographs Frank Thomas SP	200.00	90.00	25.00
1996 Leaf Signature Autographs Ozzie Timmons	3.00	1.35	.35
1996 Leaf Signature Autographs Michael Tucker	8.00	3.60	1.00
1996 Leaf Signature Autographs Ismael Valdes	8.00	3.60	1.00
1996 Leaf Signature Autographs Jose Valentin	3.00	1.35	.35
1996 Leaf Signature Autographs Todd Van Poppel	3.00	1.35	.35
1996 Leaf Signature Autographs Mo Vaughn SP	100.00	45.00	12.50
1996 Leaf Signature Autographs Quilvio Veras	3.00	1.35	.35
1996 Leaf Signature Autographs Fernando Vina	3.00	1.35	.35
1996 Leaf Signature Autographs Joe Vitiello	3.00	1.35	.35
1996 Leaf Signature Autographs Jose Vizcaino	3.00	1.35	.35
1996 Leaf Signature Autographs Omar Vizquel	8.00	3.60	1.00
1996 Leaf Signature Autographs Terrell Wade	3.00	1.35	.35
1996 Leaf Signature Autographs Paul Wagner	3.00	1.35	.35
1996 Leaf Signature Autographs Matt Walbeck	3.00	1.35	.35
1996 Leaf Signature Autographs Jerome Walton	3.00	1.35	.35

1996 Leaf Signature Autographs Turner Ward	3.00	1.35	.35
1996 Leaf Signature Autographs Allen Watson	3.00	1.35	.35
1996 Leaf Signature Autographs David Weathers	3.00	1.35	.35
1996 Leaf Signature Autographs Walt Weiss	3.00	1.35	.35
1996 Leaf Signature Autographs Turk Wendell	3.00	1.35	.35
1996 Leaf Signature Autographs Rondell White	8.00	3.60	1.00
1996 Leaf Signature Autographs Brian Williams	3.00	1.35	.35
1996 Leaf Signature Autographs George Williams	3.00	1.35	.35
1996 Leaf Signature Autographs Paul Wilson	3.00	1.35	.35
1996 Leaf Signature Autographs Bobby Witt	3.00	1.35	.35
1996 Leaf Signature Autographs Bob Wolcott	3.00	1.35	.35
1996 Leaf Signature Autographs Eric Young	3.00	1.35	.35
1996 Leaf Signature Autographs Ernie Young	3.00	1.35	.35
1996 Leaf Signature Autographs Greg Zaun	3.00	1.35	.35
1996 Leaf Signature Autographs F.Thomas Jumbo AU	80.00	36.00	10.00

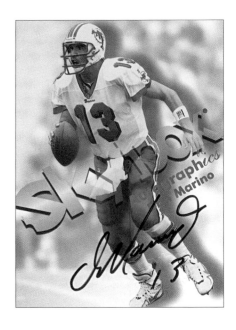

1996 Leaf Signature Autographs Gold

COMPLETE SET (252) 4000.00   1800.00   500.00

Randomly inserted primarily in first series packs, this 252-card set is parallel to the regular set and is similar in design with the exception of the gold foil printing on each card front. Each player signed 500 cards, except for the SP's of which only 100 of each are signed. Jim Thome erroneously signed 514 Gold cards.

	MINT	NRMT	EXC
1996 Leaf Signature Autographs Gold COMMON (1-252)	8.00	3.60	1.00
1996 Leaf Signature Autographs Gold 2.5X to X BRONZE CARDS			
1996 Leaf Signature Autographs Gold Raul Mondesi SP	120.00	55.00	15.00
1996 Leaf Signature Autographs Gold Jim Thome SP514	80.00	36.00	10.00

1996 Leaf Signature Extended Autographs

COMPLETE SET (217) 2500.00   1100.00   300.00

At least two autographed cards from this 217-card set were inserted in every Extended Series pack. Super Packs with four autographed cards were seeded one in every 12 packs. Most players signed 5000 cards, but short prints (500-2500 of each) do exist. On average, one in every nine packs contains a short print. All short print cards are individually noted below. By mistake, Andruw Jones, Ryan Klesko, Andy Pettitte, Kirby Puckett and Frank Thomas signed a few hundred of each of their cards in blue ink instead of black. No difference in price has been noted. Also, the Juan Gonzalez, Andruw Jones and Alex Rodriguez cards available in packs were not signed. All three cards had information on the back on how to mail them into Donruss/Leaf for an actual signed version. The deadline to exchange these cards was December 31st, 1998. In addition, middle relievers Doug Creek and Steve Parris failed to sign all 5000 of their cards. Creek submitted 1,950 cards and Parris submitted 1,800. Finally, an autographed jumbo version of the Extended Series Frank Thomas card was distributed to dealers in March, 1997. Dealers received either this card or the first series jumbo Thomas for every Extended Series case ordered. Each Extended Thomas jumbo is individually serial numbered to 1,500.

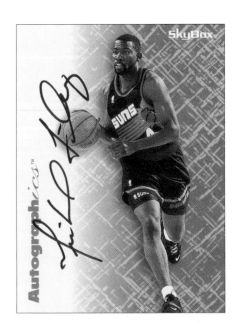

	MINT	NRMT	EXC
1996 Leaf Signature Extended Autographs COMMON (1-217)	4.00	1.80	.50
1996 Leaf Signature Extended Autographs Scott Aldred	4.00	1.80	.50
1996 Leaf Signature Extended Autographs Mike Aldrete	4.00	1.80	.50
1996 Leaf Signature Extended Autographs Rich Amaral	4.00	1.80	.50
1996 Leaf Signature Extended Autographs Alex Arias	4.00	1.80	.50
1996 Leaf Signature Extended Autographs Paul Assenmacher	4.00	1.80	.50
1996 Leaf Signature Extended Autographs Roger Bailey	4.00	1.80	.50
1996 Leaf Signature Extended Autographs Erik Bennett	4.00	1.80	.50
1996 Leaf Signature Extended Autographs Sean Bergman	4.00	1.80	.50
1996 Leaf Signature Extended Autographs Doug Bochtler	4.00	1.80	.50
1996 Leaf Signature Extended Autographs Tim Bogar	4.00	1.80	.50
1996 Leaf Signature Extended Autographs Pat Borders	4.00	1.80	.50
1996 Leaf Signature Extended Autographs Pedro Borbon	4.00	1.80	.50
1996 Leaf Signature Extended Autographs Shawn Boskie	4.00	1.80	.50
1996 Leaf Signature Extended Autographs Rafael Bournigal	4.00	1.80	.50
1996 Leaf Signature Extended Autographs Mark Brandenburg	4.00	1.80	.50
1996 Leaf Signature Extended Autographs John Briscoe	4.00	1.80	.50
1996 Leaf Signature Extended Autographs Jorge Brito	4.00	1.80	.50
1996 Leaf Signature Extended Autographs Doug Brocail	4.00	1.80	.50
1996 Leaf Signature Extended Autographs Jay Buhner SP1000	30.00	13.50	3.70

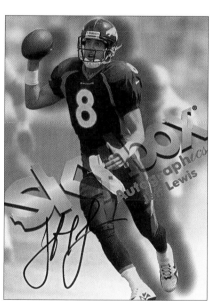

1996 Leaf Signature Extended Autographs Scott Bullett . . . . 4.00   1.80   .50
1996 Leaf Signature Extended Autographs Dave Burba . . . . 4.00   1.80   .50
1996 Leaf Signature Extended Ken Caminiti SP1000 . . . . 40.00   18.00   5.00
1996 Leaf Signature Extended Autographs John Cangelosi . . . . 4.00   1.80   .50
1996 Leaf Signature Extended Autographs Cris Carpenter . . . . 4.00   1.80   .50
1996 Leaf Signature Extended Autographs Chuck Carr . . . . 4.00   1.80   .50
1996 Leaf Signature Extended Autographs Larry Casian . . . . 4.00   1.80   .50
1996 Leaf Signature Extended Autographs Tony Castillo . . . . 4.00   1.80   .50
1996 Leaf Signature Extended Autographs Jason Christiansen . . . . 4.00   1.80   .50
1996 Leaf Signature Extended Autographs Archi Cianfrocco . . . . 4.00   1.80   .50
1996 Leaf Signature Extended Autographs Mark Clark . . . . 4.00   1.80   .50
1996 Leaf Signature Extended Autographs Terry Clark . . . . 4.00   1.80   .50
1996 Leaf Signature Extended Roger Clemens SP1000 . . . . 150.00 70.00   19.00
1996 Leaf Signature Extended Autographs Jim Converse . . . . 4.00   1.80   .50
1996 Leaf Signature Extended Autographs Dennis Cook . . . . 4.00   1.80   .50
1996 Leaf Signature Extended Autographs Francisco Cordova . . . . 4.00   1.80   .50
1996 Leaf Signature Extended Autographs Jim Corsi . . . . 4.00   1.80   .50
1996 Leaf Signature Extended Autographs Tim Crabtree . . . . 4.00   1.80   .50
1996 Leaf Signature Extended Doug Creek SP1950 . . . . 10.00   4.50   1.25
1996 Leaf Signature Extended Autographs John Cummings . . . . 4.00   1.80   .50
1996 Leaf Signature Extended Autographs Omar Daal . . . . 4.00   1.80   .50
1996 Leaf Signature Extended Autographs Rich DeLucia . . . . 4.00   1.80   .50
1996 Leaf Signature Extended Autographs Mark Dewey . . . . 4.00   1.80   .50
1996 Leaf Signature Extended Autographs Alex Diaz . . . . 4.00   1.80   .50
1996 Leaf Signature Extended Jermaine Dye SP2500 . . . . 8.00   3.60   1.00
1996 Leaf Signature Extended Autographs Ken Edenfield . . . . 4.00   1.80   .50
1996 Leaf Signature Extended Autographs Mark Eichhorn . . . . 4.00   1.80   .50
1996 Leaf Signature Extended Autographs John Ericks . . . . 4.00   1.80   .50
1996 Leaf Signature Extended Autographs Darin Erstad 40.00   18.00   5.00
1996 Leaf Signature Extended Autographs Alvaro Espinoza . . . . 4.00   1.80   .50
1996 Leaf Signature Extended Autographs Jorge Fabregas . . . . 4.00   1.80   .50
1996 Leaf Signature Extended Autographs Mike Fetters . . . . 4.00   1.80   .50
1996 Leaf Signature Extended Autographs John Flaherty . . . . 4.00   1.80   .50
1996 Leaf Signature Extended Autographs Bryce Florie . . . . 4.00   1.80   .50
1996 Leaf Signature Extended Autographs Tony Fossas . . . . 4.00   1.80   .50
1996 Leaf Signature Extended Autographs Lou Frazier . . . . 4.00   1.80   .50
1996 Leaf Signature Extended Autographs Mike Gallego . . . . 4.00   1.80   .50
1996 Leaf Signature Extended Karim Garcia SP2500 . . . . 12.00   5.50   1.50
1996 Leaf Signature Extended Autographs Jason Giambi . . . . 6.00   2.70   .75
1996 Leaf Signature Extended Autographs Ed Giovanola . . . . 4.00   1.80   .50
1996 Leaf Signature Extended Tom Glavine SP1250 . . . . 40.00   18.00   5.00
1996 Leaf Signature Extended Juan Gonzalez SP1000 . . . . 150.00 70.00   19.00
1996 Leaf Signature Extended Autographs Craig Grebeck . . . . 4.00   1.80   .50
1996 Leaf Signature Extended Autographs Buddy Groom . . . . 4.00   1.80   .50
1996 Leaf Signature Extended Autographs Kevin Gross . . . . 4.00   1.80   .50
1996 Leaf Signature Extended Autographs Eddie Guardado . . . . 4.00   1.80   .50
1996 Leaf Signature Extended Autographs Mark Guthrie . . . . 4.00   1.80   .50
1996 Leaf Signature Extended Tony Gwynn SP1000 . . . . 150.00 70.00   19.00
1996 Leaf Signature Extended Autographs Chip Hale . . . . 4.00   1.80   .50
1996 Leaf Signature Extended Autographs Darren Hall . . . . 4.00   1.80   .50
1996 Leaf Signature Extended Autographs Lee Hancock . . . . 4.00   1.80   .50
1996 Leaf Signature Extended Autographs Dave Hansen . . . . 4.00   1.80   .50
1996 Leaf Signature Extended Autographs Bryan Harvey . . . . 4.00   1.80   .50
1996 Leaf Signature Extended Autographs Bill Haselman . . . . 4.00   1.80   .50
1996 Leaf Signature Extended Autographs Mike Henneman . . . . 4.00   1.80   .50
1996 Leaf Signature Extended Autographs Doug Henry . . . . 4.00   1.80   .50
1996 Leaf Signature Extended Autographs Gil Heredia . . . . 4.00   1.80   .50
1996 Leaf Signature Extended Autographs Carlos Hernandez . . . . 4.00   1.80   .50
1996 Leaf Signature Extended Autographs Jose Hernandez . . . . 4.00   1.80   .50
1996 Leaf Signature Extended Autographs Darren Holmes . . . . 4.00   1.80   .50
1996 Leaf Signature Extended Autographs Mark Holzemer . . . . 4.00   1.80   .50
1996 Leaf Signature Extended Autographs Rick Honeycutt . . . . 4.00   1.80   .50
1996 Leaf Signature Extended Autographs Chris Hook . . . . 4.00   1.80   .50
1996 Leaf Signature Extended Autographs Chris Howard . . . . 4.00   1.80   .50

1996 Leaf Signature Extended Autographs Jack Howell . . . . 4.00   1.80   .50
1996 Leaf Signature Extended Autographs David Hulse . . . . 4.00   1.80   .50
1996 Leaf Signature Extended Autographs Edwin Hurtado . . . . 4.00   1.80   .50
1996 Leaf Signature Extended Autographs Jeff Huson . . . . 4.00   1.80   .50
1996 Leaf Signature Extended Autographs Mike James . . . . 4.00   1.80   .50
1996 Leaf Signature Extended Autographs Derek Jeter SP1000 . . . . 150.00   70.00   19.00
1996 Leaf Signature Extended Autographs Brian Johnson . . . . 4.00   1.80   .50
1996 Leaf Signature Extended Randy Johnson SP1000 . . . . 60.00   27.00   7.50
1996 Leaf Signature Extended Autographs Mark Johnson . . . . 4.00   1.80   .50
1996 Leaf Signature Extended Andruw Jones SP2000 . . . . 60.00   27.00   7.50
1996 Leaf Signature Extended Autographs Chris Jones . . . . 4.00   1.80   .50
1996 Leaf Signature Extended Autographs Ricky Jordan . . . . 4.00   1.80   .50
1996 Leaf Signature Extended Autographs Matt Karchner . . . . 4.00   1.80   .50
1996 Leaf Signature Extended Autographs Scott Karl . . . . 4.00   1.80   .50
1996 Leaf Signature Extended Jason Kendall SP2500 . . . . 25.00   11.00   3.10
1996 Leaf Signature Extended Autographs Brian Keyser . . . . 4.00   1.80   .50
1996 Leaf Signature Extended Autographs Mike Kingery . . . . 4.00   1.80   .50
1996 Leaf Signature Extended Autographs Wayne Kirby . . . . 4.00   1.80   .50
1996 Leaf Signature Extended Ryan Klesko SP1000 . . . . 25.00   11.00   3.10
1996 Leaf Signature Extended Chuck Knoblauch SP1000 . . . . 50.00   22.00   6.25
1996 Leaf Signature Extended Autographs Chad Kreuter . . . . 4.00   1.80   .50
1996 Leaf Signature Extended Autographs Tom Lampkin . . . . 4.00   1.80   .50
1996 Leaf Signature Extended Autographs Scott Leius . . . . 4.00   1.80   .50
1996 Leaf Signature Extended Autographs Jon Lieber . . . . 4.00   1.80   .50
1996 Leaf Signature Extended Autographs Nelson Liriano . . . . 4.00   1.80   .50
1996 Leaf Signature Extended Autographs Scott Livingstone . . . . 4.00   1.80   .50
1996 Leaf Signature Extended Autographs Graeme Lloyd . . . . 4.00   1.80   .50
1996 Leaf Signature Extended Kenny Lofton SP1000 . . . . 60.00   27.00   7.50
1996 Leaf Signature Extended Autographs Luis Lopez . . . . 4.00   1.80   .50
1996 Leaf Signature Extended Autographs Torey Lovullo . . . . 4.00   1.80   .50
1996 Leaf Signature Extended Greg Maddux SP500 . . . . 400.00   180.00   50.00
1996 Leaf Signature Extended Autographs Mike Maddux . . . . 4.00   1.80   .50
1996 Leaf Signature Extended Autographs Dave Magadan . . . . 4.00   1.80   .50
1996 Leaf Signature Extended Autographs Mike Magnante . . . . 4.00   1.80   .50
1996 Leaf Signature Extended Autographs Joe Magrane . . . . 4.00   1.80   .50
1996 Leaf Signature Extended Autographs Pat Mahomes . . . . 4.00   1.80   .50
1996 Leaf Signature Extended Autographs Matt Mantei . . . . 4.00   1.80   .50
1996 Leaf Signature Extended Autographs John Marzano . . . . 4.00   1.80   .50
1996 Leaf Signature Extended Autographs Terry Mathews . . . . 4.00   1.80   .50
1996 Leaf Signature Extended Autographs Chuck McElroy . . . . 4.00   1.80   .50
1996 Leaf Signature Extended Fred McGriff SP1000 . . . . 40.00   18.00   5.00
1996 Leaf Signature Extended Autographs Mark McLemore . . . . 4.00   1.80   .50
1996 Leaf Signature Extended Autographs Greg McMichael . . . . 4.00   1.80   .50
1996 Leaf Signature Extended Autographs Blas Minor . . . . 4.00   1.80   .50
1996 Leaf Signature Extended Autographs Dave Mlicki . . . . 4.00   1.80   .50
1996 Leaf Signature Extended Autographs Mike Mohler . . . . 4.00   1.80   .50
1996 Leaf Signature Extended Paul Molitor SP1000 . . . . 80.00   36.00   10.00
1996 Leaf Signature Extended Autographs Steve Montgomery . . . . 4.00   1.80   .50
1996 Leaf Signature Extended Autographs Mike Mordecai . . . . 4.00   1.80   .50
1996 Leaf Signature Extended Autographs Mike Morgan . . . . 4.00   1.80   .50
1996 Leaf Signature Extended Autographs Mike Munoz . . . . 4.00   1.80   .50
1996 Leaf Signature Extended Autographs Greg Myers . . . . 4.00   1.80   .50
1996 Leaf Signature Extended Autographs Jimmy Myers . . . . 4.00   1.80   .50
1996 Leaf Signature Extended Autographs Mike Myers . . . . 4.00   1.80   .50
1996 Leaf Signature Extended Autographs Bob Natal . . . . 4.00   1.80   .50
1996 Leaf Signature Extended Autographs Dan Naulty . . . . 4.00   1.80   .50
1996 Leaf Signature Extended Autographs Jeff Nelson . . . . 4.00   1.80   .50
1996 Leaf Signature Extended Autographs Warren Newson . . . . 4.00   1.80   .50
1996 Leaf Signature Extended Autographs Chris Nichting . . . . 4.00   1.80   .50
1996 Leaf Signature Extended Autographs Melvin Nieves . . . . 4.00   1.80   .50
1996 Leaf Signature Extended Autographs Charlie O'Brien . . . . 4.00   1.80   .50
1996 Leaf Signature Extended Autographs Alex Ochoa . . . . 4.00   1.80   .50
1996 Leaf Signature Extended Autographs Omar Olivares . . . . 4.00   1.80   .50
1996 Leaf Signature Extended Autographs Joe Oliver . . . . 4.00   1.80   .50

1996 Leaf Signature Extended Autographs Lance Painter	4.00	1.80	.50
1996 Leaf Signature Extended Rafael Palmeiro SP2000	25.00	11.00	3.10
1996 Leaf Signature Extended Autographs Mark Parent	4.00	1.80	.50
1996 Leaf Signature Extended Steve Parris SP1800	10.00	4.50	1.25
1996 Leaf Signature Extended Autographs Bob Patterson	4.00	1.80	.50
1996 Leaf Signature Extended Autographs Tony Pena	4.00	1.80	.50
1996 Leaf Signature Extended Autographs Eddie Perez	4.00	1.80	.50
1996 Leaf Signature Extended Autographs Yorkis Perez	4.00	1.80	.50
1996 Leaf Signature Extended Autographs Robert Person	4.00	1.80	.50
1996 Leaf Signature Extended Autographs Mark Petkovsek	4.00	1.80	.50
1996 Leaf Signature Extended Andy Pettitte SP1000	50.00	22.00	6.25
1996 Leaf Signature Extended Autographs J.R. Phillips	4.00	1.80	.50
1996 Leaf Signature Extended Autographs Hipolito Pichardo	4.00	1.80	.50
1996 Leaf Signature Extended Autographs Eric Plunk	4.00	1.80	.50
1996 Leaf Signature Extended Autographs Jimmy Poole	4.00	1.80	.50
1996 Leaf Signature Extended Kirby Puckett SP1000	120.00	55.00	15.00
1996 Leaf Signature Extended Autographs Paul Quantrill	4.00	1.80	.50
1996 Leaf Signature Extended Autographs Tom Quinlan	4.00	1.80	.50
1996 Leaf Signature Extended Autographs Jeff Reboulet	4.00	1.80	.50
1996 Leaf Signature Extended Autographs Jeff Reed	4.00	1.80	.50
1996 Leaf Signature Extended Autographs Steve Reed	4.00	1.80	.50
1996 Leaf Signature Extended Autographs Carlos Reyes	4.00	1.80	.50
1996 Leaf Signature Extended Autographs Bill Risley	4.00	1.80	.50
1996 Leaf Signature Extended Autographs Kevin Ritz	4.00	1.80	.50
1996 Leaf Signature Extended Autographs Kevin Roberson	4.00	1.80	.50
1996 Leaf Signature Extended Autographs Rich Robertson	4.00	1.80	.50
1996 Leaf Signature Extended Alex Rodriguez SP500	300.00	135.00	38.00
1996 Leaf Signature Extended Ivan Rodriguez SP1250	80.00	36.00	10.00
1996 Leaf Signature Extended Autographs Bruce Ruffin	4.00	1.80	.50
1996 Leaf Signature Extended Autographs Juan Samuel	4.00	1.80	.50
1996 Leaf Signature Extended Autographs Tim Scott	4.00	1.80	.50
1996 Leaf Signature Extended Autographs Kevin Sefcik	4.00	1.80	.50
1996 Leaf Signature Extended Autographs Jeff Shaw	4.00	1.80	.50
1996 Leaf Signature Extended Autographs Danny Sheaffer	4.00	1.80	.50
1996 Leaf Signature Extended Autographs Craig Shipley	4.00	1.80	.50
1996 Leaf Signature Extended Autographs Dave Silvestri	4.00	1.80	.50
1996 Leaf Signature Extended Autographs Aaron Small	4.00	1.80	.50
1996 Leaf Signature Extended John Smoltz SP1000	30.00	13.50	3.70
1996 Leaf Signature Extended Autographs Luis Sojo	4.00	1.80	.50
1996 Leaf Signature Extended Sammy Sosa SP1000	150.00	70.00	19.00
1996 Leaf Signature Extended Autographs Steve Sparks	4.00	1.80	.50
1996 Leaf Signature Extended Autographs Tim Spehr	4.00	1.80	.50
1996 Leaf Signature Extended Autographs Russ Springer	4.00	1.80	.50
1996 Leaf Signature Extended Autographs Matt Stairs	4.00	1.80	.50
1996 Leaf Signature Extended Autographs Andy Stankiewicz	4.00	1.80	.50
1996 Leaf Signature Extended Autographs Mike Stanton	4.00	1.80	.50
1996 Leaf Signature Extended Autographs Kelly Stinnett	4.00	1.80	.50
1996 Leaf Signature Extended Autographs Doug Strange	4.00	1.80	.50
1996 Leaf Signature Extended Autographs Mark Sweeney	4.00	1.80	.50
1996 Leaf Signature Extended Autographs Jeff Tabaka	4.00	1.80	.50
1996 Leaf Signature Extended Autographs Jesus Tavarez	4.00	1.80	.50
1996 Leaf Signature Extended Frank Thomas SP1000	150.00	70.00	19.00
1996 Leaf Signature Extended Autographs Larry Thomas	4.00	1.80	.50
1996 Leaf Signature Extended Autographs Mark Thompson	4.00	1.80	.50
1996 Leaf Signature Extended Autographs Mike Timlin	4.00	1.80	.50
1996 Leaf Signature Extended Autographs Steve Trachsel	4.00	1.80	.50
1996 Leaf Signature Extended Autographs Tom Urbani	4.00	1.80	.50
1996 Leaf Signature Extended Autographs Julio Valera	4.00	1.80	.50
1996 Leaf Signature Extended Autographs Dave Valle	4.00	1.80	.50
1996 Leaf Signature Extended William VanLandingham	4.00	1.80	.50
1996 Leaf Signature Extended Autographs Mo Vaughn SP1000	80.00	36.00	10.00
1996 Leaf Signature Extended Autographs Dave Veres	4.00	1.80	.50
1996 Leaf Signature Extended Autographs Ed Vosberg	4.00	1.80	.50
1996 Leaf Signature Extended Autographs Don Wengert	4.00	1.80	.50

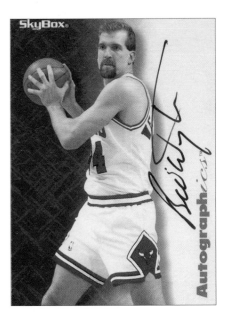

	MINT	NRMT	EXC
1996 Leaf Signature Extended Autographs Matt Whiteside	4.00	1.80	.50
1996 Leaf Signature Extended Autographs Bob Wickman	4.00	1.80	.50
1996 Leaf Signature Extended Matt Williams SP1250	30.00	13.50	3.70
1996 Leaf Signature Extended Autographs Mike Williams	4.00	1.80	.50
1996 Leaf Signature Extended Autographs Woody Williams	4.00	1.80	.50
1996 Leaf Signature Extended Autographs Craig Worthington	4.00	1.80	.50
1996 Leaf Signature Extended F.Thomas Jumbo AU	80.00	36.00	10.00

1996 Leaf Signature Extended Autographs Century Marks

	MINT	NRMT	EXC
COMPLETE SET (31)	3500.00	1600.00	450.00

Randomly inserted exclusively into Extended Series packs, cards from this 31-card parallel set feature a selection of star and rising young prospect players taken from the more comprehensive 217-card Extended Autograph set. The cards differ by a special blue holographic foil treatment. Only 100 of each card exists. In addition, Juan Gonzalez, Derek Jeter, Andruw Jones, Rafael Palmeiro and Alex Rodriguez did not sign the cards distributed in packs. All of these players cards had information on the back on how to mail them into Leaf/Donruss to receive a signed version.

	MINT	NRMT	EXC
1996 Leaf Sig. Extended Century Marks COMMON (1-31)	40.00	18.00	5.00
1996 Leaf Sig. Extended Autographs Century Marks Jay Buhner	80.00	36.00	10.00
1996 Leaf Sig. Extended Autographs Century Marks Ken Caminiti	100.00	45.00	12.50
1996 Leaf Sig. Extended Autographs Century Marks Roger Clemens	400.00	180.00	50.00
1996 Leaf Sig. Extended Autographs Century Marks Jermaine Dye	40.00	18.00	5.00
1996 Leaf Sig. Extended Autographs Century Marks Darin Erstad	200.00	90.00	25.00
1996 Leaf Sig. Extended Autographs Century Marks Karim Garcia	60.00	27.00	7.50
1996 Leaf Sig. Extended Autographs Century Marks Jason Giambi	60.00	27.00	7.50
1996 Leaf Sig. Extended Autographs Century Marks Tom Glavine	120.00	55.00	15.00
1996 Leaf Sig. Extended Autographs Century Marks Juan Gonzalez	400.00	180.00	50.00
1996 Leaf Sig. Extended Autographs Century Marks Tony Gwynn	400.00	180.00	50.00
1996 Leaf Sig. Extended Autographs Century Marks Derek Jeter	300.00	135.00	38.00
1996 Leaf Sig. Extended Autographs Century Marks Randy Johnson	150.00	70.00	19.00
1996 Leaf Sig. Extended Autographs Century Marks Andruw Jones	250.00	110.00	31.00
1996 Leaf Sig. Extended Autographs Century Marks Jason Kendall	100.00	45.00	12.50
1996 Leaf Sig. Extended Autographs Century Marks Ryan Klesko	60.00	27.00	7.50
1996 Leaf Sig. Extended Autographs Century Marks Chuck Knoblauch	120.00	55.00	15.00
1996 Leaf Sig. Extended Autographs Century Marks Kenny Lofton	150.00	70.00	19.00
1996 Leaf Sig. Extended Autographs Century Marks Greg Maddux	600.00	275.00	75.00
1996 Leaf Sig. Extended Autographs Century Marks Fred McGriff	100.00	45.00	12.50
1996 Leaf Sig. Extended Autographs Century Marks Paul Molitor	150.00	70.00	19.00
1996 Leaf Sig. Extended Autographs Century Marks Alex Ochoa	40.00	18.00	5.00
1996 Leaf Sig. Extended Autographs Century Marks Rafael Palmeiro	100.00	45.00	12.50
1996 Leaf Sig. Extended Autographs Century Marks Andy Pettitte	120.00	55.00	15.00
1996 Leaf Sig. Extended Autographs Century Marks Kirby Puckett	250.00	110.00	31.00
1996 Leaf Sig. Extended Autographs Century Marks Alex Rodriguez	400.00	180.00	50.00
1996 Leaf Sig. Extended Autographs Century Marks Ivan Rodriguez	200.00	90.00	25.00
1996 Leaf Sig. Extended Autographs Century Marks John Smoltz	80.00	36.00	10.00
1996 Leaf Sig. Extended Autographs Century Marks Sammy Sosa	400.00	180.00	50.00
1996 Leaf Sig. Extended Autographs Century Marks Frank Thomas	400.00	180.00	50.00
1996 Leaf Sig. Extended Autographs Century Marks Mo Vaughn	200.00	90.00	25.00
1996 Leaf Sig. Extended Autographs Century Marks Matt Williams	80.00	36.00	10.00

1997 Bowman Certified Blue Ink Autographs

	MINT	NRMT	EXC
COMPLETE SET (90)	1500.00	700.00	190.00

Randomly inserted in first and second series packs at a rate of one in 96, this 90-card set features color player photos of top prospects with blue ink autographs and printed on sturdy 16 pt. card stock with the Topps Certified Autograph Issue Stamp. The Derek Jeter blue ink and green ink versions are seeded in every 1,928 packs.

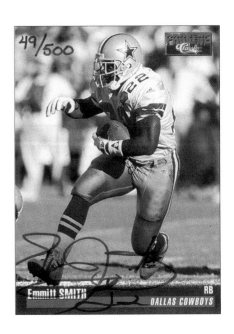

	MINT	NRMT	EXC
1997 Bowman Certified Blue Ink Autographs COMMON (1-90)	10.00	4.50	1.25
1997 Bowman Certified Blue Ink Autographs BLACK INK: .75X TO 1.5X BASIC CARDS			
1997 Bowman Certified Blue Ink Autographs BLACK STATED ODDS 1:503, ANCO 1:600			
1997 Bowman Certified Blue Ink Autographs GOLD INK: 1.5X TO 3X BASE CARDS			
1997 Bowman Certified Blue Ink Autographs GOLD: STATED ODDS 1:1509, ANCO 1:1795			
1997 Bowman Certified Blue Ink Autographs Jeff Abbott	15.00	6.75	1.85
1997 Bowman Certified Blue Ink Autographs Bob Abreu	15.00	6.75	1.85
1997 Bowman Certified Blue Ink Autographs Willie Adams	10.00	4.50	1.25

1997 Bowman Certified Blue Ink Autographs Brian Banks	10.00	4.50	1.25
1997 Bowman Certified Blue Ink Autographs Kris Benson	25.00	11.00	3.10
1997 Bowman Certified Blue Ink Autographs Darin Blood	10.00	4.50	1.25
1997 Bowman Certified Blue Ink Autographs Jaime Bluma	10.00	4.50	1.25
1997 Bowman Certified Blue Ink Autographs Kevin L. Brown	10.00	4.50	1.25
1997 Bowman Certified Blue Ink Autographs Ray Brown	10.00	4.50	1.25
1997 Bowman Certified Blue Ink Autographs Homer Bush	10.00	4.50	1.25
1997 Bowman Certified Blue Ink Autographs Mike Cameron	15.00	6.75	1.85
1997 Bowman Certified Blue Ink Autographs Jay Canizaro	10.00	4.50	1.25
1997 Bowman Certified Blue Ink Autographs Luis Castillo	15.00	6.75	1.85
1997 Bowman Certified Blue Ink Autographs Dave Coggin	10.00	4.50	1.25
1997 Bowman Certified Blue Ink Autographs Bartolo Colon	20.00	9.00	2.50
1997 Bowman Certified Blue Ink Autographs Rocky Coppinger	10.00	4.50	1.25
1997 Bowman Certified Blue Ink Autographs Jacob Cruz	10.00	4.50	1.25
1997 Bowman Certified Blue Ink Autographs Jose Cruz Jr.	60.00	27.00	7.50
1997 Bowman Certified Blue Ink Autographs Jeff D'Amico	10.00	4.50	1.25
1997 Bowman Certified Blue Ink Autographs Ben Davis	25.00	11.00	3.10
1997 Bowman Certified Blue Ink Autographs Mike Drumright	15.00	6.75	1.85
1997 Bowman Certified Blue Ink Autographs Scott Elarton	15.00	6.75	1.85
1997 Bowman Certified Blue Ink Autographs Darin Erstad	40.00	18.00	5.00
1997 Bowman Certified Blue Ink Autographs Bobby Estalella	15.00	6.75	1.85
1997 Bowman Certified Blue Ink Autographs Joe Fontenot	15.00	6.75	1.85
1997 Bowman Certified Blue Ink Autographs Tom Fordham	15.00	6.75	1.85
1997 Bowman Certified Blue Ink Autographs Brad Fullmer	25.00	11.00	3.10
1997 Bowman Certified Blue Ink Autographs Chris Fussell	10.00	4.50	1.25
1997 Bowman Certified Blue Ink Autographs Karim Garcia	15.00	6.75	1.85
1997 Bowman Certified Blue Ink Autographs Kris Detmers	10.00	4.50	1.25
1997 Bowman Certified Blue Ink Autographs Todd Greene	15.00	6.75	1.85
1997 Bowman Certified Blue Ink Autographs Ben Grieve	60.00	27.00	7.50
1997 Bowman Certified Blue Ink Autographs Vladimir Guerrero	50.00	22.00	6.25
1997 Bowman Certified Blue Ink Autographs Jose Guillen	30.00	13.50	3.70
1997 Bowman Certified Blue Ink Autographs Roy Halladay	20.00	9.00	2.50
1997 Bowman Certified Blue Ink Autographs Wes Helms	15.00	6.75	1.85
1997 Bowman Certified Blue Ink Autographs Chad Hermansen	50.00	22.00	6.25
1997 Bowman Certified Blue Ink Autographs Richard Hidalgo	15.00	6.75	1.85
1997 Bowman Certified Blue Ink Autographs Todd Hollandsworth	10.00	4.50	1.25
1997 Bowman Certified Blue Ink Autographs Damian Jackson	10.00	4.50	1.25
1997 Bowman Certified Blue Ink Autographs Derek Jeter Blue DP	80.00	36.00	10.00
1997 Bowman Certified Blue Ink Autographs Andruw Jones	40.00	18.00	5.00
1997 Bowman Certified Blue Ink Autographs Brooks Kieschnick	10.00	4.50	1.25
1997 Bowman Certified Blue Ink Autographs Eugene Kingsale	15.00	6.75	1.85
1997 Bowman Certified Blue Ink Autographs Paul Konerko	25.00	11.00	3.10
1997 Bowman Certified Blue Ink Autographs Marc Kroon	10.00	4.50	1.25
1997 Bowman Certified Blue Ink Autographs Derrek Lee	20.00	9.00	2.50
1997 Bowman Certified Blue Ink Autographs Travis Lee	120.00	55.00	15.00
1997 Bowman Certified Blue Ink Autographs Terrence Long	10.00	4.50	1.25
1997 Bowman Certified Blue Ink Autographs Curt Lyons	10.00	4.50	1.25
1997 Bowman Certified Blue Ink Autographs Eli Marrero	15.00	6.75	1.85
1997 Bowman Certified Blue Ink Autographs Rafael Medina	15.00	6.75	1.85
1997 Bowman Certified Blue Ink Autographs Juan Melo	15.00	6.75	1.85
1997 Bowman Certified Blue Ink Autographs Shane Monahan	15.00	6.75	1.85
1997 Bowman Certified Blue Ink Autographs Julio Mosquera	10.00	4.50	1.25
1997 Bowman Certified Blue Ink Autographs Heath Murray	10.00	4.50	1.25
1997 Bowman Certified Blue Ink Autographs Ryan Nye	15.00	6.75	1.85
1997 Bowman Certified Blue Ink Autographs Kevin Orie	10.00	4.50	1.25
1997 Bowman Certified Blue Ink Autographs Russ Ortiz	10.00	4.50	1.25
1997 Bowman Certified Blue Ink Autographs Carl Pavano	25.00	11.00	3.10
1997 Bowman Certified Blue Ink Autographs Jay Payton	10.00	4.50	1.25
1997 Bowman Certified Blue Ink Autographs Neifi Perez	15.00	6.75	1.85
1997 Bowman Certified Blue Ink Autographs Sidney Ponson	15.00	6.75	1.85
1997 Bowman Certified Blue Ink Autographs Calvin Reese	10.00	4.50	1.25
1997 Bowman Certified Blue Ink Autographs Ray Ricken	10.00	4.50	1.25
1997 Bowman Certified Blue Ink Autographs Brad Rigby	10.00	4.50	1.25
1997 Bowman Certified Blue Ink Autographs Adam Riggs	10.00	4.50	1.25

1997 Bowman Certified Blue Ink Autographs Ruben Rivera	15.00	6.75	1.85
1997 Bowman Certified Blue Ink Autographs J.J. Johnson	10.00	4.50	1.25
1997 Bowman Certified Blue Ink Autographs Scott Rolen	60.00	27.00	7.50
1997 Bowman Certified Blue Ink Autographs Tony Saunders	20.00	9.00	2.50
1997 Bowman Certified Blue Ink Autographs Donnie Sadler	15.00	6.75	1.85
1997 Bowman Certified Blue Ink Autographs Richie Sexson	25.00	11.00	3.10
1997 Bowman Certified Blue Ink Autographs Scott Spiezio	15.00	6.75	1.85
1997 Bowman Certified Blue Ink Autographs Everett Stull	10.00	4.50	1.25
1997 Bowman Certified Blue Ink Autographs Mike Sweeney	10.00	4.50	1.25
1997 Bowman Certified Blue Ink Autographs Fernando Tatis	25.00	11.00	3.10
1997 Bowman Certified Blue Ink Autographs Miguel Tejada	30.00	13.50	3.70
1997 Bowman Certified Blue Ink Autographs Justin Thompson	15.00	6.75	1.85
1997 Bowman Certified Blue Ink Autographs Justin Towle	20.00	9.00	2.50
1997 Bowman Certified Blue Ink Autographs Billy Wagner	15.00	6.75	1.85
1997 Bowman Certified Blue Ink Autographs Todd Walker	25.00	11.00	3.10
1997 Bowman Certified Blue Ink Autographs Luke Wilcox	10.00	4.50	1.25
1997 Bowman Certified Blue Ink Autographs Paul Wilder	25.00	11.00	3.10
1997 Bowman Certified Blue Ink Autographs Enrique Wilson	15.00	6.75	1.85
1997 Bowman Certified Blue Ink Autographs Kerry Wood	150.00	70.00	19.00
1997 Bowman Certified Blue Ink Autographs Jamey Wright	10.00	4.50	1.25
1997 Bowman Certified Blue Ink Autographs Ron Wright	20.00	9.00	2.50
1997 Bowman Certified Blue Ink Autographs Dmitri Young	15.00	6.75	1.85
1997 Bowman Certified Blue Ink Autographs Nelson Figueroa	15.00	6.75	1.85

1997 Bowman's Best Autographs

COMPLETE SET (10)	500.00	220.00	60.00

Randomly inserted in packs at a rate of 1:170, this 10-card set features five silver rookie cards and five gold veteran cards with authentic autographs and a "Certified Autograph Issue" stamp.

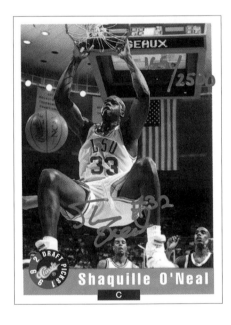

	MINT	NRMT	EXC
1997 Bowman's Best Autographs COMMON CARD	12.00	5.50	1.50
1997 Bowman's Best Autographs REF.STARS: 1X TO 2.5X BASIC CARDS			
1997 Bowman's Best Autographs REF.YOUNG STARS: .75X TO 2X BASIC CARDS			
1997 Bowman's Best Autographs REF.CRUZ JR: .6X TO 1.5X BASIC AUTO			
1997 Bowman's Best Autographs ATOMIC STARS: 2.5X TO 5X BASIC CARDS			
1997 Bowman's Best Autographs ATOMIC YOUNG STARS: 2X TO 4X BASIC CARDS			
1997 Bowman's Best Autographs ATOMIC CRUZ JR: 1.5X TO 3X BASIC AUTO			
1997 Bowman's Best Autographs Tony Gwynn	120.00	55.00	15.00
1997 Bowman's Best Autographs Paul Molitor	50.00	22.00	6.25
1997 Bowman's Best Autographs Derek Jeter	100.00	45.00	12.50
1997 Bowman's Best Autographs Brady Anderson	25.00	11.00	3.10
1997 Bowman's Best Autographs Tim Salmon	40.00	18.00	5.00
1997 Bowman's Best Autographs Todd Walker	25.00	11.00	3.10
1997 Bowman's Best Autographs Wilton Guerrero	12.00	5.50	1.50
1997 Bowman's Best Autographs Scott Spiezio	15.00	6.75	1.85
1997 Bowman's Best Autographs Jose Cruz Jr.	60.00	27.00	7.50
1997 Bowman's Best Autographs Scott Rolen	80.00	36.00	10.00

1997 Circa Emerald Autographs

COMPLETE SET (6)	300.00	135.00	38.00

These autographed cards were made available only to those collectors lucky enough to pull one of the scarce Circa Emerald Autograph Redemption cards (randomly seeded into 1:1000 1997 Circa packs). These cards are identical to the regular issue Circa cards except, of course, for the player's autograph on the card front and an embossed Fleer seal for authenticity. The deadline to redeem these cards was May 1st, 1998. In addition, an Emerald Autograph Redemption program entitled "Collect and Win" was featured in 1997 Fleer 2 packs. One in every 4 packs contained one of ten different redemption cards. The object was for collectors to piece together all ten cards and then mail them in to receive a complete set of the Circa Emerald Autographs. The catch was that card #7 was extremely short-printed (official numbers were not released but speculation is that only a handful of #7 cards made their way into packs). The exchange deadline on this "collect and win" promotion was August 1st, 1998.

	MINT	NRMT	EXC
1997 Circa Emerald Autographs COMMON CARD	12.00	5.50	1.50
1997 Circa Emerald Autographs EXCH CARDS: .1X TO .25X HI COLUMN			
1997 Circa Emerald Autographs EXCH CARDS STATED ODDS 1:1000 PACKS			
1997 Circa Emerald Autographs Alex Rodriguez AU	150.00	70.00	19.00

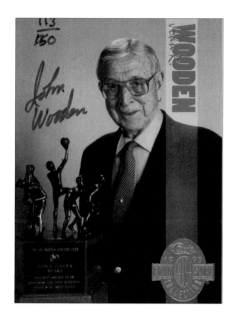

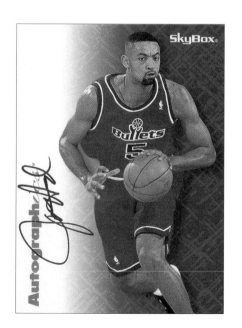

1997 Circa Emerald Autographs Darin Erstad AU	50.00	22.00	6.25
1997 Circa Emerald Autographs Todd Hollandsworth AU	12.00	5.50	1.50
1997 Circa Emerald Autographs Scott Rolen AU	80.00	36.00	10.00
1997 Circa Emerald Autographs Alex Ochoa AU	12.00	5.50	1.50
1997 Circa Emerald Autographs Todd Walker AU	25.00	11.00	3.10

1997 Donruss Elite Passing the Torch Autographs

COMPLETE SET (12) 5000.00 2200.00 600.00

This 12-card set consists of the first 150 sets of the regular "Passing the Torch" set with each card displaying an authentic player autograph. The set features a double front design which captures eight of the league's top superstars, alternating one of four different megastars on the flipside. An individual card for each of the eight players rounds out the set. Each set is sequentially numbered to 150.

	MINT	NRMT	EXC
1997 Donruss Elite Passing the Torch Autographs COMMON (1-12)	100.00	45.00	12.50
1997 Donruss Elite Passing the Torch Autographs Cal Ripken	600.00	275.00	75.00
1997 Donruss Elite Passing the Torch Autographs Alex Rodriguez	500.00	220.00	60.00
1997 Donruss Elite Passing the Torch Cal Ripken / Alex Rodriguez	1200.00	550.00	150.00
1997 Donruss Elite Passing the Torch Autographs Kirby Puckett	300.00	135.00	38.00
1997 Donruss Elite Passing the Torch Autographs Andruw Jones	150.00	70.00	19.00
1997 Donruss Elite Passing the Torch Kirby Puckett / Andruw Jones	400.00	180.00	50.00
1997 Donruss Elite Passing the Torch Autographs Cecil Fielder	100.00	45.00	12.50
1997 Donruss Elite Passing the Torch Autographs Frank Thomas	500.00	220.00	60.00
1997 Donruss Elite Passing the Torch Cecil Fielder / Frank Thomas	500.00	220.00	60.00
1997 Donruss Elite Passing the Torch Autographs Ozzie Smith	300.00	135.00	38.00
1997 Donruss Elite Passing the Torch Autographs Derek Jeter	300.00	135.00	38.00
1997 Donruss Elite Passing the Torch Ozzie Smith / Derek Jeter	400.00	180.00	50.00

1997 Donruss Signature Autographs

COMPLETE SET (117) 2000.00 900.00 250.00

Inserted one per pack, this 117-card set features color player autographed photos. The first 100 cards each player signed were blue, sequentially numbered to 100, and designated as "Century Marks." The next 100 cards signed were green, sequentially numbered 101-1,100, and designated as "Millenium Marks." Player autographs surpassing 1100 were red and were not numbered. Some autographed signature cards were not available at first and were designated by blank-backed redemption cards which could be redeemed by mail for the player's autograph card. The cards are checklisted below in alphabetical order. Asterisk cards were found in both Series A and B. Print runs for how many cards each player signed is noted below next to the players name.

	MINT	NRMT	EXC
1997 Donruss Signature Autographs COMMON CARD	5.00	2.20	.60
1997 Donruss Signature Autographs Jeff Abbott/3900	8.00	3.60	1.00
1997 Donruss Signature Autographs Bob Abreu/3900	8.00	3.60	1.00
1997 Donruss Signature Autographs Edgardo Alfonzo/3900	8.00	3.60	1.00
1997 Donruss Signature Autographs Roberto Alomar/150 *	120.00	55.00	15.00
1997 Donruss Signature Autographs Sandy Alomar Jr./1400	15.00	6.75	1.85
1997 Donruss Signature Autographs Moises Alou/900	30.00	13.50	3.70
1997 Donruss Signature Autographs Garret Anderson/3900	10.00	4.50	1.25
1997 Donruss Signature Autographs Andy Ashby/3900	5.00	2.20	.60
1997 Donruss Signature Autographs Trey Beamon/3900	5.00	2.20	.60
1997 Donruss Signature Autographs Alan Benes/3900	8.00	3.60	1.00
1997 Donruss Signature Autographs Geronimo Berroa/3900	5.00	2.20	.60
1997 Donruss Signature Autographs Wade Boggs/150 *	120.00	55.00	15.00
1997 Donruss Signature Autographs Kevin Brown C/3900	5.00	2.20	.60
1997 Donruss Signature Autographs Brett Butler/1400	20.00	9.00	2.50
1997 Donruss Signature Autographs Mike Cameron/3900	8.00	3.60	1.00
1997 Donruss Signature Autographs Giovanni Carrara/2900	5.00	2.20	.60
1997 Donruss Signature Autographs Luis Castillo/3900	8.00	3.60	1.00
1997 Donruss Signature Autographs Tony Clark/3900	15.00	6.75	1.85
1997 Donruss Signature Autographs Will Clark/1400	30.00	13.50	3.70
1997 Donruss Signature Autographs Lou Collier/3900	5.00	2.20	.60
1997 Donruss Signature Autographs Bartolo Colon/3900	12.00	5.50	1.50
1997 Donruss Signature Autographs Ron Coomer/3900	5.00	2.20	.60
1997 Donruss Signature Autographs Marty Cordova/3900	5.00	2.20	.60
1997 Donruss Signature Autographs Jacob Cruz/3900 *	5.00	2.20	.60
1997 Donruss Signature Autographs Jose Cruz Jr./900 *	80.00	36.00	10.00

1997 Donruss Signature Autographs Russ Davis/3900	5.00	2.20	.60
1997 Donruss Signature Autographs Jason Dickson/3900	8.00	3.60	1.00
1997 Donruss Signature Autographs Todd Dunwoody/3900	10.00	4.50	1.25
1997 Donruss Signature Autographs Jermaine Dye/3900	5.00	2.20	.60
1997 Donruss Signature Autographs Jim Edmonds/3900	15.00	6.75	1.85
1997 Donruss Signature Autographs Darin Erstad/900 *	50.00	22.00	6.25
1997 Donruss Signature Autographs Bobby Estalella/3900	8.00	3.60	1.00
1997 Donruss Signature Autographs Shawn Estes/3900	8.00	3.60	1.00
1997 Donruss Signature Autographs Jeff Fassero/3900	5.00	2.20	.60
1997 Donruss Signature Autographs Andres Galarraga/900	40.00	18.00	5.00
1997 Donruss Signature Autographs Karim Garcia/3900	8.00	3.60	1.00
1997 Donruss Signature Autographs Derrick Gibson/3900	10.00	4.50	1.25
1997 Donruss Signature Autographs Brian Giles/3900	8.00	3.60	1.00
1997 Donruss Signature Autographs Tom Glavine/150	100.00	45.00	12.50
1997 Donruss Signature Autographs Rick Gorecki/900	10.00	4.50	1.25
1997 Donruss Signature Autographs Shawn Green/1900	15.00	6.75	1.85
1997 Donruss Signature Autographs Todd Greene/3900	12.00	5.50	1.50
1997 Donruss Signature Autographs Rusty Greer/3900	10.00	4.50	1.25
1997 Donruss Signature Autographs Ben Grieve/3900	30.00	13.50	3.70
1997 Donruss Signature Autographs Mark Grudzielanek/3900	8.00	3.60	1.00
1997 Donruss Signature Autographs Vladimir Guerrero/1900 *	40.00	18.00	5.00
1997 Donruss Signature Autographs Wilton Guerrero/2150	10.00	4.50	1.25
1997 Donruss Signature Autographs Jose Guillen/2900	15.00	6.75	1.85
1997 Donruss Signature Autographs Jeffrey Hammonds/2150	10.00	4.50	1.25
1997 Donruss Signature Autographs Todd Helton/1400	30.00	13.50	3.70
1997 Donruss Signature Autographs Todd Hollandsworth/2900	10.00	4.50	1.25
1997 Donruss Signature Autographs Trenidad Hubbard/900	10.00	4.50	1.25
1997 Donruss Signature Autographs Todd Hundley/1400	15.00	6.75	1.85
1997 Donruss Signature Autographs Bobby Jones/3900	5.00	2.20	.60
1997 Donruss Signature Autographs Brian Jordan/1400	15.00	6.75	1.85
1997 Donruss Signature Autographs David Justice/900	40.00	18.00	5.00
1997 Donruss Signature Autographs Eric Karros/650	25.00	11.00	3.10
1997 Donruss Signature Autographs Jason Kendall/3900	10.00	4.50	1.25
1997 Donruss Signature Autographs Jimmy Key/3900	8.00	3.60	1.00
1997 Donruss Signature Autographs Brooks Kieschnick/3900	5.00	2.20	.60
1997 Donruss Signature Autographs Ryan Klesko/225	40.00	18.00	5.00
1997 Donruss Signature Autographs Paul Konerko/3900	12.00	5.50	1.50
1997 Donruss Signature Autographs Mark Kotsay/2400	20.00	9.00	2.50
1997 Donruss Signature Autographs Ray Lankford/3900	10.00	4.50	1.25
1997 Donruss Signature Autographs Barry Larkin/150 *	80.00	36.00	10.00
1997 Donruss Signature Autographs Derrek Lee/3900	12.00	5.50	1.50
1997 Donruss Signature Autographs Esteban Loaiza/3900	5.00	2.20	.60
1997 Donruss Signature Autographs Javier Lopez/1400	20.00	9.00	2.50
1997 Donruss Signature Autographs Edgar Martinez/150 *	60.00	27.00	7.50
1997 Donruss Signature Autographs Pedro Martinez/900	50.00	22.00	6.25
1997 Donruss Signature Autographs Rafael Medina/3900	8.00	3.60	1.00
1997 Donruss Signature Autographs Raul Mondesi EXCH/650	40.00	18.00	5.00
1997 Donruss Signature Autographs Matt Morris/3900	8.00	3.60	1.00
1997 Donruss Signature Autographs Paul O'Neill/900	25.00	11.00	3.10
1997 Donruss Signature Autographs Kevin Orie/3900	5.00	2.20	.60
1997 Donruss Signature Autographs David Ortiz/3900	12.00	5.50	1.50
1997 Donruss Signature Autographs Rafael Palmeiro/900	30.00	13.50	3.70
1997 Donruss Signature Autographs Jay Payton/3900	5.00	2.20	.60
1997 Donruss Signature Autographs Neifi Perez/3900	8.00	3.60	1.00
1997 Donruss Signature Autographs Manny Ramirez/900	50.00	22.00	6.25
1997 Donruss Signature Autographs Joe Randa/3900	5.00	2.20	.60
1997 Donruss Signature Autographs Calvin Reese/3900	5.00	2.20	.60
1997 Donruss Signature Autographs Edgar Renteria EXCH SP	25.00	11.00	3.10
1997 Donruss Signature Autographs Dennis Reyes/3900	10.00	4.50	1.25
1997 Donruss Signature Autographs Henry Rodriguez/3900	8.00	3.60	1.00
1997 Donruss Signature Autographs Scott Rolen/1900 *	50.00	22.00	6.25
1997 Donruss Signature Autographs Kirk Rueter/2900	8.00	3.60	1.00
1997 Donruss Signature Autographs Ryne Sandberg/400	120.00	55.00	15.00
1997 Donruss Signature Autographs Dwight Smith/2900	8.00	3.60	1.00

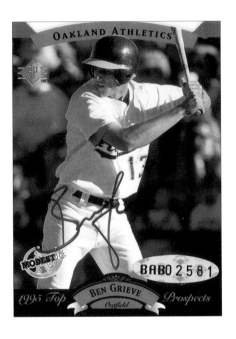

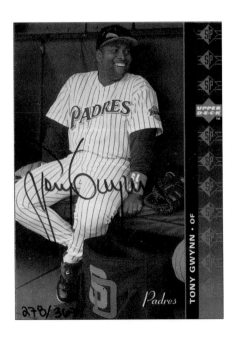

1997 Donruss Signature Autographs J.T. Snow/900 . . . . 15.00   6.75   1.85
1997 Donruss Signature Autographs Scott Spiezio/3900 . . . . 8.00   3.60   1.00
1997 Donruss Signature Autographs Shannon Stewart/2900 . . . . 10.00   4.50   1.25
1997 Donruss Signature Autographs Jeff Suppan/1900 . . . . 10.00   4.50   1.25
1997 Donruss Signature Autographs Mike Sweeney/3900 . . . . 5.00   2.20   .60
1997 Donruss Signature Autographs Miguel Tejada/3900 . . . . 15.00   6.75   1.85
1997 Donruss Signature Autographs Justin Thompson/2400 . . . . 12.00   5.50   1.50
1997 Donruss Signature Autographs Brett Tomko/3900 . . . . 8.00   3.60   1.00
1997 Donruss Signature Autographs Bubba Trammell/3900 . . . . 12.00   5.50   1.50
1997 Donruss Signature Autographs Michael Tucker/3900 . . . . 8.00   3.60   1.00
1997 Donruss Signature Autographs Javier Valentin/3900 . . . . 8.00   3.60   1.00
1997 Donruss Signature Autographs Mo Vaughn/150 * 120.00   55.00   15.00
1997 Donruss Signature Autographs Robin Ventura/1400 . . . . 20.00   9.00   2.50
1997 Donruss Signature Autographs Terrell Wade/3900 . . . . 5.00   2.20   .60
1997 Donruss Signature Autographs Billy Wagner/3900 . . . . 8.00   3.60   1.00
1997 Donruss Signature Autographs Larry Walker/900 . . . . 50.00   22.00   6.25
1997 Donruss Signature Autographs Todd Walker/2400 . . . . 15.00   6.75   1.85
1997 Donruss Signature Autographs Rondell White/3900 . . . . 8.00   3.60   1.00
1997 Donruss Signature Autographs Kevin Wickander/900 . . . . 10.00   4.50   1.25
1997 Donruss Signature Autographs Chris Widger/3900 . . . . 5.00   2.20   .60
1997 Donruss Signature Autographs Matt Williams/150 * 60.00   27.00   7.50
1997 Donruss Signature Autographs Antone Williamson/3900 . . . . 5.00   2.20   .60
1997 Donruss Signature Autographs Dan Wilson/3900 . . . . 5.00   2.20   .60
1997 Donruss Signature Autographs Tony Womack/3900 . . . . 8.00   3.60   1.00
1997 Donruss Signature Autographs Jaret Wright/3900 . . . . 30.00   13.50   3.70
1997 Donruss Signature Autographs Dmitri Young/3900 . . . . 8.00   3.60   1.00
1997 Donruss Signature Autographs Eric Young/3900 . . . . 8.00   3.60   1.00
1997 Donruss Signature Autographs Kevin Young/3900 . . . . 8.00   3.60   1.00

1997 Donruss Signature Autographs Century

COMMON CARD 40.00   18.00   5.00
Randomly inserted in packs, this set, designated as blue, features the first 100 cards signed by each player. The cards are sequentially numbered. Raul Mondesi, Eddie Murray, Edgar Renteria and Jim Thome are exchange cards. The cards are checklisted below in alphabetical order. It's believed a number of Nomar Garciaparra Century marks were lost or destroyed during packaging and as few as 62 of these cards may have been inserted into packs.

Tony Gwynn

CO-SIGNERS

	MINT	NRMT	EXC
1997 Donruss Signature Autographs Century MINOR STARS	80.00	36.00	10.00
1997 Donruss Signature Autographs Century Roberto Alomar *	150.00	70.00	19.00
1997 Donruss Signature Autographs Century Jeff Bagwell	250.00	110.00	31.00
1997 Donruss Signature Autographs Century Albert Belle	150.00	70.00	19.00
1997 Donruss Signature Autographs Century Wade Boggs *	150.00	70.00	19.00
1997 Donruss Signature Autographs Century Barry Bonds	200.00	90.00	25.00
1997 Donruss Signature Autographs Century Jay Buhner	80.00	36.00	10.00
1997 Donruss Signature Autographs Century Tony Clark	100.00	45.00	12.50
1997 Donruss Signature Autographs Century Will Clark	120.00	55.00	15.00
1997 Donruss Signature Autographs Century Roger Clemens *	300.00	135.00	38.00
1997 Donruss Signature Autographs Century Jose Cruz Jr. *	200.00	90.00	25.00
1997 Donruss Signature Autographs Century Jim Edmonds	100.00	45.00	12.50
1997 Donruss Signature Autographs Century Darin Erstad *	120.00	55.00	15.00
1997 Donruss Signature Autographs Century Andres Galarraga	120.00	55.00	15.00
1997 Donruss Signature Autographs Century Nomar Garciaparra SP62 *	500.00	220.00	60.00
1997 Donruss Signature Autographs Century Juan Gonzalez	400.00	180.00	50.00
1997 Donruss Signature Autographs Century Ben Grieve	150.00	70.00	19.00
1997 Donruss Signature Autographs Century Vladimir Guerrero *	150.00	70.00	19.00
1997 Donruss Signature Autographs Century Jose Guillen	150.00	70.00	19.00
1997 Donruss Signature Autographs Century Tony Gwynn *	400.00	180.00	50.00
1997 Donruss Signature Autographs Century Todd Helton	100.00	45.00	12.50
1997 Donruss Signature Autographs Century Derek Jeter *	400.00	180.00	50.00
1997 Donruss Signature Autographs Century Andruw Jones *	150.00	70.00	19.00
1997 Donruss Signature Autographs Century Chipper Jones *	400.00	180.00	50.00
1997 Donruss Signature Autographs Century David Justice	120.00	55.00	15.00
1997 Donruss Signature Autographs Century Ryan Klesko	100.00	45.00	12.50
1997 Donruss Signature Autographs Century Chuck Knoblauch *	120.00	55.00	15.00
1997 Donruss Signature Autographs Century Paul Konerko	100.00	45.00	12.50

1997 Donruss Signature Autographs Century Mark Kotsay 100.00 45.00 12.50
1997 Donruss Signature Autographs Century Barry Larkin * 100.00 45.00 12.50
1997 Donruss Signature Autographs Century Greg Maddux * 500.00 220.00 60.00
1997 Donruss Signature Autographs Century Edgar Martinez * 80.00 36.00 10.00
1997 Donruss Signature Autographs Century Pedro Martinez 150.00 70.00 19.00
1997 Donruss Signature Autographs Century Tino Martinez * 120.00 55.00 15.00
1997 Donruss Signature Autographs Century Raul Mondesi EXCH 100.00 45.00 12.50
1997 Donruss Signature Autographs Century Eddie Murray EXCH* 150.00 70.00 19.00
1997 Donruss Signature Autographs Century Mike Mussina 150.00 70.00 19.00
1997 Donruss Signature Autographs Century Rafael Palmeiro 100.00 45.00 12.50
1997 Donruss Signature Autographs Century Andy Pettitte * 100.00 45.00 12.50
1997 Donruss Signature Autographs Century Manny Ramirez 150.00 70.00 19.00
1997 Donruss Signature Autographs Century Cal Ripken 600.00 275.00 75.00
1997 Donruss Signature Autographs Century Alex Rodriguez 500.00 220.00 60.00
1997 Donruss Signature Autographs Century Ivan Rodriguez 200.00 90.00 25.00
1997 Donruss Signature Autographs Century Scott Rolen * 200.00 90.00 25.00
1997 Donruss Signature Autographs Century Ryne Sandberg 250.00 110.00 31.00
1997 Donruss Signature Autographs Century Gary Sheffield * 100.00 45.00 12.50
1997 Donruss Signature Autographs Century Miguel Tejada 100.00 45.00 12.50
1997 Donruss Signature Autographs Century Frank Thomas 500.00 220.00 60.00
1997 Donruss Signature Autographs Century Jim Thome EXCH 150.00 70.00 19.00
1997 Donruss Signature Autographs Century Mo Vaughn * 150.00 70.00 19.00
1997 Donruss Signature Autographs Century Larry Walker 150.00 70.00 19.00
1997 Donruss Signature Autographs Century Bernie Williams 150.00 70.00 19.00
1997 Donruss Signature Autographs Century Matt Williams * 80.00 36.00 10.00
1997 Donruss Signature Autographs Century Jaret Wright 200.00 90.00 25.00

1997 Donruss Signature Autographs Millenium

COMPLETE SET (143) 6500.00 2900.00 800.00
Randomly inserted in packs, this set, designated as green, features the second 100 cards signed by each player. The cards are sequentially numbered 101-1,100 and are checklisted below in alphabetical order. It has been noted that there are some cards in existence not serially numbered.

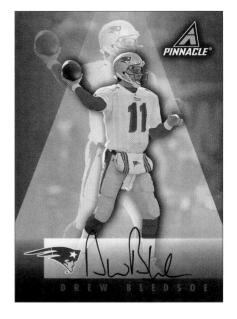

	MINT	NRMT	EXC
1997 Donruss Signature Autographs Millenium COMMON CARD	15.00	6.75	1.85
1997 Donruss Signature Autographs Millenium Jeff Abbott	30.00	13.50	3.70
1997 Donruss Signature Autographs Millenium Bob Abreu	20.00	9.00	2.50
1997 Donruss Signature Autographs Millenium Edgardo Alfonzo	20.00	9.00	2.50
1997 Donruss Signature Autographs Millenium Roberto Alomar *	60.00	27.00	7.50
1997 Donruss Signature Autographs Millenium Sandy Alomar Jr.	30.00	13.50	3.70
1997 Donruss Signature Autographs Millenium Moises Alou	40.00	18.00	5.00
1997 Donruss Signature Autographs Millenium Garret Anderson	30.00	13.50	3.70
1997 Donruss Signature Autographs Millenium Andy Ashby	15.00	6.75	1.85
1997 Donruss Signature Autographs Millenium Jeff Bagwell/400	150.00	70.00	19.00
1997 Donruss Signature Autographs Millenium Trey Beamon	15.00	6.75	1.85
1997 Donruss Signature Autographs Millenium Albert Belle/400	100.00	45.00	12.50
1997 Donruss Signature Autographs Millenium Alan Benes	30.00	13.50	3.70
1997 Donruss Signature Autographs Millenium Geronimo Berroa	15.00	6.75	1.85
1997 Donruss Signature Autographs Millenium Wade Boggs *	60.00	27.00	7.50
1997 Donruss Signature Autographs Millenium Barry Bonds/400	150.00	70.00	19.00
1997 Donruss Signature Autographs Millenium Bobby Bonilla/900 *	30.00	13.50	3.70
1997 Donruss Signature Autographs Millenium Kevin Brown/900	40.00	18.00	5.00
1997 Donruss Signature Autographs Millenium Kevin Brown C	15.00	6.75	1.85
1997 Donruss Signature Autographs Millenium Jay Buhner/900	30.00	13.50	3.70
1997 Donruss Signature Autographs Millenium Brett Butler	30.00	13.50	3.70
1997 Donruss Signature Autographs Millenium Mike Cameron	30.00	13.50	3.70
1997 Donruss Signature Autographs Millenium Giovanni Carrara	15.00	6.75	1.85
1997 Donruss Signature Autographs Millenium Luis Castillo	20.00	9.00	2.50
1997 Donruss Signature Autographs Millenium Tony Clark	40.00	18.00	5.00
1997 Donruss Signature Autographs Millenium Will Clark	50.00	22.00	6.25
1997 Donruss Signature Autographs Millenium Roger Clemens/400 * . . .	200.00	90.00	25.00
1997 Donruss Signature Autographs Millenium Lou Collier	15.00	6.75	1.85
1997 Donruss Signature Autographs Millenium Bartolo Colon	20.00	9.00	2.50
1997 Donruss Signature Autographs Millenium Ron Coomer	15.00	6.75	1.85

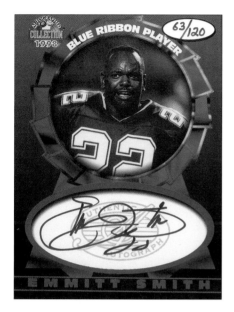

1997 Donruss Signature Autographs Millenium Marty Cordova	15.00	6.75	1.85
1997 Donruss Signature Autographs Millenium Jacob Cruz	20.00	9.00	2.50
1997 Donruss Signature Autographs Millenium Jose Cruz Jr. *	80.00	36.00	10.00
1997 Donruss Signature Autographs Millenium Russ Davis	15.00	6.75	1.85
1997 Donruss Signature Autographs Millenium Jason Dickson	20.00	9.00	2.50
1997 Donruss Signature Autographs Millenium Todd Dunwoody	30.00	13.50	3.70
1997 Donruss Signature Autographs Millenium Jermaine Dye	15.00	6.75	1.85
1997 Donruss Signature Autographs Millenium Jim Edmonds	40.00	18.00	5.00
1997 Donruss Signature Autographs Millenium Darin Erstad *	60.00	27.00	7.50
1997 Donruss Signature Autographs Millenium Bobby Estalella	20.00	9.00	2.50
1997 Donruss Signature Autographs Millenium Shawn Estes	30.00	13.50	3.70
1997 Donruss Signature Autographs Millenium Jeff Fassero	15.00	6.75	1.85
1997 Donruss Signature Autographs Millenium Andres Galarraga	50.00	22.00	6.25
1997 Donruss Signature Autographs Millenium Karim Garcia	20.00	9.00	2.50
1997 Donruss Signature Autographs Millenium Nomar Garciaparra/650 *	200.00	90.00	25.00
1997 Donruss Signature Autographs Millenium Derrick Gibson	30.00	13.50	3.70
1997 Donruss Signature Autographs Millenium Brian Giles	30.00	13.50	3.70
1997 Donruss Signature Autographs Millenium Tom Glavine	30.00	13.50	3.70
1997 Donruss Signature Autographs Millenium Juan Gonzalez/900	150.00	70.00	19.00
1997 Donruss Signature Autographs Millenium Rick Gorecki	15.00	6.75	1.85
1997 Donruss Signature Autographs Millenium Shawn Green	15.00	6.75	1.85
1997 Donruss Signature Autographs Millenium Todd Greene	20.00	9.00	2.50
1997 Donruss Signature Autographs Millenium Rusty Greer	30.00	13.50	3.70
1997 Donruss Signature Autographs Millenium Ben Grieve	60.00	27.00	7.50
1997 Donruss Signature Autographs Millenium Mark Grudzielanek	30.00	13.50	3.70
1997 Donruss Signature Autographs Millenium Vladimir Guerrero *	80.00	36.00	10.00
1997 Donruss Signature Autographs Millenium Wilton Guerrero	15.00	6.75	1.85
1997 Donruss Signature Autographs Millenium Jose Guillen	40.00	18.00	5.00
1997 Donruss Signature Autographs Millenium Tony Gwynn/900 *	150.00	70.00	19.00
1997 Donruss Signature Autographs Millenium Jeffrey Hammonds	30.00	13.50	3.70
1997 Donruss Signature Autographs Millenium Todd Helton	50.00	22.00	6.25
1997 Donruss Signature Autographs Millenium Todd Hundley	30.00	13.50	3.70
1997 Donruss Signature Autographs Millenium Todd Hollandsworth	15.00	6.75	1.85
1997 Donruss Signature Autographs Millenium Trenidad Hubbard	15.00	6.75	1.85
1997 Donruss Signature Autographs Millenium Derek Jeter/400 *	200.00	90.00	25.00
1997 Donruss Signature Autographs Millenium Andruw Jones/900 *	60.00	27.00	7.50
1997 Donruss Signature Autographs Millenium Bobby Jones	15.00	6.75	1.85
1997 Donruss Signature Autographs Millenium Chipper Jones/900 *	150.00	70.00	19.00
1997 Donruss Signature Autographs Millenium Brian Jordan	30.00	13.50	3.70
1997 Donruss Signature Autographs Millenium David Justice	50.00	22.00	6.25
1997 Donruss Signature Autographs Millenium Eric Karros	30.00	13.50	3.70
1997 Donruss Signature Autographs Millenium Jason Kendall	40.00	18.00	5.00
1997 Donruss Signature Autographs Millenium Jimmy Key	30.00	13.50	3.70
1997 Donruss Signature Autographs Millenium Brooks Kieschnick	15.00	6.75	1.85
1997 Donruss Signature Autographs Millenium Ryan Klesko	40.00	18.00	5.00
1997 Donruss Signature Autographs Millenium Chuck Knoblauch/900 *	50.00	22.00	6.25
1997 Donruss Signature Autographs Millenium Paul Konerko	40.00	18.00	5.00
1997 Donruss Signature Autographs Millenium Mark Kotsay	40.00	18.00	5.00
1997 Donruss Signature Autographs Millenium Ray Lankford	30.00	13.50	3.70
1997 Donruss Signature Autographs Millenium Barry Larkin *	40.00	18.00	5.00
1997 Donruss Signature Autographs Millenium Derrek Lee	30.00	13.50	3.70
1997 Donruss Signature Autographs Millenium Esteban Loaiza	15.00	6.75	1.85
1997 Donruss Signature Autographs Millenium Javier Lopez	30.00	13.50	3.70
1997 Donruss Signature Autographs Millenium Greg Maddux/400 *	350.00	160.00	45.00
1997 Donruss Signature Autographs Millenium Edgar Martinez *	30.00	13.50	3.70
1997 Donruss Signature Autographs Millenium Pedro Martinez	60.00	27.00	7.50
1997 Donruss Signature Autographs Millenium Tino Martinez/900 *	50.00	22.00	6.25
1997 Donruss Signature Autographs Millenium Rafael Medina	20.00	9.00	2.50
1997 Donruss Signature Autographs Millenium Raul Mondesi EXCH	40.00	18.00	5.00
1997 Donruss Signature Autographs Millenium Matt Morris	20.00	9.00	2.50
1997 Donruss Signature Autographs Millenium Eddie Murray/900 *	60.00	27.00	7.50
1997 Donruss Signature Autographs Millenium Mike Mussina/900 *	60.00	27.00	7.50
1997 Donruss Signature Autographs Millenium Paul O'Neill	30.00	13.50	3.70
1997 Donruss Signature Autographs Millenium Kevin Orie	20.00	9.00	2.50

1997 Donruss Signature Autographs Millenium David Ortiz 20.00   9.00   2.50
1997 Donruss Signature Autographs Millenium Rafael Palmeiro 40.00   18.00   5.00
1997 Donruss Signature Autographs Millenium Jay Payton 15.00   6.75   1.85
1997 Donruss Signature Autographs Millenium Neifi Perez 20.00   9.00   2.50
1997 Donruss Signature Autographs Millenium Andy Pettitte/900 * 40.00   18.00   5.00
1997 Donruss Signature Autographs Millenium Manny Ramirez 60.00   27.00   7.50
1997 Donruss Signature Autographs Millenium Joe Randa 15.00   6.75   1.85
1997 Donruss Signature Autographs Millenium Calvin Reese 15.00   6.75   1.85
1997 Donruss Signature Autographs Millenium Edgar Renteria EXCH SP . 40.00   18.00   5.00
1997 Donruss Signature Autographs Millenium Dennis Reyes 20.00   9.00   2.50
1997 Donruss Signature Autographs Millenium Cal Ripken/400 . . . . 400.00   180.00   50.00
1997 Donruss Signature Autographs Millenium Alex Rodriguez/400 . . . . 300.00   135.00   38.00
1997 Donruss Signature Autographs Millenium Henry Rodriguez 30.00   13.50   3.70
1997 Donruss Signature Autographs Millenium Ivan Rodriguez/900 . . . . 80.00   36.00   10.00
1997 Donruss Signature Autographs Millenium Scott Rolen * 80.00   36.00   10.00
1997 Donruss Signature Autographs Millenium Kirk Rueter 15.00   6.75   1.85
1997 Donruss Signature Autographs Millenium Ryne Sandberg 100.00   45.00   12.50
1997 Donruss Signature Autographs Millenium Gary Sheffield/400 * . . . 60.00   27.00   7.50
1997 Donruss Signature Autographs Millenium Dwight Smith 15.00   6.75   1.85
1997 Donruss Signature Autographs Millenium J.T. Snow 30.00   13.50   3.70
1997 Donruss Signature Autographs Millenium Scott Spiezio 20.00   9.00   2.50
1997 Donruss Signature Autographs Millenium Shannon Stewart 20.00   9.00   2.50
1997 Donruss Signature Autographs Millenium Jeff Suppan 20.00   9.00   2.50
1997 Donruss Signature Autographs Millenium Mike Sweeney 20.00   9.00   2.50
1997 Donruss Signature Autographs Millenium Miguel Tejada 40.00   18.00   5.00
1997 Donruss Signature Autographs Millenium Frank Thomas/400 . . . . . 300.00   135.00   38.00
1997 Donruss Signature Autographs Millenium Jim Thome EXCH/900 . . 60.00   27.00   7.50
1997 Donruss Signature Autographs Millenium Justin Thompson 30.00   13.50   3.70
1997 Donruss Signature Autographs Millenium Brett Tomko 20.00   9.00   2.50
1997 Donruss Signature Autographs Millenium Bubba Trammell 30.00   13.50   3.70
1997 Donruss Signature Autographs Millenium Michael Tucker 20.00   9.00   2.50
1997 Donruss Signature Autographs Millenium Javier Valentin 20.00   9.00   2.50
1997 Donruss Signature Autographs Millenium Mo Vaughn * 60.00   27.00   7.50
1997 Donruss Signature Autographs Millenium Robin Ventura 30.00   13.50   3.70
1997 Donruss Signature Autographs Millenium Terrell Wade 15.00   6.75   1.85
1997 Donruss Signature Autographs Millenium Billy Wagner 30.00   13.50   3.70
1997 Donruss Signature Autographs Millenium Larry Walker 60.00   27.00   7.50
1997 Donruss Signature Autographs Millenium Todd Walker 20.00   9.00   2.50
1997 Donruss Signature Autographs Millenium Rondell White 30.00   13.50   3.70
1997 Donruss Signature Autographs Millenium Kevin Wickander 15.00   6.75   1.85
1997 Donruss Signature Autographs Millenium Chris Widger 15.00   6.75   1.85
1997 Donruss Signature Autographs Millenium Bernie Williams/400 . . . . 100.00   45.00   12.50
1997 Donruss Signature Autographs Millenium Matt Williams * 30.00   13.50   3.70
1997 Donruss Signature Autographs Millenium Antone Williamson 15.00   6.75   1.85
1997 Donruss Signature Autographs Millenium Dan Wilson 15.00   6.75   1.85
1997 Donruss Signature Autographs Millenium Tony Womack 20.00   9.00   2.50
1997 Donruss Signature Autographs Millenium Jaret Wright 80.00   36.00   10.00
1997 Donruss Signature Autographs Millenium Dmitri Young 30.00   13.50   3.70
1997 Donruss Signature Autographs Millenium Eric Young 30.00   13.50   3.70
1997 Donruss Signature Autographs Millenium Kevin Young 30.00   13.50   3.70

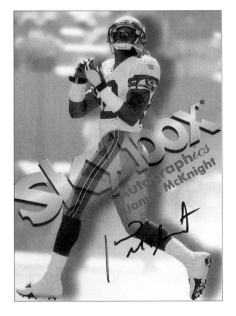

1997 Donruss Signature Notable Nicknames

COMPLETE SET (10) 1800.00   800.00   220.00
Randomly inserted in packs, this 10-card set features photos of players with notable nicknames. Only 200 of this serial numbered set were produced. The cards are unnumbered and checklisted below in alphabetical order. Roger Clemens signed a good deal of his cards without using his "Rocket" nickname. There is no difference in value between the two versions.

	MINT	NRMT	EXC
. . . .			
1997 Donruss Signature Notable Nicknames COMMON CARD	60.00	27.00	7.50
1997 Donruss Signature Notable Nicknames Ernie Banks Mr. Cub	250.00	110.00	31.00
1997 Donruss Signature Notable Nicknames Tony Clark The Tiger	100.00	45.00	12.50
1997 Donruss Signature Notable Nicknames Roger Clemens The Rocket	300.00	135.00	38.00
1997 Donruss Signature Notable Nicknames Reggie Jackson Mr. October	250.00	110.00	31.00

1997 Donruss Signature Notable Nicknames Randy Johnson The Big Unit	120.00	55.00	15.00
1997 Donruss Signature Notable Nicknames Stan Musial The Man	300.00	135.00	38.00
1997 Donruss Signature Notable Nicknames Ivan Rodriguez Pudge	150.00	70.00	19.00
1997 Donruss Signature Notable Nicknames Frank Thomas The Big Hurt	400.00	180.00	50.00
1997 Donruss Signature Notable Nicknames Mo Vaughn The Hit Dog . . .	120.00	55.00	15.00
1997 Donruss Signature Notable Nicknames Billy Wagner The Kid	60.00	27.00	7.50

1997 E-X2000 Emerald Autographs

COMPLETE SET (6) 400.00   180.00   50.00

This six-card set features autographed color player photos of some of the hottest young stars in baseball. In addition to an authentic black-ink autograph, each card is embossed with a SkyBox logo about the size of a quarter. These cards were obtained by exchanging a redemption card by mail before the May 1, 1998, deadline.

	MINT	NRMT	EXC
1997 E-X2000 Emerald Autographs COMMON CARD	15.00	6.75	1.85
1997 E-X2000 Emerald Autographs Darin Erstad	80.00	36.00	10.00
1997 E-X2000 Emerald Autographs Todd Walker	30.00	13.50	3.70
1997 E-X2000 Emerald Autographs Alex Rodriguez	200.00	90.00	25.00
1997 E-X2000 Emerald Autographs Todd Hollandsworth	15.00	6.75	1.85
1997 E-X2000 Emerald Autographs Alex Ochoa	15.00	6.75	1.85
1997 E-X2000 Emerald Autographs Scott Rolen	100.00	45.00	12.50

1997 Metal Universe Emerald Autographs

COMPLETE SET (6) 300.00   135.00   38.00

These autographed cards were distributed via mail to lucky collectors that sent in an Emerald Autograph Exchange card. The autographed cards parallel the corresponding basic cards except of course for the signature on front, coupled with special emerald foil and an embossed Fleer/SkyBox stamp. In addition, the area used for the card number on back of the regular issue card is replaced by a logo stating "certified emerald autograph". These autographed cards are unnumbered and have been assigned numbers based upon alphabetical order of each player's last name.

	MINT	NRMT	EXC
1997 Metal Universe Emerald Autographs COMMON CARD	12.00	5.50	1.50
1997 Metal Universe Emerald Autographs Darin Erstad	50.00	22.00	6.25
1997 Metal Universe Emerald Autographs Todd Hollandsworth	12.00	5.50	1.50
1997 Metal Universe Emerald Autographs Alex Ochoa	12.00	5.50	1.50
1997 Metal Universe Emerald Autographs Alex Rodriguez	150.00	70.00	19.00
1997 Metal Universe Emerald Autographs Scott Rolen	80.00	36.00	10.00
1997 Metal Universe Emerald Autographs Todd Walker	25.00	11.00	3.10

1997 SP SPx Force Autographs

COMPLETE SET (10) 3000.00   1350.00   375.00

Randomly inserted in packs, this 10-card set is an autographed parallel version of the regular SPx Force set. Only 100 of each card in this crash numbered, limited edition set were produced.

	MINT	NRMT	EXC
1997 SP SPx Force Autographs COMMON CARD (1-10)	100.00	45.00	12.50
1997 SP SPx Force Autographs Ken Griffey Jr. AU	1000.00	450.00	125.00
1997 SP SPx Force Autographs Albert Belle AU	200.00	90.00	25.00
1997 SP SPx Force Autographs Mo Vaughn AU EXCH	200.00	90.00	25.00
1997 SP SPx Force Autographs Gary Sheffield AU	120.00	55.00	15.00
1997 SP SPx Force Autographs Greg Maddux AU	500.00	220.00	60.00
1997 SP SPx Force Autographs Alex Rodriguez AU	500.00	220.00	60.00
1997 SP SPx Force Autographs Todd Hollandsworth AU	100.00	45.00	12.50
1997 SP SPx Force Autographs Roberto Alomar AU	200.00	90.00	25.00
1997 SP SPx Force Autographs Tony Gwynn AU	400.00	180.00	50.00
1997 SP SPx Force Autographs Andruw Jones AU	200.00	90.00	25.00

1997 SP Vintage Autographs

COMMON CARD (1-31) 25.00   11.00   3.10

Randomly inserted in packs, this 31-card set features authenticated original 1993-1996 SP cards that have been autographed by the pictured player. The print runs are listed after year following the player's name in the checklist below. Some of the very short printed autographs are listed but not priced. Each card came in the pack along with a standard size certificate of authenticity. These certificates are usually included when these autographed cards are traded.

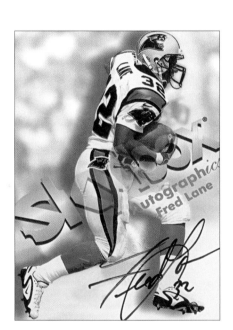

	MINT	NRMT	EXC
1997 SP Vintage Autographs Jeff Bagwell '95/173	150.00	70.00	19.00
1997 SP Vintage Autographs Jeff Bagwell '96/292	120.00	55.00	15.00
1997 SP Vintage Autographs Jeff Bagwell '96 MM/23	400.00	180.00	50.00
1997 SP Vintage Autographs Jay Buhner '95/57	100.00	45.00	12.50
1997 SP Vintage Autographs Jay Buhner '96/79	100.00	45.00	12.50
1997 SP Vintage Autographs Jay Buhner '96 FX/27	150.00	70.00	19.00
1997 SP Vintage Autographs Ken Griffey Jr. '93/16	2500.00	1100.00	300.00
1997 SP Vintage Autographs Ken Griffey Jr. '94/103	1000.00	450.00	125.00
1997 SP Vintage Autographs Ken Griffey Jr. '95/38	1500.00	700.00	190.00
1997 SP Vintage Autographs Ken Griffey Jr. '96/312	500.00	220.00	60.00
1997 SP Vintage Autographs Tony Gwynn '93/17	800.00	350.00	100.00
1997 SP Vintage Autographs Tony Gwynn '94/367	200.00	90.00	25.00
1997 SP Vintage Autographs Tony Gwynn '94 HV/31	500.00	220.00	60.00
1997 SP Vintage Autographs Tony Gwynn '95/64	400.00	180.00	50.00
1997 SP Vintage Autographs Tony Gwynn '96/20	600.00	275.00	75.00
1997 SP Vintage Autographs Todd Hollandsworth '94/167	25.00	11.00	3.10
1997 SP Vintage Autographs Chipper Jones '93/34	500.00	220.00	60.00
1997 SP Vintage Autographs Chipper Jones '95/60	400.00	180.00	50.00
1997 SP Vintage Autographs Chipper Jones '96/102	300.00	135.00	38.00
1997 SP Vintage Autographs R.Ordonez '96/111	30.00	13.50	3.70
1997 SP Vintage Autographs Rey Ordonez '96 MM/40	50.00	22.00	6.25
1997 SP Vintage Autographs Alex Rodriguez '94/94	400.00	180.00	50.00
1997 SP Vintage Autographs Alex Rodriguez '95/63	500.00	220.00	60.00
1997 SP Vintage Autographs Alex Rodriguez '96/73	500.00	220.00	60.00
1997 SP Vintage Autographs Gary Sheffield '94/130	80.00	36.00	10.00
1997 SP Vintage Autographs Gary Sheffield '95/221	60.00	27.00	7.50
1997 SP Vintage Autographs Gary Sheffield '96/58	100.00	45.00	12.50
1997 SP Vintage Autographs Mo Vaughn '97 EXCH/250	80.00	36.00	10.00

1997 Sports Illustrated Autographed Mini-Covers

COMPLETE SET (6)	1000.00	450.00	125.00

Redemptions for these autographed cards were randomly inserted in packs. This six-card set features color photos of three current and three retired players on miniature SI covers. Only 250 of each card was produced and serially numbered and autographed.

	MINT	NRMT	EXC
1997 Sports Illustrated Autographed Mini-Covers COMMON CARD (1-6)	80.00	36.00	10.00
1997 Sports Illustrated Autographed Mini-Covers Alex Rodriguez	250.00	110.00	31.00
1997 Sports Illustrated Autographed Mini-Covers Cal Ripken	300.00	135.00	38.00
1997 Sports Illustrated Autographed Mini-Covers Kirby Puckett	120.00	55.00	15.00
1997 Sports Illustrated Autographed Mini-Covers Willie Mays	200.00	90.00	25.00
1997 Sports Illustrated Autographed Mini-Covers Frank Robinson	80.00	36.00	10.00
1997 Sports Illustrated Autographed Mini-Covers Hank Aaron	150.00	70.00	19.00

1997 SPx Bound for Glory Supreme Signatures

COMPLETE SET (5)	1200.00	550.00	150.00

Randomly inserted in packs, this five-card set features unnumbered autographed Bound for Glory cards. Only 250 of each card was produced and signed and are sequentially numbered. The cards are checklisted below in alphabetical order.

	MINT	NRMT	EXC
1997 SPx Bound for Glory Supreme Signatures COMMON CARD (1-5 .)	60.00	27.00	7.50
1997 SPx Bound for Glory Supreme Signatures Jeff Bagwell	150.00	70.00	19.00
1997 SPx Bound for Glory Supreme Signatures Ken Griffey Jr.	500.00	220.00	60.00
1997 SPx Bound for Glory Supreme Signatures Andruw Jones	120.00	55.00	15.00
1997 SPx Bound for Glory Supreme Signatures Alex Rodriguez	300.00	135.00	38.00
1997 SPx Bound for Glory Supreme Signatures Gary Sheffield	60.00	27.00	7.50

1997 Stadium Club Co-Signers

COMPLETE SET (10)	600.00	275.00	75.00

Randomly inserted in first series eight-card hobby packs at a rate of one in 168 and first series 13-card hobby collector packs at a rate of one in 96, cards (CO1-CO5) from this dual-sided, dual-player set feature color action player photos printed on 20pt. card stock with authentic signatures of two major league stand-outs per card. The last five cards (CO6-CO10) were randomly inserted in second series 10-card hobby packs with a rate of one in 168 and inserted with a rate of one in 96 hobby collector packs.

	MINT	NRMT	EXC
1997 Stadium Club Co-Signers COMPLETE SERIES 1 (5) 300.00	135.00	38.00
1997 Stadium Club Co-Signers COMPLETE SERIES 2 (5) 300.00	135.00	38.00
1997 Stadium Club Co-Signers COMMON CARD (CO1-CO10) 20.00	9.00	2.50
1997 Stadium Club Co-Signers Andy Pettitte / Derek Jeter 120.00	55.00	15.00
1997 Stadium Club Co-Signers Paul Wilson / Todd Hundley 25.00	11.00	3.10
1997 Stadium Club Co-Signers Jermaine Dye / Mark Wohlers 20.00	9.00	2.50
1997 Stadium Club Co-Signers Scott Rolen / Gregg Jefferies 100.00	45.00	12.50
1997 Stadium Club Co-Signers Todd Hollandsworth / Jason Kendall 40.00	18.00	5.00
1997 Stadium Club Co-Signers Alan Benes / Robin Ventura 40.00	18.00	5.00
1997 Stadium Club Co-Signers Eric Karros / Raul Mondesi 50.00	22.00	6.25
1997 Stadium Club Co-Signers Rey Ordonez / Nomar Garciaparra 120.00	55.00	15.00
1997 Stadium Club Co-Signers Rondell White / Marty Cordova 25.00	11.00	3.10
1997 Stadium Club Co-Signers Tony Gwynn / Karim Garcia 120.00	55.00	15.00

1998 Bowman Certified Blue Autographs

	MINT	NRMT	EXC
COMPLETE SET (70) 1500.00	700.00	190.00

Randomly inserted in Bowman's second series only, this 70-card set was inserted in packs at a rate of one in 122, and printed in gold, blue and silver ink variations.

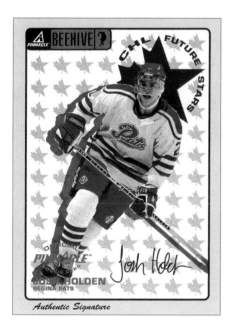

	MINT	NRMT	EXC
1998 Bowman Certified Blue Autographs COMMON CARD (1-70) 15.00	6.75	1.85
1998 Bowman Certified Blue Autographs Adrian Beltre 50.00	22.00	6.25
1998 Bowman Certified Blue Autographs Brad Fullmer 20.00	9.00	2.50
1998 Bowman Certified Blue Autographs Ricky Ledee 20.00	9.00	2.50
1998 Bowman Certified Blue Autographs David Ortiz 20.00	9.00	2.50
1998 Bowman Certified Blue Autographs Fernando Tatis 15.00	6.75	1.85
1998 Bowman Certified Blue Autographs Kerry Wood 120.00	55.00	15.00
1998 Bowman Certified Blue Autographs Mel Rosario 15.00	6.75	1.85
1998 Bowman Certified Blue Autographs Cole Liniak 15.00	6.75	1.85
1998 Bowman Certified Blue Autographs A.J. Hinch 20.00	9.00	2.50
1998 Bowman Certified Blue Autographs Jhensy Sandoval 25.00	11.00	3.10
1998 Bowman Certified Blue Autographs Jose Cruz Jr. 40.00	18.00	5.00
1998 Bowman Certified Blue Autographs Richard Hidalgo 15.00	6.75	1.85
1998 Bowman Certified Blue Autographs Geoff Jenkins 15.00	6.75	1.85
1998 Bowman Certified Blue Autographs Carl Pavano 20.00	9.00	2.50
1998 Bowman Certified Blue Autographs Richie Sexson 25.00	11.00	3.10
1998 Bowman Certified Blue Autographs Tony Womack 15.00	6.75	1.85
1998 Bowman Certified Blue Autographs Scott Rolen 80.00	36.00	10.00
1998 Bowman Certified Blue Autographs Ryan Minor 30.00	13.50	3.70
1998 Bowman Certified Blue Autographs Eli Marrero 15.00	6.75	1.85
1998 Bowman Certified Blue Autographs Jason Marquis 15.00	6.75	1.85
1998 Bowman Certified Blue Autographs Mike Lowell 20.00	9.00	2.50
1998 Bowman Certified Blue Autographs Todd Helton 40.00	18.00	5.00
1998 Bowman Certified Blue Autographs Chad Green 15.00	6.75	1.85
1998 Bowman Certified Blue Autographs Scott Elarton 15.00	6.75	1.85
1998 Bowman Certified Blue Autographs Russell Branyan 20.00	9.00	2.50
1998 Bowman Certified Blue Autographs Mike Drumright 15.00	6.75	1.85
1998 Bowman Certified Blue Autographs Ben Grieve 60.00	27.00	7.50
1998 Bowman Certified Blue Autographs Jacque Jones 15.00	6.75	1.85
1998 Bowman Certified Blue Autographs Jared Sandberg 25.00	11.00	3.10
1998 Bowman Certified Blue Autographs Grant Roberts 15.00	6.75	1.85
1998 Bowman Certified Blue Autographs Mike Stoner 30.00	13.50	3.70
1998 Bowman Certified Blue Autographs Brian Rose 15.00	6.75	1.85
1998 Bowman Certified Blue Autographs Randy Winn 15.00	6.75	1.85
1998 Bowman Certified Blue Autographs Justin Towle 15.00	6.75	1.85
1998 Bowman Certified Blue Autographs Anthony Sanders 15.00	6.75	1.85
1998 Bowman Certified Blue Autographs Rafael Medina 15.00	6.75	1.85
1998 Bowman Certified Blue Autographs Corey Lee 15.00	6.75	1.85
1998 Bowman Certified Blue Autographs Mike Kinkade 15.00	6.75	1.85
1998 Bowman Certified Blue Autographs Norm Hutchins 15.00	6.75	1.85

1998 Bowman Certified Blue Autographs Jason Brester 15.00   6.75   1.85
1998 Bowman Certified Blue Autographs Ben Davis 20.00   9.00   2.50
1998 Bowman Certified Blue Autographs Nomar Garciaparra 100.00   45.00   12.50
1998 Bowman Certified Blue Autographs Jeff Liefer 15.00   6.75   1.85
1998 Bowman Certified Blue Autographs Eric Milton 15.00   6.75   1.85
1998 Bowman Certified Blue Autographs Preston Wilson 15.00   6.75   1.85
1998 Bowman Certified Blue Autographs Miguel Tejada 20.00   9.00   2.50
1998 Bowman Certified Blue Autographs Luis Ordaz 15.00   6.75   1.85
1998 Bowman Certified Blue Autographs Travis Lee 80.00   36.00   10.00
1998 Bowman Certified Blue Autographs Kris Benson 15.00   6.75   1.85
1998 Bowman Certified Blue Autographs Jacob Cruz 15.00   6.75   1.85
1998 Bowman Certified Blue Autographs Dermal Brown 20.00   9.00   2.50
1998 Bowman Certified Blue Autographs Marc Kroon 15.00   6.75   1.85
1998 Bowman Certified Blue Autographs Chad Hermansen 30.00   13.50   3.70
1998 Bowman Certified Blue Autographs Roy Halladay 15.00   6.75   1.85
1998 Bowman Certified Blue Autographs Eric Chavez 40.00   18.00   5.00
1998 Bowman Certified Blue Autographs Jason Conti 15.00   6.75   1.85
1998 Bowman Certified Blue Autographs Juan Encarnacion 20.00   9.00   2.50
1998 Bowman Certified Blue Autographs Paul Wilder 15.00   6.75   1.85
1998 Bowman Certified Blue Autographs Aramis Ramirez 40.00   18.00   5.00
1998 Bowman Certified Blue Autographs Cliff Politte 15.00   6.75   1.85
1998 Bowman Certified Blue Autographs Todd Dunwoody 15.00   6.75   1.85
1998 Bowman Certified Blue Autographs Paul Konerko 25.00   11.00   3.10
1998 Bowman Certified Blue Autographs Shane Monahan 15.00   6.75   1.85
1998 Bowman Certified Blue Autographs Alex Sanchez 15.00   6.75   1.85
1998 Bowman Certified Blue Autographs Jeff Abbott 15.00   6.75   1.85
1998 Bowman Certified Blue Autographs John Patterson 15.00   6.75   1.85
1998 Bowman Certified Blue Autographs Peter Munro 15.00   6.75   1.85
1998 Bowman Certified Blue Autographs Jarrod Washburn 15.00   6.75   1.85
1998 Bowman Certified Blue Autographs Derrek Lee 20.00   9.00   2.50
1998 Bowman Certified Blue Autographs Ramon Hernandez 20.00   9.00   2.50

1998 Donruss Elite Back to the Future Autographs

COMPLETE SET (8) 3500.00   1600.00   450.00
Randomly inserted in packs, this seven-card set is a parallel version of the the regular 1998 Donruss Elite Back to the Future insert set and contains the first 100 cards of the regular set signed by both pictured players. Card number six does not exist. Cal Ripken did not sign card #1 along with Paul Konerko. Ripken eventually signed 200 separate cards. One hundred special redemptions (rather bland black and white text-based cards) were issued for the Ripken card and randomly seeded into packs. In addition, lucky collectors that pulled one of the first 100 serial #'d Back to the Future Konerko autograph cards could exchange it for a Ripken autograph AND still receive their Konerko autograph back.

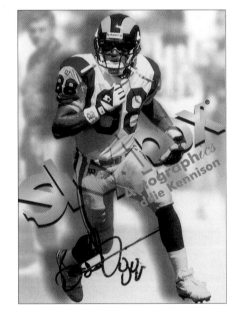

	MINT	NRMT	EXC
1998 Donruss Elite Back to the Future Autographs COMMON (1A-5/7-8) 60.00		27.00	7.50
1998 Donruss Elite Back to the Future Cal Ripken / Paul Konerko 60.00		27.00	7.50
Redeemed/100#(Redeemed card signed only by Konerko)			
1998 Donruss Elite Back to the Future Cal Ripken AU Redeemed/200 . . 500.00		220.00	60.00
Redeemed card signed only by Ripken			
1998 Donruss Elite Back to the Future Jeff Bagwell / Todd Helton 250.00		110.00	31.00
1998 Donruss Elite Back to the Future Eddie Matthews / Chipper Jones . 400.00		180.00	50.00
1998 Donruss Elite Back to the Future Juan Gonzalez / Ben Grieve 400.00		180.00	50.00
1998 Donruss Elite Back to the Future Hank Aaron / Jose Cruz Jr. 400.00		180.00	50.00
1998 Donruss Elite Back to the Future Nolan Ryan / Greg Maddux 1200.00		550.00	150.00
1998 Donruss Elite Back to Future Alex Rodriguez / Nomar Garciaparra . 600.00		275.00	75.00
1998 Donruss Elite Back to the Future Cal Ripken AU EXCH100 . . . . 500.00		220.00	60.00

1998 Donruss Signature Series Previews

	MINT	NRMT	EXC
1998 Donruss Signature Series Previews COMMON CARD 30.00		13.50	3.70
1998 Donruss Signature Series Previews Sandy Alomar Jr./96 . . . . 50.00		22.00	6.25
1998 Donruss Signature Series Previews Andy Benes/135 . . . . 40.00		18.00	5.00
1998 Donruss Signature Series Previews Russell Branyan/188 . . . . 40.00		18.00	5.00
1998 Donruss Signature Series Previews Tony Clark/188 . . . . 60.00		27.00	7.50
1998 Donruss Signature Series Previews Juan Encarnacion/193 . . . . 40.00		18.00	5.00

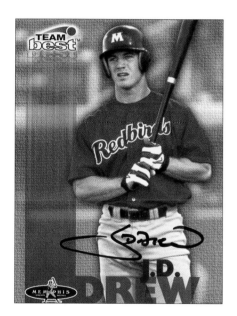

1998 Donruss Signature Series Previews Brad Fullmer/396	30.00	13.50	3.70
1998 Donruss Signature Series Previews Juan Gonzalez/108	300.00	135.00	38.00
1998 Donruss Signature Series Previews Ben Grieve/100	150.00	70.00	19.00
1998 Donruss Signature Series Previews Todd Helton/101	100.00	45.00	12.50
1998 Donruss Signature Series Previews Richard Hidalgo/380	30.00	13.50	3.70
1998 Donruss Signature Series Previews A.J. Hinch/400	30.00	13.50	3.70
1998 Donruss Signature Series Previews Damian Jackson/15	120.00	55.00	15.00
1998 Donruss Signature Series Previews Chipper Jones/112	300.00	135.00	38.00
1998 Donruss Signature Series Previews Chuck Knoblauch/98	100.00	45.00	12.50
1998 Donruss Signature Series Previews Travis Lee/101	200.00	90.00	25.00
1998 Donruss Signature Series Previews Mike Lowell/450	30.00	13.50	3.70
1998 Donruss Signature Series Previews Greg Maddux/92	400.00	180.00	50.00
1998 Donruss Signature Series Previews Kevin Millwood/395	80.00	36.00	10.00
1998 Donruss Signature Series Previews Magglio Ordonez/420	40.00	18.00	5.00
1998 Donruss Signature Series Previews David Ortiz/393	30.00	13.50	3.70
1998 Donruss Signature Series Previews Rafael Palmeiro/107	80.00	36.00	10.00
1998 Donruss Signature Series Previews Cal Ripken/22	1200.00	550.00	150.00
1998 Donruss Signature Series Previews Alex Rodriguez/23	1000.00	450.00	125.00
1998 Donruss Signature Series Previews Curt Schilling/100	80.00	36.00	10.00
1998 Donruss Signature Series Previews Randall Simon/380	30.00	13.50	3.70
1998 Donruss Signature Series Previews Fernando Tatis/400	30.00	13.50	3.70
1998 Donruss Signature Series Previews Miguel Tejada/375	30.00	13.50	3.70
1998 Donruss Signature Series Previews Robin Ventura/95	60.00	27.00	7.50
1998 Donruss Signature Series Previews Kerry Wood/373	150.00	70.00	19.00

1998 SP Authentic Chirography

COMPLETE SET (30) 2000.00 900.00 250.00

Randomly inserted in packs at a rate of one in 25, this 31-card set is autographed by the league's top players. The Ken Griffey Jr. card was actually not available in packs. Instead, an exchange card was printed and seeded into packs. Collectors had until July 27th, 1999 to redeem these Griffey exchange cards.

	MINT	NRMT	EXC
1998 SP Authentic Chirography COMMON CARD	30.00	13.50	3.70
1998 SP Authentic Chirography Andruw Jones	50.00	22.00	6.25
1998 SP Authentic Chirography Alex Rodriguez SP800	150.00	70.00	19.00
1998 SP Authentic Chirography Ben Grieve	80.00	36.00	10.00
1998 SP Authentic Chirography Charles Johnson	30.00	13.50	3.70
1998 SP Authentic Chirography Chipper Jones SP800	120.00	55.00	15.00
1998 SP Authentic Chirography Darin Erstad	50.00	22.00	6.25
1998 SP Authentic Chirography Gary Sheffield	30.00	13.50	3.70
1998 SP Authentic Chirography Ivan Rodriguez	60.00	27.00	7.50
1998 SP Authentic Chirography Jose Cruz Jr.	50.00	22.00	6.25
1998 SP Authentic Chirography Ken Griffey Jr. SP400 EXCH	300.00	135.00	38.00
1998 SP Authentic Chirography Livan Hernandez	30.00	13.50	3.70
1998 SP Authentic Chirography Mark Kotsay	30.00	13.50	3.70
1998 SP Authentic Chirography Mike Mussina	50.00	22.00	6.25
1998 SP Authentic Chirography Miguel Tejada	30.00	13.50	3.70
1998 SP Authentic Chirography Mo Vaughn SP800	60.00	27.00	7.50
1998 SP Authentic Chirography Nomar Garciaparra SP400	150.00	70.00	19.00
1998 SP Authentic Chirography Paul Konerko	30.00	13.50	3.70
1998 SP Authentic Chirography Paul Molitor SP800	60.00	27.00	7.50
1998 SP Authentic Chirography Roberto Alomar SP800	60.00	27.00	7.50
1998 SP Authentic Chirography Russell Branyan	30.00	13.50	3.70
1998 SP Authentic Chirography Roger Clemens SP400	150.00	70.00	19.00
1998 SP Authentic Chirography Ray Lankford	30.00	13.50	3.70
1998 SP Authentic Chirography Sean Casey	30.00	13.50	3.70
1998 SP Authentic Chirography Scott Rolen	80.00	36.00	10.00
1998 SP Authentic Chirography Tony Clark	30.00	13.50	3.70
1998 SP Authentic Chirography Tony Gwynn SP850	120.00	55.00	15.00
1998 SP Authentic Chirography Todd Helton	50.00	22.00	6.25
1998 SP Authentic Chirography Travis Lee	100.00	45.00	12.50
1998 SP Authentic Chirography Vladimir Guerrero	60.00	27.00	7.50

1998 Sports Illustrated Then and Now Autograph Redemptions

COMPLETE SET (6) 750.00   350.00   95.00

Randomly inserted in packs, these six different redemption cards could be exchanged prior to the November 1st, 1999 deadline for special signed cards. Four of the six cards in the set (#'s 2, 3, 4 and 5) were serial numbered by hand to 250. The other two cards (#'s 1 and 6) were serial numbered by hand to 500. All of the cards except for Gibson and Rolen utilize the same card fronts as seen in the more common Covers insert set (featuring reproductions of classic SI covers). The Gibson and Rolen cards feature unique card fronts. All six card backs feature guidelines for the exchange program. The cards are unnumbered and checklisted below alphabetically.

	MINT	NRMT	EXC
1998 Sports Illustrated Then and Now Autograph Red. COMMON (1-6) .	80.00	36.00	10.00
1998 Sports Illustrated Then and Now Autograph Red. Roger Clemens/250	150.00	70.00	19.00
1998 Sports Illustrated Then and Now Autograph Red. Bob Gibson/500	80.00	36.00	10.00
1998 Sports Illustrated Then and Now Autograph Red. Tony Gwynn/250	150.00	70.00	19.00
1998 Sports Illustrated Then and Now Red. Harmon Killebrew/500	80.00	36.00	10.00
1998 Sports Illustrated Then and Now Autograph Red. Willie Mays/250 .	200.00	90.00	25.00
1998 Sports Illustrated Then and Now Autograph Red. Scott Rolen/250 .	120.00	55.00	15.00

1998 Stadium Club Co-Signers

COMMON CARD (CS1-CS36) 50.00   22.00   6.25

Randomly inserted exclusively in first and second series hobby and Home Team Advantage packs, this 36-card set features color photos of two top players on each card along with their autographs. These cards were released in three different levels of scarcity: A, B and C. Seeding rates are as follows: Series 1 Group A 1:4372 hobby and 1:2623 HTA, Series 1 Group B 1:1457 hobby and 1:874 HTA, Series 1 Group C 1:121 hobby and 1:73 HTA, Series 2 Group A 1:4702 hobby and 1:2821 HTA, Series 2 Group B 1:1567 hobby and 1:940 HTA and Series 2 Group C 1:131 hobby and 1:78 HTA. The scarce group A cards (rumored to be only 25 of each made) are the most difficult to obtain and are not priced due to lack of market information.

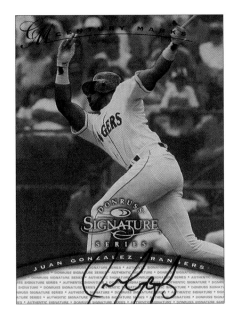

	MINT	NRMT	EXC
1998 Stadium Club Co-Signers Nomar Garciaparra A / Scott Rolen			
1998 Stadium Club Co-Signers Nomar Garciaparra B / Derek Jeter	300.00	135.00	38.00
1998 Stadium Club Co-Signers Nomar Garciaparra C / Eric Karros	120.00	55.00	15.00
1998 Stadium Club Co-Signers Scott Rolen C / Derek Jeter	150.00	70.00	19.00
1998 Stadium Club Co-Signers Scott Rolen B / Eric Karros	200.00	90.00	25.00
1998 Stadium Club Co-Signers Derek Jeter A / Eric Karros			
1998 Stadium Club Co-Signers Travis Lee B / Jose Cruz Jr.	250.00	110.00	31.00
1998 Stadium Club Co-Signers Travis Lee C / Mark Kotsay	120.00	55.00	15.00
1998 Stadium Club Co-Signers Travis Lee A / Paul Konerko			
1998 Stadium Club Co-Signers Jose Cruz Jr. A / Mark Kotsay			
1998 Stadium Club Co-Signers Jose Cruz Jr. C / Paul Konerko	80.00	36.00	10.00
1998 Stadium Club Co-Signers Mark Kotsay B / Paul Konerko	100.00	45.00	12.50
1998 Stadium Club Co-Signers Tony Gwynn A / Larry Walker			
1998 Stadium Club Co-Signers Tony Gwynn C / Mark Grudzielanek	120.00	55.00	15.00
1998 Stadium Club Co-Signers Tony Gwynn B / Andres Galarraga	250.00	110.00	31.00
1998 Stadium Club Co-Signers Larry Walker B / Mark Grudzielanek	100.00	45.00	12.50
1998 Stadium Club Co-Signers Larry Walker C / Andres Galarraga	80.00	36.00	10.00
1998 Stadium Club Co-Signers Mark Grudzielanek A / Andres Galarraga			
1998 Stadium Club Co-Signers Sandy Alomar A / Roberto Alomar			
1998 Stadium Club Co-Signers Sandy Alomar C / Andy Pettitte	50.00	22.00	6.25
1998 Stadium Club Co-Signers Sandy Alomar B / Tino Martinez	80.00	36.00	10.00
1998 Stadium Club Co-Signers Roberto Alomar B / Andy Pettitte	120.00	55.00	15.00
1998 Stadium Club Co-Signers Roberto Alomar C / Tino Martinez	60.00	27.00	7.50
1998 Stadium Club Co-Signers Andy Pettitte A / Tino Martinez			
1998 Stadium Club Co-Signers Tony Clark A / Todd Hundley			
1998 Stadium Club Co-Signers Tony Clark B / Tim Salmon	100.00	45.00	12.50
1998 Stadium Club Co-Signers Tony Clark C / Robin Ventura	50.00	22.00	6.25
1998 Stadium Club Co-Signers Todd Hundley C / Tim Salmon	50.00	22.00	6.25
1998 Stadium Club Co-Signers Todd Hundley B / Robin Ventura	50.00	22.00	6.25
1998 Stadium Club Co-Signers Tim Salmon A / Robin Ventura			
1998 Stadium Club Co-Signers Roger Clemens B / Randy Johnson	250.00	110.00	31.00
1998 Stadium Club Co-Signers Roger Clemens A / Jaret Wright			
1998 Stadium Club Co-Signers Roger Clemens C / Matt Morris	100.00	45.00	12.50
1998 Stadium Club Co-Signers Randy Johnson C / Jaret Wright	80.00	36.00	10.00
1998 Stadium Club Co-Signers Randy Johnson A / Matt Morris			
1998 Stadium Club Co-Signers Jaret Wright B / Matt Morris	100.00	45.00	12.50

1998 Topps Stars Rookie Reprints Autographs

COMPLETE SET (5) 400.00   180.00   50.00
Stated odds are around 1:273 packs.

	MINT	NRMT	EXC
1998 Topps Stars Rookie Reprints Autographs COMMON CARD (1-5) . .	60.00	27.00	7.50
1998 Topps Stars Rookie Reprints Autographs Johnny Bench	100.00	45.00	12.50
1998 Topps Stars Rookie Reprints Autographs Whitey Ford	60.00	27.00	7.50
1998 Topps Stars Rookie Reprints Autographs Joe Morgan	60.00	27.00	7.50
1998 Topps Stars Rookie Reprints Autographs Mike Schmidt	120.00	55.00	15.00
1998 Topps Stars Rookie Reprints Autographs Carl Yastrzemski	100.00	45.00	12.50

1995 Action Packed Hall of Fame

COMPLETE SET (35) 800.00   350.00   100.00

1995 Action Packed Hall of Fame Signature series I was released in January, with series II released in time for the playoffs. Except for Pete Maravich, every player in the set autographed at least 500 cards. Bill Russell and Bob Cousy are featured only on signed cards, not unsigned ones; thus, the regular set consists of 38 cards, but the signed set contains 40. Redemption cards for the autographs were randomly inserted. Every box contained one autograph redemption card and one 24K gold card; gold versions of all 38 cards exist. Action Packed limited the product to 2,000 cases. "Greats of the Game" autograph cards were inserted one per case. The fronts feature either color or black-and- white embossed player photos inside gold borders. The player's name is reversed out in the top wider gold border. His facsimile autograph is inscribed in gold across the picture. On a ghosted version of the front photo, the backs present biography and career summary. The third series is subdivided as follows: Hall of Fame (1-31), Class of '94 (32-36), and Greats of the Game (37-40). 24K cards are valued at 20 times the listed prices below. Redeemed autograph cards are valued at 60 times the listed prices below. The autographed Russell and Cousy cards are priced individually below.

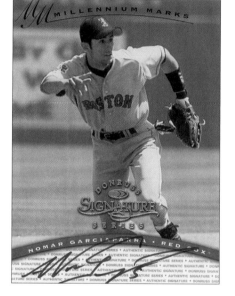

	MINT	NRMT	EXC
1995 Action Packed Hall of Fame COMPLETE SERIES 1 (20)	400.00	180.00	50.00
1995 Action Packed Hall of Fame COMPLETE SERIES 2 (17)	400.00	180.00	50.00
1995 Action Packed Hall of Fame COMMON CARD (1-38)	15.00	6.75	1.85
1995 Action Packed Hall of Fame Nate Archibald	25.00	11.00	3.10
1995 Action Packed Hall of Fame Dick McGuire	15.00	6.75	1.85
1995 Action Packed Hall of Fame Lou Carnesecca	15.00	6.75	1.85
1995 Action Packed Hall of Fame Red Holzman	15.00	6.75	1.85
1995 Action Packed Hall of Fame Rick Barry	25.00	11.00	3.10
1995 Action Packed Hall of Fame Billy Cunningham	25.00	11.00	3.10
1995 Action Packed Hall of Fame Connie Hawkins	30.00	13.50	3.70
1995 Action Packed Hall of Fame Dan Issel	25.00	11.00	3.10
1995 Action Packed Hall of Fame Walt Bellamy	15.00	6.75	1.85
1995 Action Packed Hall of Fame Elvin Hayes	30.00	13.50	3.70
1995 Action Packed Hall of Fame Calvin Murphy	25.00	11.00	3.10
1995 Action Packed Hall of Fame Bob Knight	30.00	13.50	3.70
1995 Action Packed Hall of Fame Al McGuire	25.00	11.00	3.10
1995 Action Packed Hall of Fame K.C. Jones	15.00	6.75	1.85
1995 Action Packed Hall of Fame Jack Ramsay	15.00	6.75	1.85
1995 Action Packed Hall of Fame John Wooden	30.00	13.50	3.70
1995 Action Packed Hall of Fame Ray Meyer	15.00	6.75	1.85
1995 Action Packed Hall of Fame Lenny Wilkens	25.00	11.00	3.10
1995 Action Packed Hall of Fame Dean Smith	30.00	13.50	3.70
1995 Action Packed Hall of Fame Ed Macauley	15.00	6.75	1.85
1995 Action Packed Hall of Fame Nate Thurmond	25.00	11.00	3.10
1995 Action Packed Hall of Fame Dolph Schayes	30.00	13.50	3.70
1995 Action Packed Hall of Fame Bill Sharman	25.00	11.00	3.10
1995 Action Packed Hall of Fame Jerry Lucas	25.00	11.00	3.10
1995 Action Packed Hall of Fame Frank Ramsey	15.00	6.75	1.85
1995 Action Packed Hall of Fame Bob Pettit	30.00	13.50	3.70
1995 Action Packed Hall of Fame Hal Greer	15.00	6.75	1.85
1995 Action Packed Hall of Fame Bill Walton	30.00	13.50	3.70
1995 Action Packed Hall of Fame Bill Bradley	30.00	13.50	3.70
1995 Action Packed Hall of Fame Tom Gola	15.00	6.75	1.85
1995 Action Packed Hall of Fame Carol Blazejowski	15.00	6.75	1.85
1995 Action Packed Hall of Fame Denny Crum	15.00	6.75	1.85
1995 Action Packed Hall of Fame Chuck Daly	15.00	6.75	1.85

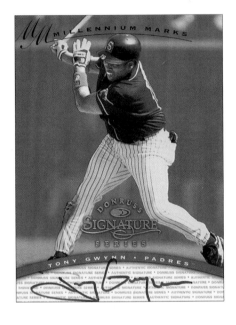

1995 Action Packed Hall of Fame Buddy Jeanette	15.00	6.75	1.85
1995 Action Packed Hall of Fame Cesare Rubini	15.00	6.75	1.85
1995 Action Packed Hall of Fame Bill Bradley	30.00	13.50	3.70
1995 Action Packed Hall of Fame Bill Walton	30.00	13.50	3.70
1995 Action Packed Hall of Fame Bob Cousy AU	100.00	45.00	12.50
1995 Action Packed Hall of Fame Bill Russell AU	400.00	180.00	50.00

1994 SkyBox USA Autographs

COMPLETE SET (7) 750.00   350.00   95.00

These scarce chase cards were inserted in SkyBox USA packs at a rate of about two per case. Each player signed his "Trademark Move" card from the regular issue set. These are the only seven players known to have signed cards for this product. The signatures are in gold paint, and the cards are embossed with the SkyBox seal to distinguish them from any cards signed after the product's release.

	MINT	NRMT	EXC
1994 SkyBox USA Autographs COMMON AUTOGRAPH CARD	75.00	34.00	9.50
1994 SkyBox USA Autographs Larry Johnson	75.00	34.00	9.50
1994 SkyBox USA Autographs Shawn Kemp	200.00	90.00	25.00
1994 SkyBox USA Autographs Dominique Wilkins	100.00	45.00	12.50
1994 SkyBox USA Autographs Isiah Thomas	100.00	45.00	12.50
1994 SkyBox USA Autographs Joe Dumars	100.00	45.00	12.50
1994 SkyBox USA Autographs Dan Majerle	75.00	34.00	9.50
1994 SkyBox USA Autographs Tim Hardaway	150.00	70.00	19.00

1994-95 Collector's Choice Blow-Ups

COMPLETE SET (5) 10.00   4.50   1.25

One of these oversized (5" by 7") cards was inserted exclusively into each series 2 hobby box. Each Blow-Up is identical in design and numbering to their corresponding basic issue card. According to information provided by Upper Deck at least 3,000 of these cards were autographed and randomly seeded into boxes. There are far fewer autographed Michael Jordan Blow-Ups than the other four players featured.

	MINT	NRMT	EXC
1994-95 Collector's Choice Blow-Ups COMMON CARD (40/76/132) . . .	50	.23	.06
1994-95 Collector's Choice Blow-Ups Michael Jordan BB	8.00	3.60	1.00
1994-95 Collector's Choice Blow-Ups Calbert Cheaney	.75	.35	.09
1994-95 Collector's Choice Blow-Ups Shawn Bradley	.75	.35	.09
1994-95 Collector's Choice Blow-Ups Bobby Hurley	.50	.23	.06
1994-95 Collector's Choice Blow-Ups Shawn Kemp	2.00	.90	.25
1994-95 Collector's Choice Blow-Ups Michael Jordan AU	5000.00	2200.00	600.00
1994-95 Collector's Choice Blow-Ups Calbert Cheaney AU	30.00	13.50	3.70
1994-95 Collector's Choice Blow-Ups Shawn Bradley AU	30.00	13.50	3.70
1994-95 Collector's Choice Blow-Ups Bobby Hurley AU	30.00	13.50	3.70
1994-95 Collector's Choice Blow-Ups Shawn Kemp AU	150.00	70.00	19.00

1996-97 SkyBox Premium Autographics Black

COMP.BLACK AU SET (95) 3500.00   1600.00   450.00

Randomly inserted in the following 1996-97 products: Hoops series one and two, SkyBox series one and two, SkyBox Z-Force series one and two and SkyBox EX2000 all at a rate of one in 72, this set features autographs of some of the top stars in the NBA. Card design is identical for each issue and several players had their cards seeded into more than one of the aforementioned products. Card fronts feature a background in the particular player's team colors and an action shot of the player. Most of the cards were autographed vertically along the left side. Card backs are black with a spotlight photo, the player's name and career statistics. The first 100 cards of each player were autographed in blue ink and the remaining number were in black. A couple exceptions include Hakeem Olajuwon and Scottie Pippen, who autographed all of their cards in blue ink only. Also, Kevin Garnett autographed two-thirds of his cards in blue and the rest in black. The cards below are not numbered and are listed alphabetically. As far as set value, the set is considered complete with the Kevin Garnett Black, Hakeem Olajuwon Blue and the Scottie Pippen Blue. Both Olajuwon and Pippen are also listed under the Blue set. Recently, some news of counterfeits have surfaced. The focal cards being reproduced include the Grant Hill, Kevin Garnett and Scottie Pippen. These cards feature no chipping on the edges, a lighter color of black on the back, a fuzzy copyright line and, in general, a poor autograph. These do, however, have the SkyBox logo stamped on the card.

	MINT	NRMT	EXC
1996-97 SkyBox Premium Auto. Black COMMON BLACK AU CARD . . .	10.00	4.50	1.25
1996-97 SkyBox Premium Autographics Black Ray Allen	80.00	36.00	10.00

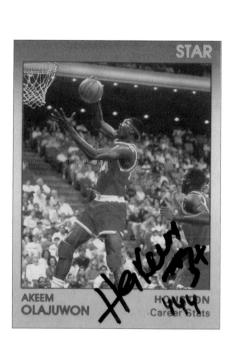

1996-97 SkyBox Premium Autographics Black Kenny Anderson 35.00 16.00 4.40
1996-97 SkyBox Premium Autographics Black Nick Anderson 30.00 13.50 3.70
1996-97 SkyBox Premium Autographics Black B.J. Armstrong 10.00 4.50 1.25
1996-97 SkyBox Premium Autographics Black Vincent Askew 10.00 4.50 1.25
1996-97 SkyBox Premium Autographics Black Dana Barros 10.00 4.50 1.25
1996-97 SkyBox Premium Autographics Black Brent Barry 20.00 9.00 2.50
1996-97 SkyBox Premium Autographics Black Travis Best 10.00 4.50 1.25
1996-97 SkyBox Premium Autographics Black Muggsy Bogues 10.00 4.50 1.25
1996-97 SkyBox Premium Autographics Black P.J. Brown 10.00 4.50 1.25
1996-97 SkyBox Premium Autographics Black Randy Brown 20.00 9.00 2.50
1996-97 SkyBox Premium Autographics Black Marcus Camby 60.00 27.00 7.50
1996-97 SkyBox Premium Autographics Black Chris Childs 15.00 6.75 1.85
1996-97 SkyBox Premium Autographics Black Dell Curry 10.00 4.50 1.25
1996-97 SkyBox Premium Autographics Black Andrew DeClercq 10.00 4.50 1.25
1996-97 SkyBox Premium Autographics Black Tony Delk 35.00 16.00 4.40
1996-97 SkyBox Premium Autographics Black Sherman Douglas 10.00 4.50 1.25
1996-97 SkyBox Premium Autographics Black Clyde Drexler 150.00 70.00 19.00
1996-97 SkyBox Premium Autographics Black Tyus Edney 10.00 4.50 1.25
1996-97 SkyBox Premium Autographics Black Michael Finley 40.00 18.00 5.00
1996-97 SkyBox Premium Autographics Black Rick Fox 10.00 4.50 1.25
1996-97 SkyBox Premium Autographics Black Kevin Garnett 300.00 135.00 38.00
1996-97 SkyBox Premium Autographics Black Matt Geiger 10.00 4.50 1.25
1996-97 SkyBox Premium Autographics Black Kendall Gill 30.00 13.50 3.70
1996-97 SkyBox Premium Autographics Black Brian Grant 10.00 4.50 1.25
1996-97 SkyBox Premium Autographics Black Tim Hardaway 60.00 27.00 7.50
1996-97 SkyBox Premium Autographics Black Grant Hill 300.00 135.00 38.00
1996-97 SkyBox Premium Autographics Black Tyrone Hill 10.00 4.50 1.25
1996-97 SkyBox Premium Autographics Black Allan Houston 30.00 13.50 3.70
1996-97 SkyBox Premium Autographics Black Juwan Howard 250.00 110.00 31.00
1996-97 SkyBox Premium Autographics Black Zydrunas Ilgauskas 35.00 16.00 4.40
1996-97 SkyBox Premium Autographics Black Jim Jackson 15.00 6.75 1.85
1996-97 SkyBox Premium Autographics Black Mark Jackson 15.00 6.75 1.85
1996-97 SkyBox Premium Autographics Black Eddie Jones 125.00 55.00 15.50
1996-97 SkyBox Premium Autographics Black Adam Keefe 10.00 4.50 1.25
1996-97 SkyBox Premium Autographics Black Steve Kerr 20.00 9.00 2.50
1996-97 SkyBox Premium Autographics Black Kerry Kittles 80.00 36.00 10.00
1996-97 SkyBox Premium Autographics Black Toni Kukoc 40.00 18.00 5.00
1996-97 SkyBox Premium Autographics Black Andrew Lang 10.00 4.50 1.25
1996-97 SkyBox Premium Autographics Black Voshon Lenard 15.00 6.75 1.85
1996-97 SkyBox Premium Autographics Black Grant Long 10.00 4.50 1.25
1996-97 SkyBox Premium Autographics Black Luc Longley 30.00 13.50 3.70
1996-97 SkyBox Premium Autographics Black George Lynch 10.00 4.50 1.25
1996-97 SkyBox Premium Autographics Black Don MacLean 10.00 4.50 1.25
1996-97 SkyBox Premium Autographics Black Stephon Marbury 150.00 70.00 19.00
1996-97 SkyBox Premium Autographics Black Lee Mayberry 10.00 4.50 1.25
1996-97 SkyBox Premium Autographics Black Walter McCarty 30.00 13.50 3.70
1996-97 SkyBox Premium Autographics Black George McCloud 60.00 27.00 7.50
1996-97 SkyBox Premium Autographics Black Antonio McDyess 90.00 40.00 11.00
1996-97 SkyBox Premium Autographics Black Nate McMillan 10.00 4.50 1.25
1996-97 SkyBox Premium Autographics Black Chris Mills 10.00 4.50 1.25
1996-97 SkyBox Premium Autographics Black Sam Mitchell 10.00 4.50 1.25
1996-97 SkyBox Premium Autographics Black Eric Montross 10.00 4.50 1.25
1996-97 SkyBox Premium Autographics Black Chris Morris 10.00 4.50 1.25
1996-97 SkyBox Premium Autographics Black Lawrence Moten 10.00 4.50 1.25
1996-97 SkyBox Premium Autographics Black Alonzo Mourning 175.00 80.00 22.00
1996-97 SkyBox Premium Autographics Black Gheorghe Muresan 10.00 4.50 1.25
1996-97 SkyBox Premium Autographics Black Steve Nash 70.00 32.00 8.75
1996-97 SkyBox Premium Autographics Black Ed O'Bannon 10.00 4.50 1.25
1996-97 SkyBox Premium Autographics Black Charles Oakley 25.00 11.00 3.10
1996-97 SkyBox Premium Autographics Black Hakeem Olajuwon Blue .. 200.00 90.00 25.00
1996-97 SkyBox Premium Autographics Black Greg Ostertag 10.00 4.50 1.25
1996-97 SkyBox Premium Autographics Black Billy Owens 10.00 4.50 1.25
1996-97 SkyBox Premium Autographics Black Sam Perkins 15.00 6.75 1.85
1996-97 SkyBox Premium Autographics Black Chuck Person 10.00 4.50 1.25

1996-97 SkyBox Premium Autographics Black Wesley Person 10.00 4.50 1.25
1996-97 SkyBox Premium Autographics Black Bobby Phills 10.00 4.50 1.25
1996-97 SkyBox Premium Autographics Black Scottie Pippen (blue ink) . 300.00 135.00 38.00
1996-97 SkyBox Premium Autographics Black Theo Ratliff 10.00 4.50 1.25
1996-97 SkyBox Premium Autographics Black Glen Rice 60.00 27.00 7.50
1996-97 SkyBox Premium Autographics Black Rodney Rogers 10.00 4.50 1.25
1996-97 SkyBox Premium Autographics Black Byron Scott 15.00 6.75 1.85
1996-97 SkyBox Premium Autographics Black Dennis Scott 10.00 4.50 1.25
1996-97 SkyBox Premium Autographics Black Joe Smith 60.00 27.00 7.50
1996-97 SkyBox Premium Autographics Black Kenny Smith 10.00 4.50 1.25
1996-97 SkyBox Premium Autographics Black Rik Smits 15.00 6.75 1.85
1996-97 SkyBox Premium Autographics Black Eric Snow 10.00 4.50 1.25
1996-97 SkyBox Premium Autographics Black Latrell Sprewell 25.00 11.00 3.10
1996-97 SkyBox Premium Autographics Black Jerry Stackhouse 50.00 22.00 6.25
1996-97 SkyBox Premium Autographics Black John Starks 30.00 13.50 3.70
1996-97 SkyBox Premium Autographics Black Bryant Stith 10.00 4.50 1.25
1996-97 SkyBox Premium Autographics Black Damon Stoudamire 150.00 70.00 19.00
1996-97 SkyBox Premium Autographics Black Rod Strickland 120.00 55.00 15.00
1996-97 SkyBox Premium Autographics Black Bob Sura 15.00 6.75 1.85
1996-97 SkyBox Premium Autographics Black Zan Tabak 10.00 4.50 1.25
1996-97 SkyBox Premium Autographics Black Loy Vaught 15.00 6.75 1.85
1996-97 SkyBox Premium Autographics Black Antoine Walker 150.00 70.00 19.00
1996-97 SkyBox Premium Autographics Black Samaki Walker 25.00 11.00 3.10
1996-97 SkyBox Premium Autographics Black John Wallace 60.00 27.00 7.50
1996-97 SkyBox Premium Autographics Black Bill Wennington 15.00 6.75 1.85
1996-97 SkyBox Premium Autographics Black David Wesley 10.00 4.50 1.25
1996-97 SkyBox Premium Autographics Black Doug West 10.00 4.50 1.25
1996-97 SkyBox Premium Autographics Black Monty Williams 10.00 4.50 1.25
1996-97 SkyBox Premium Autographics Black Joe Wolf 10.00 4.50 1.25
1996-97 SkyBox Premium Autographics Black Sharone Wright 10.00 4.50 1.25

1996-97 SkyBox Premium Autographics Blue

COMPLETE SET (94) 7000.00 3200.00 900.00
Randomly inserted in the following 1996-97 products: Hoops series one and two, SkyBox series one and two, SkyBox Z-Force series one and two and SkyBox E-X2000, this set features the first 100 autographs of some of the top stars in the NBA. Hakeem Olajuwon and Scottie Pippen autographed all of their cards in blue ink only. The cards below are not numbered and are listed alphabetically. Note: John Wallace did not sign any blue cards, so this set is actually complete at 94 cards.

	MINT	NRMT	EXC
1996-97 SkyBox Premium Auto. Blue COMMON BLUE AU CARD	20.00	9.00	2.50
1996-97 SkyBox Premium Autographics Blue Ray Allen	150.00	70.00	19.00
1996-97 SkyBox Premium Autographics Blue Kenny Anderson	70.00	32.00	8.75
1996-97 SkyBox Premium Autographics Blue Nick Anderson	60.00	27.00	7.50
1996-97 SkyBox Premium Autographics Blue B.J. Armstrong	20.00	9.00	2.50
1996-97 SkyBox Premium Autographics Blue Vincent Askew	20.00	9.00	2.50
1996-97 SkyBox Premium Autographics Blue Dana Barros	20.00	9.00	2.50
1996-97 SkyBox Premium Autographics Blue Brent Barry	40.00	18.00	5.00
1996-97 SkyBox Premium Autographics Blue Travis Best	20.00	9.00	2.50
1996-97 SkyBox Premium Autographics Blue Muggsy Bogues	20.00	9.00	2.50
1996-97 SkyBox Premium Autographics Blue P.J. Brown	20.00	9.00	2.50
1996-97 SkyBox Premium Autographics Blue Randy Brown	40.00	18.00	5.00
1996-97 SkyBox Premium Autographics Blue Marcus Camby	120.00	55.00	15.00
1996-97 SkyBox Premium Autographics Blue Chris Childs	30.00	13.50	3.70
1996-97 SkyBox Premium Autographics Blue Dell Curry	20.00	9.00	2.50
1996-97 SkyBox Premium Autographics Blue Andrew DeClercq	20.00	9.00	2.50
1996-97 SkyBox Premium Autographics Blue Tony Delk	70.00	32.00	8.75
1996-97 SkyBox Premium Autographics Blue Sherman Douglas	20.00	9.00	2.50
1996-97 SkyBox Premium Autographics Blue Clyde Drexler	300.00	135.00	38.00
1996-97 SkyBox Premium Autographics Blue Tyus Edney	20.00	9.00	2.50
1996-97 SkyBox Premium Autographics Blue Michael Finley	80.00	36.00	10.00
1996-97 SkyBox Premium Autographics Blue Rick Fox	20.00	9.00	2.50
1996-97 SkyBox Premium Autographics Blue Kevin Garnett	275.00	125.00	34.00
1996-97 SkyBox Premium Autographics Blue Matt Geiger	20.00	9.00	2.50

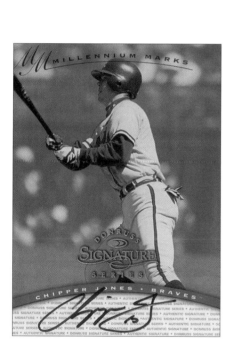

1996-97 SkyBox Premium Autographics Blue Kendall Gill	60.00	27.00	7.50
1996-97 SkyBox Premium Autographics Blue Brian Grant	20.00	9.00	2.50
1996-97 SkyBox Premium Autographics Blue Tim Hardaway	120.00	55.00	15.00
1996-97 SkyBox Premium Autographics Blue Grant Hill	600.00	275.00	75.00
1996-97 SkyBox Premium Autographics Blue Tyrone Hill	20.00	9.00	2.50
1996-97 SkyBox Premium Autographics Blue Allan Houston	60.00	27.00	7.50
1996-97 SkyBox Premium Autographics Blue Juwan Howard	500.00	220.00	60.00
1996-97 SkyBox Premium Autographics Blue Zydrunas Ilgauskas	70.00	32.00	8.75
1996-97 SkyBox Premium Autographics Blue Jim Jackson	30.00	13.50	3.70
1996-97 SkyBox Premium Autographics Blue Mark Jackson	30.00	13.50	3.70
1996-97 SkyBox Premium Autographics Blue Eddie Jones	250.00	110.00	31.00
1996-97 SkyBox Premium Autographics Blue Adam Keefe	20.00	9.00	2.50
1996-97 SkyBox Premium Autographics Blue Steve Kerr	40.00	18.00	5.00
1996-97 SkyBox Premium Autographics Blue Kerry Kittles	150.00	70.00	19.00
1996-97 SkyBox Premium Autographics Blue Toni Kukoc	80.00	36.00	10.00
1996-97 SkyBox Premium Autographics Blue Andrew Lang	20.00	9.00	2.50
1996-97 SkyBox Premium Autographics Blue Voshon Lenard	30.00	13.50	3.70
1996-97 SkyBox Premium Autographics Blue Grant Long	20.00	9.00	2.50
1996-97 SkyBox Premium Autographics Blue Luc Longley	60.00	27.00	7.50
1996-97 SkyBox Premium Autographics Blue George Lynch	20.00	9.00	2.50
1996-97 SkyBox Premium Autographics Blue Don MacLean	20.00	9.00	2.50
1996-97 SkyBox Premium Autographics Blue Stephon Marbury	300.00	135.00	38.00
1996-97 SkyBox Premium Autographics Blue Lee Mayberry	20.00	9.00	2.50
1996-97 SkyBox Premium Autographics Blue Walter McCarty	60.00	27.00	7.50
1996-97 SkyBox Premium Autographics Blue George McCloud	80.00	36.00	10.00
1996-97 SkyBox Premium Autographics Blue Antonio McDyess	175.00	80.00	22.00
1996-97 SkyBox Premium Autographics Blue Nate McMillan	20.00	9.00	2.50
1996-97 SkyBox Premium Autographics Blue Chris Mills	20.00	9.00	2.50
1996-97 SkyBox Premium Autographics Blue Sam Mitchell	20.00	9.00	2.50
1996-97 SkyBox Premium Autographics Blue Eric Montross	20.00	9.00	2.50
1996-97 SkyBox Premium Autographics Blue Chris Morris	20.00	9.00	2.50
1996-97 SkyBox Premium Autographics Blue Lawrence Moten	20.00	9.00	2.50
1996-97 SkyBox Premium Autographics Blue Alonzo Mourning	350.00	160.00	45.00
1996-97 SkyBox Premium Autographics Blue Gheorghe Muresan	30.00	13.50	3.70
1996-97 SkyBox Premium Autographics Blue Steve Nash	120.00	55.00	15.00
1996-97 SkyBox Premium Autographics Blue Ed O'Bannon	20.00	9.00	2.50
1996-97 SkyBox Premium Autographics Blue Charles Oakley	50.00	22.00	6.25
1996-97 SkyBox Premium Autographics Blue Hakeem Olajuwon	200.00	90.00	25.00
1996-97 SkyBox Premium Autographics Blue Greg Ostertag	20.00	9.00	2.50
1996-97 SkyBox Premium Autographics Blue Billy Owens	20.00	9.00	2.50
1996-97 SkyBox Premium Autographics Blue Sam Perkins	30.00	13.50	3.70
1996-97 SkyBox Premium Autographics Blue Chuck Person	20.00	9.00	2.50
1996-97 SkyBox Premium Autographics Blue Wesley Person	20.00	9.00	2.50
1996-97 SkyBox Premium Autographics Blue Bobby Phills	20.00	9.00	2.50
1996-97 SkyBox Premium Autographics Blue Scottie Pippen	300.00	135.00	38.00
1996-97 SkyBox Premium Autographics Blue Theo Ratliff	20.00	9.00	2.50
1996-97 SkyBox Premium Autographics Blue Glen Rice	120.00	55.00	15.00
1996-97 SkyBox Premium Autographics Blue Rodney Rogers	20.00	9.00	2.50
1996-97 SkyBox Premium Autographics Blue Byron Scott	30.00	13.50	3.70
1996-97 SkyBox Premium Autographics Blue Dennis Scott	20.00	9.00	2.50
1996-97 SkyBox Premium Autographics Blue Joe Smith	120.00	55.00	15.00
1996-97 SkyBox Premium Autographics Blue Kenny Smith	20.00	9.00	2.50
1996-97 SkyBox Premium Autographics Blue Rik Smits	30.00	13.50	3.70
1996-97 SkyBox Premium Autographics Blue Eric Snow	20.00	9.00	2.50
1996-97 SkyBox Premium Autographics Blue Latrell Sprewell	50.00	22.00	6.25
1996-97 SkyBox Premium Autographics Blue Jerry Stackhouse	120.00	55.00	15.00
1996-97 SkyBox Premium Autographics Blue John Starks	60.00	27.00	7.50
1996-97 SkyBox Premium Autographics Blue Bryant Stith	20.00	9.00	2.50
1996-97 SkyBox Premium Autographics Blue Damon Stoudamire	300.00	135.00	38.00
1996-97 SkyBox Premium Autographics Blue Rod Strickland	250.00	110.00	31.00
1996-97 SkyBox Premium Autographics Blue Bob Sura	30.00	13.50	3.70
1996-97 SkyBox Premium Autographics Blue Zan Tabak	20.00	9.00	2.50
1996-97 SkyBox Premium Autographics Blue Loy Vaught	30.00	13.50	3.70
1996-97 SkyBox Premium Autographics Blue Antoine Walker	300.00	135.00	38.00

1996-97 SkyBox Premium Autographics Blue Samaki Walker 50.00   22.00   6.25
1996-97 SkyBox Premium Autographics Blue Bill Wennington 30.00   13.50   3.70
1996-97 SkyBox Premium Autographics Blue David Wesley 20.00   9.00   2.50
1996-97 SkyBox Premium Autographics Blue Doug West 20.00   9.00   2.50
1996-97 SkyBox Premium Autographics Blue Monty Williams 20.00   9.00   2.50
1996-97 SkyBox Premium Autographics Blue Joe Wolf 20.00   9.00   2.50
1996-97 SkyBox Premium Autographics Blue Sharone Wright 20.00   9.00   2.50

1997 SPx ProMotion Autographs

COMPLETE SET (5) 3000.00   1350.00   375.00

This five-card set is a parallel set to the regular SPx Pro Motion set and is similar in design. The difference is the autograph of the pictured player on the card. Only 100 of these autographed cards are available for each player and are hand numbered.

	MINT	NRMT	EXC
1997 SPx ProMotion Autographs COMMON CARD (1-5)	125.00	55.00	15.50
1997 SPx ProMotion Autographs Michael Jordan	2500.00	1100.00	300.00
1997 SPx ProMotion Autographs Damon Stoudamire	250.00	110.00	31.00
1997 SPx ProMotion Autographs Anfernee Hardaway	400.00	180.00	50.00
1997 SPx ProMotion Autographs Shawn Kemp	300.00	135.00	38.00
1997 SPx ProMotion Autographs Antonio McDyess	125.00	55.00	15.50

1997-98 Bowman's Best Autograph Atomic Refractors

COMPLETE SET (11) 2500.00   1100.00   300.00

This 11-card parallel set was randomly inserted into packs at a rate of one in 5,961 packs. The cards feature autographs against an atomic refractor background.

	MINT	NRMT	EXC
1997-98 Bowman's Best Autograph Atomic Refractors COMMON CARD	90.00	40.00	11.00
1997-98 Bowman's Best Autograph Atomic Refractors Glenn Robinson ..	175.00	80.00	22.00
1997-98 Bowman's Best Autograph Atomic Refractors Karl Malone	250.00	110.00	31.00
1997-98 Bowman's Best Autograph Atomic Refractors Dikembe Mutombo	90.00	40.00	11.00
1997-98 Bowman's Best Autograph Atomic Refractors Steve Smith	90.00	40.00	11.00
1997-98 Bowman's Best Autograph Atomic Refractors Mitch Richmond .	175.00	80.00	22.00
1997-98 Bowman's Best Autograph Atomic Refractors Tony Battie	175.00	80.00	22.00
1997-98 Bowman's Best Autograph Atomic Refractors Keith Van Horn ..	750.00	350.00	95.00
1997-98 Bowman's Best Autograph Atomic Refractors Chauncey Billups .	250.00	110.00	31.00
1997-98 Bowman's Best Autograph Atomic Refractors Ron Mercer	450.00	200.00	55.00
1997-98 Bowman's Best Autograph Atomic Refractors Adonal Foyle	90.00	40.00	11.00
1997-98 Bowman's Best Autograph Atomic Refractors Karl Malone MVP .	300.00	135.00	38.00

1997-98 Bowman's Best Autograph Refractors

COMPLETE SET (11) 1700.00   750.00   210.00

This 11-card parallel set was randomly inserted into packs at a rate of one in 1,987 packs. The cards feature autographs against a refractor background.

	MINT	NRMT	EXC
1997-98 Bowman's Best Autograph Refractors COMMON CARD	60.00	27.00	7.50
1997-98 Bowman's Best Autograph Refractors Glenn Robinson	120.00	55.00	15.00
1997-98 Bowman's Best Autograph Refractors Karl Malone	150.00	70.00	19.00
1997-98 Bowman's Best Autograph Refractors Dikembe Mutombo	60.00	27.00	7.50
1997-98 Bowman's Best Autograph Refractors Steve Smith	60.00	27.00	7.50
1997-98 Bowman's Best Autograph Refractors Mitch Richmond	120.00	55.00	15.00
1997-98 Bowman's Best Autograph Refractors Tony Battie	120.00	55.00	15.00
1997-98 Bowman's Best Autograph Refractors Keith Van Horn	500.00	220.00	60.00
1997-98 Bowman's Best Autograph Refractors Chauncey Billups	150.00	70.00	19.00
1997-98 Bowman's Best Autograph Refractors Ron Mercer	300.00	135.00	38.00
1997-98 Bowman's Best Autograph Refractors Adonal Foyle	60.00	27.00	7.50
1997-98 Bowman's Best Autograph Refractors Karl Malone MVP	200.00	90.00	25.00

1997-98 Bowman's Best Autographs

COMPLETE SET (11) 700.00   325.00   90.00

Randomly inserted into packs at a rate of one in 373, this 11-card set features autographs on the regular player cards. The only exception is Karl Malone, who has a regular autograph and a special MVP card autograph. There is no special insertion rate for the MVP card.

	MINT	NRMT	EXC
1997-98 Bowman's Best Autographs COMMON CARD 30.00	13.50	3.70
1997-98 Bowman's Best Autographs Glenn Robinson 60.00	27.00	7.50
1997-98 Bowman's Best Autographs Karl Malone 80.00	36.00	10.00
1997-98 Bowman's Best Autographs Dikembe Mutombo 30.00	13.50	3.70
1997-98 Bowman's Best Autographs Steve Smith 30.00	13.50	3.70
1997-98 Bowman's Best Autographs Mitch Richmond 60.00	27.00	7.50
1997-98 Bowman's Best Autographs Tony Battie 60.00	27.00	7.50
1997-98 Bowman's Best Autographs Keith Van Horn 150.00	70.00	19.00
1997-98 Bowman's Best Autographs Chauncey Billups 60.00	27.00	7.50
1997-98 Bowman's Best Autographs Ron Mercer 120.00	55.00	15.00
1997-98 Bowman's Best Autographs Adonal Foyle 30.00	13.50	3.70
1997-98 Bowman's Best Autographs Karl Malone MVP 100.00	45.00	12.50

1997-98 SkyBox Premium Autographics

COMPLETE SET (119) 4800.00   2200.00   600.00

Randomly inserted in packs of all Fleer/SkyBox products, this set features autographs of some of the NBA's best players. For Hoops 1, these were inserted at a rate of one in 240 hobby and retail packs. For Hoops 2, these were inserted at a rate of one in 144 hobby and retail. For Metal and Metal Championship, these cards were inserted one in 120 hobby and retail. For SkyBox Premium 1 and 2, these cards were inserted one in 72 packs. For SkyBox E-X2001, these cards were inserted one in 60 packs. For SkyBox Z-Force 1 and 2, these cards were inserted one in 120 packs. Both Tracy McGrady and Rasheed Wallace only have Century Marks cards - no regular ones. Those cards are included in the set price, but are priced in the Century Mark set. The cards are not numbered and listed below alphabetically.

15

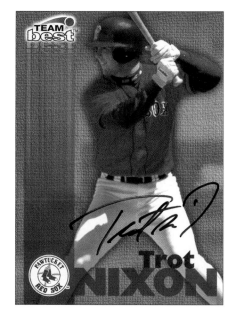

	MINT	NRMT	EXC
1997-98 SkyBox Premium Autographics COMMON AUTOGRAPH 10.00	4.50	1.25
1997-98 SkyBox Premium Autographics Shareef Abdur-Rahim 150.00	70.00	19.00
1997-98 SkyBox Premium Autographics Cory Alexander 10.00	4.50	1.25
1997-98 SkyBox Premium Autographics Kenny Anderson 25.00	11.00	3.10
1997-98 SkyBox Premium Autographics Nick Anderson 20.00	9.00	2.50
1997-98 SkyBox Premium Autographics Stacey Augmon 10.00	4.50	1.25
1997-98 SkyBox Premium Autographics Isaac Austin 10.00	4.50	1.25
1997-98 SkyBox Premium Autographics Vin Baker 80.00	36.00	10.00
1997-98 SkyBox Premium Autographics Charles Barkley 300.00	135.00	38.00
1997-98 SkyBox Premium Autographics Dana Barros 10.00	4.50	1.25
1997-98 SkyBox Premium Autographics Brent Barry 10.00	4.50	1.25
1997-98 SkyBox Premium Autographics Tony Battie 30.00	13.50	3.70
1997-98 SkyBox Premium Autographics Travis Best 10.00	4.50	1.25
1997-98 SkyBox Premium Autographics Corie Blount 10.00	4.50	1.25
1997-98 SkyBox Premium Autographics P.J. Brown 10.00	4.50	1.25
1997-98 SkyBox Premium Autographics Randy Brown 20.00	9.00	2.50
1997-98 SkyBox Premium Autographics Jud Buechler 20.00	9.00	2.50
1997-98 SkyBox Premium Autographics Marcus Camby 50.00	22.00	6.25
1997-98 SkyBox Premium Autographics Elden Campbell 15.00	6.75	1.85
1997-98 SkyBox Premium Autographics Chris Carr 10.00	4.50	1.25
1997-98 SkyBox Premium Autographics Kelvin Cato 40.00	18.00	5.00
1997-98 SkyBox Premium Autographics Duane Causwell 10.00	4.50	1.25
1997-98 SkyBox Premium Autographics Rex Chapman 35.00	16.00	4.40
1997-98 SkyBox Premium Autographics Calbert Cheaney 10.00	4.50	1.25
1997-98 SkyBox Premium Autographics Randolph Childress 10.00	4.50	1.25
1997-98 SkyBox Premium Autographics Derrick Coleman 30.00	13.50	3.70
1997-98 SkyBox Premium Autographics Austin Croshere 25.00	11.00	3.10
1997-98 SkyBox Premium Autographics Dell Curry 10.00	4.50	1.25
1997-98 SkyBox Premium Autographics Ben Davis 10.00	4.50	1.25
1997-98 SkyBox Premium Autographics Mark Davis 10.00	4.50	1.25
1997-98 SkyBox Premium Autographics Andrew DeClercq 10.00	4.50	1.25
1997-98 SkyBox Premium Autographics Tony Delk 25.00	11.00	3.10
1997-98 SkyBox Premium Autographics Vlade Divac 15.00	6.75	1.85
1997-98 SkyBox Premium Autographics Clyde Drexler 125.00	55.00	15.50
1997-98 SkyBox Premium Autographics Joe Dumars 40.00	18.00	5.00
1997-98 SkyBox Premium Autographics Howard Eisley 10.00	4.50	1.25

1997-98 SkyBox Premium Autographics Danny Ferry 10.00   4.50   1.25
1997-98 SkyBox Premium Autographics Michael Finley 25.00   11.00   3.10
1997-98 SkyBox Premium Autographics Derek Fisher 25.00   11.00   3.10
1997-98 SkyBox Premium Autographics Danny Fortson 40.00   18.00   5.00
1997-98 SkyBox Premium Autographics Todd Fuller 10.00   4.50   1.25
1997-98 SkyBox Premium Autographics Chris Gatling 10.00   4.50   1.25
1997-98 SkyBox Premium Autographics Matt Geiger 10.00   4.50   1.25
1997-98 SkyBox Premium Autographics Brian Grant 10.00   4.50   1.25
1997-98 SkyBox Premium Autographics Tom Gugliotta 70.00   32.00   8.75
1997-98 SkyBox Premium Autographics Tim Hardaway 80.00   36.00   10.00
1997-98 SkyBox Premium Autographics Ron Harper 25.00   11.00   3.10
1997-98 SkyBox Premium Autographics Othella Harrington 10.00   4.50   1.25
1997-98 SkyBox Premium Autographics Grant Hill 250.00   110.00   31.00
1997-98 SkyBox Premium Autographics Tyrone Hill 10.00   4.50   1.25
1997-98 SkyBox Premium Autographics Allan Houston 35.00   16.00   4.40
1997-98 SkyBox Premium Autographics Juwan Howard 80.00   36.00   10.00
1997-98 SkyBox Premium Autographics Lindsey Hunter 30.00   13.50   3.70
1997-98 SkyBox Premium Autographics Bobby Hurley 10.00   4.50   1.25
1997-98 SkyBox Premium Autographics Jim Jackson 20.00   9.00   2.50
1997-98 SkyBox Premium Autographics Avery Johnson 10.00   4.50   1.25
1997-98 SkyBox Premium Autographics Eddie Johnson 10.00   4.50   1.25
1997-98 SkyBox Premium Autographics Ervin Johnson 10.00   4.50   1.25
1997-98 SkyBox Premium Autographics Larry Johnson 40.00   18.00   5.00
1997-98 SkyBox Premium Autographics Popeye Jones 10.00   4.50   1.25
1997-98 SkyBox Premium Autographics Adam Keefe 10.00   4.50   1.25
1997-98 SkyBox Premium Autographics Steve Kerr 20.00   9.00   2.50
1997-98 SkyBox Premium Autographics Kerry Kittles 75.00   34.00   9.50
1997-98 SkyBox Premium Autographics Brevin Knight 50.00   22.00   6.25
1997-98 SkyBox Premium Autographics Travis Knight 20.00   9.00   2.50
1997-98 SkyBox Premium Autographics George Lynch 10.00   4.50   1.25
1997-98 SkyBox Premium Autographics Don MacLean 10.00   4.50   1.25
1997-98 SkyBox Premium Autographics Stephon Marbury 175.00   80.00   22.00
1997-98 SkyBox Premium Autographics Donny Marshall 10.00   4.50   1.25
1997-98 SkyBox Premium Autographics Walter McCarty 10.00   4.50   1.25
1997-98 SkyBox Premium Autographics Antonio McDyess 60.00   27.00   7.50
1997-98 SkyBox Premium Autographics Ron Mercer 150.00   70.00   19.00

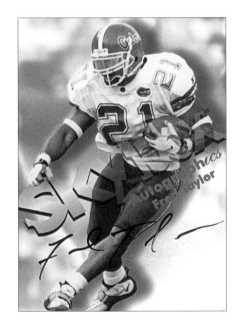

1997-98 SkyBox Premium Autographics Reggie Miller 200.00   90.00   25.00
1997-98 SkyBox Premium Autographics Chris Mills 10.00   4.50   1.25
1997-98 SkyBox Premium Autographics Sam Mitchell 10.00   4.50   1.25
1997-98 SkyBox Premium Autographics Chris Morris 10.00   4.50   1.25
1997-98 SkyBox Premium Autographics Alonzo Mourning 100.00   45.00   12.50
1997-98 SkyBox Premium Autographics Chris Mullin 35.00   16.00   4.40
1997-98 SkyBox Premium Autographics Dikembe Mutombo 50.00   22.00   6.25
1997-98 SkyBox Premium Autographics Anthony Parker 25.00   11.00   3.10
1997-98 SkyBox Premium Autographics Sam Perkins 15.00   6.75   1.85
1997-98 SkyBox Premium Autographics Elliott Perry 10.00   4.50   1.25
1997-98 SkyBox Premium Autographics Bobby Phills 10.00   4.50   1.25
1997-98 SkyBox Premium Autographics Eric Piatkowski 10.00   4.50   1.25
1997-98 SkyBox Premium Autographics Scottie Pippen 250.00   110.00   31.00
1997-98 SkyBox Premium Autographics Vitaly Potapenko 10.00   4.50   1.25
1997-98 SkyBox Premium Autographics Brent Price 10.00   4.50   1.25
1997-98 SkyBox Premium Autographics Theo Ratliff 10.00   4.50   1.25
1997-98 SkyBox Premium Autographics Glen Rice 60.00   27.00   7.50
1997-98 SkyBox Premium Autographics Glenn Robinson 50.00   22.00   6.25
1997-98 SkyBox Premium Autographics Dennis Rodman 400.00   180.00   50.00
1997-98 SkyBox Premium Autographics Roy Rogers 10.00   4.50   1.25
1997-98 SkyBox Premium Autographics Malik Rose 10.00   4.50   1.25
1997-98 SkyBox Premium Autographics Joe Smith 60.00   27.00   7.50
1997-98 SkyBox Premium Autographics Tony Smith 10.00   4.50   1.25
1997-98 SkyBox Premium Autographics Eric Snow 10.00   4.50   1.25
1997-98 SkyBox Premium Auto. Jerry Stackhouse (Pistons uniform) 80.00   36.00   10.00
1997-98 SkyBox Premium Auto. Jerry Stackhouse (Sixers uniform) 50.00   22.00   6.25
1997-98 SkyBox Premium Autographics John Starks 30.00   13.50   3.70
1997-98 SkyBox Premium Autographics Bryant Stith 10.00   4.50   1.25

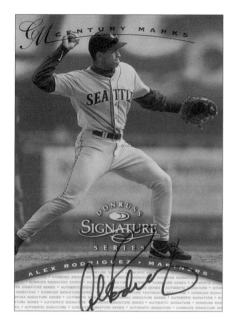

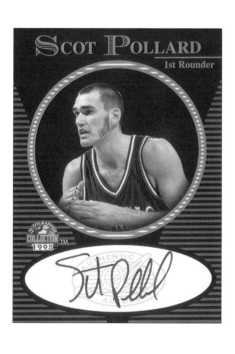

1997-98 SkyBox Premium Autographics Erick Strickland 15.00   6.75   1.85
1997-98 SkyBox Premium Autographics Rod Strickland 50.00   22.00   6.25
1997-98 SkyBox Premium Autographics Nick Van Exel 60.00   27.00   7.50
1997-98 SkyBox Premium Autographics Keith Van Horn 175.00   80.00   22.00
1997-98 SkyBox Premium Autographics David Vaughn 10.00   4.50   1.25
1997-98 SkyBox Premium Autographics Jacque Vaughn 20.00   9.00   2.50
1997-98 SkyBox Premium Autographics Antoine Walker 150.00   70.00   19.00
1997-98 SkyBox Premium Autographics Clarence Weatherspoon 10.00   4.50   1.25
1997-98 SkyBox Premium Autographics David Wesley 10.00   4.50   1.25
1997-98 SkyBox Premium Autographics Dominique Wilkins 60.00   27.00   7.50
1997-98 SkyBox Premium Autographics Gerald Wilkins 10.00   4.50   1.25
1997-98 SkyBox Premium Autographics Eric Williams 10.00   4.50   1.25
1997-98 SkyBox Premium Autographics John Williams 10.00   4.50   1.25
1997-98 SkyBox Premium Autographics Lorenzo Williams 10.00   4.50   1.25
1997-98 SkyBox Premium Autographics Monty Williams 10.00   4.50   1.25
1997-98 SkyBox Premium Autographics Scott Williams 10.00   4.50   1.25
1997-98 SkyBox Premium Autographics Walt Williams 10.00   4.50   1.25
1997-98 SkyBox Premium Autographics Lorenzen Wright 10.00   4.50   1.25

1997-98 SkyBox Premium Autographics Century Marks

COMMON CARD 30.00   13.50   3.70

Hand numbered to 100, these embossed cards make up the first hundred cards signed by each athlete. To determine where each card was issued, please refer to the regular SkyBox Autographics set. The cards are not numbered and are listed below alphabetically.

	MINT	NRMT	EXC
1997-98 SkyBox Premium Auto. Century Marks Shareef Abdur-Rahim ..	450.00	200.00	55.00
1997-98 SkyBox Premium Autographics Century Marks Cory Alexander .	30.00	13.50	3.70
1997-98 SkyBox Premium Autographics Century Marks Kenny Anderson	75.00	34.00	9.50
1997-98 SkyBox Premium Autographics Century Marks Nick Anderson .	60.00	27.00	7.50
1997-98 SkyBox Premium Autographics Century Marks Stacey Augmon .	30.00	13.50	3.70
1997-98 SkyBox Premium Autographics Century Marks Isaac Austin	30.00	13.50	3.70
1997-98 SkyBox Premium Autographics Century Marks Vin Baker	300.00	135.00	38.00
1997-98 SkyBox Premium Autographics Century Marks Charles Barkley .	900.00	400.00	110.00
1997-98 SkyBox Premium Autographics Century Marks Dana Barros ...	30.00	13.50	3.70
1997-98 SkyBox Premium Autographics Century Marks Brent Barry	30.00	13.50	3.70
1997-98 SkyBox Premium Autographics Century Marks Tony Battie	120.00	55.00	15.00
1997-98 SkyBox Premium Autographics Century Marks Travis Best	30.00	13.50	3.70
1997-98 SkyBox Premium Autographics Century Marks Corie Blount ...	30.00	13.50	3.70
1997-98 SkyBox Premium Autographics Century Marks P.J. Brown	30.00	13.50	3.70
1997-98 SkyBox Premium Autographics Century Marks Randy Brown ...	60.00	27.00	7.50
1997-98 SkyBox Premium Autographics Century Marks Jud Buechler ...	60.00	27.00	7.50
1997-98 SkyBox Premium Autographics Century Marks Marcus Camby .	150.00	70.00	19.00
1997-98 SkyBox Premium Autographics Century Marks Elden Campbell .	50.00	22.00	6.25
1997-98 SkyBox Premium Autographics Century Marks Chris Carr	30.00	13.50	3.70
1997-98 SkyBox Premium Autographics Century Marks Kelvin Cato	120.00	55.00	15.00
1997-98 SkyBox Premium Autographics Century Marks Duane Causwell .	30.00	13.50	3.70
1997-98 SkyBox Premium Autographics Century Marks Rex Chapman ..	100.00	45.00	12.50
1997-98 SkyBox Premium Autographics Century Marks Calbert Cheaney	30.00	13.50	3.70
1997-98 SkyBox Premium Auto. Century Marks Randolph Childress	30.00	13.50	3.70
1997-98 SkyBox Premium Autographics Century Marks Derrick Coleman	100.00	45.00	12.50
1997-98 SkyBox Premium Autographics Century Marks Austin Croshere	75.00	34.00	9.50
1997-98 SkyBox Premium Autographics Century Marks Dell Curry	30.00	13.50	3.70
1997-98 SkyBox Premium Autographics Century Marks Ben Davis	30.00	13.50	3.70
1997-98 SkyBox Premium Autographics Century Marks Mark Davis	30.00	13.50	3.70
1997-98 SkyBox Premium Autographics Century Marks Andrew DeClercq	30.00	13.50	3.70
1997-98 SkyBox Premium Autographics Century Marks Tony Delk	75.00	34.00	9.50
1997-98 SkyBox Premium Autographics Century Marks Vlade Divac	50.00	22.00	6.25
1997-98 SkyBox Premium Autographics Century Marks Clyde Drexler ..	350.00	160.00	45.00
1997-98 SkyBox Premium Autographics Century Marks Joe Dumars	150.00	70.00	19.00
1997-98 SkyBox Premium Autographics Century Marks Howard Eisley ..	30.00	13.50	3.70
1997-98 SkyBox Premium Autographics Century Marks Danny Ferry ...	30.00	13.50	3.70
1997-98 SkyBox Premium Autographics Century Marks Michael Finley ..	75.00	34.00	9.50
1997-98 SkyBox Premium Autographics Century Marks Derek Fisher ...	75.00	34.00	9.50

1997-98 SkyBox Premium Autographics Century Marks Danny Fortson . 120.00   55.00   15.00
1997-98 SkyBox Premium Autographics Century Marks Todd Fuller 30.00   13.50   3.70
1997-98 SkyBox Premium Autographics Century Marks Chris Gatling . . . 30.00   13.50   3.70
1997-98 SkyBox Premium Autographics Century Marks Matt Geiger 30.00   13.50   3.70
1997-98 SkyBox Premium Autographics Century Marks Brian Grant 30.00   13.50   3.70
1997-98 SkyBox Premium Autographics Century Marks Tom Gugliotta . . 200.00   90.00   25.00
1997-98 SkyBox Premium Autographics Century Marks Tim Hardaway . . 225.00   100.00   28.00
1997-98 SkyBox Premium Autographics Century Marks Ron Harper 75.00   34.00   9.50
1997-98 SkyBox Premium Auto. Century Marks Othella Harrington 30.00   13.50   3.70
1997-98 SkyBox Premium Autographics Century Marks Grant Hill 900.00   400.00   110.00
1997-98 SkyBox Premium Autographics Century Marks Tyrone Hill 30.00   13.50   3.70
1997-98 SkyBox Premium Autographics Century Marks Allan Houston . . 100.00   45.00   12.50
1997-98 SkyBox Premium Autographics Century Marks Juwan Howard . . 300.00   135.00   38.00
1997-98 SkyBox Premium Autographics Century Marks Lindsey Hunter . 90.00   40.00   11.00
1997-98 SkyBox Premium Autographics Century Marks Bobby Hurley . . 30.00   13.50   3.70
1997-98 SkyBox Premium Autographics Century Marks Jim Jackson 60.00   27.00   7.50
1997-98 SkyBox Premium Autographics Century Marks Avery Johnson . . 30.00   13.50   3.70
1997-98 SkyBox Premium Autographics Century Marks Eddie Johnson . . 30.00   13.50   3.70
1997-98 SkyBox Premium Autographics Century Marks Ervin Johnson . . 30.00   13.50   3.70
1997-98 SkyBox Premium Autographics Century Marks Larry Johnson . . 150.00   70.00   19.00
1997-98 SkyBox Premium Autographics Century Marks Popeye Jones . . 30.00   13.50   3.70
1997-98 SkyBox Premium Autographics Century Marks Adam Keefe . . . 30.00   13.50   3.70
1997-98 SkyBox Premium Autographics Century Marks Steve Kerr 60.00   27.00   7.50
1997-98 SkyBox Premium Autographics Century Marks Kerry Kittles 225.00   100.00   28.00
1997-98 SkyBox Premium Autographics Century Marks Brevin Knight . . 175.00   80.00   22.00
1997-98 SkyBox Premium Autographics Century Marks Travis Knight . . . 60.00   27.00   7.50
1997-98 SkyBox Premium Autographics Century Marks George Lynch . . 30.00   13.50   3.70
1997-98 SkyBox Premium Autographics Century Marks Don MacLean . . 30.00   13.50   3.70
1997-98 SkyBox Premium Autographics Century Marks Stephon Marbury 500.00   220.00   60.00
1997-98 SkyBox Premium Autographics Century Marks Donny Marshall . 30.00   13.50   3.70
1997-98 SkyBox Premium Autographics Century Marks Walter McCarty . 30.00   13.50   3.70
1997-98 SkyBox Premium Auto. Century Marks Antonio McDyess 200.00   90.00   25.00
1997-98 SkyBox Premium Autographics Century Marks Tracy McGrady . 350.00   160.00   45.00
1997-98 SkyBox Premium Autographics Century Marks Ron Mercer 450.00   200.00   55.00
1997-98 SkyBox Premium Autographics Century Marks Reggie Miller . . . 600.00   275.00   75.00
1997-98 SkyBox Premium Autographics Century Marks Chris Mills 30.00   13.50   3.70
1997-98 SkyBox Premium Autographics Century Marks Sam Mitchell . . . 30.00   13.50   3.70
1997-98 SkyBox Premium Autographics Century Marks Chris Morris . . . 30.00   13.50   3.70
1997-98 SkyBox Premium Auto. Century Marks Alonzo Mourning 300.00   135.00   38.00
1997-98 SkyBox Premium Autographics Century Marks Chris Mullin 90.00   40.00   11.00
1997-98 SkyBox Premium Auto. Century Marks Dikembe Mutombo 150.00   70.00   19.00
1997-98 SkyBox Premium Autographics Century Marks Anthony Parker . 75.00   34.00   9.50
1997-98 SkyBox Premium Autographics Century Marks Sam Perkins . . . 50.00   22.00   6.25
1997-98 SkyBox Premium Autographics Century Marks Elliot Perry 30.00   13.50   3.70
1997-98 SkyBox Premium Autographics Century Marks Bobby Phills . . . 30.00   13.50   3.70
1997-98 SkyBox Premium Autographics Century Marks Eric Piatkowski . 30.00   13.50   3.70
1997-98 SkyBox Premium Autographics Century Marks Scottie Pippen . . 750.00   350.00   95.00
1997-98 SkyBox Premium Autographics Century Marks Vitaly Potapenko 30.00   13.50   3.70
1997-98 SkyBox Premium Autographics Century Marks Brent Price 30.00   13.50   3.70
1997-98 SkyBox Premium Autographics Century Marks Theo Ratliff 30.00   13.50   3.70
1997-98 SkyBox Premium Autographics Century Marks Glen Rice 175.00   80.00   22.00
1997-98 SkyBox Premium Autographics Century Marks Glenn Robinson . 175.00   80.00   22.00
1997-98 SkyBox Premium Autographics Century Marks Dennis Rodman . 1300.00   575.00   160.00
1997-98 SkyBox Premium Autographics Century Marks Roy Rogers 30.00   13.50   3.70
1997-98 SkyBox Premium Autographics Century Marks Malik Rose 30.00   13.50   3.70
1997-98 SkyBox Premium Autographics Century Marks Joe Smith 175.00   80.00   22.00
1997-98 SkyBox Premium Autographics Century Marks Tony Smith 30.00   13.50   3.70
1997-98 SkyBox Premium Autographics Century Marks Eric Snow 30.00   13.50   3.70
1997-98 SkyBox Prem. Cent. Marks Jerry Stackhouse (Pistons uniform) . 225.00   100.00   28.00
1997-98 SkyBox Prem. Century Marks Jerry Stackhouse (Sixers uniform) 175.00   80.00   22.00
1997-98 SkyBox Premium Autographics Century Marks John Starks . . . 90.00   40.00   11.00
1997-98 SkyBox Premium Autographics Century Marks Bryant Stith 30.00   13.50   3.70
1997-98 SkyBox Premium Autographics Century Marks Erick Strickland . 50.00   22.00   6.25
1997-98 SkyBox Premium Autographics Century Marks Rod Strickland . . 150.00   70.00   19.00

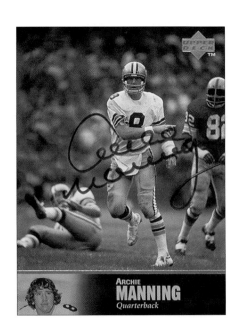

	MINT	NRMT	EXC
1997-98 SkyBox Premium Autographics Century Marks Nick Van Exel .. 200.00	90.00	25.00
1997-98 SkyBox Premium Autographics Century Marks Keith Van Horn . 750.00	350.00	95.00
1997-98 SkyBox Premium Autographics Century Marks David Vaughn .. 30.00	13.50	3.70
1997-98 SkyBox Premium Autographics Century Marks Jacque Vaughn .. 90.00	40.00	11.00
1997-98 SkyBox Premium Autographics Century Marks Antoine Walker . 450.00	200.00	55.00
1997-98 SkyBox Premium Autographics Century Marks Rasheed Wallace 150.00	70.00	19.00
1997-98 SkyBox Premium Auto. Century Marks Clarence Weatherspoon 30.00	13.50	3.70
1997-98 SkyBox Premium Autographics Century Marks David Wesley .. 30.00	13.50	3.70
1997-98 SkyBox Premium Auto. Century Marks Dominique Wilkins 175.00	80.00	22.00
1997-98 SkyBox Premium Autographics Century Marks Gerald Wilkins .. 30.00	13.50	3.70
1997-98 SkyBox Premium Autographics Century Marks Eric Williams ... 30.00	13.50	3.70
1997-98 SkyBox Premium Autographics Century Marks John Williams .. 30.00	13.50	3.70
1997-98 SkyBox Premium Auto. Century Marks Lorenzo Williams 30.00	13.50	3.70
1997-98 SkyBox Premium Autographics Century Marks Monty Williams . 30.00	13.50	3.70
1997-98 SkyBox Premium Autographics Century Marks Scott Williams .. 30.00	13.50	3.70
1997-98 SkyBox Premium Autographics Century Marks Walt Williams ... 30.00	13.50	3.70
1997-98 SkyBox Premium Autographics Century Marks Lorenzen Wright 30.00	13.50	3.70

1997-98 SP Authentic BuyBack

COMMON CARD (1-15) 60.00   27.00   7.50

Randomly inserted into packs at a rate of one in 309 packs, this 36-card set features 15 different player autographs on past SP issued cards and/or inserts. Each card is different in regards to how many each player signed, but those numbers were not disclosed. Some cards are not priced below due to insufficient market information.

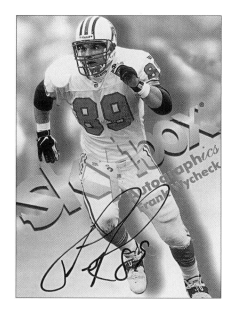

	MINT	NRMT	EXC
1997-98 SP Authentic BuyBack Shareef Abdur-Rahim '96/7 .... 100.00	45.00	12.50
1997-98 SP Authentic BuyBack Vin Baker '94/5		
1997-98 SP Authentic BuyBack Vin Baker '95/6 .... 100.00	45.00	12.50
1997-98 SP Authentic BuyBack Vin Baker '95/6AS 175.00	80.00	22.00
1997-98 SP Authentic BuyBack Clyde Drexler '94/5 .... 100.00	45.00	12.50
1997-98 SP Authentic BuyBack Clyde Drexler '95/6 .... 100.00	45.00	12.50
1997-98 SP Authentic BuyBack Clyde Drexler '96/7 .... 125.00	55.00	15.50
1997-98 SP Authentic BuyBack Anfernee Hardaway '94/5 .... 250.00	110.00	31.00
1997-98 SP Authentic BuyBack Anfernee Hardaway '95/6 .... 200.00	90.00	25.00
1997-98 SP Authentic BuyBack Anfernee Hardaway '96/7 .... 400.00	180.00	50.00
1997-98 SP Authentic BuyBack Tim Hardaway '94/5 .... 80.00	36.00	10.00
1997-98 SP Authentic BuyBack Tim Hardaway '95/6		
1997-98 SP Authentic BuyBack Tim Hardaway '96/7		
1997-98 SP Authentic BuyBack Juwan Howard '94/5 .... 100.00	45.00	12.50
1997-98 SP Authentic BuyBack Juwan Howard '95/6 .... 70.00	32.00	8.75
1997-98 SP Authentic BuyBack Juwan Howard '95/6AS 100.00	45.00	12.50
1997-98 SP Authentic BuyBack Juwan Howard '96/7 .... 125.00	55.00	15.50
1997-98 SP Authentic BuyBack Eddie Jones '94/5 .... 125.00	55.00	15.50
1997-98 SP Authentic BuyBack Eddie Jones '95/6 .... 80.00	36.00	10.00
1997-98 SP Authentic BuyBack Eddie Jones '96/7		
1997-98 SP Authentic BuyBack Michael Jordan '94MJ1R 3500.00	1600.00	450.00
1997-98 SP Authentic BuyBack Jason Kidd '94/5 .... 125.00	55.00	15.50
1997-98 SP Authentic BuyBack Jason Kidd '95/6		
1997-98 SP Authentic BuyBack Jason Kidd '95/6AS		
1997-98 SP Authentic BuyBack Jason Kidd '96/7		
1997-98 SP Authentic BuyBack Kerry Kittles '96/7 .... 75.00	34.00	9.50
1997-98 SP Authentic BuyBack Karl Malone '94/5 .... 125.00	55.00	15.50
1997-98 SP Authentic BuyBack Karl Malone '95/6 .... 200.00	90.00	25.00
1997-98 SP Authentic BuyBack Glen Rice '95/6AS 60.00	27.00	7.50
1997-98 SP Authentic BuyBack Glen Rice '96/7 .... 80.00	36.00	10.00
1997-98 SP Authentic BuyBack Mitch Richmond '94/5 .... 60.00	27.00	7.50
1997-98 SP Authentic BuyBack Mitch Richmond '95/6 .... 60.00	27.00	7.50
1997-98 SP Authentic BuyBack Mitch Richmond '96/7 .... 125.00	55.00	15.50
1997-98 SP Authentic BuyBack Damon Stoudamire '95/6 .... 150.00	70.00	19.00
1997-98 SP Authentic BuyBack Damon Stoudamire '96/7 .... 150.00	70.00	19.00
1997-98 SP Authentic BuyBack Antoine Walker '96/7 .... 150.00	70.00	19.00

1997-98 Stadium Club Co-Signers

COMMON CARD (CO1-24) 80.00   36.00   10.00

Randomly inserted in both series, with series one inserted at one in 387 hobby and series two at one in 309 hobby, this 12-card set features a color action photo of a different player on each side of the card along with an authentic authograph of each player. Each of these double-sided cards are stamped with the Topps Certified Autograph issue stamp to ensure authenticity. The cards were inserted within three groups at different levels. Group "A", or cards CO1-CO4 were inserted at one in15,483. Group "B", or cards CO5-CO8 were inserted at one in 5,161. Group "C", or cards CO9-CO12 were inserted at one in 430 packs. Card backs carry a CO prefix.

	MINT	NRMT	EXC
1997-98 Stadium Club Co-Signers Karl Malone / Kobe Bryant	1200.00	550.00	150.00
1997-98 Stadium Club Co-Signers Juwan Howard / Hakeem Olajuwon	350.00	160.00	45.00
1997-98 Stadium Club Co-Signers John Starks / Joe Smith	250.00	110.00	31.00
1997-98 Stadium Club Co-Signers Clyde Drexler / Tim Hardaway	400.00	180.00	50.00
1997-98 Stadium Club Co-Signers Kobe Bryant / John Starks	450.00	200.00	55.00
1997-98 Stadium Club Co-Signers Hakeem Olajuwon / Clyde Drexler	200.00	90.00	25.00
1997-98 Stadium Club Co-Signers Tim Hardaway / Juwan Howard	150.00	70.00	19.00
1997-98 Stadium Club Co-Signers Joe Smith / Karl Malone	125.00	55.00	15.50
1997-98 Stadium Club Co-Signers Juwan Howard / Clyde Drexler	100.00	45.00	12.50
1997-98 Stadium Club Co-Signers Hakeem Olajuwon / Tim Hardaway	110.00	50.00	14.00
1997-98 Stadium Club Co-Signers Joe Smith / Kobe Bryant	225.00	100.00	28.00
1997-98 Stadium Club Co-Signers Karl Malone / John Starks	80.00	36.00	10.00
1997-98 Stadium Club Co-Sign. Dikembe Mutombo / Chauncey Billups	200.00	90.00	25.00
1997-98 Stadium Club Co-Signers Keith Van Horn / Chris Webber	600.00	275.00	75.00
1997-98 Stadium Club Co-Signers Karl Malone / Kerry Kittles	300.00	135.00	38.00
1997-98 Stadium Club Co-Signers Ron Mercer / Antoine Walker	600.00	275.00	75.00
1997-98 Stadium Club Co-Signers Chris Webber / Karl Malone	150.00	70.00	19.00
1997-98 Stadium Club Co-Signers Antoine Walker / Dikembe Mutombo	125.00	55.00	15.50
1997-98 Stadium Club Co-Signers Kerry Kittles / Keith Van Horn	300.00	135.00	38.00
1997-98 Stadium Club Co-Signers Chauncey Billups / Ron Mercer	250.00	110.00	31.00
1997-98 Stadium Club Co-Signers Antoine Walker / Chauncey Billups	150.00	70.00	19.00
1997-98 Stadium Club Co-Signers Dikembe Mutombo / Ron Mercer	80.00	36.00	10.00
1997-98 Stadium Club Co-Signers Keith Van Horn / Karl Malone	200.00	90.00	25.00
1997-98 Stadium Club Co-Signers Chris Webber / Kerry Kittles	80.00	36.00	10.00

1989-97 Goal Line HOF Autographs

COMPLETE SET (141) 3500.00   1600.00   450.00

These attractive cards were issued by subscription per series and are often found autographed. Although the cards were not released signed, the set is popular with autograph collectors and commonly traded signed.

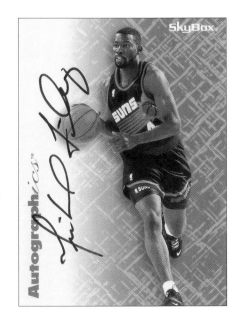

	MINT	NRMT	EXC
1989-97 Goal Line HOF Autographs COMMON AUTO	15.00	6.75	1.85
1989-97 Goal Line HOF Autographs Lance Alworth	25.00	11.00	3.10
1989-97 Goal Line HOF Autographs Red Badgro	15.00	6.75	1.85
1989-97 Goal Line HOF Autographs Mel Blount	15.00	6.75	1.85
1989-97 Goal Line HOF Autographs Terry Bradshaw	30.00	13.50	3.70
1989-97 Goal Line HOF Autographs Jim Brown	30.00	13.50	3.70
1989-97 Goal Line HOF Autographs George Connor	15.00	6.75	1.85
1989-97 Goal Line HOF Autographs Tom Fears	15.00	6.75	1.85
1989-97 Goal Line HOF Autographs Frank Gifford	25.00	11.00	3.10
1989-97 Goal Line HOF Autographs Otto Graham	30.00	13.50	3.70
1989-97 Goal Line HOF Autographs Red Grange	150.00	70.00	19.00
1989-97 Goal Line HOF Autographs Sam Huff	20.00	9.00	2.50
1989-97 Goal Line HOF Autographs Dick(Night Train) Lane	15.00	6.75	1.85
1989-97 Goal Line HOF Autographs Sid Luckman	30.00	13.50	3.70
1989-97 Goal Line HOF Autographs Bobby Mitchell	15.00	6.75	1.85
1989-97 Goal Line HOF Autographs Merlin Olsen	20.00	9.00	2.50
1989-97 Goal Line HOF Autographs Jim Parker	15.00	6.75	1.85
1989-97 Goal Line HOF Autographs Joe Perry	15.00	6.75	1.85
1989-97 Goal Line HOF Autographs Pete Rozelle	125.00	55.00	15.50
1989-97 Goal Line HOF Autographs Art Shell	20.00	9.00	2.50
1989-97 Goal Line HOF Autographs Fran Tarkenton	35.00	16.00	4.40
1989-97 Goal Line HOF Autographs Paul Warfield	15.00	6.75	1.85
1989-97 Goal Line HOF Autographs Larry Wilson	15.00	6.75	1.85
1989-97 Goal Line HOF Autographs Willie Wood	15.00	6.75	1.85
1989-97 Goal Line HOF Autographs Doug Atkins	15.00	6.75	1.85
1989-97 Goal Line HOF Autographs Bobby Bell	15.00	6.75	1.85

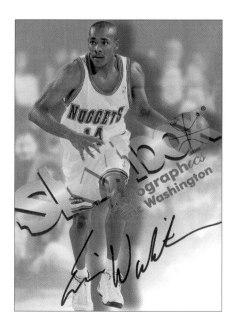

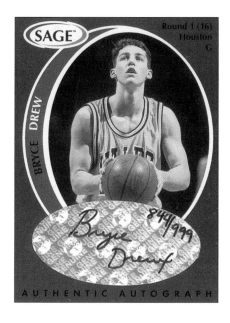

1989-97 Goal Line HOF Autographs Raymond Berry	20.00	9.00	2.50
1989-97 Goal Line HOF Autographs Paul Brown	100.00	45.00	12.50
1989-97 Goal Line HOF Autographs Len Dawson	20.00	9.00	2.50
1989-97 Goal Line HOF Autographs Mike Ditka	25.00	11.00	3.10
1989-97 Goal Line HOF Autographs Dan Fortmann	50.00	22.00	6.25
1989-97 Goal Line HOF Autographs Frank Gatski	15.00	6.75	1.85
1989-97 Goal Line HOF Autographs Elroy Hirsch	20.00	9.00	2.50
1989-97 Goal Line HOF Autographs Paul Hornung	20.00	9.00	2.50
1989-97 Goal Line HOF Autographs John Henry Johnson	20.00	9.00	2.50
1989-97 Goal Line HOF Autographs Yale Lary	15.00	6.75	1.85
1989-97 Goal Line HOF Autographs George McAfee	15.00	6.75	1.85
1989-97 Goal Line HOF Autographs Joe Namath	50.00	22.00	6.25
1989-97 Goal Line HOF Autographs Ray Nitschke	25.00	11.00	3.10
1989-97 Goal Line HOF Autographs Jim Ringo	15.00	6.75	1.85
1989-97 Goal Line HOF Autographs Charley Taylor	20.00	9.00	2.50
1989-97 Goal Line HOF Autographs Charley Trippi	15.00	6.75	1.85
1989-97 Goal Line HOF Autographs Fred Biletnikoff	15.00	6.75	1.85
1989-97 Goal Line HOF Autographs Buck Buchanan	50.00	22.00	6.25
1989-97 Goal Line HOF Autographs Dick Butkus	25.00	11.00	3.10
1989-97 Goal Line HOF Autographs Earl Campbell	20.00	9.00	2.50
1989-97 Goal Line HOF Autographs Tony Canadeo	15.00	6.75	1.85
1989-97 Goal Line HOF Autographs Art Donovan	20.00	9.00	2.50
1989-97 Goal Line HOF Autographs Ray Flaherty	40.00	18.00	5.00
1989-97 Goal Line HOF Autographs Forrest Gregg	15.00	6.75	1.85
1989-97 Goal Line HOF Autographs Lou Groza	15.00	6.75	1.85
1989-97 Goal Line HOF Autographs John Hannah	20.00	9.00	2.50
1989-97 Goal Line HOF Autographs Don Hutson	75.00	34.00	9.50
1989-97 Goal Line HOF Autographs Deacon Jones	20.00	9.00	2.50
1989-97 Goal Line HOF Autographs Stan Jones	15.00	6.75	1.85
1989-97 Goal Line HOF Autographs Sonny Jurgensen	20.00	9.00	2.50
1989-97 Goal Line HOF Autographs Ollie Matson	20.00	9.00	2.50
1989-97 Goal Line HOF Autographs Mike McCormack	15.00	6.75	1.85
1989-97 Goal Line HOF Autographs Marion Motley	20.00	9.00	2.50
1989-97 Goal Line HOF Autographs George Musso	15.00	6.75	1.85
1989-97 Goal Line HOF Autographs Clarence(Ace) Parker	20.00	9.00	2.50
1989-97 Goal Line HOF Autographs Pete Pihos	15.00	6.75	1.85
1989-97 Goal Line HOF Autographs Tex Schramm	15.00	6.75	1.85
1989-97 Goal Line HOF Autographs Roger Staubach	35.00	16.00	4.40
1989-97 Goal Line HOF Autographs Jan Stenerud	15.00	6.75	1.85
1989-97 Goal Line HOF Autographs Y.A. Tittle	20.00	9.00	2.50
1989-97 Goal Line HOF Autographs Bulldog Turner	25.00	11.00	3.10
1989-97 Goal Line HOF Autographs Steve Van Buren	15.00	6.75	1.85
1989-97 Goal Line HOF Autographs Herb Adderley	15.00	6.75	1.85
1989-97 Goal Line HOF Autographs Lem Barney	15.00	6.75	1.85
1989-97 Goal Line HOF Autographs Sammy Baugh	50.00	22.00	6.25
1989-97 Goal Line HOF Autographs Chuck Bednarik	20.00	9.00	2.50
1989-97 Goal Line HOF Autographs Willie Brown	15.00	6.75	1.85
1989-97 Goal Line HOF Autographs Al Davis	100.00	45.00	12.50
1989-97 Goal Line HOF Autographs Bill Dudley	15.00	6.75	1.85
1989-97 Goal Line HOF Autographs Weeb Ewbank	15.00	6.75	1.85
1989-97 Goal Line HOF Autographs Sid Gillman	15.00	6.75	1.85
1989-97 Goal Line HOF Autographs Jack Ham	20.00	9.00	2.50
1989-97 Goal Line HOF Autographs Dante Lavelli	15.00	6.75	1.85
1989-97 Goal Line HOF Autographs Bob Lilly	15.00	6.75	1.85
1989-97 Goal Line HOF Autographs John Mackey	15.00	6.75	1.85
1989-97 Goal Line HOF Autographs Hugh McElhenny	20.00	9.00	2.50
1989-97 Goal Line HOF Autographs Ron Mix	15.00	6.75	1.85
1989-97 Goal Line HOF Autographs Leo Nomellini	15.00	6.75	1.85
1989-97 Goal Line HOF Autographs Alan Page	20.00	9.00	2.50
1989-97 Goal Line HOF Autographs John Riggins	100.00	45.00	12.50
1989-97 Goal Line HOF Autographs Gale Sayers	25.00	11.00	3.10
1989-97 Goal Line HOF Autographs Gene Upshaw	15.00	6.75	1.85
1989-97 Goal Line HOF Autographs Alex Wojciechowicz	800.00	350.00	100.00
1989-97 Goal Line HOF Autographs George Blanda	25.00	11.00	3.10

1989-97 Goal Line HOF Autographs Larry Csonka 30.00   13.50   3.70
1989-97 Goal Line HOF Autographs Dan Fouts 25.00   11.00   3.10
1989-97 Goal Line HOF Autographs Bob Griese 25.00   11.00   3.10
1989-97 Goal Line HOF Autographs Ken Houston 15.00   6.75   1.85
1989-97 Goal Line HOF Autographs Lamar Hunt OWN 15.00   6.75   1.85
1989-97 Goal Line HOF Autographs Jack Lambert 25.00   11.00   3.10
1989-97 Goal Line HOF Autographs Tom Landry 20.00   9.00   2.50
1989-97 Goal Line HOF Autographs Willie Lanier 20.00   9.00   2.50
1989-97 Goal Line HOF Autographs Larry Little 15.00   6.75   1.85
1989-97 Goal Line HOF Autographs Don Maynard 15.00   6.75   1.85
1989-97 Goal Line HOF Autographs Lenny Moore 20.00   9.00   2.50
1989-97 Goal Line HOF Autographs Chuck Noll CO 20.00   9.00   2.50
1989-97 Goal Line HOF Autographs Jim Otto 15.00   6.75   1.85
1989-97 Goal Line HOF Autographs Walter Payton 40.00   18.00   5.00
1989-97 Goal Line HOF Autographs Andy Robustelli 15.00   6.75   1.85
1989-97 Goal Line HOF Autographs Bob St. Clair 15.00   6.75   1.85
1989-97 Goal Line HOF Autographs Joe Schmidt 15.00   6.75   1.85
1989-97 Goal Line HOF Autographs Jim Taylor 20.00   9.00   2.50
1989-97 Goal Line HOF Autographs Doak Walker 25.00   11.00   3.10
1989-97 Goal Line HOF Autographs Bill Walsh CO 20.00   9.00   2.50
1989-97 Goal Line HOF Autographs Arnie Weinmeister 20.00   9.00   2.50
1989-97 Goal Line HOF Autographs Bill Willis 15.00   6.75   1.85
1989-97 Goal Line HOF Autographs Roosevelt Brown 15.00   6.75   1.85
1989-97 Goal Line HOF Autographs Willie Davis 15.00   6.75   1.85
1989-97 Goal Line HOF Autographs Tony Dorsett 25.00   11.00   3.10
1989-97 Goal Line HOF Autographs Bud Grant 20.00   9.00   2.50
1989-97 Goal Line HOF Autographs Joe Greene 20.00   9.00   2.50
1989-97 Goal Line HOF Autographs Franco Harris 20.00   9.00   2.50
1989-97 Goal Line HOF Autographs Ted Hendricks 20.00   9.00   2.50
1989-97 Goal Line HOF Autographs Jim Johnson 15.00   6.75   1.85
1989-97 Goal Line HOF Autographs Leroy Kelly 20.00   9.00   2.50
1989-97 Goal Line HOF Autographs Jim Langer 15.00   6.75   1.85
1989-97 Goal Line HOF Autographs Gino Marchetti 20.00   9.00   2.50
1989-97 Goal Line HOF Autographs O.J. Simpson 100.00   45.00   12.50
1989-97 Goal Line HOF Autographs Jackie Smith 15.00   6.75   1.85
1989-97 Goal Line HOF Autographs Bart Starr 25.00   11.00   3.10
1989-97 Goal Line HOF Autographs Ernie Stautner 15.00   6.75   1.85
1989-97 Goal Line HOF Autographs Johnny Unitas 60.00   27.00   7.50
1989-97 Goal Line HOF Autographs Randy White 25.00   11.00   3.10
1989-97 Goal Line HOF Autographs Steve Largent 25.00   11.00   3.10
1989-97 Goal Line HOF Autographs Lee Roy Selmon 15.00   6.75   1.85
1989-97 Goal Line HOF Autographs Kellen Winslow 15.00   6.75   1.85
1989-97 Goal Line HOF Autographs Lou Creekmur 15.00   6.75   1.85
1989-97 Goal Line HOF Autographs Dan Dierdorf 15.00   6.75   1.85
1989-97 Goal Line HOF Autographs Joe Gibbs 20.00   9.00   2.50
1989-97 Goal Line HOF Autographs Charlie Joiner 20.00   9.00   2.50
1989-97 Goal Line HOF Autographs Mel Renfro 15.00   6.75   1.85
1989-97 Goal Line HOF Autographs Mike Haynes 15.00   6.75   1.85
1989-97 Goal Line HOF Autographs Wellington Mara 25.00   11.00   3.10
1989-97 Goal Line HOF Autographs Don Shula CO 50.00   22.00   6.25
1989-97 Goal Line HOF Autographs Mike Webster 25.00   11.00   3.10

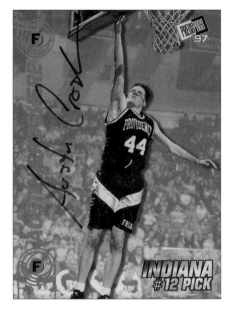

1991 Pro Line Portraits Autographs

COMPLETE SET (301) 5500.00   2500.00   700.00

This 300-card standard-size set features some of the NFL's most popular players in non-game shots. These certified autographed cards were randomly included into packs as unnumbered cards. They are listed below according to the numbers assigned to them in the regular series. It has been reported by collectors that an autographed card is found with a frequency of about one per three boxes of 1991 ProLine. The Tim McDonald card (163) is not included in the set price or listings as only one card is known to exist. Cards with signatures cut in half are considered to have major defects. The autographed Santa cards are not considered part of the set.

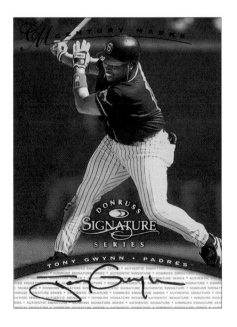

	MINT	NRMT	EXC
1991 Pro Line Portraits Autographs COMMON CARD (1-300)	5.00	2.20	.60
1991 Pro Line Portraits Autographs Jim Kelly (Autopenned)	15.00	6.75	1.85

1991 Pro Line Portraits Autographs Jim Kelly (Real signature)	150.00	70.00	19.00
1991 Pro Line Portraits Autographs Carl Banks	5.00	2.20	.60
1991 Pro Line Portraits Autographs Neal Anderson	8.00	3.60	1.00
1991 Pro Line Portraits Autographs James Brooks	8.00	3.60	1.00
1991 Pro Line Portraits Autographs Reggie Langhorne	50.00	22.00	6.25
1991 Pro Line Portraits Autographs Robert Awalt	5.00	2.20	.60
1991 Pro Line Portraits Autographs Greg Kragen	5.00	2.20	.60
1991 Pro Line Portraits Autographs Steve Young	100.00	45.00	12.50
1991 Pro Line Portraits Autographs Nick Bell	5.00	2.20	.60
1991 Pro Line Portraits Autographs Ray Childress	8.00	3.60	1.00
1991 Pro Line Portraits Autographs Albert Bentley	5.00	2.20	.60
1991 Pro Line Portraits Auto. Albert Lewis (Most signatures are cut off)	50.00	22.00	6.25
1991 Pro Line Portraits Autographs Howie Long	25.00	11.00	3.10
1991 Pro Line Portraits Autographs Flipper Anderson	8.00	3.60	1.00
1991 Pro Line Portraits Autographs Mark Clayton	8.00	3.60	1.00
1991 Pro Line Portraits Autographs Jarrod Bunch	5.00	2.20	.60
1991 Pro Line Portraits Autographs Bruce Armstrong	5.00	2.20	.60
1991 Pro Line Portraits Autographs Vinnie Clark	5.00	2.20	.60
1991 Pro Line Portraits Autographs Rob Moore	12.00	5.50	1.50
1991 Pro Line Portraits Autographs Eric Allen	5.00	2.20	.60
1991 Pro Line Portraits Autographs Timm Rosenbach	5.00	2.20	.60
1991 Pro Line Portraits Autographs Gary Anderson K	5.00	2.20	.60
1991 Pro Line Portraits Autographs Martin Bayless	5.00	2.20	.60
1991 Pro Line Portraits Autographs Kevin Fagan	5.00	2.20	.60
1991 Pro Line Portraits Autographs Brian Blades	8.00	3.60	1.00
1991 Pro Line Portraits Autographs Gary Anderson RB	8.00	3.60	1.00
1991 Pro Line Portraits Autographs Earnest Byner	8.00	3.60	1.00
1991 Pro Line Portraits Autographs O.J. Simpson RET	200.00	90.00	25.00
1991 Pro Line Portraits Autographs Dan Henning CO	5.00	2.20	.60
1991 Pro Line Portraits Autographs Sean Landeta	5.00	2.20	.60
1991 Pro Line Portraits Autographs James Lofton	20.00	9.00	2.50
1991 Pro Line Portraits Autographs Mike Singletary	35.00	16.00	4.40
1991 Pro Line Portraits Autographs David Fulcher	5.00	2.20	.60
1991 Pro Line Portraits Autographs Mark Murphy	5.00	2.20	.60
1991 Pro Line Portraits Autographs Issiac Holt	5.00	2.20	.60
1991 Pro Line Portraits Autographs Dennis Smith	5.00	2.20	.60
1991 Pro Line Portraits Autographs Lomas Brown	5.00	2.20	.60
1991 Pro Line Portraits Autographs Ernest Givins	8.00	3.60	1.00
1991 Pro Line Portraits Autographs Duane Bickett	5.00	2.20	.60
1991 Pro Line Portraits Autographs Barry Word	5.00	2.20	.60
1991 Pro Line Portraits Autographs Tony Mandarich	5.00	2.20	.60
1991 Pro Line Portraits Autographs Cleveland Gary	5.00	2.20	.60
1991 Pro Line Portraits Autographs Ferrell Edmunds	5.00	2.20	.60
1991 Pro Line Portraits Autographs Randal Hill	8.00	3.60	1.00
1991 Pro Line Portraits Autographs Irving Fryar	12.00	5.50	1.50
1991 Pro Line Portraits Autographs Henry Jones	5.00	2.20	.60
1991 Pro Line Portraits Autographs Blair Thomas	5.00	2.20	.60
1991 Pro Line Portraits Autographs Andre Waters	5.00	2.20	.60
1991 Pro Line Portraits Autographs J.T. Smith	5.00	2.20	.60
1991 Pro Line Portraits Autographs Thomas Everett	5.00	2.20	.60
1991 Pro Line Portraits Autographs Marion Butts	8.00	3.60	1.00
1991 Pro Line Portraits Autographs Tom Rathman	5.00	2.20	.60
1991 Pro Line Portraits Autographs Vann McElroy	5.00	2.20	.60
1991 Pro Line Portraits Autographs Mark Carrier WR	8.00	3.60	1.00
1991 Pro Line Portraits Autographs Jim Lachey	5.00	2.20	.60
1991 Pro Line Portraits Autographs Joe Theismann RET	25.00	11.00	3.10
1991 Pro Line Portraits Autographs Jerry Glanville CO	5.00	2.20	.60
1991 Pro Line Portraits Autographs Doug Riesenberg	5.00	2.20	.60
1991 Pro Line Portraits Autographs Cornelius Bennett	12.00	5.50	1.50
1991 Pro Line Portraits Autographs Mark Carrier DB	100.00	45.00	12.50
1991 Pro Line Portraits Autographs Rodney Holman	225.00	100.00	28.00
1991 Pro Line Portraits Autographs Leroy Hoard	5.00	2.20	.60
1991 Pro Line Portraits Autographs Michael Irvin	40.00	18.00	5.00
1991 Pro Line Portraits Autographs Bobby Humphrey	5.00	2.20	.60

1991 Pro Line Portraits Autographs Mel Gray 8.00   3.60   1.00
1991 Pro Line Portraits Autographs Brian Noble . . . . 5.00   2.20   .60
1991 Pro Line Portraits Autographs Al Smith . . . . 5.00   2.20   .60
1991 Pro Line Portraits Autographs Eric Dickerson 25.00   11.00   3.10
1991 Pro Line Portraits Autographs Steve DeBerg 8.00   3.60   1.00
1991 Pro Line Portraits Autographs Jay Schroeder . . . . 5.00   2.20   .60
1991 Pro Line Portraits Autographs Irv Pankey . . . . 5.00   2.20   .60
1991 Pro Line Portraits Autographs Reggie Roby . . . . 5.00   2.20   .60
1991 Pro Line Portraits Autographs Wade Wilson . . . . 5.00   2.20   .60
1991 Pro Line Portraits Autographs Johnny Rembert . . . . 5.00   2.20   .60
1991 Pro Line Portraits Autographs Russell Maryland 8.00   3.60   1.00
1991 Pro Line Portraits Autographs Al Toon 8.00   3.60   1.00
1991 Pro Line Portraits Autographs Randall Cunningham 30.00   13.50   3.70
1991 Pro Line Portraits Autographs Lonnie Young . . . . 5.00   2.20   .60
1991 Pro Line Portraits Autographs Carnell Lake 8.00   3.60   1.00
1991 Pro Line Portraits Autographs Burt Grossman . . . . 5.00   2.20   .60
1991 Pro Line Portraits Autographs Jim Mora CO . . . . 5.00   2.20   .60
1991 Pro Line Portraits Autographs Dave Krieg 8.00   3.60   1.00
1991 Pro Line Portraits Autographs Bruce Hill . . . . 5.00   2.20   .60
1991 Pro Line Portraits Autographs Ricky Sanders . . . . 5.00   2.20   .60
1991 Pro Line Portraits Autographs Roger Staubach RET 125.00   55.00   15.50
1991 Pro Line Portraits Autographs Richard Williamson CO . . . . 5.00   2.20   .60
1991 Pro Line Portraits Autographs Everson Walls . . . . 5.00   2.20   .60
1991 Pro Line Portraits Autographs Shane Conlan . . . . 5.00   2.20   .60
1991 Pro Line Portraits Autographs Mike Ditka CO 30.00   13.50   3.70
1991 Pro Line Portraits Autographs Mark Bortz . . . . 5.00   2.20   .60
1991 Pro Line Portraits Autographs Tim McGee . . . . 5.00   2.20   .60
1991 Pro Line Portraits Autographs Michael Dean Perry 8.00   3.60   1.00
1991 Pro Line Portraits Autographs Danny Noonan . . . . 5.00   2.20   .60
1991 Pro Line Portraits Autographs Mark Jackson . . . . 5.00   2.20   .60
1991 Pro Line Portraits Autographs Chris Miller 8.00   3.60   1.00
1991 Pro Line Portraits Autographs Ed McCaffrey . . . . 5.00   2.20   .60
1991 Pro Line Portraits Autographs Lorenzo White . . . . 5.00   2.20   .60
1991 Pro Line Portraits Autographs Ray Donaldson . . . . 5.00   2.20   .60
1991 Pro Line Portraits Autographs Nick Lowery (May be autopenned) . . 5.00   2.20   .60
1991 Pro Line Portraits Autographs Steve Smith . . . . 5.00   2.20   .60
1991 Pro Line Portraits Autographs Jackie Slater . . . . 5.00   2.20   .60
1991 Pro Line Portraits Autographs Louis Oliver . . . . 5.00   2.20   .60
1991 Pro Line Portraits Autographs Kanavis McGhee . . . . 5.00   2.20   .60
1991 Pro Line Portraits Autographs Ray Agnew . . . . 5.00   2.20   .60
1991 Pro Line Portraits Autographs Sam Mills 8.00   3.60   1.00
1991 Pro Line Portraits Autographs Bill Pickel . . . . 5.00   2.20   .60
1991 Pro Line Portraits Autographs Keith Byars 8.00   3.60   1.00
1991 Pro Line Portraits Autographs Ricky Proehl . . . . 5.00   2.20   .60
1991 Pro Line Portraits Autographs Merril Hoge . . . . 5.00   2.20   .60
1991 Pro Line Portraits Autographs Rod Bernstine . . . . 5.00   2.20   .60
1991 Pro Line Portraits Autographs Andy Heck . . . . 5.00   2.20   .60
1991 Pro Line Portraits Autographs Broderick Thomas . . . . 5.00   2.20   .60
1991 Pro Line Portraits Autographs Andre Collins . . . . 5.00   2.20   .60
1991 Pro Line Portraits Autographs Paul Warfield RET 20.00   9.00   2.50
1991 Pro Line Portraits Autographs Bill Belichick CO . . . . 5.00   2.20   .60
1991 Pro Line Portraits Autographs Ottis Anderson 8.00   3.60   1.00
1991 Pro Line Portraits Autographs Andre Reed 20.00   9.00   2.50
1991 Pro Line Portraits Autographs Andre Rison (Ball-point pen) 12.00   5.50   1.50
1991 Pro Line Portraits Autographs Andre Rison (Signed in Sharpie) 30.00   13.50   3.70
1991 Pro Line Portraits Autographs Dexter Carter . . . . 5.00   2.20   .60
1991 Pro Line Portraits Autographs Anthony Munoz 12.00   5.50   1.50
1991 Pro Line Portraits Autographs Bernie Kosar 8.00   3.60   1.00
1991 Pro Line Portraits Autographs Alonzo Highsmith 60.00   27.00   7.50
1991 Pro Line Portraits Autographs David Treadwell . . . . 5.00   2.20   .60
1991 Pro Line Portraits Autographs Rodney Peete 8.00   3.60   1.00
1991 Pro Line Portraits Autographs Haywood Jeffires 8.00   3.60   1.00
1991 Pro Line Portraits Autographs Clarence Verdin . . . . 5.00   2.20   .60
1991 Pro Line Portraits Autographs Christian Okoye . . . . 5.00   2.20   .60

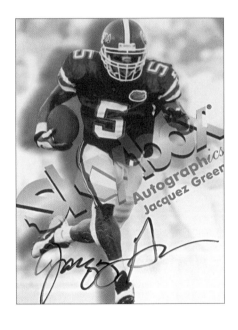

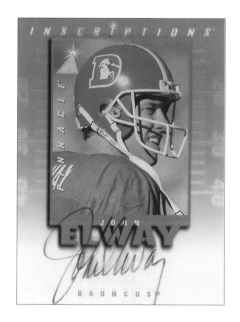

1991 Pro Line Portraits Autographs Greg Townsend	125.00	55.00	15.50
1991 Pro Line Portraits Autographs Tom Newberry	5.00	2.20	.60
1991 Pro Line Portraits Autographs Keith Sims	5.00	2.20	.60
1991 Pro Line Portraits Autographs Myron Guyton	5.00	2.20	.60
1991 Pro Line Portraits Autographs Andre Tippett	8.00	3.60	1.00
1991 Pro Line Portraits Autographs Steve Walsh	5.00	2.20	.60
1991 Pro Line Portraits Autographs Erik McMillan	5.00	2.20	.60
1991 Pro Line Portraits Autographs Jim McMahon	250.00	110.00	31.00
1991 Pro Line Portraits Autographs Derek Hill	5.00	2.20	.60
1991 Pro Line Portraits Autographs D.J. Johnson	5.00	2.20	.60
1991 Pro Line Portraits Autographs Leslie O'Neal	8.00	3.60	1.00
1991 Pro Line Portraits Autographs Pierce Holt	5.00	2.20	.60
1991 Pro Line Portraits Autographs Cortez Kennedy	8.00	3.60	1.00
1991 Pro Line Portraits Autographs Danny Peebles	5.00	2.20	.60
1991 Pro Line Portraits Autographs Alvin Walton	5.00	2.20	.60
1991 Pro Line Portraits Autographs Drew Pearson RET	12.00	5.50	1.50
1991 Pro Line Portraits Autographs Dick MacPherson CO	5.00	2.20	.60
1991 Pro Line Portraits Autographs Erik Howard	5.00	2.20	.60
1991 Pro Line Portraits Autographs Steve Tasker	8.00	3.60	1.00
1991 Pro Line Portraits Autographs Bill Fralic	5.00	2.20	.60
1991 Pro Line Portraits Autographs Don Warren	5.00	2.20	.60
1991 Pro Line Portraits Autographs Eric Thomas	5.00	2.20	.60
1991 Pro Line Portraits Autographs Jack Pardee CO	5.00	2.20	.60
1991 Pro Line Portraits Autographs Gary Zimmerman	5.00	2.20	.60
1991 Pro Line Portraits Autographs Leonard Marshall (Frequently miscut)	5.00	2.20	.60
1991 Pro Line Portraits Autographs Chris Spielman	8.00	3.60	1.00
1991 Pro Line Portraits Autographs Sam Wyche CO	5.00	2.20	.60
1991 Pro Line Portraits Autographs Rohn Stark	5.00	2.20	.60
1991 Pro Line Portraits Autographs Stephone Paige	5.00	2.20	.60
1991 Pro Line Auto. Lionel Washington (Most signatures are cut off)	100.00	45.00	12.50
1991 Pro Line Portraits Autographs Henry Ellard	8.00	3.60	1.00
1991 Pro Line Portraits Autographs Dan Marino	200.00	90.00	25.00
1991 Pro Line Portraits Autographs Lindy Infante CO	5.00	2.20	.60
1991 Pro Line Portraits Autographs Dan McGwire	5.00	2.20	.60
1991 Pro Line Portraits Autographs Ken O'Brien	8.00	3.60	1.00
1991 Pro Line Portraits Autographs Louis Lipps	8.00	3.60	1.00
1991 Pro Line Portraits Autographs Billy Joe Tolliver	5.00	2.20	.60
1991 Pro Line Portraits Autographs Harris Barton	5.00	2.20	.60
1991 Pro Line Portraits Autographs Tony Woods	5.00	2.20	.60
1991 Pro Line Portraits Autographs Matt Millen	8.00	3.60	1.00
1991 Pro Line Portraits Autographs Gale Sayers RET	40.00	18.00	5.00
1991 Pro Line Portraits Autographs Ron Meyer CO	5.00	2.20	.60
1991 Pro Line Portraits Autographs William Roberts	5.00	2.20	.60
1991 Pro Line Portraits Autographs Thurman Thomas	25.00	11.00	3.10
1991 Pro Line Portraits Autographs Steve McMichael	8.00	3.60	1.00
1991 Pro Line Portraits Autographs Ickey Woods	5.00	2.20	.60
1991 Pro Line Portraits Autographs Eugene Lockhart	5.00	2.20	.60
1991 Pro Line Portraits Autographs George Seifert CO	8.00	3.60	1.00
1991 Pro Line Portraits Autographs Keith Jones	5.00	2.20	.60
1991 Pro Line Portraits Autographs Jack Trudeau	5.00	2.20	.60
1991 Pro Line Portraits Autographs Kevin Porter	5.00	2.20	.60
1991 Pro Line Portraits Autographs Ronnie Lott	20.00	9.00	2.50
1991 Pro Line Portraits Autographs Marty Schottenheimer CO	8.00	3.60	1.00
1991 Pro Line Portraits Autographs Morten Andersen	8.00	3.60	1.00
1991 Pro Line Portraits Autographs Anthony Thompson	5.00	2.20	.60
1991 Pro Line Portraits Autographs Tim Worley	5.00	2.20	.60
1991 Pro Line Portraits Autographs Billy Ray Smith	5.00	2.20	.60
1991 Pro Line Portraits Autographs David Whitmore	5.00	2.20	.60
1991 Pro Line Portraits Autographs Jacob Green	5.00	2.20	.60
1991 Pro Line Portraits Autographs Browning Nagle	5.00	2.20	.60
1991 Pro Line Portraits Franco Harris RET (Most signatures are cut off)	40.00	18.00	5.00
1991 Pro Line Portraits Autographs Art Shell CO	20.00	9.00	2.50
1991 Pro Line Portraits Autographs Bart Oates	5.00	2.20	.60
1991 Pro Line Portraits Autographs William Perry	8.00	3.60	1.00

1991 Pro Line Portraits Autographs Chuck Noll CO 25.00   11.00   3.10
1991 Pro Line Portraits Autographs Troy Aikman 100.00   45.00   12.50
1991 Pro Line Portraits Autographs Jeff George 12.00   5.50   1.50
1991 Pro Line Portraits Autographs Derrick Thomas 20.00   9.00   2.50
1991 Pro Line Portraits Autographs Roger Craig 12.00   5.50   1.50
1991 Pro Line Portraits Autographs John Fourcade . . . . 5.00   2.20   .60
1991 Pro Line Portraits Autographs Rod Woodson 20.00   9.00   2.50
1991 Pro Line Portraits Autographs Anthony Miller 8.00   3.60   1.00
1991 Pro Line Portraits Autographs Jerry Rice 135.00   60.00   17.00
1991 Pro Line Portraits Autographs Eugene Robinson 8.00   3.60   1.00
1991 Pro Line Portraits Autographs Charles Mann . . . . 5.00   2.20   .60
1991 Pro Line Portraits Autographs Mel Blount RET 12.00   5.50   1.50
1991 Pro Line Portraits Autographs Don Shula CO 40.00   18.00   5.00
1991 Pro Line Portraits Autographs Jumbo Elliott . . . . 5.00   2.20   .60
1991 Pro Line Portraits Autographs Jay Hilgenberg . . . . 5.00   2.20   .60
1991 Pro Line Portraits Autographs Deron Cherry . . . . 5.00   2.20   .60
1991 Pro Line Portraits Autographs Dan Reeves CO 12.00   5.50   1.50
1991 Pro Line Portraits Autographs Roman Phifer . . . . 5.00   2.20   .60
1991 Pro Line Portraits Autographs David Little . . . . 5.00   2.20   .60
1991 Pro Line Portraits Autographs Lee Williams . . . . 5.00   2.20   .60
1991 Pro Line Portraits Autographs John Taylor 8.00   3.60   1.00
1991 Pro Line Portraits Autographs Monte Coleman . . . . 5.00   2.20   .60
1991 Pro Line Portraits Autographs Walter Payton RET 100.00   45.00   12.50
1991 Pro Line Portraits Autographs John Robinson CO . . . . 5.00   2.20   .60
1991 Pro Line Portraits Autographs Pepper Johnson . . . . 5.00   2.20   .60
1991 Pro Line Portraits Autographs Tom Thayer . . . . 5.00   2.20   .60
1991 Pro Line Portraits Autographs Dan Saleaumua . . . . 5.00   2.20   .60
1991 Pro Line Portraits Autographs Ernest Spears . . . . 5.00   2.20   .60
1991 Pro Line Portraits Autographs Bubby Brister (Signed Bubby 6) . . . . 5.00   2.20   .60
1991 Pro Line Portraits Autographs Junior Seau 20.00   9.00   2.50
1991 Pro Line Portraits Autographs Brent Jones 8.00   3.60   1.00
1991 Pro Line Portraits Autographs Rufus Porter . . . . 5.00   2.20   .60
1991 Pro Line Portraits Autographs Jack Kemp RET (Autopenned) 30.00   13.50   3.70
1991 Pro Line Portraits Autographs Wayne Fontes CO . . . . 5.00   2.20   .60
1991 Pro Line Portraits Autographs Phil Simms 25.00   11.00   3.10
1991 Pro Line Portraits Autographs Shaun Gayle . . . . 5.00   2.20   .60
1991 Pro Line Portraits Autographs Bill Maas . . . . 5.00   2.20   .60
1991 Pro Line Portraits Autographs Renaldo Turnbull 8.00   3.60   1.00
1991 Pro Line Portraits Autographs Bryan Hinkle . . . . 5.00   2.20   .60
1991 Pro Line Portraits Autographs Gary Plummer . . . . 5.00   2.20   .60
1991 Pro Line Portraits Autographs Jerry Burns CO . . . . 5.00   2.20   .60
1991 Pro Line Portraits Autographs Lawrence Taylor 35.00   16.00   4.40
1991 Pro Line Portraits Autographs Joe Gibbs CO 20.00   9.00   2.50
1991 Pro Line Portraits Auto. Neil Smith (Most signatures are cut off) . . . 60.00   27.00   7.50
1991 Pro Line Portraits Autographs Rich Kotite CO . . . . 5.00   2.20   .60
1991 Pro Line Portraits Autographs Jim Covert . . . . 5.00   2.20   .60
1991 Pro Line Portraits Tim Grunhard (Two different signatures known) . 5.00   2.20   .60
1991 Pro Line Portraits Autographs Joe Bugel CO . . . . 5.00   2.20   .60
1991 Pro Line Portraits Autographs David Wyman . . . . 5.00   2.20   .60
1991 Pro Line Portraits Autographs Maury Buford . . . . 5.00   2.20   .60
1991 Pro Line Portraits Autographs Kevin Ross . . . . 5.00   2.20   .60
1991 Pro Line Portraits Autographs Jimmy Johnson CO 40.00   18.00   5.00
1991 Pro Line Portraits Autographs Jim Morrissey . . . . 5.00   2.20   .60
1991 Pro Line Portraits Autographs Jeff Hostetler 8.00   3.60   1.00
1991 Pro Line Portraits Autographs Andre Ware 8.00   3.60   1.00
1991 Pro Line Portraits Autographs Steve Largent RET 35.00   16.00   4.40
1991 Pro Line Portraits Autographs Chuck Knox CO 8.00   3.60   1.00
1991 Pro Line Portraits Autographs Boomer Esiason 12.00   5.50   1.50
1991 Pro Line Portraits Autographs Kevin Butler . . . . 5.00   2.20   .60
1991 Pro Line Portraits Autographs Bruce Smith 20.00   9.00   2.50
1991 Pro Line Portraits Autographs Webster Slaughter 8.00   3.60   1.00
1991 Pro Line Portraits Autographs Mike Sherrard . . . . 5.00   2.20   .60
1991 Pro Line Portraits Autographs Steve Broussard . . . . 5.00   2.20   .60
1991 Pro Line Portraits Autographs Warren Moon 30.00   13.50   3.70

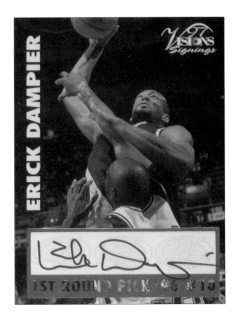

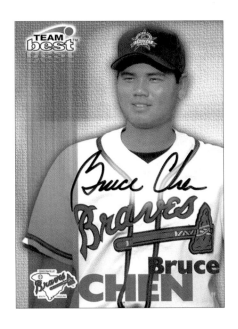

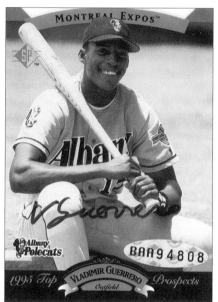

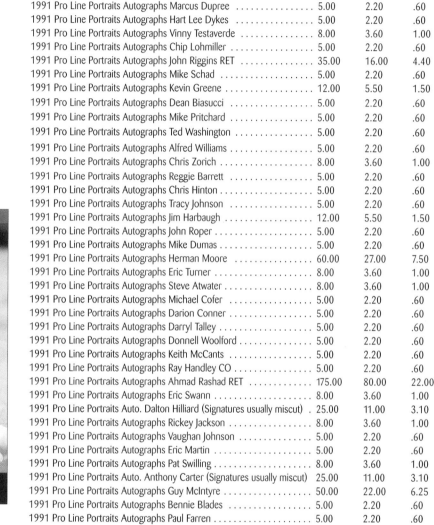

1991 Pro Line Portraits Autographs John Elway 120.00   55.00   15.00
1991 Pro Line Portraits Autographs Bob Golic . . . . 5.00   2.20   .60
1991 Pro Line Portraits Autographs Jim Everett 8.00   3.60   1.00
1991 Pro Line Portraits Autographs Bruce Coslet CO . . . . 5.00   2.20   .60
1991 Pro Line Portraits Autographs James Francis 250.00   110.00   31.00
1991 Pro Line Portraits Autographs Eric Dorsey . . . . 5.00   2.20   .60
1991 Pro Line Portraits Autographs Marcus Dupree . . . . 5.00   2.20   .60
1991 Pro Line Portraits Autographs Hart Lee Dykes . . . . 5.00   2.20   .60
1991 Pro Line Portraits Autographs Vinny Testaverde 8.00   3.60   1.00
1991 Pro Line Portraits Autographs Chip Lohmiller . . . . 5.00   2.20   .60
1991 Pro Line Portraits Autographs John Riggins RET 35.00   16.00   4.40
1991 Pro Line Portraits Autographs Mike Schad . . . . 5.00   2.20   .60
1991 Pro Line Portraits Autographs Kevin Greene 12.00   5.50   1.50
1991 Pro Line Portraits Autographs Dean Biasucci . . . . 5.00   2.20   .60
1991 Pro Line Portraits Autographs Mike Pritchard . . . . 5.00   2.20   .60
1991 Pro Line Portraits Autographs Ted Washington . . . . 5.00   2.20   .60
1991 Pro Line Portraits Autographs Alfred Williams . . . . 5.00   2.20   .60
1991 Pro Line Portraits Autographs Chris Zorich 8.00   3.60   1.00
1991 Pro Line Portraits Autographs Reggie Barrett . . . . 5.00   2.20   .60
1991 Pro Line Portraits Autographs Chris Hinton . . . . 5.00   2.20   .60
1991 Pro Line Portraits Autographs Tracy Johnson . . . . 5.00   2.20   .60
1991 Pro Line Portraits Autographs Jim Harbaugh 12.00   5.50   1.50
1991 Pro Line Portraits Autographs John Roper . . . . 5.00   2.20   .60
1991 Pro Line Portraits Autographs Mike Dumas . . . . 5.00   2.20   .60
1991 Pro Line Portraits Autographs Herman Moore 60.00   27.00   7.50
1991 Pro Line Portraits Autographs Eric Turner 8.00   3.60   1.00
1991 Pro Line Portraits Autographs Steve Atwater 8.00   3.60   1.00
1991 Pro Line Portraits Autographs Michael Cofer . . . . 5.00   2.20   .60
1991 Pro Line Portraits Autographs Darion Conner . . . . 5.00   2.20   .60
1991 Pro Line Portraits Autographs Darryl Talley . . . . 5.00   2.20   .60
1991 Pro Line Portraits Autographs Donnell Woolford . . . . 5.00   2.20   .60
1991 Pro Line Portraits Autographs Keith McCants . . . . 5.00   2.20   .60
1991 Pro Line Portraits Autographs Ray Handley CO . . . . 5.00   2.20   .60
1991 Pro Line Portraits Autographs Ahmad Rashad RET 175.00   80.00   22.00
1991 Pro Line Portraits Autographs Eric Swann 8.00   3.60   1.00
1991 Pro Line Portraits Auto. Dalton Hilliard (Signatures usually miscut) . 25.00   11.00   3.10
1991 Pro Line Portraits Autographs Rickey Jackson 8.00   3.60   1.00
1991 Pro Line Portraits Autographs Vaughan Johnson . . . . 5.00   2.20   .60
1991 Pro Line Portraits Autographs Eric Martin . . . . 5.00   2.20   .60
1991 Pro Line Portraits Autographs Pat Swilling 8.00   3.60   1.00
1991 Pro Line Portraits Auto. Anthony Carter (Signatures usually miscut) 25.00   11.00   3.10
1991 Pro Line Portraits Autographs Guy McIntyre 50.00   22.00   6.25
1991 Pro Line Portraits Autographs Bennie Blades . . . . 5.00   2.20   .60
1991 Pro Line Portraits Autographs Paul Farren . . . . 5.00   2.20   .60
1991 Pro Line Portraits Autographs Payne Stewart 80.00   36.00   10.00
1991 Pro Line Portraits Santa Claus Sendaway (Signed, not numbered) . . 30.00   13.50   3.70
1991 Pro Line Portraits Santa Claus Sendaway (Signed and numbered) . . 50.00   22.00   6.25

1991 Pro Line Portraits Wives Autographs
COMPLETE SET (7) 600.00   275.00   75.00
This seven-card standard-size set was included in the 1991 Pro Line Portraits set as inserts in the regular foil packs. These cards feature wives of some of the NFL's most popular personalities, including former television actress Jennifer Montana and star of the Cosby show, Phylicia Rashad. Less than 15 of Rashad's cards are currently known to exist. The cards are unnumbered but are listed below according to the numbers assigned to them in the regular series.

	MINT	NRMT	EXC
1991 Pro Line Portraits Wives Autographs COMMON CARD (1-7)	15.00	6.75	1.85
1991 Pro Line Portraits Wives Autographs Jennifer Montana	75.00	34.00	9.50
1991 Pro Line Portraits Wives Autographs Babette Kosar	15.00	6.75	1.85
1991 Pro Line Portraits Wives Autographs Janet Elway	15.00	6.75	1.85
1991 Pro Line Portraits Wives Autographs Michelle Oates	15.00	6.75	1.85
1991 Pro Line Portraits Wives Autographs Toni Lipps	15.00	6.75	1.85
1991 Pro Line Portraits Wives Autographs Stacey O'Brien	15.00	6.75	1.85
1991 Pro Line Portraits Wives Autographs Phylicia Rashad	500.00	220.00	60.00

1991 Score Dream Team Autographs

COMPLETE SET (11) 850.00   375.00   105.00

This 11-card standard-size set was randomly inserted in second series packs. The odds of receiving them according to Score is not less than 1 in 5000 packs. The actual signed cards are distinguishable from regular Dream Team cards (which carry facsimile autographs on the backs) because the facsimile autograph has been removed from the card-back. The two versions (signed and facsimile) are easily confused with each other so take care in examining the cards closely. The best approach is to compare a card known to be from the base set (facsimile) to the card in question. Players used a variety of inks and most signed on the cardfronts. According to Score, only 500 of each player's cards were autographed.

	MINT	NRMT	EXC
1991 Score Dream Team Autographs COMMON CARD (676-686)	30.00	13.50	3.70
1991 Score Dream Team Autographs Warren Moon	100.00	45.00	12.50
1991 Score Dream Team Autographs Barry Sanders	300.00	135.00	38.00
1991 Score Dream Team Autographs Thurman Thomas	125.00	55.00	15.50
1991 Score Dream Team Autographs Andre Reed	75.00	34.00	9.50
1991 Score Dream Team Autographs Andre Rison	75.00	34.00	9.50
1991 Score Dream Team Autographs Keith Jackson	40.00	18.00	5.00
1991 Score Dream Team Autographs Bruce Armstrong	30.00	13.50	3.70
1991 Score Dream Team Autographs Jim Lachey	30.00	13.50	3.70
1991 Score Dream Team Autographs Bruce Matthews	30.00	13.50	3.70
1991 Score Dream Team Autographs Mike Munchak	30.00	13.50	3.70
1991 Score Dream Team Autographs Don Mosebar	30.00	13.50	3.70

1992 Pro Line Portraits Autographs

COMPLETE SET (161) 1200.00   550.00   150.00

This 167-card standard-size set continues the numbering of the 1991 Pro Line Portraits set. Reportedly 35,000 ten-box cases were produced. Pro Line's goal was to have an autographed card in each box. Also autograph cards could be obtained through a mail-in offer in exchange for 12 1991 Pro Line Portraits wrappers (black) and 12 1992 Pro Line Collection wrappers (white). The fronts display full-bleed color photos in non-game shots while the backs carry personal information. The cards are unnumbered but are listed below according to the numbers assigned to them in the regular series. The following cards were not signed: 349 James Hasty, 370 Anthony Smith, 417 Dennis Green, 428 Frank Gifford, 451 Mark Rypien, 462 Richard Todd. The Santa and Mrs. Claus autographed cards are not considered part of the complete set.

	MINT	NRMT	EXC
1992 Pro Line Portraits Autographs COMMON CARD (301-467)	4.00	1.80	.50
1992 Pro Line Portraits Autographs Steve Emtman	4.00	1.80	.50
1992 Pro Line Portraits Autographs Al Edwards	4.00	1.80	.50
1992 Pro Line Portraits Autographs Wendell Davis	4.00	1.80	.50
1992 Pro Line Portraits Autographs Lewis Billups	4.00	1.80	.50
1992 Pro Line Portraits Autographs Brian Brennan	4.00	1.80	.50
1992 Pro Line Portraits Autographs John Gesek	4.00	1.80	.50
1992 Pro Line Portraits Autographs Terrell Buckley	4.00	1.80	.50
1992 Pro Line Portraits Autographs Johnny Mitchell	4.00	1.80	.50
1992 Pro Line Portraits Autographs LeRoy Butler	7.00	3.10	.85
1992 Pro Line Portraits Autographs William Fuller	7.00	3.10	.85
1992 Pro Line Portraits Autographs Bill Brooks	7.00	3.10	.85
1992 Pro Line Portraits Autographs Dino Hackett	4.00	1.80	.50
1992 Pro Line Portraits Autographs Willie Gault	7.00	3.10	.85
1992 Pro Line Portraits Autographs Aaron Cox	4.00	1.80	.50
1992 Pro Line Portraits Autographs Jeff Cross	4.00	1.80	.50
1992 Pro Line Portraits Autographs Emmitt Smith	100.00	45.00	12.50
1992 Pro Line Portraits Autographs Marv Cook	4.00	1.80	.50
1992 Pro Line Portraits Autographs Gill Fenerty	4.00	1.80	.50
1992 Pro Line Portraits Autographs Jeff Carlson	4.00	1.80	.50
1992 Pro Line Portraits Autographs Brad Baxter	4.00	1.80	.50
1992 Pro Line Portraits Autographs Fred Barnett	7.00	3.10	.85
1992 Pro Line Portraits Autographs Kurt Barber	4.00	1.80	.50
1992 Pro Line Portraits Autographs Eric Green	4.00	1.80	.50
1992 Pro Line Portraits Autographs Greg Clark	4.00	1.80	.50
1992 Pro Line Portraits Autographs Keith DeLong	4.00	1.80	.50

L E F T   W I N G
AILIER GAUCHE
AUTHENTIC SIGNATURE
WILLIE O'REE

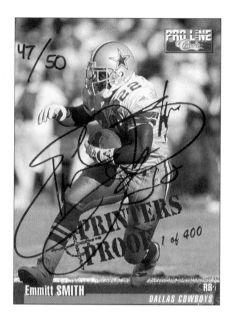

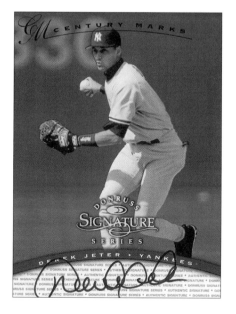

1992 Pro Line Portraits Autographs Patrick Hunter	4.00	1.80	.50
1992 Pro Line Portraits Autographs Troy Vincent	7.00	3.10	.85
1992 Pro Line Portraits Autographs Gary Clark	7.00	3.10	.85
1992 Pro Line Portraits Autographs Joe Montana	125.00	55.00	15.50
1992 Pro Line Portraits Autographs Michael Haynes	7.00	3.10	.85
1992 Pro Line Portraits Autographs Edgar Bennett	12.00	5.50	1.50
1992 Pro Line Portraits Autographs Darren Lewis	4.00	1.80	.50
1992 Pro Line Portraits Autographs Derrick Fenner	4.00	1.80	.50
1992 Pro Line Portraits Autographs Rob Burnett	4.00	1.80	.50
1992 Pro Line Portraits Autographs Alvin Harper	7.00	3.10	.85
1992 Pro Line Portraits Autographs Vance Johnson	4.00	1.80	.50
1992 Pro Line Portraits Autographs William White	4.00	1.80	.50
1992 Pro Line Portraits Autographs Sterling Sharpe	20.00	9.00	2.50
1992 Pro Line Portraits Autographs Sean Jones	7.00	3.10	.85
1992 Pro Line Portraits Autographs Jeff Herrod	4.00	1.80	.50
1992 Pro Line Portraits Autographs Chris Martin	4.00	1.80	.50
1992 Pro Line Portraits Autographs Ethan Horton	4.00	1.80	.50
1992 Pro Line Portraits Autographs Robert Delpino	4.00	1.80	.50
1992 Pro Line Portraits Autographs Mark Higgs	4.00	1.80	.50
1992 Pro Line Portraits Autographs Chris Doleman	7.00	3.10	.85
1992 Pro Line Portraits Autographs Tommy Hodson	4.00	1.80	.50
1992 Pro Line Portraits Autographs Craig Heyward	7.00	3.10	.85
1992 Pro Line Portraits Autographs Cary Conklin	4.00	1.80	.50
1992 Pro Line Portraits Autographs Antone Davis	4.00	1.80	.50
1992 Pro Line Portraits Autographs Ernie Jones	4.00	1.80	.50
1992 Pro Line Portraits Autographs Greg Lloyd	12.00	5.50	1.50
1992 Pro Line Portraits Autographs John Friesz	4.00	1.80	.50
1992 Pro Line Portraits Autographs Charles Haley	7.00	3.10	.85
1992 Pro Line Portraits Autographs Tracy Scroggins	4.00	1.80	.50
1992 Pro Line Portraits Autographs Paul Gruber	4.00	1.80	.50
1992 Pro Line Portraits Autographs Ricky Ervins	7.00	3.10	.85
1992 Pro Line Portraits Autographs Brad Muster	4.00	1.80	.50
1992 Pro Line Portraits Autographs Deion Sanders	40.00	18.00	5.00

(Sanders also signed and numbered 200 cards from his personal stock; these are worth double)

1992 Pro Line Portraits Autographs Mitch Frerotte	4.00	1.80	.50
1992 Pro Line Portraits Autographs Stan Thomas	4.00	1.80	.50
1992 Pro Line Portraits Autographs Harold Green	4.00	1.80	.50
1992 Pro Line Portraits Autographs Eric Metcalf	7.00	3.10	.85
1992 Pro Line Portraits Autographs Ken Norton Jr.	7.00	3.10	.85
1992 Pro Line Portraits Autographs Dave Widell	7.00	3.10	.85
1992 Pro Line Portraits Autographs Mike Tomczak	4.00	1.80	.50
1992 Pro Line Portraits Autographs Bubba McDowell	4.00	1.80	.50
1992 Pro Line Portraits Auto. Jessie Hester (Signed in ball-point pen)	4.00	1.80	.50
1992 Pro Line Portraits Autographs Ervin Randle	4.00	1.80	.50
1992 Pro Line Portraits Autographs Pat Terrell	4.00	1.80	.50
1992 Pro Line Portraits Autographs Jim C. Jensen	4.00	1.80	.50
1992 Pro Line Portraits Autographs Mike Merriweather	4.00	1.80	.50
1992 Pro Line Portraits Autographs Chris Singleton	4.00	1.80	.50
1992 Pro Line Portraits Autographs Floyd Turner	4.00	1.80	.50
1992 Pro Line Portraits Autographs Jim Sweeney	4.00	1.80	.50
1992 Pro Line Portraits Autographs Keith Jackson	7.00	3.10	.85
1992 Pro Line Portraits Autographs Walter Reeves	4.00	1.80	.50
1992 Pro Line Portraits Autographs Neil O'Donnell	12.00	5.50	1.50
1992 Pro Line Portraits Autographs Nate Lewis	4.00	1.80	.50
1992 Pro Line Portraits Autographs Keith Henderson	4.00	1.80	.50
1992 Pro Line Portraits Autographs Kelly Stouffer	4.00	1.80	.50
1992 Pro Line Portraits Autographs Ricky Reynolds	4.00	1.80	.50
1992 Pro Line Portraits Autographs Joe Jacoby	4.00	1.80	.50
1992 Pro Line Portraits Autographs Fred Biletnikoff RET	250.00	110.00	31.00
1992 Pro Line Portraits Autographs Jessie Tuggle	4.00	1.80	.50
1992 Pro Line Portraits Autographs Tom Waddle	4.00	1.80	.50
1992 Pro Line Portraits Autographs David Shula CO	4.00	1.80	.50
1992 Pro Line Portraits Autographs Van Waiters	4.00	1.80	.50
1992 Pro Line Portraits Autographs Jay Novacek	7.00	3.10	.85

1992 Pro Line Portraits Autographs Michael Young . . . . 4.00   1.80   .50
1992 Pro Line Portraits Autographs Mike Holmgren CO . . . . 7.00   3.10   .85
1992 Pro Line Portraits Autographs Doug Smith . . . . 4.00   1.80   .50
1992 Pro Line Portraits Autographs Mike Prior . . . . 4.00   1.80   .50
1992 Pro Line Portraits Autographs Harvey Williams . . . . 7.00   3.10   .85
1992 Pro Line Portraits Autographs Aaron Wallace . . . . 4.00   1.80   .50
1992 Pro Line Portraits Autographs Tony Zendejas . . . . 4.00   1.80   .50
1992 Pro Line Portraits Autographs Sammie Smith . . . . 4.00   1.80   .50
1992 Pro Line Portraits Autographs Henry Thomas . . . . 4.00   1.80   .50
1992 Pro Line Portraits Autographs Jon Vaughn . . . . 4.00   1.80   .50
1992 Pro Line Portraits Autographs Brian Washington . . . . 4.00   1.80   .50
1992 Pro Line Portraits Autographs Leon Searcy . . . . 4.00   1.80   .50
1992 Pro Line Portraits Autographs Lance Smith . . . . 4.00   1.80   .50
1992 Pro Line Portraits Autographs Warren Williams . . . . 4.00   1.80   .50
1992 Pro Line Portraits Autographs Bobby Ross CO . . . . 4.00   1.80   .50
1992 Pro Line Portraits Autographs Harry Sydney . . . . 4.00   1.80   .50
1992 Pro Line Portraits Autographs John L. Williams . . . . 7.00   3.10   .85
1992 Pro Line Portraits Autographs Ken Willis . . . . 4.00   1.80   .50
1992 Pro Line Portraits Autographs Brian Mitchell . . . . 7.00   3.10   .85
1992 Pro Line Portraits Autographs Dick Butkus RET 20.00   9.00   2.50
1992 Pro Line Portraits Autographs Chuck Knox CO . . . . 4.00   1.80   .50
1992 Pro Line Portraits Autographs Robert Porcher . . . . 4.00   1.80   .50
1992 Pro Line Portraits Autographs Calvin Williams . . . . 7.00   3.10   .85
1992 Pro Line Portraits Autographs Bill Cowher CO . . . . 7.00   3.10   .85
1992 Pro Line Portraits Autographs Eric Moore . . . . 4.00   1.80   .50
1992 Pro Line Portraits Autographs Derek Brown TE . . . . 4.00   1.80   .50
1992 Pro Line Portraits Autographs Tom Flores CO . . . . 7.00   3.10   .85
1992 Pro Line Portraits Autographs Dale Carter . . . . 7.00   3.10   .85
1992 Pro Line Portraits Autographs Tony Dorsett RET 20.00   9.00   2.50
1992 Pro Line Portraits Autographs Marco Coleman . . . . 7.00   3.10   .85
1992 Pro Line Portraits Autographs Sam Wyche CO . . . . 7.00   3.10   .85
1992 Pro Line Portraits Autographs Ray Crockett . . . . 4.00   1.80   .50
1992 Pro Line Portraits Autographs Dan Fouts RET 15.00   6.75   1.85
1992 Pro Line Portraits Autographs Hugh Millen . . . . 4.00   1.80   .50
1992 Pro Line Portraits Autographs Quentin Coryatt . . . . 7.00   3.10   .85
1992 Pro Line Portraits Autographs Brian Jordan 12.00   5.50   1.50
1992 Pro Line Portraits Autographs Toby Caston . . . . 7.00   3.10   .85
1992 Pro Line Portraits Autographs Ted Marchibroda CO . . . . 7.00   3.10   .85
1992 Pro Line Portraits Autographs Cris Carter 30.00   13.50   3.70
1992 Pro Line Portraits Autographs Tim Krumrie . . . . 4.00   1.80   .50
1992 Pro Line Portraits Autographs Otto Graham RET 20.00   9.00   2.50
1992 Pro Line Portraits Autographs Vaughn Dunbar . . . . 4.00   1.80   .50
1992 Pro Line Portraits Autographs John Fina . . . . 4.00   1.80   .50
1992 Pro Line Portraits Autographs Sonny Jurgensen RET 20.00   9.00   2.50
1992 Pro Line Portraits Autographs Robert Jones . . . . 4.00   1.80   .50
1992 Pro Line Portraits Autographs Steve DeOssie . . . . 4.00   1.80   .50
1992 Pro Line Portraits Autographs Eddie LeBaron RET 12.00   5.50   1.50
1992 Pro Line Portraits Autographs Chester McGlockton . . . . 7.00   3.10   .85
1992 Pro Line Portraits Autographs Ken Stabler RET 30.00   13.50   3.70
1992 Pro Line Portraits Autographs Joe DeLamielleure RET . . . . 4.00   1.80   .50
1992 Pro Line Portraits Autographs Charley Taylor RET 12.00   5.50   1.50
1992 Pro Line Portraits Autographs Greg Skrepenak . . . . 4.00   1.80   .50
1992 Pro Line Portraits Autographs Y.A. Tittle RET 20.00   9.00   2.50
1992 Pro Line Portraits Autographs Chuck Smith . . . . 4.00   1.80   .50
1992 Pro Line Portraits Autographs Kellen Winslow RET 12.00   5.50   1.50
1992 Pro Line Portraits Autographs Kevin Smith . . . . 7.00   3.10   .85
1992 Pro Line Portraits Autographs Phillippi Sparks . . . . 4.00   1.80   .50
1992 Pro Line Portraits Autographs Alonzo Spellman . . . . 4.00   1.80   .50
1992 Pro Line Portraits Autographs Darryl Williams . . . . 4.00   1.80   .50
1992 Pro Line Portraits Autographs Tommy Vardell . . . . 7.00   3.10   .85
1992 Pro Line Portraits Autographs Tommy Maddox . . . . 4.00   1.80   .50
1992 Pro Line Portraits Autographs Steve Israel . . . . 4.00   1.80   .50
1992 Pro Line Portraits Autographs Marquez Pope . . . . 4.00   1.80   .50

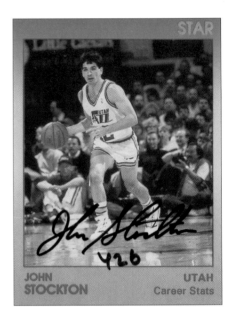

JOHN STOCKTON   UTAH
Career Stats

1992 Pro Line Portraits Autographs Eugene Chung .... 4.00   1.80   .50
1992 Pro Line Portraits Autographs Lynn Swann RET 75.00   34.00   9.50
1992 Pro Line Portraits Autographs Sean Gilbert .... 7.00   3.10   .85
1992 Pro Line Portraits Autographs Chris Mims .... 7.00   3.10   .85
1992 Pro Line Portraits Autographs Al Davis OWN 350.00   160.00   45.00
1992 Pro Line Portraits Autographs Mike Fox .... 4.00   1.80   .50
1992 Pro Line Portraits Autographs David Klingler .... 7.00   3.10   .85
1992 Pro Line Portraits Autographs Darren Woodson .... 7.00   3.10   .85
1992 Pro Line Portraits Autographs Jason Hanson .... 7.00   3.10   .85
1992 Pro Line Portraits Autographs Lem Barney RET .... 7.00   3.10   .85
1992 Pro Line Portraits Autographs Santa Claus 20.00   9.00   2.50
1992 Pro Line Portraits Autographs Mrs. Santa Claus 20.00   9.00   2.50

1992 Pro Line Portraits Team NFL Autographs

COMPLETE SET (5) 200.00   90.00   25.00

This five-card standard-size set marks the debut of Pro Line's Team NFL Collectible cards, which features stars from other sports as well as celebrities from the entertainment world. On the fronts, each personality is pictured wearing attire of their favorite NFL team. The horizontal backs have team color-coded stripes at the top and an extended quote on a silver panel. The cards are unnumbered but are listed below according to the numbers assigned to them in the regular series. Card #1B, of which Muhammad Ali signed a limited number with his birth name, Cassius Clay, is not included in the set price.

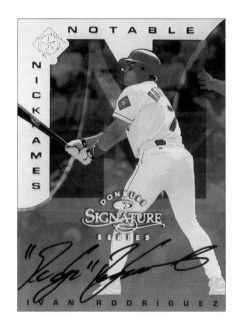

	MINT	NRMT	EXC
1992 Pro Line Portraits Team NFL Autographs COMMON CARD (1-5) ..	10.00	4.50	1.25
1992 Pro Line Portraits Team NFL Autographs Muhammad Ali	125.00	55.00	15.50
1992 Pro Line Portraits NFL Auto. Muhammad Ali (Signed Cassius Clay) .	500.00	220.00	60.00
1992 Pro Line Portraits Team NFL Autographs Milton Berle	25.00	11.00	3.10
1992 Pro Line Portraits Team NFL Autographs Don Mattingly	35.00	16.00	4.40
1992 Pro Line Portraits Team NFL Autographs Martin Mull	10.00	4.50	1.25
1992 Pro Line Portraits NFL Auto. Isiah Thomas (Card is signed Isiah) ...	15.00	6.75	1.85

1996 Laser View Inscriptions

COMPLETE SET (25) 1500.00   700.00   190.00

Randomly inserted in packs at a rate of one in 24, this set is a 25-card, sequentially numbered set featuring autographs of some of the top players in the NFL. The cards are unnumbered and listed below alphabetically. The number of autographs that each player signed is listed after his name.

	MINT	NRMT	EXC
1996 Laser View Inscriptions COMMON CARD (1-25)	20.00	9.00	2.50
1996 Laser View Inscriptions Jeff Blake/3125	25.00	11.00	3.10
1996 Laser View Inscriptions Drew Bledsoe/2775	80.00	36.00	10.00
1996 Laser View Inscriptions Dave Brown/3100	20.00	9.00	2.50
1996 Laser View Inscriptions Mark Brunell/3200	80.00	36.00	10.00
1996 Laser View Inscriptions Kerry Collins/3000	30.00	13.50	3.70
1996 Laser View Inscriptions John Elway/3100	120.00	55.00	15.00
1996 Laser View Inscriptions Boomer Esiason/1500	175.00	80.00	22.00
1996 Laser View Inscriptions Jim Everett/3100	20.00	9.00	2.50
1996 Laser View Inscriptions Brett Favre/4850	120.00	55.00	15.00
1996 Laser View Inscriptions Jeff George/2900	25.00	11.00	3.10
1996 Laser View Inscriptions Jim Harbaugh/3500	25.00	11.00	3.10
1996 Laser View Inscriptions Jeff Hostetler/3750	20.00	9.00	2.50
1996 Laser View Inscriptions Michael Irvin/3050	25.00	11.00	3.10
1996 Laser View Inscriptions Jim Kelly/3100	40.00	18.00	5.00
1996 Laser View Inscriptions Bernie Kosar/3200	20.00	9.00	2.50
1996 Laser View Inscriptions Erik Kramer/3150	20.00	9.00	2.50
1996 Laser View Inscriptions Rick Mirer/3150	25.00	11.00	3.10
1996 Laser View Inscriptions Scott Mitchell/4900	20.00	9.00	2.50
1996 Laser View Inscriptions Warren Moon/2800	25.00	11.00	3.10
1996 Laser View Inscriptions Neil O'Donnell/1600	50.00	22.00	6.25
1996 Laser View Inscriptions Jerry Rice/900	350.00	160.00	45.00
1996 Laser View Inscriptions Barry Sanders/2900	140.00	65.00	17.50
1996 Laser View Inscriptions Junior Seau/3000	25.00	11.00	3.10
1996 Laser View Inscriptions Heath Shuler/3100	25.00	11.00	3.10
1996 Laser View Inscriptions Steve Young/1950	100.00	45.00	12.50

1996 Pro Line Autographs

COMP.GOLD SET (73) 2800.00   1250.00   350.00

This 73-card set features borderless color action player photos with a gold foil player autograph. We have priced the gold foil versions which were inserted at a rate of every 170 packs in hobby and retail packs and one every 200 in jumbo packs. The blue foil varieties were inserted more frequently. Blue foil versions were inserted one ever 25 hobby and retail packs and one every 90 jumbo packs. Since the cards are not numbered we have sequenced them alphabetically.

	MINT	NRMT	EXC
1996 Pro Line Autographs COMMON GOLD FOIL	12.00	5.50	1.50
1996 Pro Line Autographs COMP.BLUE SET (68)	650.00	300.00	80.00
1996 Pro Line Autographs COMMON BLUE FOIL	6.00	2.70	.75
1996 Pro Line Autographs *BLUE FOIL CARDS: .3X TO .6X GOLDS			
1996 Pro Line Autographs Troy Aikman (Emmitt Smith; Gold Only)	500.00	220.00	60.00
1996 Pro Line Autographs Eric Allen	12.00	5.50	1.50
1996 Pro Line Autographs Mike Alstott	70.00	32.00	8.75
1996 Pro Line Autographs Tony Banks	60.00	27.00	7.50
1996 Pro Line Autographs Blaine Bishop	12.00	5.50	1.50
1996 Pro Line Autographs Drew Bledsoe	150.00	70.00	19.00
1996 Pro Line Autographs Tim Brown	20.00	9.00	2.50
1996 Pro Line Autographs Marion Butts	12.00	5.50	1.50
1996 Pro Line Autographs Sedric Clark	12.00	5.50	1.50
1996 Pro Line Autographs Duane Clemons	12.00	5.50	1.50
1996 Pro Line Autographs Marco Coleman	12.00	5.50	1.50
1996 Pro Line Autographs Eric Davis	12.00	5.50	1.50
1996 Pro Line Autographs Derrick Deese	12.00	5.50	1.50
1996 Pro Line Autographs Jack Del Rio	12.00	5.50	1.50
1996 Pro Line Autographs Ty Detmer	20.00	9.00	2.50
1996 Pro Line Autographs Chris Doering	12.00	5.50	1.50
1996 Pro Line Autographs Jumbo Elliott	12.00	5.50	1.50
1996 Pro Line Autographs Marshall Faulk	50.00	22.00	6.25
1996 Pro Line Autographs Glenn Foley	12.00	5.50	1.50
1996 Pro Line Autographs John Friesz	12.00	5.50	1.50
1996 Pro Line Autographs Daryl Gardener	20.00	9.00	2.50
1996 Pro Line Autographs Randall Godfrey	12.00	5.50	1.50
1996 Pro Line Autographs Scott Greene	12.00	5.50	1.50
1996 Pro Line Autographs Rhett Hall	12.00	5.50	1.50
1996 Pro Line Autographs Merton Hanks	12.00	5.50	1.50
1996 Pro Line Autographs Kevin Hardy	12.00	5.50	1.50
1996 Pro Line Autographs Richard Huntley	12.00	5.50	1.50
1996 Pro Line Autographs Michael Jackson	12.00	5.50	1.50
1996 Pro Line Autographs Ron Jaworski	20.00	9.00	2.50
1996 Pro Line Autographs Andre Johnson	12.00	5.50	1.50
1996 Pro Line Autographs Keyshawn Johnson	60.00	27.00	7.50
1996 Pro Line Auto. Keyshawn Johnson (Neil O'Donnell – Gold Only)	175.00	80.00	22.00
1996 Pro Line Autographs Mike Jones	12.00	5.50	1.50
1996 Pro Line Autographs Jim Kiick	30.00	13.50	3.70
1996 Pro Line Autographs Jeff Lewis	20.00	9.00	2.50
1996 Pro Line Autographs Tommy Maddox	12.00	5.50	1.50
1996 Pro Line Autographs Arthur Marshall	12.00	5.50	1.50
1996 Pro Line Autographs Russell Maryland	12.00	5.50	1.50
1996 Pro Line Autographs Derrick Mayes	30.00	13.50	3.70
1996 Pro Line Autographs Ed McCaffrey	12.00	5.50	1.50
1996 Pro Line Autographs Keenan McCardell	20.00	9.00	2.50
1996 Pro Line Autographs Terry McDaniel	12.00	5.50	1.50
1996 Pro Line Autographs Tim McDonald	12.00	5.50	1.50
1996 Pro Line Autographs Willie McGinest	12.00	5.50	1.50
1996 Pro Line Autographs Mark McMillian	12.00	5.50	1.50
1996 Pro Line Autographs Johnny McWilliams	12.00	5.50	1.50
1996 Pro Line Autographs Ray Mickens	12.00	5.50	1.50
1996 Pro Line Autographs Anthony Miller	12.00	5.50	1.50
1996 Pro Line Autographs Rick Mirer	30.00	13.50	3.70
1996 Pro Line Autographs Alex Molden	12.00	5.50	1.50
1996 Pro Line Autographs Johnnie Morton	20.00	9.00	2.50

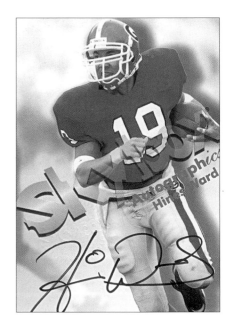

1996 Pro Line Autographs Eric Moulds	30.00	13.50	3.70
1996 Pro Line Autographs Roman Oben	12.00	5.50	1.50
1996 Pro Line Autographs Neil O'Donnell (Gold Only)	60.00	27.00	7.50
1996 Pro Line Autographs Leslie O'Neal	12.00	5.50	1.50
1996 Pro Line Autographs Roman Phifer	12.00	5.50	1.50
1996 Pro Line Autographs Gary Plummer	12.00	5.50	1.50
1996 Pro Line Autographs Jim Plunkett	30.00	13.50	3.70
1996 Pro Line Autographs Stanley Pritchett	20.00	9.00	2.50
1996 Pro Line Autographs John Randle	12.00	5.50	1.50
1996 Pro Line Autographs Brian Roche	12.00	5.50	1.50
1996 Pro Line Autographs Orpheus Roye	12.00	5.50	1.50
1996 Pro Line Autographs Mark Seay	12.00	5.50	1.50
1996 Pro Line Autographs Mike Sherrard	12.00	5.50	1.50
1996 Pro Line Autographs Chris Slade	12.00	5.50	1.50
1996 Pro Line Autographs Scott Slutzker	12.00	5.50	1.50
1996 Pro Line Autographs Emmitt Smith (Gold Only)	350.00	160.00	45.00
1996 Pro Line Autographs Steve Taneyhill	12.00	5.50	1.50
1996 Pro Line Autographs Robb Thomas	12.00	5.50	1.50
1996 Pro Line Autographs William Thomas	12.00	5.50	1.50
1996 Pro Line Autographs Alex Van Dyke	30.00	13.50	3.70
1996 Pro Line Autographs Randy White	30.00	13.50	3.70
1996 Pro Line Autographs Steve Young (Gold Only)	150.00	70.00	19.00

1996 Pro Line Memorabilia Rookie Autographs

COMPLETE SET (15) 800.00   350.00   100.00

Randomly inserted in packs at the rate of one in 12, this 15-card set features borderless color action player photos of NFL rookies with the player's autograph on the front. A limited number of each card was signed by the pictured player and are sequentially numbered. The cards are unnumbered and checklisted below alphabetically.

Diamond Best
Kenny **WOOD** p

	MINT	NRMT	EXC
1996 Pro Line Memorabilia Rookie Autographs COMMON CARD	15.00	6.75	1.85
1996 Pro Line Memorabilia Rookie Autographs Tim Biakabutuka/210	70.00	32.00	8.75
1996 Pro Line Memorabilia Rookie Tim Biakabutuka/600 Eddie George	175.00	80.00	22.00
1996 Pro Line Memorabilia Rookie Autographs Duane Clemons/1255	15.00	6.75	1.85
1996 Pro Line Memorabilia Rookie Autographs Daryl Gardener/1390	20.00	9.00	2.50
1996 Pro Line Memorabilia Rookie Autographs Eddie George/395	200.00	90.00	25.00
1996 Pro Line Memorabilia Rookie Terry Glenn/600 Keyshawn Johnson	120.00	55.00	15.00
1996 Pro Line Memorabilia Rookie Autographs Kevin Hardy/940	20.00	9.00	2.50
1996 Pro Line Memorabilia Rookie Autographs Jeff Hartings/1370	15.00	6.75	1.85
1996 Pro Line Memorabilia Rookie Autographs Andre Johnson/1370	15.00	6.75	1.85
1996 Pro Line Memorabilia Rookie Autographs Keyshawn Johnson/195	100.00	45.00	12.50
1996 Pro Line Memorabilia Rookie Autographs Pete Kendall/1495	15.00	6.75	1.85
1996 Pro Line Memorabilia Rookie Autographs Alex Molden/1320	15.00	6.75	1.85
1996 Pro Line Memorabilia Rookie Autographs Eric Moulds/1010	30.00	13.50	3.70
1996 Pro Line Memorabilia Rookie Autographs Jamain Stephens/795	15.00	6.75	1.85
1996 Pro Line Memorabilia Rookie Autographs Jerome Woods/1375	15.00	6.75	1.85

1996 Score Board NFL Lasers Autographs

COMPLETE SET (7) 900.00   400.00   110.00

Randomly inserted in packs at a rate of one in 150, this seven-card set features color player images over a black shadow player image and the player's autograph in the yellow bar near the bottom. Only 400 of each card was hand-signed. A Die Cut version was also produced and numbered of 100-sets made.

	MINT	NRMT	EXC
1996 Score Board NFL Lasers Autographs COMMON CARD (1-7)	80.00	36.00	10.00
1996 Score Board NFL Lasers Autographs *DIE CUTS: 1X TO 2X BASIC CARDS			
1996 Score Board NFL Lasers Autographs Troy Aikman	150.00	70.00	19.00
1996 Score Board NFL Lasers Autographs Drew Bledsoe	120.00	55.00	15.00
1996 Score Board NFL Lasers Autographs Marshall Faulk	80.00	36.00	10.00
1996 Score Board NFL Lasers Autographs Keyshawn Johnson	80.00	36.00	10.00
1996 Score Board NFL Lasers Autographs Emmitt Smith	200.00	90.00	25.00
1996 Score Board NFL Lasers Autographs Kordell Stewart	150.00	70.00	19.00
1996 Score Board NFL Lasers Autographs Steve Young	120.00	55.00	15.00

1996 SkyBox Premium Autographs

COMPLETE SET (6) 400.00   180.00   50.00

Randomly inserted in packs at a rate of one in 900, this six-card set features color photos of players signed as SkyBox spokesmen. Each card is hand-signed.

	MINT	NRMT	EXC
1996 SkyBox Premium Autographs COMMON CARD (1-6)	25.00	11.00	3.10
1996 SkyBox Premium Autographs Trent Dilfer	40.00	18.00	5.00
1996 SkyBox Premium Autographs Brett Favre	250.00	110.00	31.00
1996 SkyBox Premium Autographs William Floyd	40.00	18.00	5.00
1996 SkyBox Premium Autographs Daryl Johnston	25.00	11.00	3.10
1996 SkyBox Premium Autographs Dave Meggett	25.00	11.00	3.10
1996 SkyBox Premium Autographs Eric Turner	25.00	11.00	3.10

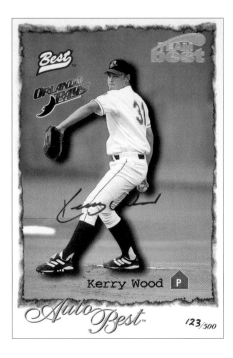

1997 Leaf Signature Autographs

COMMON CARD (1-107) 15.00   6.75   1.85

Randomly inserted one in every pack, this set features borderless color player photos measuring 8" by 10" and printed on super-premium card stock with foil treatment and a signable UV coating. Each card is autographed and displays an "Authentic Signature" designation. The cards are unnumbered and checklisted below in alphabetical order.

	MINT	NRMT	EXC
1997 Leaf Signature Autographs *FIRST DOWN MARKERS: 1X TO 2X . .			
1997 Leaf Signature Autographs Karim Abdul-Jabbar/2500	20.00	9.00	2.50
1997 Leaf Signature Autographs Derrick Alexander WR/4000	20.00	9.00	2.50
1997 Leaf Signature Autographs Terry Allen/3000	30.00	13.50	3.70
1997 Leaf Signature Autographs Mike Alstott/4000	30.00	13.50	3.70
1997 Leaf Signature Autographs Jamal Anderson/4000	20.00	9.00	2.50
1997 Leaf Signature Autographs Reidel Anthony/2000	30.00	13.50	3.70
1997 Leaf Signature Autographs Darnell Autry/4000	30.00	13.50	3.70
1997 Leaf Signature Autographs Tony Banks/500	40.00	18.00	5.00
1997 Leaf Signature Autographs Tiki Barber/4000	30.00	13.50	3.70
1997 Leaf Signature Autographs Pat Barnes/4000	30.00	13.50	3.70
1997 Leaf Signature Autographs Jerome Bettis/500	60.00	27.00	7.50
1997 Leaf Signature Autographs Tim Biakabutuka/3000	15.00	6.75	1.85
1997 Leaf Signature Autographs Will Blackwell/2500	30.00	13.50	3.70
1997 Leaf Signature Autographs Jeff Blake/500	40.00	18.00	5.00
1997 Leaf Signature Autographs Drew Bledsoe/500	135.00	60.00	17.00
1997 Leaf Signature Autographs Peter Boulware/4000	20.00	9.00	2.50
1997 Leaf Signature Autographs Robert Brooks/1000	20.00	9.00	2.50
1997 Leaf Signature Autographs Dave Brown/500	40.00	18.00	5.00
1997 Leaf Signature Autographs Tim Brown/2500	30.00	13.50	3.70
1997 Leaf Signature Autographs Isaac Bruce/2500	30.00	13.50	3.70
1997 Leaf Signature Autographs Mark Brunell/500	135.00	60.00	17.00
1997 Leaf Signature Autographs Rae Carruth/5000	20.00	9.00	2.50
1997 Leaf Signature Autographs Cris Carter/2500	30.00	13.50	3.70
1997 Leaf Signature Autographs Larry Centers/4000	20.00	9.00	2.50
1997 Leaf Signature Autographs Ben Coates/4000	20.00	9.00	2.50
1997 Leaf Signature Autographs Todd Collins/4000	20.00	9.00	2.50
1997 Leaf Signature Autographs Albert Connell/4000	15.00	6.75	1.85
1997 Leaf Signature Autographs Curtis Conway/3000	20.00	9.00	2.50
1997 Leaf Signature Autographs Terrell Davis/2500	100.00	45.00	12.50
1997 Leaf Signature Autographs Troy Davis/4000	30.00	13.50	3.70
1997 Leaf Signature Autographs Trent Dilfer/500	50.00	22.00	6.25
1997 Leaf Signature Autographs Corey Dillon/4000	60.00	27.00	7.50
1997 Leaf Signature Autographs Jim Druckenmiller/5000	40.00	18.00	5.00
1997 Leaf Signature Autographs Warrick Dunn/2000	100.00	45.00	12.50
1997 Leaf Signature Autographs John Elway/500	175.00	80.00	22.00
1997 Leaf Signature Autographs Bert Emanuel/4000	20.00	9.00	2.50
1997 Leaf Signature Autographs Bobby Engram/3000	20.00	9.00	2.50
1997 Leaf Signature Autographs Boomer Esiason/500	50.00	22.00	6.25
1997 Leaf Signature Autographs Jim Everett/500	40.00	18.00	5.00
1997 Leaf Signature Autographs Marshall Faulk/3000	30.00	13.50	3.70
1997 Leaf Signature Autographs Antonio Freeman/2000	30.00	13.50	3.70
1997 Leaf Signature Autographs Gus Frerotte/500	40.00	18.00	5.00
1997 Leaf Signature Autographs Irving Fryar/3000	20.00	9.00	2.50

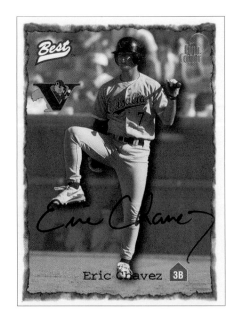

Ruben Mateo

1997 Leaf Signature Autographs Joey Galloway/3000	30.00	13.50	3.70
1997 Leaf Signature Autographs Eddie George/300	175.00	80.00	22.00
1997 Leaf Signature Autographs Jeff George/500	40.00	18.00	5.00
1997 Leaf Signature Autographs Tony Gonzalez/4000	30.00	13.50	3.70
1997 Leaf Signature Autographs Jay Graham/1000	30.00	13.50	3.70
1997 Leaf Signature Autographs Elvis Grbac/500	40.00	18.00	5.00
1997 Leaf Signature Autographs Darrell Green/2500	15.00	6.75	1.85
1997 Leaf Signature Autographs Yatil Green/5000	30.00	13.50	3.70
1997 Leaf Signature Autographs Rodney Hampton/4000	20.00	9.00	2.50
1997 Leaf Signature Autographs Byron Hanspard/4000	30.00	13.50	3.70
1997 Leaf Signature Autographs Jim Harbaugh/500	40.00	18.00	5.00
1997 Leaf Signature Autographs Marvin Harrison/3000	30.00	13.50	3.70
1997 Leaf Signature Autographs Garrison Hearst/4000	20.00	9.00	2.50
1997 Leaf Signature Autographs Greg Hill/4000	20.00	9.00	2.50
1997 Leaf Signature Autographs Ike Hilliard/2000	30.00	13.50	3.70
1997 Leaf Signature Autographs Jeff Hostetler/500	40.00	18.00	5.00
1997 Leaf Signature Autographs Brad Johnson/2000	40.00	18.00	5.00
1997 Leaf Signature Autographs Keyshawn Johnson/1000	35.00	16.00	4.40
1997 Leaf Signature Autographs Daryl Johnston/3000	20.00	9.00	2.50
1997 Leaf Signature Autographs Jim Kelly/500	60.00	27.00	7.50
1997 Leaf Signature Autographs Eddie Kennison/3000	30.00	13.50	3.70
1997 Leaf Signature Autographs Joey Kent/4000	30.00	13.50	3.70
1997 Leaf Signature Autographs Bernie Kosar/500	40.00	18.00	5.00
1997 Leaf Signature Autographs Erik Kramer/500	40.00	18.00	5.00
1997 Leaf Signature Autographs Dorsey Levens/3000	30.00	13.50	3.70
1997 Leaf Signature Autographs Kevin Lockett/4000	20.00	9.00	2.50
1997 Leaf Signature Autographs Tony Martin/4000	20.00	9.00	2.50
1997 Leaf Signature Autographs Leeland McElroy/4000	20.00	9.00	2.50
1997 Leaf Signature Autographs Natrone Means/3000	30.00	13.50	3.70
1997 Leaf Signature Autographs Eric Metcalf/4000	20.00	9.00	2.50
1997 Leaf Signature Autographs Anthony Miller/3000	20.00	9.00	2.50
1997 Leaf Signature Autographs Rick Mirer/500	40.00	18.00	5.00
1997 Leaf Signature Autographs Scott Mitchell/500	40.00	18.00	5.00
1997 Leaf Signature Autographs Warren Moon/500	50.00	22.00	6.25
1997 Leaf Signature Autographs Herman Moore/2500	30.00	13.50	3.70
1997 Leaf Signature Autographs Muhsin Muhammad/3000	15.00	6.75	1.85
1997 Leaf Signature Autographs Adrian Murrell/3000	30.00	13.50	3.70
1997 Leaf Signature Autographs Neil O'Donnell/500	40.00	18.00	5.00
1997 Leaf Signature Autographs Terrell Owens/3000	35.00	16.00	4.40
1997 Leaf Signature Autographs Brett Perriman/1000	15.00	6.75	1.85
1997 Leaf Signature Autographs Lawrence Phillips/1000	20.00	9.00	2.50
1997 Leaf Signature Autographs Jake Plummer/5000	60.00	27.00	7.50
1997 Leaf Signature Autographs Andre Reed/3000	20.00	9.00	2.50
1997 Leaf Signature Autographs Darrell Russell/2000	15.00	6.75	1.85
1997 Leaf Signature Autographs Rashaan Salaam/3000	20.00	9.00	2.50
1997 Leaf Signature Autographs Barry Sanders/400	250.00	110.00	31.00
1997 Leaf Signature Autographs Chris Sanders/3000	20.00	9.00	2.50
1997 Leaf Signature Autographs Frank Sanders/3000	20.00	9.00	2.50
1997 Leaf Signature Autographs Darnay Scott/2000	20.00	9.00	2.50
1997 Leaf Signature Autographs Junior Seau/500	40.00	18.00	5.00
1997 Leaf Signature Autographs Shannon Sharpe/1000	20.00	9.00	2.50
1997 Leaf Signature Autographs Sedrick Shaw/4000	30.00	13.50	3.70
1997 Leaf Signature Autographs Heath Shuler/500	40.00	18.00	5.00
1997 Leaf Signature Autographs Antowain Smith/5000	50.00	22.00	6.25
1997 Leaf Signature Autographs Emmitt Smith/200	300.00	135.00	38.00
1997 Leaf Signature Autographs Kordell Stewart/500	135.00	60.00	17.00
1997 Leaf Signature Autographs J.J. Stokes/3000	20.00	9.00	2.50
1997 Leaf Signature Autographs Vinny Testaverde/200	80.00	36.00	10.00
1997 Leaf Signature Autographs Thurman Thomas/2500	30.00	13.50	3.70
1997 Leaf Signature Autographs Tamarick Vanover/4000	20.00	9.00	2.50
1997 Leaf Signature Autographs Herschel Walker/3000	20.00	9.00	2.50
1997 Leaf Signature Autographs Michael Westbrook/3000	15.00	6.75	1.85
1997 Leaf Signature Autographs Danny Wuerffel/4000	30.00	13.50	3.70
1997 Leaf Signature Autographs Steve Young/500	125.00	55.00	15.50

1997 Pinnacle Inscriptions Autographs

COMPLETE SET (30) 3500.00   1600.00   450.00

This 30-card set features autographed cards of players in the Pinnacle Inscriptions set. Each player signed a certain amount of cards and that number is featured immediately after the players name. The odds of finding an autograph card was reported by the manufacturer to be one every 23 packs.

	MINT	NRMT	EXC
1997 Pinnacle Inscriptions Autographs COMMON CARD (1-30)	25.00	11.00	3.10
1997 Pinnacle Inscriptions Autographs Tony Banks/1925	60.00	27.00	7.50
1997 Pinnacle Inscriptions Autographs Jeff Blake/1470	60.00	27.00	7.50
1997 Pinnacle Inscriptions Autographs Drew Bledsoe/1970	100.00	45.00	12.50
1997 Pinnacle Inscriptions Autographs Dave Brown/1970	25.00	11.00	3.10
1997 Pinnacle Inscriptions Autographs Mark Brunell/2000	100.00	45.00	12.50
1997 Pinnacle Inscriptions Autographs Kerry Collins/1300	80.00	36.00	10.00
1997 Pinnacle Inscriptions Autographs Trent Dilfer/1950	60.00	27.00	7.50
1997 Pinnacle Inscriptions Autographs John Elway/1975	150.00	70.00	19.00
1997 Pinnacle Inscriptions Autographs Jim Everett/2000	25.00	11.00	3.10
1997 Pinnacle Inscriptions Autographs Brett Favre/215	700.00	325.00	90.00
1997 Pinnacle Inscriptions Autographs Gus Frerotte/1975	60.00	27.00	7.50
1997 Pinnacle Inscriptions Autographs Jeff George/1935	40.00	18.00	5.00
1997 Pinnacle Inscriptions Autographs Elvis Grbac/1985	40.00	18.00	5.00
1997 Pinnacle Inscriptions Autographs Jim Harbaugh/1975	40.00	18.00	5.00
1997 Pinnacle Inscriptions Autographs Jeff Hostetler/2000	25.00	11.00	3.10
1997 Pinnacle Inscriptions Autographs Jim Kelly/1925	60.00	27.00	7.50
1997 Pinnacle Inscriptions Autographs Bernie Kosar/1975	25.00	11.00	3.10
1997 Pinnacle Inscriptions Autographs Erik Kramer/2000	25.00	11.00	3.10
1997 Pinnacle Inscriptions Autographs Dan Marino/440	500.00	220.00	60.00
1997 Pinnacle Inscriptions Autographs Rick Mirer/2000	40.00	18.00	5.00
1997 Pinnacle Inscriptions Autographs Scott Mitchell/1995	40.00	18.00	5.00
1997 Pinnacle Inscriptions Autographs Warren Moon/1975	60.00	27.00	7.50
1997 Pinnacle Inscriptions Autographs Neil O'Donnell/1990	40.00	18.00	5.00
1997 Pinnacle Inscriptions Autographs Jerry Rice/950	250.00	110.00	31.00
1997 Pinnacle Inscriptions Autographs Barry Sanders/2053 SP	500.00	220.00	60.00
1997 Pinnacle Inscriptions Autographs Junior Seau/1900	40.00	18.00	5.00
1997 Pinnacle Inscriptions Autographs Heath Shuler/1865	40.00	18.00	5.00
1997 Pinnacle Inscriptions Autographs Emmitt Smith/220	600.00	275.00	75.00
1997 Pinnacle Inscriptions Autographs Kordell Stewart/1495	135.00	60.00	17.00
1997 Pinnacle Inscriptions Autographs Vinny Testaverde/1975	40.00	18.00	5.00
1997 Pinnacle Inscriptions Autographs Steve Young/1900	100.00	45.00	12.50

1997 Pinnacle Inside Autographs

COMPLETE SET (25) 2000.00   900.00   250.00

Randomly inserted in cans at the rate of one in 251, this 25-card set features color photos of members of the Quarterback Club with their genuine autographs displayed on the card. The unnumbered backs carry another player photo and player information. Several of the cards were only available via a mail-in redemption card that was inserted into packs. The redemption card was to be exchanged for a random signed card. The offer expired March 31, 1998.

	MINT	NRMT	EXC
1997 Pinnacle Inside Autographs COMMON CARD (1-25)	40.00	18.00	5.00
1997 Pinnacle Inside Autographs Tony Banks	70.00	32.00	8.75
1997 Pinnacle Inside Autographs Jeff Blake	60.00	27.00	7.50
1997 Pinnacle Inside Autographs Drew Bledsoe	175.00	80.00	22.00
1997 Pinnacle Inside Autographs Dave Brown	40.00	18.00	5.00
1997 Pinnacle Inside Autographs Mark Brunell	175.00	80.00	22.00
1997 Pinnacle Inside Autographs Kerry Collins	60.00	27.00	7.50
1997 Pinnacle Inside Autographs Trent Dilfer	60.00	27.00	7.50
1997 Pinnacle Inside Autographs John Elway	250.00	110.00	31.00
1997 Pinnacle Inside Autographs Jim Everett	40.00	18.00	5.00
1997 Pinnacle Inside Autographs Gus Frerotte	60.00	27.00	7.50
1997 Pinnacle Inside Autographs Jeff George	60.00	27.00	7.50
1997 Pinnacle Inside Autographs Elvis Grbac	60.00	27.00	7.50
1997 Pinnacle Inside Autographs Jim Harbaugh	60.00	27.00	7.50
1997 Pinnacle Inside Autographs Jeff Hostetler	40.00	18.00	5.00

	MINT	NRMT	EXC
1997 Pinnacle Inside Autographs Jim Kelly	100.00	45.00	12.50
1997 Pinnacle Inside Autographs Bernie Kosar	40.00	18.00	5.00
1997 Pinnacle Inside Autographs Erik Kramer	40.00	18.00	5.00
1997 Pinnacle Inside Autographs Scott Mitchell	60.00	27.00	7.50
1997 Pinnacle Inside Autographs Rick Mirer	60.00	27.00	7.50
1997 Pinnacle Inside Autographs Warren Moon	60.00	27.00	7.50
1997 Pinnacle Inside Autographs Barry Sanders	200.00	100.00	30.00
1997 Pinnacle Inside Autographs Junior Seau	60.00	27.00	7.50
1997 Pinnacle Inside Autographs Heath Shuler	60.00	27.00	7.50
1997 Pinnacle Inside Autographs Kordell Stewart	175.00	80.00	22.00
1997 Pinnacle Inside Autographs Vinny Testaverde	60.00	27.00	7.50
1997 Pinnacle Inside Autographs Steve Young	175.00	80.00	22.00

1997 Pro Line Autographs

COMPLETE SET (52)	1600.00	700.00	200.00

Signed cards of top NFL players were randomly inserted at the rate of 1:28 packs. Unlike previous issues, each card is not a parallel of the base set but has been completely re-designed. A white box appears on the cardfront containing the signature. Cardbacks are unnumbered and contain a congratulatory message. The cards are checklisted below alphabetically.

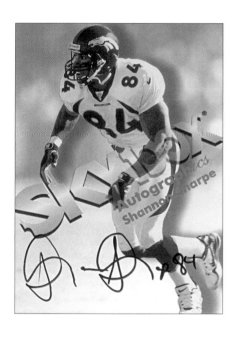

	MINT	NRMT	EXC
1997 Pro Line Autographs COMMON CARD	15.00	6.75	1.85
1997 Pro Line Autographs Karim Abdul-Jabbar	50.00	22.00	6.25
1997 Pro Line Autographs Troy Aikman	175.00	80.00	22.00
1997 Pro Line Autographs Eric Allen	15.00	6.75	1.85
1997 Pro Line Autographs Mike Alstott	60.00	27.00	7.50
1997 Pro Line Autographs Marco Battaglia	15.00	6.75	1.85
1997 Pro Line Autographs Eric Bjornson	15.00	6.75	1.85
1997 Pro Line Autographs Peter Boulware	20.00	9.00	2.50
1997 Pro Line Autographs Ray Buchanon	15.00	6.75	1.85
1997 Pro Line Autographs Rae Carruth	20.00	9.00	2.50
1997 Pro Line Autographs Kerry Collins	40.00	18.00	5.00
1997 Pro Line Autographs Stephen Davis	15.00	6.75	1.85
1997 Pro Line Autographs Terrell Davis	150.00	70.00	19.00
1997 Pro Line Autographs Derrick Deese	15.00	6.75	1.85
1997 Pro Line Autographs Koy Detmer	15.00	6.75	1.85
1997 Pro Line Autographs Ken Dilger	15.00	6.75	1.85
1997 Pro Line Autographs Corey Dillon	70.00	32.00	8.75
1997 Pro Line Autographs Hugh Douglas	15.00	6.75	1.85
1997 Pro Line Autographs Jason Dunn	15.00	6.75	1.85
1997 Pro Line Autographs Warrick Dunn	100.00	45.00	12.50
1997 Pro Line Autographs Ray Farmer	15.00	6.75	1.85
1997 Pro Line Autographs Brett Favre	225.00	100.00	28.00
1997 Pro Line Autographs Joey Galloway	30.00	13.50	3.70
1997 Pro Line Autographs Norberto Garrido	15.00	6.75	1.85
1997 Pro Line Autographs Terry Glenn	60.00	27.00	7.50
1997 Pro Line Autographs Byron Hanspard	30.00	13.50	3.70
1997 Pro Line Autographs Kevin Hardy	20.00	9.00	2.50
1997 Pro Line Autographs Steve Israel	15.00	6.75	1.85
1997 Pro Line Autographs Brad Johnson	30.00	13.50	3.70
1997 Pro Line Autographs Keyshawn Johnson	60.00	27.00	7.50
1997 Pro Line Autographs Greg Jones	15.00	6.75	1.85
1997 Pro Line Autographs Mike Jones	15.00	6.75	1.85
1997 Pro Line Autographs Danny Kanell	30.00	13.50	3.70
1997 Pro Line Autographs David LaFleur	30.00	13.50	3.70
1997 Pro Line Autographs Keenan McCardell	20.00	9.00	2.50
1997 Pro Line Autographs Leeland McElroy	20.00	9.00	2.50
1997 Pro Line Autographs Willie McGinest	15.00	6.75	1.85
1997 Pro Line Autographs Mark McMillian	15.00	6.75	1.85
1997 Pro Line Autographs Nate Newton	15.00	6.75	1.85
1997 Pro Line Autographs Jake Plummer	90.00	40.00	11.00
1997 Pro Line Autographs John Randle	15.00	6.75	1.85
1997 Pro Line Autographs Simeon Rice	20.00	9.00	2.50
1997 Pro Line Autographs Jon Runyan	15.00	6.75	1.85

1997 Pro Line Autographs Chris Slade 15.00   6.75   1.85
1997 Pro Line Autographs Antowain Smith 60.00   27.00   7.50
1997 Pro Line Autographs Emmitt Smith 200.00   90.00   25.00
1997 Pro Line Autographs Jimmy Smith 20.00   9.00   2.50
1997 Pro Line Autographs Matt Stevens 15.00   6.75   1.85
1997 Pro Line Autographs Kordell Stewart 120.00   55.00   15.00
1997 Pro Line Autographs Mark Tuinei 15.00   6.75   1.85
1997 Pro Line Autographs Bryant Westbrook 20.00   9.00   2.50
1997 Pro Line Autographs Brian Williams LB 15.00   6.75   1.85
1997 Pro Line Autographs Dusty Zeigler 15.00   6.75   1.85

1997 Pro Line Autographs Emerald

COMPLETE SET (43)

Score Board produced a parallel set to its 1997 Pro Line Autograph series. Each card includes Emerald colored foil on the front along with the player's autograph. All Autographs were randomly inserted at the rate of 1:28 packs. Each of the Emerald cards was also individually numbered, unlike the base Autograph set. We've numbered the cards below according to their base set counterparts.

	MINT	NRMT	EXC
1997 Pro Line Autographs Emerald COMMON CARD	25.00	11.00	3.10
1997 Pro Line Autographs Emerald Karim Abdul-Jabbar/190	120.00	55.00	15.00
1997 Pro Line Autographs Emerald Troy Aikman/40	600.00	275.00	75.00
1997 Pro Line Autographs Emerald Eric Allen/250	25.00	11.00	3.10
1997 Pro Line Autographs Emerald Marco Battaglia/500	25.00	11.00	3.10
1997 Pro Line Autographs Emerald Eric Bjornson/390	25.00	11.00	3.10
1997 Pro Line Autographs Emerald Peter Boulware/430	30.00	13.50	3.70
1997 Pro Line Autographs Emerald Ray Buchanon/390	25.00	11.00	3.10
1997 Pro Line Autographs Emerald Rae Carruth/525	40.00	18.00	5.00
1997 Pro Line Autographs Emerald Kerry Collins/170	120.00	55.00	15.00
1997 Pro Line Autographs Emerald Stephen Davis/530	25.00	11.00	3.10
1997 Pro Line Autographs Emerald Terrell Davis/100	400.00	180.00	50.00
1997 Pro Line Autographs Emerald Ken Dilger/525	25.00	11.00	3.10
1997 Pro Line Autographs Emerald Corey Dillon/470	100.00	45.00	12.50
1997 Pro Line Autographs Emerald Hugh Douglas/400	25.00	11.00	3.10
1997 Pro Line Autographs Emerald Jason Dunn/525	25.00	11.00	3.10
1997 Pro Line Autographs Emerald Warrick Dunn/430	175.00	80.00	22.00
1997 Pro Line Autographs Emerald Ray Farmer/340	25.00	11.00	3.10
1997 Pro Line Autographs Emerald Brett Favre/100	600.00	275.00	75.00
1997 Pro Line Autographs Emerald Joey Galloway/300	60.00	27.00	7.50
1997 Pro Line Autographs Emerald Terry Glenn/380	150.00	70.00	19.00
1997 Pro Line Autographs Emerald Byron Hanspard/500	40.00	18.00	5.00
1997 Pro Line Autographs Emerald Kevin Hardy/500	30.00	13.50	3.70
1997 Pro Line Autographs Emerald Brad Johnson/410	50.00	22.00	6.25
1997 Pro Line Autographs Emerald Keyshawn Johnson/100	150.00	70.00	19.00
1997 Pro Line Autographs Emerald Greg Jones/470	25.00	11.00	3.10
1997 Pro Line Autographs Emerald Danny Kanell/450	40.00	18.00	5.00
1997 Pro Line Autographs Emerald David LaFleur/500	25.00	11.00	3.10
1997 Pro Line Autographs Emerald Keenan McCardell/220	30.00	13.50	3.70
1997 Pro Line Autographs Emerald Leeland McElroy/440	30.00	13.50	3.70
1997 Pro Line Autographs Emerald Willie McGinest/210	25.00	11.00	3.10
1997 Pro Line Autographs Emerald Nate Newton/340	25.00	11.00	3.10
1997 Pro Line Autographs Emerald Jake Plummer/440	160.00	70.00	20.00
1997 Pro Line Autographs Emerald John Randle/400	25.00	11.00	3.10
1997 Pro Line Autographs Emerald Simeon Rice/375	30.00	13.50	3.70
1997 Pro Line Autographs Emerald Jon Runyan/500	25.00	11.00	3.10
1997 Pro Line Autographs Emerald Chris Slade/260	25.00	11.00	3.10
1997 Pro Line Autographs Emerald Emmitt Smith/200	350.00	160.00	45.00
1997 Pro Line Autographs Emerald Jimmy Smith/280	30.00	13.50	3.70
1997 Pro Line Autographs Emerald Matt Stevens/450	25.00	11.00	3.10
1997 Pro Line Autographs Emerald Kordell Stewart/130	300.00	135.00	38.00
1997 Pro Line Autographs Emerald Mark Tuinei/400	25.00	11.00	3.10
1997 Pro Line Autographs Emerald Bryant Westbrook/525	30.00	13.50	3.70
1997 Pro Line Autographs Emerald Dusty Zeigler/480	25.00	11.00	3.10

1997 Pro Line DC3 Autographs

COMPLETE SET (6) 800.00   350.00   100.00

Randomly inserted at the rate of only one per case, this six-card insert set features color player photos of six hot, up-and-coming NFL stars. Only a maximum of 300 cards were signed by each player.

	MINT	NRMT	EXC
1997 Pro Line DC3 Autographs COMMON CARD (1-6)	60.00	27.00	7.50
1997 Pro Line DC3 Autographs Kordell Stewart	160.00	70.00	20.00
1997 Pro Line DC3 Autographs Kerry Collins	60.00	27.00	7.50
1997 Pro Line DC3 Autographs Terrell Davis	200.00	90.00	25.00
1997 Pro Line DC3 Autographs Eddie George	200.00	90.00	25.00
1997 Pro Line DC3 Autographs Karim Abdul-Jabbar	70.00	32.00	8.75
1997 Pro Line DC3 Autographs Keyshawn Johnson	60.00	27.00	7.50

1997 SkyBox Premium Autographics

COMPLETE SET (70) 3000.00   1350.00   375.00

The Autographics inserts set was distributed across the line of 1997 SkyBox football products and includes 68-different cards. SkyBox Impact packs contained 48-different cards inserted at the rate of 1:120 packs. Each card features an authentic player signature along with an embossed SkyBox seal. SkyBox Premium packs included 65-cards inserted at the rate of 1:72 packs. SkyBox E-X2000 included 51-cards random inserted at the rate of 1:60 packs. We've combined the listings below since many cards were inserted in more than one product type (S= SkyBox Premium, IM= SkyBox Impact, EX= SkyBox E-X2000). The first 100-signed of each card was printed with holographic foil layering and individually numbered; called Century Marks. Brett Favre and Reggie White were only produced as Century Marks. All other cards were printed in both versions. The unnumbered cards are listed below alphabetically.

	MINT	NRMT	EXC
1997 SkyBox Premium Autographics COMMON CARD	10.00	4.50	1.25
1997 SkyBox Premium Autographics CENTURY MARKS: .75X TO 1.5X BASIC CARDS			
1997 SkyBox Premium Autographics Karim Abdul-Jabbar	50.00	22.00	6.25
1997 SkyBox Premium Autographics Larry Allen IM/S	10.00	4.50	1.25
1997 SkyBox Premium Autographics Terry Allen IM/S	40.00	18.00	5.00
1997 SkyBox Premium Autographics Mike Alstott IM/MU/S	70.00	32.00	8.75
1997 SkyBox Premium Autographics Darnell Autry EX/IM/MU/S	40.00	18.00	5.00
1997 SkyBox Premium Autographics Tony Banks IM	50.00	22.00	6.25
1997 SkyBox Premium Autographics Pat Barnes EX/S	40.00	18.00	5.00
1997 SkyBox Premium Autographics Jeff Blake S	40.00	18.00	5.00
1997 SkyBox Premium Autographics Michael Booker IM/S	10.00	4.50	1.25
1997 SkyBox Premium Autographics Rueben Brown EX/S	10.00	4.50	1.25
1997 SkyBox Premium Autographics Rae Carruth EX/IM/MU/S	20.00	9.00	2.50
1997 SkyBox Premium Autographics Cris Carter EX/IM/S	40.00	18.00	5.00
1997 SkyBox Premium Autographics Ben Coates EX/IM/S	20.00	9.00	2.50
1997 SkyBox Premium Autographics Ernie Conwell EX/IM/S	10.00	4.50	1.25
1997 SkyBox Premium Autographics Terrell Davis EX/IM/S	150.00	70.00	19.00
1997 SkyBox Premium Autographics Ty Detmer EX/IM/MU/S	20.00	9.00	2.50
1997 SkyBox Premium Autographics Ken Dilger EX/IM/S	10.00	4.50	1.25
1997 SkyBox Premium Autographics Corey Dillon IM/S	90.00	40.00	11.00
1997 SkyBox Premium Autographics Jim Druckenmiller EX/S	60.00	27.00	7.50
1997 SkyBox Premium Autographics Rickey Dudley EX/IM/S	20.00	9.00	2.50
1997 SkyBox Premium Autographics Brett Favre CENT.EX	600.00	275.00	75.00
1997 SkyBox Premium Autographics Antonio Freeman EX/IM/S	50.00	22.00	6.25
1997 SkyBox Premium Autographics Daryl Gardener EX/IM/S	10.00	4.50	1.25
1997 SkyBox Premium Autographics Chris Gedney IM/S	10.00	4.50	1.25
1997 SkyBox Premium Autographics Eddie George S	150.00	70.00	19.00
1997 SkyBox Premium Autographics Hunter Goodwin EX/IM/S	10.00	4.50	1.25
1997 SkyBox Premium Autographics Marvin Harrison EX/S	40.00	18.00	5.00
1997 SkyBox Premium Autographics Garrison Hearst EX/S	20.00	9.00	2.50
1997 SkyBox Premium Autographics William Henderson EX/IM/S	10.00	4.50	1.25
1997 SkyBox Premium Autographics Michael Jackson EX/IM/S	20.00	9.00	2.50
1997 SkyBox Premium Autographics Tory James EX/IM/S	10.00	4.50	1.25
1997 SkyBox Premium Autographics Rob Johnson EX/IM/S	50.00	22.00	6.25
1997 SkyBox Premium Autographics Chris T. Jones IM/S	20.00	9.00	2.50
1997 SkyBox Premium Autographics Pete Kendall EX/S	10.00	4.50	1.25
1997 SkyBox Premium Autographics Eddie Kennison EX/MU/S	40.00	18.00	5.00

1997 SkyBox Premium Autographics David LaFleur EX/IM/S 40.00   18.00   5.00
1997 SkyBox Premium Autographics Jeff Lewis EX/IM/S 10.00   4.50   1.25
1997 SkyBox Premium Autographics Thomas Lewis IM/S 10.00   4.50   1.25
1997 SkyBox Premium Autographics Kevin Lockett EX/IM/S 20.00   9.00   2.50
1997 SkyBox Premium Autographics Brian Manning IM/MU/S 10.00   4.50   1.25
1997 SkyBox Premium Autographics Dan Marino S 400.00   180.00   50.00
1997 SkyBox Premium Autographics Ed McCaffrey EX/IM/MU/S 10.00   4.50   1.25
1997 SkyBox Premium Autographics Keenan McCardell EX/S 20.00   9.00   2.50
1997 SkyBox Premium Autographics Glyn Milburn EX/IM/S 10.00   4.50   1.25
1997 SkyBox Premium Autographics Alex Molden EX/IM/S 10.00   4.50   1.25
1997 SkyBox Premium Autographics Johnnie Morton IM/S 20.00   9.00   2.50
1997 SkyBox Premium Autographics Winslow Oliver EX/S 10.00   4.50   1.25
1997 SkyBox Premium Autographics Jerry Rice MU 400.00   180.00   50.00
1997 SkyBox Premium Autographics Rashaan Salaam EX/S 20.00   9.00   2.50
1997 SkyBox Premium Autographics Frank Sanders EX/IM/S 20.00   9.00   2.50
1997 SkyBox Premium Autographics Shannon Sharpe EX/IM/MU/S ... 20.00   9.00   2.50
1997 SkyBox Premium Autographics Sedrick Shaw EX/IM/S 40.00   18.00   5.00
1997 SkyBox Premium Autographics Alex Smith EX/IM/S 10.00   4.50   1.25
1997 SkyBox Premium Autographics Antowain Smith EX/S 70.00   32.00   8.75
1997 SkyBox Premium Autographics Emmitt Smith EX 300.00   135.00   38.00
1997 SkyBox Premium Autographics Jimmy Smith IM/S 20.00   9.00   2.50
1997 SkyBox Premium Autographics Shawn Springs S 20.00   9.00   2.50
1997 SkyBox Premium Autographics James O.Stewart EX/IM/S 20.00   9.00   2.50
1997 SkyBox Premium Autographics Kordell Stewart IM 150.00   70.00   19.00
1997 SkyBox Premium Autographics Rodney Thomas EX/S 10.00   4.50   1.25
1997 SkyBox Premium Autographics Amani Toomer EX/IM/S 20.00   9.00   2.50
1997 SkyBox Premium Autographics Floyd Turner EX/IM/S 10.00   4.50   1.25
1997 SkyBox Premium Autographics Alex Van Dyke EX/IM/S 10.00   4.50   1.25
1997 SkyBox Premium Autographics Mike Vrabel IM/MU/S 10.00   4.50   1.25
1997 SkyBox Premium Autographics Charles Way EX/S 20.00   9.00   2.50
1997 SkyBox Premium Autographics Chris Warren EX/MU/S 20.00   9.00   2.50
1997 SkyBox Premium Autographics Reggie White CENT. EX/S 100.00   45.00   12.50
1997 SkyBox Premium Autographics Ricky Whittle EX/IM/S 10.00   4.50   1.25
1997 SkyBox Premium Autographics Sherman Williams EX/IM/S 10.00   4.50   1.25
1997 SkyBox Premium Autographics Jon Witman EX/IM/S 10.00   4.50   1.25

1997 SP Authentic Sign of the Times

COMPLETE SET (28) 2000.00   900.00   250.00

Randomly inserted in packs at the rate of one in 24, this 28-card set features redemption cards for favorite current NFL stars with a white instructional sticker mounted to the cardfront. Collectors could redeem the cards for signed prize cards. The cards are unnumbered and checklisted below in alphabetical order. Foiled and non-foiled versions of some card were mailed asredemptions. While some player's cards have been found in both versions, others have only been reported as either non-foiled or foiled.

	MINT	NRMT	EXC
1997 SP Authentic Sign of the Times COMMON CARD (1-28)	15.00	6.75	1.85
1997 SP Authentic Sign of the Times Karim Abdul-Jabbar (white stock) ..	30.00	13.50	3.70
1997 SP Authentic Sign of the Times Troy Aikman	200.00	90.00	25.00
1997 SP Authentic Sign of the Times Terry Allen	30.00	13.50	3.70
1997 SP Authentic Sign of the Times Reidel Anthony	30.00	13.50	3.70
1997 SP Authentic Sign of the Times Jerome Bettis	30.00	13.50	3.70
1997 SP Authentic Sign of the Times Will Blackwell	25.00	11.00	3.10
1997 SP Authentic Sign of the Times Jeff Blake	30.00	13.50	3.70
1997 SP Authentic Sign of the Times Robert Brooks	15.00	6.75	1.85
1997 SP Authentic Sign of the Times Tim Brown	30.00	13.50	3.70
1997 SP Authentic Sign of the Times Isaac Bruce	30.00	13.50	3.70
1997 SP Authentic Sign of the Times Rae Carruth (white stock)	15.00	6.75	1.85
1997 SP Authentic Sign of the Times Kerry Collins	60.00	27.00	7.50
1997 SP Authentic Sign of the Times Terrell Davis	135.00	60.00	17.00
1997 SP Authentic Sign of the Times Jim Druckenmiller	40.00	18.00	5.00
1997 SP Authentic Sign of the Times Warrick Dunn	100.00	45.00	12.50
1997 SP Authentic Sign of the Times Marshall Faulk	30.00	13.50	3.70
1997 SP Authentic Sign of the Times Joey Galloway	30.00	13.50	3.70
1997 SP Authentic Sign of the Times Eddie George (silver foil stock)	100.00	45.00	12.50

	MINT	NRMT	EXC
1997 SP Authentic Sign of the Times Tony Gonzalez	25.00	11.00	3.10
1997 SP Authentic Sign of the Times George Jones	15.00	6.75	1.85
1997 SP Authentic Sign of the Times Napoleon Kaufman	60.00	27.00	7.50
1997 SP Authentic Sign of the Times Dan Marino (silver foil stock)	350.00	160.00	45.00
1997 SP Authentic Sign of the Times Dan Marino (white stock)	300.00	135.00	38.00
1997 SP Authentic Sign of the Times Curtis Martin (silver foil stock)	80.00	36.00	10.00
1997 SP Authentic Sign of the Times Herman Moore	30.00	13.50	3.70
1997 SP Authentic Sign of the Times Jerry Rice (silver foil stock)	250.00	110.00	31.00
1997 SP Authentic Sign of the Times Rashaan Salaam	15.00	6.75	1.85
1997 SP Authentic Sign of the Times Antowain Smith	40.00	18.00	5.00
1997 SP Authentic Sign of the Times Emmitt Smith (silver foil stock)	300.00	135.00	38.00

1998 Bowman Rookie Autographs

	MINT	NRMT	EXC
COMP.BLUE SET (11)	800.00	350.00	100.00

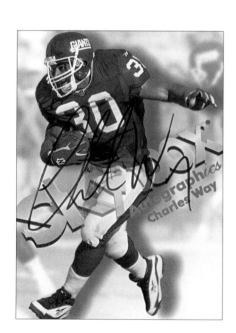

	MINT	NRMT	EXC
1998 Bowman Rookie Autographs COMMON BLUE (A1-A11)	30.00	13.50	3.70
1998 Bowman Rookie Autographs *GOLD FOILS: 1.5X TO 3X BLUE			
1998 Bowman Rookie Autographs *SILVER FOILS: 1X TO 2X BLUE			
1998 Bowman Rookie Autographs Peyton Manning	150.00	70.00	19.00
1998 Bowman Rookie Autographs Andre Wadsworth	30.00	13.50	3.70
1998 Bowman Rookie Autographs Brian Griese	60.00	27.00	7.50
1998 Bowman Rookie Autographs Ryan Leaf	120.00	55.00	15.00
1998 Bowman Rookie Autographs Fred Taylor	80.00	36.00	10.00
1998 Bowman Rookie Autographs Robert Edwards	80.00	36.00	10.00
1998 Bowman Rookie Autographs Randy Moss	225.00	100.00	28.00
1998 Bowman Rookie Autographs Curtis Enis	80.00	36.00	10.00
1998 Bowman Rookie Autographs Kevin Dyson	40.00	18.00	5.00
1998 Bowman Rookie Autographs Charles Woodson	60.00	27.00	7.50
1998 Bowman Rookie Autographs Tim Dwight	40.00	18.00	5.00

1998 CE Supreme Season Review Pro-Signature Authentic

	MINT	NRMT	EXC
COMPLETE SET (6)	2000.00	900.00	250.00

Randomly inserted in packs at the rate of one in 2300, this seven-card set features color player photos printed on 50-point, silver holofoil card stock with rainbow holofoil embossing and the hand-written autograph by the featured player. The backs contain a statement of authenticity.

	MINT	NRMT	EXC
1998 CE Supreme Season Review Pro-Signature Auth. COMMON (1-6)	150.00	70.00	19.00
1998 CE Supreme Season Review Pro-Signature Authentic Troy Aikman	500.00	220.00	60.00
1998 CE Supreme Season Review Pro-Signature Authentic Marcus Allen	225.00	100.00	28.00
1998 CE Supreme Season Review Pro-Signature Authentic Terrell Davis	500.00	220.00	60.00
1998 CE Supreme Season Review Pro-Signature Authentic Desmond Howard	150.00	70.00	19.00
1998 CE Supreme Season Review Pro-Signature Authentic Jerry Rice	500.00	220.00	60.00
1998 CE Sup. Sea. Rev. Pro-Sig. (Ryan Leaf or Peyton Manning card)	150.00	70.00	19.00

1998 Playoff Absolute Dan Marino Milestones

	MINT	NRMT	EXC
COMPLETE SET (10)	2000.00	900.00	250.00

The 1998 Playoff Absolute Marino Milestones set consists of 5 cards and is an insert to the 1998 Playoff Absolute base set. The cards are randomly inserted in packs at a rate of one in 397. The set offers authentic Dan Marino autographed cards commemorating records set by the NFL great.

	MINT	NRMT	EXC
1998 Playoff Absolute Dan Marino Milestones COMMON CARD (1-10)	200.00	90.00	25.00
1998 Playoff Absolute Dan Marino Milestones Dan Marino	200.00	90.00	25.00
1998 Playoff Absolute Dan Marino Milestones Dan Marino	200.00	90.00	25.00
1998 Playoff Absolute Dan Marino Milestones Dan Marino	200.00	90.00	25.00
1998 Playoff Absolute Dan Marino Milestones Dan Marino	200.00	90.00	25.00
1998 Playoff Absolute Dan Marino Milestones Dan Marino	200.00	90.00	25.00
1998 Playoff Absolute Dan Marino Milestones Dan Marino - 7452	200.00	90.00	25.00
1998 Playoff Absolute Dan Marino Milestones Dan Marino - 56/9	200.00	90.00	25.00
1998 Playoff Absolute Dan Marino Milestones Dan Marino - 5084	200.00	90.00	25.00
1998 Playoff Absolute Dan Marino Milestones Dan Marino - 9	200.00	90.00	25.00
1998 Playoff Absolute Dan Marino Milestones Dan Marino - 96.0	200.00	90.00	25.00

1998 Topps Autographs

	MINT	NRMT	EXC
COMPLETE SET (15)	700.00	325.00	90.00
1998 Topps Autographs COMMON CARD (A1-A15)	20.00	9.00	2.50
1998 Topps Autographs Randy Moss	175.00	80.00	22.00
1998 Topps Autographs Mike Alstott	40.00	18.00	5.00
1998 Topps Autographs Jake Plummer	75.00	34.00	9.50
1998 Topps Autographs Corey Dillon	50.00	22.00	6.25
1998 Topps Autographs Kordell Stewart	75.00	34.00	9.50
1998 Topps Autographs Eddie George	60.00	27.00	7.50
1998 Topps Autographs Jason Sehorn	20.00	9.00	2.50
1998 Topps Autographs Joey Galloway	30.00	13.50	3.70
1998 Topps Autographs Ryan Leaf	100.00	45.00	12.50
1998 Topps Autographs Peyton Manning	125.00	55.00	15.50
1998 Topps Autographs Dwight Stephenson	25.00	11.00	3.10
1998 Topps Autographs Anthony Munoz	40.00	18.00	5.00
1998 Topps Autographs Mike Singletary	40.00	18.00	5.00
1998 Topps Autographs Tommy McDonald	25.00	11.00	3.10
1998 Topps Autographs Paul Krause	30.00	13.50	3.70

1994 Parkhurst Missing Link Autographs

COMPLETE SET (6) 750.00   350.00   95.00

The 1994 Parkhurst Missing Link Autograph set is comprised of six Hall of Famers. Randomly inserted in Missing Link packs, the cards are autographed on the front and numbered "X of 956" on the back. The cards are also numbered for set purposes A1-A6. The design is different from those found in the Missing Link issue. Card fronts are color, but do not contain the player's name (except for autograph) or team name. The backs provide a congratulatory note to the collector.

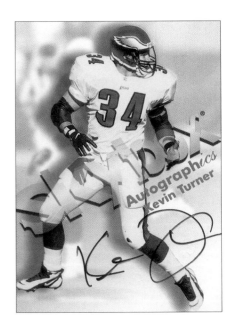

	MINT	NRMT	EXC
1994 Parkhurst Missing Link Autographs COMMON CARD (1-6)	100.00	45.00	12.50
1994 Parkhurst Missing Link Autographs Gordie Howe	200.00	90.00	25.00
1994 Parkhurst Missing Link Autographs Maurice Richard	175.00	80.00	22.00
1994 Parkhurst Missing Link Autographs Bernie Geoffrion	100.00	45.00	12.50
1994 Parkhurst Missing Link Autographs Gump Worsley	100.00	45.00	12.50
1994 Parkhurst Missing Link Autographs Jean Beliveau	150.00	70.00	19.00
1994 Parkhurst Missing Link Autographs Frank Mahovlich	100.00	45.00	12.50

1994 Parkhurst Tall Boys Autographs

COMPLETE SET (6) 500.00   220.00   60.00

964 of each of these six cards were randomly inserted throughout the production run of 1994 Parkhurst Tall Boys. The cards featured an isolated player photo over a team color-coded background. The player's autograph appears in a white, oblong box along the bottom. A congratulatory note, which serves to authenticate the signature, appears on the back along with a whimsical caricature of company mascot, Mr. Parkie. The cards are serially numbered out of 964 on the back.

	MINT	NRMT	EXC
1994 Parkhurst Tall Boys Autographs COMMON CARD (A1-A6)	50.00	22.00	6.25
1994 Parkhurst Tall Boys Autographs Rod Gilbert	50.00	22.00	6.25
1994 Parkhurst Tall Boys Autographs Yvan Cournoyer	60.00	27.00	7.50
1994 Parkhurst Tall Boys Autographs Bobby Hull	125.00	55.00	15.50
1994 Parkhurst Tall Boys Autographs Phil Esposito	100.00	45.00	12.50
1994 Parkhurst Tall Boys Autographs Gordie Howe	150.00	70.00	19.00
1994 Parkhurst Tall Boys Autographs Dave Keon	80.00	36.00	10.00

1996-97 SP SPx Force Autographs

COMPLETE SET (4) 3000.00   1350.00   375.00

These four different autograph cards were randomly inserted one in 2,500 packs of 1996-97 SP. Besides the player's signature, the cards are parallel to the more common, unsigned SPx Force inserts. Only 100 cards were signed by each player.

	MINT	NRMT	EXC
1996-97 SP SPx Force Autographs COMMON CARD (SPX1-SPX4)	200.00	90.00	25.00
1996-97 SP SPx Force Autographs Wayne Gretzky AU	1800.00	800.00	220.00

1996-97 SP SPx Force Autographs Jaromir Jagr AU 700.00   325.00   90.00
1996-97 SP SPx Force Autographs Martin Brodeur AU 400.00   180.00   50.00
1996-97 SP SPx Force Autographs Jarome Iginla AU 200.00   90.00   25.00

1997-98 Donruss Elite Back to the Future Autographs
COMPLETE SET (8) 2800.00   1250.00   350.00
Randomly inserted in packs, this eight-card set if parallel to the regular Back to the Future insert set and consists of the first 100 cards of the regular set autographed by both players.

	MINT	NRMT	EXC
1997-98 Donruss Elite Back to the Future Autographs COMMON (1-8) .	150.00	70.00	19.00
1997-98 Donruss Elite Back to the Future Eric Lindros / Joe Thornton . . .	400.00	180.00	50.00
1997-98 Donruss Elite Back to the Future Jocelyn Thibault / Marc Denis .	150.00	70.00	19.00
1997-98 Donruss Elite Back to Future Teemu Selanne / Patrick Marleau .	300.00	135.00	38.00
1997-98 Donruss Elite Back to the Future Jaromir Jagr / Daniel Cleary . . .	300.00	135.00	38.00
1997-98 Donruss Elite Back to the Future Sergei Fedorov / Peter Forsberg	400.00	180.00	50.00
1997-98 Donruss Elite Back to the Future Brett Hull / Bobby Hull	300.00	135.00	38.00
1997-98 Donruss Elite Back to Future Martin Brodeur / Roberto Luongo .	300.00	135.00	38.00
1997-98 Donruss Elite Back to the Future Gordie Howe / Steve Yzerman	600.00	275.00	75.00

1997-98 SP Authentic Mark of a Legend
COMPLETE SET (6) 1400.00   650.00   180.00
Randomly inserted in packs at the rate of one in 198, this six-card set features autographed color portraits of six of the NHL's greatest all-time players.

	MINT	NRMT	EXC
1997-98 SP Authentic Mark of a Legend COMMON CARD (M1-M6) . . .	50.00	22.00	6.25
1997-98 SP Authentic Mark of a Legend Gordie Howe/112	500.00	220.00	60.00
1997-98 SP Authentic Mark of a Legend Billy Smith/560	50.00	22.00	6.25
1997-98 SP Authentic Mark of a Legend Cam Neely/560	100.00	45.00	12.50
1997-98 SP Authentic Mark of a Legend Bryan Trottier/560	50.00	22.00	6.25
1997-98 SP Authentic Mark of a Legend Bobby Hull/560	120.00	55.00	15.00
1997-98 SP Authentic Mark of a Legend Wayne Gretzky/560	600.00	275.00	75.00

1997-98 SP Authentic Tradition
COMPLETE SET (6) 2000.00   900.00   250.00
Randomly inserted in packs at the rate of one in 340, this six-card set features color action dual photos and autographs of a current star and NHL legend from the same team.

	MINT	NRMT	EXC
1997-98 SP Authentic Tradition COMMON CARD (T1-T6)	80.00	36.00	10.00
1997-98 SP Authentic Tradition W.Gretzky/G.Howe	1200.00	550.00	150.00
1997-98 SP Authentic Tradition P.Roy/B.Smith/333	300.00	135.00	38.00
1997-98 SP Authentic Tradition J.Thornton/C.Neely/352	120.00	55.00	15.00
1997-98 SP Authentic Tradition B.Berard/B.Trottier/352	70.00	32.00	8.75
1997-98 SP Authentic Tradition B.Hull/B.Hull	250.00	110.00	31.00
1997-98 SP Authentic Tradition R.Bourque/C.Neely/140	250.00	110.00	31.00

1997-98 SPx DuoView Autographs
COMPLETE SET (6) 3500.00   1600.00   450.00
Randomly inserted in packs, this six-card set is a partial parallel version of the DuoView insert set featuring gold foil enhancements and the pictured player's autograph. Only 100 of each each card was produced and are sequentially hand numbered.

	MINT	NRMT	EXC
1997-98 SPx DuoView Autographs COMMON CARD (1-6)	100.00	45.00	12.50
1997-98 SPx DuoView Autographs Wayne Gretzky	1500.00	700.00	190.00
1997-98 SPx DuoView Autographs Jaromir Jagr	600.00	275.00	75.00
1997-98 SPx DuoView Autographs Martin Brodeur	300.00	135.00	38.00
1997-98 SPx DuoView Autographs Jarome Iginla	100.00	45.00	12.50
1997-98 SPx DuoView Autographs Patrick Roy	1000.00	450.00	125.00
1997-98 SPx DuoView Autographs Doug Weight	100.00	45.00	12.50

1997 Visions Signings Artistry Autographs

COMPLETE SET (20) 2000.00   900.00   250.00

These certified autographed cards feature Score Board's "exclusive printing technology" and were inserted at a rate of 1:18 packs. These 20 cards are autographed parallels of the Artistry insert set.

	MINT	NRMT	EXC
1997 Visions Signings Artistry Autographs COMMON AUTO (A1-A20) .	25.00	11.00	3.10
1997 Visions Signings Artistry Autographs Jose Cruz Jr.	60.00	27.00	7.50
1997 Visions Signings Artistry Autographs Allen Iverson	125.00	55.00	15.50
1997 Visions Signings Artistry Autographs Marcus Camby	50.00	22.00	6.25
1997 Visions Signings Artistry Autographs Shareef Abdur-Rahim	80.00	36.00	10.00
1997 Visions Signings Artistry Autographs Stephon Marbury	125.00	55.00	15.50
1997 Visions Signings Artistry Autographs Ray Allen	70.00	32.00	8.75
1997 Visions Signings Artistry Autographs Antoine Walker	140.00	65.00	17.50
1997 Visions Signings Artistry Autographs Kobe Bryant	200.00	90.00	25.00
1997 Visions Signings Artistry Autographs Clyde Drexler	150.00	70.00	19.00
1997 Visions Signings Artistry Autographs Scottie Pippen	250.00	110.00	31.00
1997 Visions Signings Artistry Autographs Alonzo Mourning	70.00	32.00	8.75
1997 Visions Signings Artistry Autographs Eddie George	125.00	55.00	15.50
1997 Visions Signings Artistry Autographs Warrick Dunn	150.00	70.00	19.00
1997 Visions Signings Artistry Autographs Darrell Russell	30.00	13.50	3.70
1997 Visions Signings Artistry Autographs Peter Boulware	30.00	13.50	3.70
1997 Visions Signings Artistry Autographs Shawn Springs	30.00	13.50	3.70
1997 Visions Signings Artistry Autographs Yatil Green	30.00	13.50	3.70
1997 Visions Signings Artistry Autographs Brett Favre	300.00	135.00	38.00
1997 Visions Signings Artistry Autographs Emmitt Smith	250.00	110.00	31.00
1997 Visions Signings Artistry Autographs Dainius Zubrus	40.00	18.00	5.00

1997 Visions Signings Autographs

COMMON AUTOGRAPH 8.00   3.60   1.00

Each 1997 Visions Signings pack contains either an autographed card or an insert card. One in six packs contain a regular autograph card. Three cards, #2 Troy Aikman, #29 Allen Iverson, and #53 Emmitt Smith, never made their way into packs as slated, so the complete set only contains 63 cards.

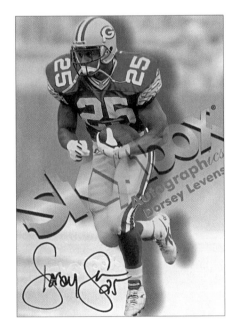

	MINT	NRMT	EXC
1997 Visions Signings Autographs SEMISTARS	12.00	5.50	1.50
1997 Visions Signings Autographs UNLISTED STARS	15.00	6.75	1.85
1997 Visions Signings Autographs Shareef Abdur-Rahim	50.00	22.00	6.25
1997 Visions Signings Autographs Ray Allen	50.00	22.00	6.25
1997 Visions Signings Autographs Tony Banks	25.00	11.00	3.10
1997 Visions Signings Autographs Michael Booker	8.00	3.60	1.00
1997 Visions Signings Autographs Peter Boulware	12.00	5.50	1.50
1997 Visions Signings Autographs Dante Calabria	8.00	3.60	1.00
1997 Visions Signings Autographs Rae Carruth	25.00	11.00	3.10
1997 Visions Signings Autographs Jose Cruz Jr.	40.00	18.00	5.00
1997 Visions Signings Autographs Erick Dampier	8.00	3.60	1.00
1997 Visions Signings Autographs Tony Delk	12.00	5.50	1.50
1997 Visions Signings Autographs Koy Detmer	15.00	6.75	1.85
1997 Visions Signings Autographs Corey Dillon	50.00	22.00	6.25
1997 Visions Signings Autographs Warrick Dunn	75.00	34.00	9.50
1997 Visions Signings Autographs Tyus Edney	8.00	3.60	1.00
1997 Visions Signings Autographs Brian Evans	8.00	3.60	1.00
1997 Visions Signings Autographs Derek Fisher	12.00	5.50	1.50
1997 Visions Signings Autographs Yatil Green	25.00	11.00	3.10
1997 Visions Signings Autographs Ben Grieve	50.00	22.00	6.25
1997 Visions Signings Autographs Vladimir Guerrero	40.00	18.00	5.00
1997 Visions Signings Autographs Steve Hamer	8.00	3.60	1.00
1997 Visions Signings Autographs Byron Hanspard	25.00	11.00	3.10
1997 Visions Signings Autographs Kevin Hardy	8.00	3.60	1.00
1997 Visions Signings Autographs Othella Harrington	8.00	3.60	1.00
1997 Visions Signings Autographs Wes Helms	25.00	11.00	3.10
1997 Visions Signings Autographs Richard Hidalgo	8.00	3.60	1.00
1997 Visions Signings Autographs Josh Holden	8.00	3.60	1.00
1997 Visions Signings Autographs DeRon Jenkins	8.00	3.60	1.00

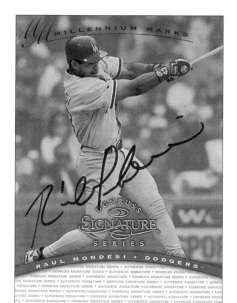

1997 Visions Signings Autographs Andre Johnson	8.00	3.60	1.00
1997 Visions Signings Autographs Greg Jones	8.00	3.60	1.00
1997 Visions Signings Autographs Danny Kanell	12.00	5.50	1.50
1997 Visions Signings Autographs Jason Kendall	12.00	5.50	1.50
1997 Visions Signings Autographs Pete Kendall	8.00	3.60	1.00
1997 Visions Signings Autographs Travis Knight	25.00	11.00	3.10
1997 Visions Signings Autographs David LaFleur	12.00	5.50	1.50
1997 Visions Signings Autographs Jeff Lewis	8.00	3.60	1.00
1997 Visions Signings Autographs Stephon Marbury	75.00	34.00	9.50
1997 Visions Signings Autographs Dave McCarty	8.00	3.60	1.00
1997 Visions Signings Autographs Walter McCarty	8.00	3.60	1.00
1997 Visions Signings Autographs Leeland McElroy	15.00	6.75	1.85
1997 Visions Signings Autographs Ray Mickens	8.00	3.60	1.00
1997 Visions Signings Autographs Jay Payton	25.00	11.00	3.10
1997 Visions Signings Autographs Vitaly Potopenko	8.00	3.60	1.00
1997 Visions Signings Autographs Trevor Pryce	8.00	3.60	1.00
1997 Visions Signings Autographs Efthlmas Retzias	8.00	3.60	1.00
1997 Visions Signings Autographs Roy Rogers	8.00	3.60	1.00
1997 Visions Signings Autographs Malik Rose	8.00	3.60	1.00
1997 Visions Signings Autographs Darrell Russell	8.00	3.60	1.00
1997 Visions Signings Autographs Sergei Samsonov	40.00	18.00	5.00
1997 Visions Signings Autographs Antowain Smith	40.00	18.00	5.00
1997 Visions Signings Autographs Kurt Thomas	8.00	3.60	1.00
1997 Visions Signings Autographs Joe Thornton	30.00	13.50	3.70
1997 Visions Signings Autographs Amani Toomer	15.00	6.75	1.85
1997 Visions Signings Autographs Antoine Walker	90.00	40.00	11.00
1997 Visions Signings Autographs John Wallace	12.00	5.50	1.50
1997 Visions Signings Autographs Bryant Westbrook	8.00	3.60	1.00
1997 Visions Signings Autographs Jerome Williams	8.00	3.60	1.00
1997 Visions Signings Autographs Stepfret Williams	8.00	3.60	1.00
1997 Visions Signings Autographs Paul Wilson	15.00	6.75	1.85
1997 Visions Signings Autographs Kerry Wood	75.00	34.00	9.50
1997 Visions Signings Autographs Lorenzen Wright	12.00	5.50	1.50
1997 Visions Signings Autographs Dainius Zubrus	25.00	11.00	3.10
1997 Visions Signings Autographs Andrei Zyuzin	8.00	3.60	1.00

1998 Press Pass Autographs

COMMON CARD 8.00   3.60   1.00

This 38-card set is a quasi-parallel of the base set with 32 different players/coaches signing versions of their respective cards. Peyton Manning, Ryan Leaf, Germane Crowell, Shaun Williams, John Avery, Robert Holcombe were only made available through redemption cards. Andre Wadsworth, Donald Hayes, Jason Peter, Anthony Simmons, Skip Hicks, Ahman Green, Jacquez Green were available in packs and also as redemptions. Redemption cards have an expiration date of May 31, 1999. Autographs were inserted 1:18 hobby packs and 1:36 retail packs. There was also a limited edition Peyton Manning autograph card that was only made available to attendees of the SportsFest card show in Philadelphia via a redemption for opened wrappers at the Press Pass company booth.

	MINT	NRMT	EXC
1998 Press Pass Autographs Peyton Manning	100.00	45.00	12.50
1998 Press Pass Autographs Ryan Leaf	100.00	45.00	12.50
1998 Press Pass Autographs Andre Wadsworth	25.00	11.00	3.10
1998 Press Pass Autographs Randy Moss	120.00	55.00	15.00
1998 Press Pass Autographs Curtis Enis	40.00	18.00	5.00
1998 Press Pass Autographs Jason Peter	8.00	3.60	1.00
1998 Press Pass Autographs Brian Simmons	8.00	3.60	1.00
1998 Press Pass Autographs Takeo Spikes	15.00	6.75	1.85
1998 Press Pass Autographs Michael Myers	8.00	3.60	1.00
1998 Press Pass Autographs Kevin Dyson	20.00	9.00	2.50
1998 Press Pass Autographs Grant Wistrom	15.00	6.75	1.85
1998 Press Pass Autographs Fred Taylor	40.00	18.00	5.00
1998 Press Pass Autographs Germane Crowell	20.00	9.00	2.50
1998 Press Pass Autographs Anthony Simmons LB	10.00	4.50	1.25
1998 Press Pass Autographs Robert Edwards	40.00	18.00	5.00
1998 Press Pass Autographs Shaun Williams	8.00	3.60	1.00
1998 Press Pass Autographs Phil Savoy	15.00	6.75	1.85

1998 Press Pass Autographs John Avery	25.00	11.00	3.10
1998 Press Pass Autographs Vonnie Holliday	20.00	9.00	2.50
1998 Press Pass Autographs Tim Dwight	15.00	6.75	1.85
1998 Press Pass Autographs Donovin Darius	8.00	3.60	1.00
1998 Press Pass Autographs Alonzo Mayes	8.00	3.60	1.00
1998 Press Pass Autographs Brian Kelly	8.00	3.60	1.00
1998 Press Pass Autographs Hines Ward	20.00	9.00	2.50
1998 Press Pass Autographs Jacquez Green	30.00	13.50	3.70
1998 Press Pass Autographs Marcus Nash	20.00	9.00	2.50
1998 Press Pass Autographs Ahman Green	30.00	13.50	3.70
1998 Press Pass Autographs Joe Jurevicius	20.00	9.00	2.50
1998 Press Pass Autographs Tavian Banks	20.00	9.00	2.50
1998 Press Pass Autographs Donald Hayes	10.00	4.50	1.25
1998 Press Pass Autographs Robert Holcombe	30.00	13.50	3.70
1998 Press Pass Autographs Skip Hicks	20.00	9.00	2.50
1998 Press Pass Autographs Pat Johnson	10.00	4.50	1.25
1998 Press Pass Autographs Alan Faneca	10.00	4.50	1.25
1998 Press Pass Autographs Steve Spurrier CO	30.00	13.50	3.70
1998 Press Pass Autographs Mike Price CO	10.00	4.50	1.25
1998 Press Pass Autographs Bobby Bowden CO	10.00	4.50	1.25
1998 Press Pass Autographs Tom Osborne CO	40.00	18.00	5.00
1998 Press Pass Autographs Peyton Manning SportsFest	100.00	45.00	12.50

1998 Press Pass Autographs

COMPLETE SET (38)	600.00	275.00	75.00

These autographed cards were inserted 1:18 hobby and 1:36 retail packs. Either an autograph or redemption card was inserted. While some players were available via both packs and redemption cards, nine players were only made available via redemption cards: Keon Clark, Bonzi Wells, Paul Pierce, Brian Skinner, Michael Dickerson, Tyronn Lue, Jeff Sheppard, DeMarco Johnson and Miles Simon.

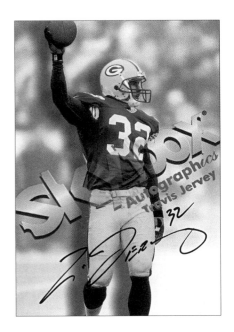

	MINT	NRMT	EXC
1998 Press Pass Autographs COMMON CARD	8.00	3.60	1.00
1998 Press Pass Autographs SEMISTARS	10.00	4.50	1.25
1998 Press Pass Autographs Toby Bailey	10.00	4.50	1.25
1998 Press Pass Autographs Mike Bibby	60.00	27.00	7.50
1998 Press Pass Autographs Earl Boykins	10.00	4.50	1.25
1998 Press Pass Autographs Torraye Braggs	8.00	3.60	1.00
1998 Press Pass Autographs Cory Carr	8.00	3.60	1.00
1998 Press Pass Autographs Anthony Carter	8.00	3.60	1.00
1998 Press Pass Autographs Vince Carter	50.00	22.00	6.25
1998 Press Pass Autographs Keon Clark	12.00	5.50	1.50
1998 Press Pass Autographs Michael Dickerson	20.00	9.00	2.50
1998 Press Pass Autographs Michael Doleac	15.00	6.75	1.85
1998 Press Pass Autographs Bryce Drew	20.00	9.00	2.50
1998 Press Pass Autographs Pat Garrity	12.00	5.50	1.50
1998 Press Pass Autographs Matt Harpring	12.00	5.50	1.50
1998 Press Pass Autographs Al Harrington	20.00	9.00	2.50
1998 Press Pass Autographs J.R. Henderson	8.00	3.60	1.00
1998 Press Pass Autographs Larry Hughes	25.00	11.00	3.10
1998 Press Pass Autographs DeMarco Johnson	8.00	3.60	1.00
1998 Press Pass Autographs Malcolm Johnson	8.00	3.60	1.00
1998 Press Pass Autographs Mike Jones	8.00	3.60	1.00
1998 Press Pass Autographs Raef Lafrentz	50.00	22.00	6.25
1998 Press Pass Autographs Tyronn Lue	10.00	4.50	1.25
1998 Press Pass Autographs Roshown McLeod	10.00	4.50	1.25
1998 Press Pass Autographs Brad Miller	8.00	3.60	1.00
1998 Press Pass Autographs Nazr Mohammed	15.00	6.75	1.85
1998 Press Pass Autographs Michael Olowokandi	60.00	27.00	7.50
1998 Press Pass Autographs Andrae Patterson	10.00	4.50	1.25
1998 Press Pass Autographs Paul Pierce	8.00	3.60	1.00
1998 Press Pass Autographs Casey Shaw	8.00	3.60	1.00
1998 Press Pass Autographs Jeff Sheppard	8.00	3.60	1.00
1998 Press Pass Autographs Clayton Shields	8.00	3.60	1.00
1998 Press Pass Autographs Miles Simon	12.00	5.50	1.50

	MINT	NRMT	EXC
1998 Press Pass Autographs Brian Skinner	8.00	3.60	1.00
1998 Press Pass Autographs Robert Traylor	50.00	22.00	6.25
1998 Press Pass Autographs Saddi Washington	8.00	3.60	1.00
1998 Press Pass Autographs Bonzi Wells	20.00	9.00	2.50
1998 Press Pass Autographs Jahidi Wells	8.00	3.60	1.00
1998 Press Pass Autographs Jason Williams	25.00	11.00	3.10
1998 Press Pass Autographs Shammond Williams	8.00	3.60	1.00

1998 Press Pass Double Threat Rookie Script Autographs

COMPLETE SET (34) 8.00   3.60   1.00

Michael Olowokandi, Jason Williams, Keon Clark, Bonzi Wells, Michael Dickerson, Roshown McLeod, Paul Pierce, Miles Simon, Toby Baily and Robert Patterson where only made available via redemption cards.

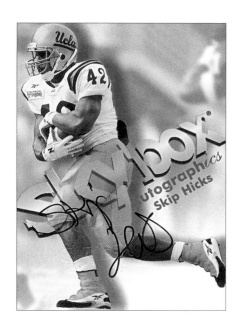

	MINT	NRMT	EXC
1998 Press Pass Double Threat Rookie Script Autographs COMMON	8.00	3.60	1.00
1998 Press Pass Double Threat Rookie Script Autographs SEMISTARS	10.00	4.50	1.25
1998 Press Pass Double Threat Rookie Script UNLISTED STARS	12.00	5.50	1.50
1998 Press Pass Double Threat Rookie Script Autographs Toby Bailey	8.00	3.60	1.00
1998 Press Pass Double Threat Rookie Script Autographs Mike Bibby	60.00	27.00	7.50
1998 Press Pass Double Threat Rookie Script Autographs Torraye Braggs	8.00	3.60	1.00
1998 Press Pass Double Threat Rookie Script Autographs Cory Carr	8.00	3.60	1.00
1998 Press Pass Double Threat Rookie Script Autographs Vince Carter	50.00	22.00	6.25
1998 Press Pass Double Threat Rookie Script Autographs Keon Clark	8.00	3.60	1.00
1998 Press Pass Double Threat Rookie Script Michael Dickerson	8.00	3.60	1.00
1998 Press Pass Double Threat Rookie Script Autographs Michael Doleac	15.00	6.75	1.85
1998 Press Pass Double Threat Rookie Script Autographs Bryce Drew	20.00	9.00	2.50
1998 Press Pass Double Threat Rookie Script Autographs Pat Garrity	8.00	3.60	1.00
1998 Press Pass Double Threat Rookie Script Autographs Matt Harpring	8.00	3.60	1.00
1998 Press Pass Double Threat Rookie Script Autographs Al Harrington	20.00	9.00	2.50
1998 Press Pass Double Threat Rookie Script Autographs J.R. Henderson	8.00	3.60	1.00
1998 Press Pass Double Threat Rookie Script Autographs Larry Hughes	25.00	11.00	3.10
1998 Press Pass Double Threat Rookie Script Autographs Sam Jacobson	8.00	3.60	1.00
1998 Press Pass Double Threat Rookie Script DeMarco Johnson	8.00	3.60	1.00
1998 Press Pass Double Threat Rookie Script Autographs Raef LaFrentz	50.00	22.00	6.25
1998 Press Pass Double Threat Rookie Script Autographs Tyronn Lue	8.00	3.60	1.00
1998 Press Pass Double Threat Rookie Script Autographs Sean Marks	8.00	3.60	1.00
1998 Press Pass Double Threat Rookie Script Roshown McLeod	8.00	3.60	1.00
1998 Press Pass Double Threat Rookie Script Nazr Mohammed	15.00	6.75	1.85
1998 Press Pass Double Threat Rookie Script Michael Olowokandi	8.00	3.60	1.00
1998 Press Pass Double Threat Rookie Script Andrae Patterson	8.00	3.60	1.00
1998 Press Pass Double Threat Rookie Script Ruben Patterson	8.00	3.60	1.00
1998 Press Pass Double Threat Rookie Script Autographs Paul Pierce	8.00	3.60	1.00
1998 Press Pass Double Threat Rookie Script Autographs Casey Shaw	8.00	3.60	1.00
1998 Press Pass Double Threat Rookie Script Autographs Miles Simon	8.00	3.60	1.00
1998 Press Pass Double Threat Rookie Script Autographs Brian Skinner	8.00	3.60	1.00
1998 Press Pass Double Threat Rookie Script Autographs Robert Traylor	50.00	22.00	6.25
1998 Press Pass Double Threat Rookie Script Autographs Bonzi Wells	8.00	3.60	1.00
1998 Press Pass Double Threat Rookie Script Autographs Tyson Wheeler	8.00	3.60	1.00
1998 Press Pass Double Threat Rookie Script Autographs Jahidi White	8.00	3.60	1.00
1998 Press Pass Double Threat Rookie Script Autographs Jason Williams	8.00	3.60	1.00
1998 Press Pass Double Threat Rookie Script Shammond Williams	8.00	3.60	1.00

1992 Traks Autographs

COMPLETE SET (10) 450.00   200.00   55.00

This set was distributed randomly throughout 1992 Traks packs. A maximum of 5000 cards were signed by each driver and many cards can be found, as well, without signatures. The Ricky Rudd card is considered a short print signed due to the seemingly large number of available copies unsigned. Unsigned cards typically sell for a fraction of autographed issues. The set is highlighted by a dually signed Dale Earnhardt and Richard Petty card (#A1).

	MINT	NRMT	EXC
1992 Traks Autographs COMMON CARD (A1-A9)	20.00	9.00	2.50
1992 Traks Autographs Dale Earnhardt / Richard Petty	200.00	90.00	25.00
1992 Traks Autographs Rusty Wallace	75.00	34.00	9.50
1992 Traks Autographs Harry Gant	40.00	18.00	5.00

1992 Traks Autographs Ernie Irvan 60.00   27.00   7.50
1992 Traks Autographs Ricky Rudd SP 50.00   22.00   6.25
1992 Traks Autographs Kyle Petty 40.00   18.00   5.00
1992 Traks Autographs Jeff Gordon 100.00   45.00   12.50
1992 Traks Autographs Bobby Labonte 40.00   18.00   5.00
1992 Traks Autographs Benny Parsons 20.00   9.00   2.50

1993 Finish Line NHRA Autographs
COMPLETE SET (9) 180.00   80.00   22.00
Finish Line produced this nine-card set with each card individually signed by the featured driver. The cards were randomly inserted in 1993 Finish Line foil and jumbo packs.

	MINT	NRMT	EXC
1993 Finish Line NHRA Autographs COMMON AUTO (1-9)	16.00	7.25	2.00
1993 Finish Line NHRA Autographs Joe Amato	20.00	9.00	2.50
1993 Finish Line NHRA Autographs Cory McClenathan	20.00	9.00	2.50
1993 Finish Line NHRA Autographs Kenny Bernstein	30.00	13.50	3.70
1993 Finish Line NHRA Autographs Cruz Pedregon	20.00	9.00	2.50
1993 Finish Line NHRA Autographs John Force	50.00	22.00	6.25
1993 Finish Line NHRA Autographs Al Hofmann	16.00	7.25	2.00
1993 Finish Line NHRA Autographs Warren Johnson	20.00	9.00	2.50
1993 Finish Line NHRA Autographs Scott Geoffrion	16.00	7.25	2.00
1993 Finish Line NHRA Autographs Jerry Eckman	16.00	7.25	2.00

1993 Maxx Jeff Gordon
COMPLETE SET (20) 8.00   3.60   1.00
This 20-card set was produced by Maxx and was distributed only in set form through Club Maxx for $4.95 per set. It highlights his career from his early childhood to debut on the Winston Cup circuit. 1,000 Jeff Gordon autographed cards were randomly inserted into the sets at a 1:100 ratio.

	MINT	NRMT	EXC
1993 Maxx Jeff Gordon COMMON CARD (1-20)	.50	.23	.06
1993 Maxx Jeff Gordon Jeff Gordon AUTO	140.00	65.00	17.50

1994 Finish Line Gold Autographs
COMPLETE SET (19) 300.00   135.00   38.00
Nineteen drivers and crew members signed copies of their regular 1994 Finish Line Gold cards to be randomly inserted into packs (approximately one per box). The autographs were signed using a gold paint pen and limited to less than 2000 copies of each card.

	MINT	NRMT	EXC
1994 Finish Line Gold Autographs COMMON AUTO	8.00	3.60	1.00
1994 Finish Line Gold Autographs COMMON DRIVER	15.00	6.75	1.85
1994 Finish Line Gold Autographs Lake Speed	15.00	6.75	1.85
1994 Finish Line Gold Autographs Morgan Shepherd	15.00	6.75	1.85
1994 Finish Line Gold Autographs Buddy Parrott	8.00	3.60	1.00
1994 Finish Line Gold Autographs Robert Pressley	15.00	6.75	1.85
1994 Finish Line Gold Autographs Terry Labonte	50.00	22.00	6.25
1994 Finish Line Gold Autographs Kenny Wallace	15.00	6.75	1.85
1994 Finish Line Gold Autographs Dale Jarrett	40.00	18.00	5.00
1994 Finish Line Gold Autographs Ricky Craven	20.00	9.00	2.50
1994 Finish Line Gold Autographs Tony Glover	8.00	3.60	1.00
1994 Finish Line Gold Autographs Ray Evernham	8.00	3.60	1.00
1994 Finish Line Gold Autographs Ken Schrader	20.00	9.00	2.50
1994 Finish Line Gold Autographs Hermie Sadler	15.00	6.75	1.85
1994 Finish Line Gold Autographs Ernie Irvan	40.00	18.00	5.00
1994 Finish Line Gold Autographs Mark Martin	50.00	22.00	6.25
1994 Finish Line Gold Autographs Michael Waltrip	20.00	9.00	2.50
1994 Finish Line Gold Autographs David Green	15.00	6.75	1.85
1994 Finish Line Gold Autographs Ricky Rudd	20.00	9.00	2.50
1994 Finish Line Gold Autographs Jimmy Makar	8.00	3.60	1.00
1994 Finish Line Gold Autographs Brett Bodine	15.00	6.75	1.85

1994 Maxx Autographs

COMPLETE SET (16) 900.00   400.00   110.00

Maxx packaged the 37 Autographs cards throughout the print run of 1994 series two and Medallion products. Although a few older Maxx issues were included, most of the cards signed were from series one 1994 Maxx and the Rookie Class of '94 insert sets. Wrapper stated odds for pulling an autographed card from series two was 1:200 packs. To pull a signed card from Maxx Medallion collectors faced wrapper stated odds of 1:18 packs. Each signed card was crimped with Maxx's corporate seal which reads "J.R. Maxx Inc. Corporate Seal 1988 North Carolina."

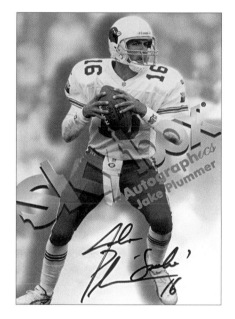

	MINT	NRMT	EXC
1994 Maxx Autographs COMMON CARD	12.00	5.50	1.50
1994 Maxx Autographs COMMON DRIVER	20.00	9.00	2.50
1994 Maxx Autographs Rick Mast	20.00	9.00	2.50
1994 Maxx Autographs Steve Grissom Rookie Class	20.00	9.00	2.50
1994 Maxx Autographs Joe Nemechek Rookie Class	20.00	9.00	2.50
1994 Maxx Autographs John Andretti Rookie Class	20.00	9.00	2.50
1994 Maxx Autographs Ricky Rudd	25.00	11.00	3.10
1994 Maxx Autographs Mark Martin	75.00	34.00	9.50
1994 Maxx Autographs Loy Allen Jr. Rookie Class	20.00	9.00	2.50
1994 Maxx Autographs Jeremy Mayfield Rookie Class	20.00	9.00	2.50
1994 Maxx Autographs Bill Elliott '91 Maxx	100.00	45.00	12.50
1994 Maxx Autographs Loy Allen Jr. Rookie Class	20.00	9.00	2.50
1994 Maxx Autographs Bill Elliott '92 Maxx Red	75.00	34.00	9.50
1994 Maxx Autographs Terry Labonte	75.00	34.00	9.50
1994 Maxx Autographs Dale Jarrett	60.00	27.00	7.50
1994 Maxx Autographs Buddy Baker '92 Maxx Black	20.00	9.00	2.50
1994 Maxx Autographs Buddy Baker '92 Maxx Red	20.00	9.00	2.50
1994 Maxx Autographs Bobby Labonte	25.00	11.00	3.10
1994 Maxx Autographs Jeff Gordon	250.00	110.00	31.00
1994 Maxx Autographs Ken Schrader	20.00	9.00	2.50
1994 Maxx Autographs Harry Gant	25.00	11.00	3.10
1994 Maxx Autographs Loy Allen Jr.	20.00	9.00	2.50
1994 Maxx Autographs Kyle Petty	20.00	9.00	2.50
1994 Maxx Autographs Phil Parsons	20.00	9.00	2.50
1994 Maxx Autographs Rich Bickle	20.00	9.00	2.50
1994 Maxx Autographs Glen Wood	12.00	5.50	1.50
1994 Maxx Autographs Len Wood	12.00	5.50	1.50
1994 Maxx Autographs Eddie Wood	12.00	5.50	1.50
1994 Maxx Autographs Larry McReynolds	12.00	5.50	1.50
1994 Maxx Autographs Steve Grissom	20.00	9.00	2.50
1994 Maxx Autographs Joe Nemechek	20.00	9.00	2.50
1994 Maxx Autographs Ward Burton	20.00	9.00	2.50
1994 Maxx Autographs Mike Wallace	20.00	9.00	2.50
1994 Maxx Autographs Jeff Burton	25.00	11.00	3.10
1994 Maxx Autographs Shawna Robinson	20.00	9.00	2.50
1994 Maxx Autographs Mark Martin	75.00	34.00	9.50
1994 Maxx Autographs Kenny Wallace	20.00	9.00	2.50
1994 Maxx Autographs Robert Pressley	20.00	9.00	2.50
1994 Maxx Autographs Buddy Baker	20.00	9.00	2.50

1994 Traks Autographs

COMPLETE SET (13) 200.00   90.00   25.00

Randomly inserted in both series one and two packs, these inserts are a specially designed card with each signed by the featured driver. A 13th card (cover/checklist card) was also inserted. A maximum of 3500 of each card was signed.

	MINT	NRMT	EXC
1994 Traks Autographs COMMON AUTO (A1-A12)	12.00	5.50	1.50
1994 Traks Autographs Todd Bodine	12.00	5.50	1.50
1994 Traks Autographs Jeff Burton / Ward Burton	30.00	13.50	3.70
1994 Traks Autographs Harry Gant	20.00	9.00	2.50
1994 Traks Autographs Jeff Gordon	75.00	34.00	9.50
1994 Traks Autographs Steve Grissom	12.00	5.50	1.50
1994 Traks Autographs Ernie Irvan	30.00	13.50	3.70
1994 Traks Autographs Sterling Marlin	30.00	13.50	3.70

	MINT	NRMT	EXC
1994 Traks Autographs Mark Martin	40.00	18.00	5.00
1994 Traks Autographs Joe Nemechek	12.00	5.50	1.50
1994 Traks Autographs Robert Pressley	12.00	5.50	1.50
1994 Traks Autographs Ken Schrader	12.00	5.50	1.50
1994 Traks Autographs Rusty Wallace	40.00	18.00	5.00
1994 Traks Autographs Cover Card (Checklist back)	12.00	5.50	1.50

1995 Action Packed NHRA Autographs

COMPLETE SET (16) 700.00   325.00   90.00

This 16-card insert set features the top drivers in the NHRA signatures. Each card is hand numbered of 500. The Kenny Bernstein and John Force cards were numbered of 125. The cards were availble one per 24 packs.

	MINT	NRMT	EXC
1995 Action Packed NHRA Autographs COMMON CARD	30.00	13.50	3.70
1995 Action Packed NHRA Autographs Scott Kalitta	30.00	13.50	3.70
1995 Action Packed NHRA Autographs Larry Dixon	30.00	13.50	3.70
1995 Action Packed NHRA Autographs Cory McClenathan	40.00	18.00	5.00
1995 Action Packed NHRA Autographs K.Bernstein/125	150.00	70.00	19.00
1995 Action Packed NHRA Autographs Mike Dunn	30.00	13.50	3.70
1995 Action Packed NHRA Autographs Tommy Johnson	30.00	13.50	3.70
1995 Action Packed NHRA Autographs Shelly Anderson	30.00	13.50	3.70
1995 Action Packed NHRA Autographs John Force/125	175.00	80.00	22.00
1995 Action Packed NHRA Autographs Cruz Pedregon	40.00	18.00	5.00
1995 Action Packed NHRA Autographs Al Hofmann	30.00	13.50	3.70
1995 Action Packed NHRA Autographs Darrell Alderman	30.00	13.50	3.70
1995 Action Packed NHRA Autographs Scott Geoffrion	30.00	13.50	3.70
1995 Action Packed NHRA Autographs Warren Johnson	30.00	13.50	3.70
1995 Action Packed NHRA Autographs Jim Yates	30.00	13.50	3.70
1995 Action Packed NHRA Autographs Kurt Johnson	30.00	13.50	3.70
1995 Action Packed NHRA Autographs Eddie Hill	40.00	18.00	5.00

1995 Maxx Autographs

COMPLETE SET (48) 800.00   350.00   100.00

This 48-card sets features 1995 Maxx series one cards autographed by some of the top personalities in NASCAR. The cards were randomly inserted in 1995 Maxx series two packs. To guarantee its authenticity, each signed card was crimped with Maxx's corporate seal which reads "J.R. Maxx Inc. Corporate Seal 1988 North Carolina." Most of the Johnny Benson cards were signed on the back.

	MINT	NRMT	EXC
1995 Maxx Autographs COMMON CARD	12.00	5.50	1.50
1995 Maxx Autographs COMMON DRIVER	20.00	9.00	2.50
1995 Maxx Autographs Terry Labonte	75.00	34.00	9.50
1995 Maxx Autographs Geoff Bodine	20.00	9.00	2.50
1995 Maxx Autographs Ted Musgrave	20.00	9.00	2.50
1995 Maxx Autographs Morgan Shepherd	20.00	9.00	2.50
1995 Maxx Autographs Bobby Labonte	25.00	11.00	3.10
1995 Maxx Autographs Jeff Gordon	250.00	110.00	31.00
1995 Maxx Autographs Ken Schrader	20.00	9.00	2.50
1995 Maxx Autographs Michael Waltrip	20.00	9.00	2.50
1995 Maxx Autographs Joe Nemechek	20.00	9.00	2.50
1995 Maxx Autographs Kyle Petty	20.00	9.00	2.50
1995 Maxx Autographs Andy Petree	12.00	5.50	1.50
1995 Maxx Autographs Larry McReynolds	12.00	5.50	1.50
1995 Maxx Autographs Buddy Parrott	12.00	5.50	1.50
1995 Maxx Autographs Steve Hmiel	12.00	5.50	1.50
1995 Maxx Autographs Ken Howes	12.00	5.50	1.50
1995 Maxx Autographs Leonard Wood	12.00	5.50	1.50
1995 Maxx Autographs Bill Ingle	12.00	5.50	1.50
1995 Maxx Autographs Doug Hewitt	12.00	5.50	1.50
1995 Maxx Autographs Robin Pemberton	12.00	5.50	1.50
1995 Maxx Autographs Donnie Wingo	12.00	5.50	1.50
1995 Maxx Autographs Pete Peterson	12.00	5.50	1.50
1995 Maxx Autographs Tony Glover	12.00	5.50	1.50
1995 Maxx Autographs Gary DeHart	12.00	5.50	1.50

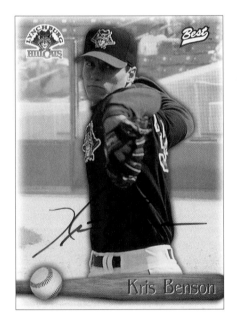

Kris Benson

1995 Maxx Autographs Jimmy Makar	12.00	5.50	1.50
1995 Maxx Autographs Mike Beam	12.00	5.50	1.50
1995 Maxx Autographs Kevin Hamlin	12.00	5.50	1.50
1995 Maxx Autographs Paul Andrews	12.00	5.50	1.50
1995 Maxx Autographs Chris Hussey	12.00	5.50	1.50
1995 Maxx Autographs Jim Long	12.00	5.50	1.50
1995 Maxx Autographs Donnie Richeson	12.00	5.50	1.50
1995 Maxx Autographs Troy Selberg	12.00	5.50	1.50
1995 Maxx Autographs Tony Furr	12.00	5.50	1.50
1995 Maxx Autographs Mike Hill	12.00	5.50	1.50
1995 Maxx Autographs Philippe Lopez	12.00	5.50	1.50
1995 Maxx Autographs Jeff Hammond	12.00	5.50	1.50
1995 Maxx Autographs Buddy Barnes	12.00	5.50	1.50
1995 Maxx Autographs Charley Pressley	12.00	5.50	1.50
1995 Maxx Autographs Doug Richert	12.00	5.50	1.50
1995 Maxx Autographs Mike Hillman	12.00	5.50	1.50
1995 Maxx Autographs Robbie Loomis	12.00	5.50	1.50
1995 Maxx Autographs Ricky Craven	20.00	9.00	2.50
1995 Maxx Autographs Chad Little	20.00	9.00	2.50
1995 Maxx Autographs Robert Pressley	20.00	9.00	2.50
1995 Maxx Autographs Johnny Benson	20.00	9.00	2.50
1995 Maxx Autographs Bobby Dotter	20.00	9.00	2.50
1995 Maxx Autographs Larry Pearson	20.00	9.00	2.50
1995 Maxx Autographs Dennis Setzer	20.00	9.00	2.50
1995 Maxx Autographs Tim Fedewa	20.00	9.00	2.50

1996 Autographed Racing Autographs

COMPLETE SET (65)	900.00	400.00	110.00

This 65-card insert set features hand-signed cards of the top names in racing. The cards were inserted at a rate of one in 12 packs. The cards featured red foil on the front along with the autograph. The backs carry the statement, "Congratulations. You've received an authentic 1996 Autographed Racing Autographed Card. There is also a "Certified" parallel version to the 65-card set. The parallel Certified version cards feature gold foil stamping on the front. In addition to the difference in foil color, each autographed is numbered. The backs of the Certified cards feature the same statement as the regular autographs. Certified autographs were inserted in packs at a rate of one in 24 packs.

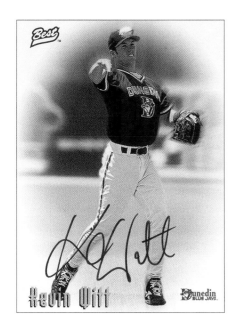

	MINT	NRMT	EXC
1996 Autographed Racing Autographs COMMON CARD (1-65)	6.00	2.70	.75
1996 Autographed Racing Autographs COMMON DRIVER (1-65)	10.00	4.50	1.25
1996 Autographed Racing Autographs COMP.CERT.AUTO SET (65)	1500.00	700.00	190.00
1996 Autographed Racing Autographs CERT.AUTO CARD: 1.25X TO X LISTED CARDS			
1996 Autographed Racing Autographs Loy Allen Jr.	10.00	4.50	1.25
1996 Autographed Racing Autographs John Andretti	10.00	4.50	1.25
1996 Autographed Racing Autographs Paul Andrews	6.00	2.70	.75
1996 Autographed Racing Autographs Johnny Benson	10.00	4.50	1.25
1996 Autographed Racing Autographs Brett Bodine	10.00	4.50	1.25
1996 Autographed Racing Autographs Geoff Bodine	10.00	4.50	1.25
1996 Autographed Racing Autographs Todd Bodine	10.00	4.50	1.25
1996 Autographed Racing Autographs Jeff Burton	10.00	4.50	1.25
1996 Autographed Racing Autographs Ward Burton	10.00	4.50	1.25
1996 Autographed Racing Autographs Richard Childress	6.00	2.70	.75
1996 Autographed Racing Autographs Ricky Craven	20.00	9.00	2.50
1996 Autographed Racing Autographs Barry Dodson	6.00	2.70	.75
1996 Autographed Racing Autographs Dale Earnhardt	175.00	80.00	22.00
1996 Autographed Racing Autographs Joe Gibbs	10.00	4.50	1.25
1996 Autographed Racing Autographs Tony Glover	6.00	2.70	.75
1996 Autographed Racing Autographs Jeff Gordon	175.00	80.00	22.00
1996 Autographed Racing Autographs David Green	10.00	4.50	1.25
1996 Autographed Racing Autographs Bobby Hamilton	10.00	4.50	1.25
1996 Autographed Racing Autographs Doug Hewitt	6.00	2.70	.75
1996 Autographed Racing Autographs Steve Hmiel	6.00	2.70	.75
1996 Autographed Racing Autographs Ernie Irvan	40.00	18.00	5.00
1996 Autographed Racing Autographs Dale Jarrett	60.00	27.00	7.50
1996 Autographed Racing Autographs Ned Jarrett	6.00	2.70	.75

1996 Autographed Racing Autographs Jason Keller 10.00   4.50   1.25
1996 Autographed Racing Autographs Bobby Labonte 20.00   9.00   2.50
1996 Autographed Racing Autographs Terry Labonte 75.00   34.00   9.50
1996 Autographed Racing Autographs Randy Lajoie 10.00   4.50   1.25
1996 Autographed Racing Autographs Jimmy Makar . . . . 6.00   2.70   .75
1996 Autographed Racing Autographs Dave Marcis 10.00   4.50   1.25
1996 Autographed Racing Autographs Sterling Marlin 20.00   9.00   2.50
1996 Autographed Racing Autographs Mark Martin 75.00   34.00   9.50
1996 Autographed Racing Autographs Rick Mast 10.00   4.50   1.25
1996 Autographed Racing Autographs Jeremy Mayfield 50.00   22.00   6.25
1996 Autographed Racing Autographs Larry McClure . . . . 6.00   2.70   .75
1996 Autographed Racing Autographs Mike McLaughlin 10.00   4.50   1.25
1996 Autographed Racing Autographs Larry McReynolds . . . . 6.00   2.70   .75
1996 Autographed Racing Autographs Patty Moise 10.00   4.50   1.25
1996 Autographed Racing Autographs Brad Parrott . . . . 6.00   2.70   .75
1996 Autographed Racing Autographs Buddy Parrott . . . . 6.00   2.70   .75
1996 Autographed Racing Autographs Todd Parrott . . . . 6.00   2.70   .75
1996 Autographed Racing Autographs Robin Pemberton . . . . 6.00   2.70   .75
1996 Autographed Racing Autographs Runt Pittman . . . . 6.00   2.70   .75
1996 Autographed Racing Autographs Charley Pressley . . . . 6.00   2.70   .75
1996 Autographed Racing Autographs Robert Pressley 10.00   4.50   1.25
1996 Autographed Racing Autographs Dr. Jerry Punch . . . . 6.00   2.70   .75
1996 Autographed Racing Autographs Chuck Rider . . . . 6.00   2.70   .75
1996 Autographed Racing Autographs Jack Roush . . . . 6.00   2.70   .75
1996 Autographed Racing Autographs Ricky Rudd 20.00   9.00   2.50
1996 Autographed Racing Autographs Elton Sawyer 10.00   4.50   1.25
1996 Autographed Racing Autographs Ken Schrader 10.00   4.50   1.25
1996 Autographed Racing Autographs Morgan Shepherd 10.00   4.50   1.25
1996 Autographed Racing Autographs Mike Skinner 10.00   4.50   1.25
1996 Autographed Racing Autographs David Smith . . . . 6.00   2.70   .75
1996 Autographed Racing Autographs Jimmy Spencer 10.00   4.50   1.25
1996 Autographed Racing Autographs Hut Stricklin 10.00   4.50   1.25
1996 Autographed Racing Autographs Dick Trickle 10.00   4.50   1.25
1996 Autographed Racing Autographs Kenny Wallace 10.00   4.50   1.25
1996 Autographed Racing Autographs Mike Wallace 10.00   4.50   1.25
1996 Autographed Racing Autographs Darrell Waltrip 20.00   9.00   2.50
1996 Autographed Racing Autographs Michael Waltrip 10.00   4.50   1.25
1996 Autographed Racing Autographs Eddie Wood . . . . 6.00   2.70   .75
1996 Autographed Racing Autographs Glen Wood . . . . 6.00   2.70   .75
1996 Autographed Racing Autographs Kim Wood . . . . 6.00   2.70   .75
1996 Autographed Racing Autographs Len Wood . . . . 6.00   2.70   .75
1996 Autographed Racing Autographs Robert Yates . . . . 6.00   2.70   .75

1996 Flair Autographs

COMPLETE SET (12) 900.00   400.00   110.00

This 12-card insert set consist of the top names in NASCAR. Autograph redemption cards were randomly inserted in packs at a rate of one in 100. The redemption card featured one of the 12 drivers on the front and instructions on how and where to redeem it.

	MINT	NRMT	EXC
1996 Flair Autographs COMMON CARD (1-12)	25.00	11.00	3.10
1996 Flair Autographs Ricky Craven	30.00	13.50	3.70
1996 Flair Autographs Dale Earnhardt	250.00	110.00	31.00
1996 Flair Autographs Bill Elliott	90.00	40.00	11.00
1996 Flair Autographs Jeff Gordon	250.00	110.00	31.00
1996 Flair Autographs Ernie Irvan	50.00	22.00	6.25
1996 Flair Autographs Dale Jarrett	75.00	34.00	9.50
1996 Flair Autographs Bobby Labonte	30.00	13.50	3.70
1996 Flair Autographs Terry Labonte	90.00	40.00	11.00
1996 Flair Autographs Sterling Marlin	40.00	18.00	5.00
1996 Flair Autographs Mark Martin	90.00	40.00	11.00
1996 Flair Autographs Ted Musgrave	25.00	11.00	3.10
1996 Flair Autographs Rusty Wallace	90.00	40.00	11.00

1996 Maxx Autographs Terry Labonte

These three cards were intended to be inserted into Maxx Signed and Sealed. Due to Maxx's bankruptcy the Signed and Sealed set was never produced. We have only received enough market information on the Jeff Gordon card to list a price.

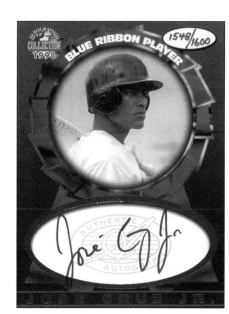

	MINT	NRMT	EXC
1996 Maxx Autographs Jeff Gordon	150.00	70.00	19.00
1996 Maxx Autographs Ken Schrader			

1996 Ultra Update Autographs

COMPLETE SET (12)	750.00	350.00	95.00

This 12-card insert set features the top names in NASCAR. The cards found in packs were redemption cards. These cards could be sent in to receive an autographed card of the driver who appeared on the front of the card. The redemption cards were seeded one in 100 packs.

	MINT	NRMT	EXC
1996 Ultra Update Autographs COMMON CARD	15.00	6.75	1.85
1996 Ultra Update Autographs Ricky Craven	20.00	9.00	2.50
1996 Ultra Update Autographs Dale Earnhardt	250.00	110.00	31.00
1996 Ultra Update Autographs Bill Elliott	70.00	32.00	8.75
1996 Ultra Update Autographs Jeff Gordon	200.00	90.00	25.00
1996 Ultra Update Autographs Ernie Irvan	40.00	18.00	5.00
1996 Ultra Update Autographs Dale Jarrett	60.00	27.00	7.50
1996 Ultra Update Autographs Bobby Labonte	20.00	9.00	2.50
1996 Ultra Update Autographs Terry Labonte	70.00	32.00	8.75
1996 Ultra Update Autographs Sterling Marlin	30.00	13.50	3.70
1996 Ultra Update Autographs Mark Martin	70.00	32.00	8.75
1996 Ultra Update Autographs Ted Musgrave	15.00	6.75	1.85
1996 Ultra Update Autographs Rusty Wallace	70.00	32.00	8.75

1996 Upper Deck Road To The Cup Autographs

COMPLETE SET (29)	700.00	325.00	90.00

Randomly inserted in hobby packs only at a rate of one in 16, this 29-card insert set features authentic signatures from the hottest motorsports drivers. Card # H7 was supposed to be Bill Elliott. Due to a crash at Talladega on April 28, 1996, Bill was unable to sign his cards and was dropped from the set.

	MINT	NRMT	EXC
1996 Upper Deck Road To The Cup COMMON CARD (H1-H30)	15.00	6.75	1.85
1996 Upper Deck Road To The Cup Autographs Jeff Gordon	250.00	110.00	31.00
1996 Upper Deck Road To The Cup Autographs Sterling Marlin	25.00	11.00	3.10
1996 Upper Deck Road To The Cup Autographs Mark Martin	75.00	34.00	9.50
1996 Upper Deck Road To The Cup Autographs Rusty Wallace	75.00	34.00	9.50
1996 Upper Deck Road To The Cup Autographs Terry Labonte	75.00	34.00	9.50
1996 Upper Deck Road To The Cup Autographs Ted Musgrave	15.00	6.75	1.85
1996 Upper Deck Road To The Cup Autographs Ricky Rudd	20.00	9.00	2.50
1996 Upper Deck Road To The Cup Autographs Bobby Labonte	20.00	9.00	2.50
1996 Upper Deck Road To The Cup Autographs Morgan Shepherd	15.00	6.75	1.85
1996 Upper Deck Road To The Cup Autographs Michael Waltrip	15.00	6.75	1.85
1996 Upper Deck Road To The Cup Autographs Dale Jarrett	60.00	27.00	7.50
1996 Upper Deck Road To The Cup Autographs Bobby Hamilton	15.00	6.75	1.85
1996 Upper Deck Road To The Cup Autographs Derrike Cope	15.00	6.75	1.85
1996 Upper Deck Road To The Cup Autographs Geoff Bodine	15.00	6.75	1.85
1996 Upper Deck Road To The Cup Autographs Ken Schrader	15.00	6.75	1.85
1996 Upper Deck Road To The Cup Autographs John Andretti	15.00	6.75	1.85
1996 Upper Deck Road To The Cup Autographs Darrell Waltrip	20.00	9.00	2.50
1996 Upper Deck Road To The Cup Autographs Brett Bodine	15.00	6.75	1.85
1996 Upper Deck Road To The Cup Autographs Kenny Wallace	15.00	6.75	1.85
1996 Upper Deck Road To The Cup Autographs Ward Burton	15.00	6.75	1.85
1996 Upper Deck Road To The Cup Autographs Lake Speed	15.00	6.75	1.85
1996 Upper Deck Road To The Cup Autographs Ricky Craven	15.00	6.75	1.85
1996 Upper Deck Road To The Cup Autographs Jimmy Spencer	15.00	6.75	1.85
1996 Upper Deck Road To The Cup Autographs Steve Grissom	15.00	6.75	1.85
1996 Upper Deck Road To The Cup Autographs Joe Nemechek	15.00	6.75	1.85

1996 Upper Deck Road To The Cup Autographs Ernie Irvan 35.00   16.00   4.40
1996 Upper Deck Road To The Cup Autographs Kyle Petty 15.00   6.75   1.85
1996 Upper Deck Road To The Cup Autographs Johnny Benson 15.00   6.75   1.85
1996 Upper Deck Road To The Cup Autographs Jeff Burton 20.00   9.00   2.50

1996 VIP Autographs
COMPLETE SET (26) 650.00   300.00   80.00
This 26-card set features desirable autographs from NASCAR's biggest stars. More than 25,000 autographs were inserted in packs of V.I.P. The autograph cards were inserted at a rate of one per 24 packs.

	MINT	NRMT	EXC
1996 VIP Autographs COMMON CARD (1-26)	8.00	3.60	1.00
1996 VIP Autographs COMMON DRIVER (1-26)	15.00	6.75	1.85
1996 VIP Autographs Jeff Andrews	8.00	3.60	1.00
1996 VIP Autographs Johnny Benson	20.00	9.00	2.50
1996 VIP Autographs Geoff Bodine	20.00	9.00	2.50
1996 VIP Autographs Jeff Burton	20.00	9.00	2.50
1996 VIP Autographs Ricky Craven	20.00	9.00	2.50
1996 VIP Autographs Dale Earnhardt	200.00	90.00	25.00
1996 VIP Autographs Danny Glad	8.00	3.60	1.00
1996 VIP Autographs Jeff Gordon	200.00	90.00	25.00
1996 VIP Autographs David Green	15.00	6.75	1.85
1996 VIP Autographs Jeff Green	15.00	6.75	1.85
1996 VIP Autographs Steve Hmiel	8.00	3.60	1.00
1996 VIP Autographs Ernie Irvan	30.00	13.50	3.70
1996 VIP Autographs Jason Keller	15.00	6.75	1.85
1996 VIP Autographs Bobby Labonte	20.00	9.00	2.50
1996 VIP Autographs Chad Little	15.00	6.75	1.85
1996 VIP Autographs Jeremy Mayfield	40.00	18.00	5.00
1996 VIP Autographs Mike McLaughlin	15.00	6.75	1.85
1996 VIP Autographs Ted Musgrave	20.00	9.00	2.50
1996 VIP Autographs Joe Nemechek	20.00	9.00	2.50
1996 VIP Autographs Robert Pressley	15.00	6.75	1.85
1996 VIP Autographs Charlie Siegars	8.00	3.60	1.00
1996 VIP Autographs Mike Skinner	20.00	9.00	2.50
1996 VIP Autographs David Smith	8.00	3.60	1.00
1996 VIP Autographs Rusty Wallace	70.00	32.00	8.75
1996 VIP Autographs Michael Waltrip	20.00	9.00	2.50
1996 VIP Autographs Rick Wetzel	8.00	3.60	1.00

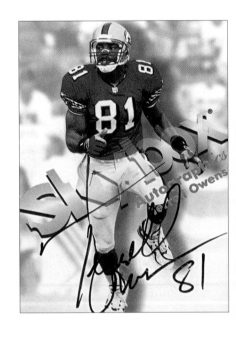

1997 Autographed Racing Autographs
COMPLETE SET (56) . . . . 4.00   1.80   .50
This insert set features hand-signed cards from the top names in racing. It is important to note that the 56-card checklist presented below may not be complete. Spokespeople at Score Board have not been able to confirm our checklist. Some of the autographed cards distributed in this product are in the form of redemption cards and cards from the 1996 Autographed Racing product. The same driver may have two or possibly three different autograph cards in this product. The cards were randomly inserted into packs at a ratio of 5:24.

	MINT	NRMT	EXC
1997 Autographed Racing Autographs COMMON CARD	4.00	1.80	.50
1997 Autographed Racing Autographs COMMON DRIVER	8.00	3.60	1.00
1997 Autographed Racing Autographs John Andretti	8.00	3.60	1.00
1997 Autographed Racing Autographs Tommy Baldwin	4.00	1.80	.50
1997 Autographed Racing Autographs Brett Bodine	8.00	3.60	1.00
1997 Autographed Racing Autographs Geoff Bodine	8.00	3.60	1.00
1997 Autographed Racing Autographs Todd Bodine	8.00	3.60	1.00
1997 Autographed Racing Autographs Jeff Burton	15.00	6.75	1.85
1997 Autographed Racing Autographs Richard Childress	4.00	1.80	.50
1997 Autographed Racing Autographs Ricky Craven	15.00	6.75	1.85
1997 Autographed Racing Autographs Wally Dallenbach Jr.	8.00	3.60	1.00
1997 Autographed Racing Autographs Gary DeHart	4.00	1.80	.50
1997 Autographed Racing Autographs Randy Dorton	4.00	1.80	.50
1997 Autographed Racing Autographs Dale Earnhardt	200.00	90.00	25.00
1997 Autographed Racing Autographs Ray Evernham	4.00	1.80	.50
1997 Autographed Racing Autographs Joe Gibbs	15.00	6.75	1.85

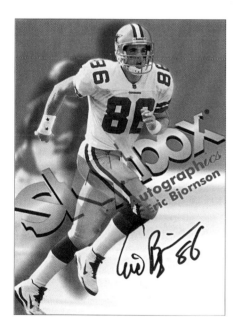

1997 Autographed Racing Autographs Tony Glover	4.00	1.80	.50
1997 Autographed Racing Autographs Jeff Gordon	200.00	90.00	25.00
1997 Autographed Racing Autographs Robby Gordon	8.00	3.60	1.00
1997 Autographed Racing Autographs Andy Graves	4.00	1.80	.50
1997 Autographed Racing Autographs Steve Grissom	8.00	3.60	1.00
1997 Autographed Racing Autographs Bobby Hamilton	8.00	3.60	1.00
1997 Autographed Racing Autographs Rick Hendrick	4.00	1.80	.50
1997 Autographed Racing Autographs Steve Hmiel	4.00	1.80	.50
1997 Autographed Racing Autographs Ron Hornaday Jr.	8.00	3.60	1.00
1997 Autographed Racing Autographs Ernie Irvan	15.00	6.75	1.85
1997 Autographed Racing Autographs Dale Jarrett	60.00	27.00	7.50
1997 Autographed Racing Autographs Jimmy Johnson	4.00	1.80	.50
1997 Autographed Racing Autographs Terry Labonte	75.00	34.00	9.50
1997 Autographed Racing Autographs Bobby Labonte	15.00	6.75	1.85
1997 Autographed Racing Autographs Randy LaJoie	8.00	3.60	1.00
1997 Autographed Racing Autographs Jimmy Makar	4.00	1.80	.50
1997 Autographed Racing Autographs Sterling Marlin	15.00	6.75	1.85
1997 Autographed Racing Autographs Dave Marcis	8.00	3.60	1.00
1997 Autographed Racing Autographs Mark Martin	75.00	34.00	9.50
1997 Autographed Racing Autographs Rick Mast	8.00	3.60	1.00
1997 Autographed Racing Autographs Jeremy Mayfield	40.00	18.00	5.00
1997 Autographed Racing Autographs Kenny Mayne	15.00	6.75	1.85
1997 Autographed Racing Autographs Larry McReynolds	4.00	1.80	.50
1997 Autographed Racing Autographs Ted Musgrave	8.00	3.60	1.00
1997 Autographed Racing Autographs Buddy Parrott	4.00	1.80	.50
1997 Autographed Racing Autographs Todd Parrott	4.00	1.80	.50
1997 Autographed Racing Autographs Robin Pemberton	4.00	1.80	.50
1997 Autographed Racing Autographs Kyle Petty	15.00	6.75	1.85
1997 Autographed Racing Autographs Shelton Pittman	4.00	1.80	.50
1997 Autographed Racing Autographs Robert Pressley	8.00	3.60	1.00
1997 Autographed Racing Autographs Dr. Jerry Punch	8.00	3.60	1.00
1997 Autographed Racing Autographs Harry Raimer	4.00	1.80	.50
1997 Autographed Racing Autographs Dave Rezendes	8.00	3.60	1.00
1997 Autographed Racing Autographs Greg Sacks	8.00	3.60	1.00
1997 Autographed Racing Autographs Morgan Shepherd	8.00	3.60	1.00
1997 Autographed Racing Autographs Hut Stricklin	8.00	3.60	1.00
1997 Autographed Racing Autographs Dick Trickle	8.00	3.60	1.00
1997 Autographed Racing Autographs Kenny Wallace	8.00	3.60	1.00
1997 Autographed Racing Autographs Mike Wallace	8.00	3.60	1.00
1997 Autographed Racing Autographs Darrell Waltrip	15.00	6.75	1.85
1997 Autographed Racing Autographs Michael Waltrip	8.00	3.60	1.00
1997 Autographed Racing Autographs Wood Brothers	4.00	1.80	.50

1997 Pinnacle Spellbound Autographs

COMPLETE SET (12) 700.00 325.00 90.00

This five-card set features the autographs of five drivers from the regular set. Each of the drivers signed 500 cards. The Jeff Gordon card inserted packs was actually a redemtpion that could be redemmed for an autogrpahed card. An insert ratio was not given for these cards.

	MINT	NRMT	EXC
1997 Pinnacle Spellbound Autographs COMMON CARD (1-12)	75.00	34.00	9.50
1997 Pinnacle Spellbound Autographs Terry Labonte	100.00	45.00	12.50
1997 Pinnacle Spellbound Autographs Dale Jarrett	75.00	34.00	9.50
1997 Pinnacle Spellbound Autographs Dale Earnhardt	300.00	135.00	38.00
1997 Pinnacle Spellbound Autographs Jeff Gordon Redemption Card	300.00	135.00	38.00
1997 Pinnacle Spellbound Autographs Jeff Gordon Autographed Card	300.00	135.00	38.00
1997 Pinnacle Spellbound Autographs Bill Elliott	100.00	45.00	12.50

1997 Race Sharks Shark Tooth Signatures

COMPLETE SET (25) 700.00 325.00 90.00

This 25-card set features autographs of Winston Cup and Busch Grand National drivers, crew chiefs, owners and other racing personalities. The cards were inserted one per 24 packs.

	MINT	NRMT	EXC
1997 Race Sharks Shark Tooth Signatures COMMON CARD (1-25)	6.00	2.70	.75
1997 Race Sharks Shark Tooth Signatures COMMON DRIVER (1-25) ...	12.00	5.50	1.50
1997 Race Sharks Shark Tooth Signatures COMP. FIRST BITE SET(25) ..	1000.00	450.00	125.00
1997 Race Sharks Shark Tooth Signatures FIRST BITE CARDS: .75X TO 1.25X CARDS			
1997 Race Sharks Shark Tooth Signatures Dale Earnhardt	200.00	90.00	25.00
1997 Race Sharks Shark Tooth Signatures Jeff Gordon	200.00	90.00	25.00
1997 Race Sharks Shark Tooth Signatures Dale Jarrett	60.00	27.00	7.50
1997 Race Sharks Shark Tooth Signatures Terry Labonte	60.00	27.00	7.50
1997 Race Sharks Shark Tooth Signatures Sterling Marlin	30.00	13.50	3.70
1997 Race Sharks Shark Tooth Signatures Bill Elliott	60.00	27.00	7.50
1997 Race Sharks Shark Tooth Signatures Ricky Craven	12.00	5.50	1.50
1997 Race Sharks Shark Tooth Signatures Robert Pressley	12.00	5.50	1.50
1997 Race Sharks Shark Tooth Signatures Jeff Burton	15.00	6.75	1.85
1997 Race Sharks Shark Tooth Signatures Ward Burton	12.00	5.50	1.50
1997 Race Sharks Shark Tooth Signatures Bobby Labonte	15.00	6.75	1.85
1997 Race Sharks Shark Tooth Signatures Joe Nemechek	12.00	5.50	1.50
1997 Race Sharks Shark Tooth Signatures Chad Little	12.00	5.50	1.50
1997 Race Sharks Shark Tooth Signatures David Green	12.00	5.50	1.50
1997 Race Sharks Shark Tooth Signatures Jeff Green	12.00	5.50	1.50
1997 Race Sharks Shark Tooth Signatures Joe Gibbs	8.00	3.60	1.00
1997 Race Sharks Shark Tooth Signatures Todd Parrott	6.00	2.70	.75
1997 Race Sharks Shark Tooth Signatures Jeff Hammond	6.00	2.70	.75
1997 Race Sharks Shark Tooth Signatures Charlie Pressley	6.00	2.70	.75
1997 Race Sharks Shark Tooth Signatures Joey Knuckles	6.00	2.70	.75
1997 Race Sharks Shark Tooth Signatures David Smith	6.00	2.70	.75
1997 Race Sharks Shark Tooth Signatures Brad Parrott	6.00	2.70	.75
1997 Race Sharks Shark Tooth Signatures Eddie Dickerson	6.00	2.70	.75
1997 Race Sharks Shark Tooth Signatures Randy Dorton	6.00	2.70	.75
1997 Race Sharks Shark Tooth Signatures Jimmy Johnson	6.00	2.70	.75

1997 SB Motorsports Autographs

COMPLETE SET (5)	700.00	325.00	90.00

The top 10 drivers from the Winston Cup circuit have hand-signed these insert cards. The cards were inserted one in 576 Packs. Each card was sequentially numbered.

	MINT	NRMT	EXC
1997 SB Motorsports Autographs COMMON CARD (AU1-AU5)	30.00	13.50	3.70
1997 SB Motorsports Autographs Dale Earnhardt	300.00	135.00	38.00
1997 SB Motorsports Autographs Jeff Gordon	300.00	135.00	38.00
1997 SB Motorsports Autographs Terry Labonte	90.00	40.00	11.00
1997 SB Motorsports Autographs Dale Jarrett	75.00	34.00	9.50
1997 SB Motorsports Autographs Robby Gordon	30.00	13.50	3.70

1997 Score Board IQ Remarques

COMPLETE SET (10)	400.00	180.00	50.00

These cards features the original artwork of renowed artist Sam Bass. Ten of his more famous artworks were reprinted on canvas stock in order to create these cards. These cards are numbered from 101 to 570 and are autographed by Bass. These cards are inserted one per 65 packs.

	MINT	NRMT	EXC
1997 Score Board IQ Remarques COMMON CARD (SB1-SB10)	20.00	9.00	2.50
1997 Score Board IQ Remarques Dale Earnhardt	120.00	55.00	15.00
1997 Score Board IQ Remarques Jeff Gordon	120.00	55.00	15.00
1997 Score Board IQ Remarques Richard Childress	20.00	9.00	2.50
1997 Score Board IQ Remarques Ernie Irvan	25.00	11.00	3.10
1997 Score Board IQ Remarques Rusty Wallace's Car	20.00	9.00	2.50
1997 Score Board IQ Remarques Darrell Waltrip	25.00	11.00	3.10
1997 Score Board IQ Remarques Richard Petty	40.00	18.00	5.00
1997 Score Board IQ Remarques Bobby Labonte	25.00	11.00	3.10
1997 Score Board IQ Remarques Alan Kulwicki	50.00	22.00	6.25
1997 Score Board IQ Remarques Terry Labonte	60.00	27.00	7.50